P9-AQP-014

NATO 1948

NATO 1948

The Birth of the Transatlantic Alliance

Lawrence S. Kaplan
with the assistance of Morris Honick

ROWMAN & LITTLEFIELD PUBLISHERS, INC.
Lanham • Boulder • New York • Toronto • Plymouth, UK

ROWMAN & LITTLEFIELD PUBLISHERS, INC.

Published in the United States of America
by Rowman & Littlefield Publishers, Inc.
A wholly owned subsidary of The Rowman & Littlefield Publishing Group, Inc.
4501 Forbes Boulevard, Suite 200, Lanham, Maryland 20706
www.rowmanlittlefield.com

Estover Road, Plymouth PL6 7PY, United Kingdom

British Library Cataloguing in Publication Information Available

Library of Congress Cataloging-in-Publication Data
Kaplan, Lawrence S.
  Nato 1948 : the birth of the Transatlantic Alliance / Lawrence S. Kaplan.
    p. cm.
  Includes bibliographical references and index.
  ISBN-13: 978-0-7425-3916-7 (cloth : alk. paper)
  ISBN-10: 0-7425-3916-4 (cloth : alk. paper)
  ISBN-13: 978-0-7425-3917-4 (pbk. : alk. paper)
  ISBN-10: 0-7425-3917-2 (pbk. : alk. paper)
  1. North Atlantic Treaty Organization—History—20th century. I. Title.
  UA646.3.K365 2007
  355'.03109182109044—dc22

                                                          2006100324

Printed in the United States of America

∞™ The paper used in this publication meets the minimum requirements of
American National Standard for Information Sciences—Permanence of Paper
for Printed Library Materials, ANSI/NISO Z39.48-1992.

U.S. undertones of superiority and resentment of that feeling of superiority frequently surfaced during negotiations. The French were the most vocal in their irritation over the inferior role Europeans were forced to play to gain the kind of support they needed from the United States—a country and a people lacking the cultural achievements of Europeans—and that was a continuing source of discomfort. Britain served to calm emotions, but even they periodically expressed their indignation at being patronized by U.S. leaders.

For the United States the obstacles to an alliance were even more daunting in light of its long isolationist tradition. Not only did the Truman administration and Congress have to be assured of the reality of Europe's promise to reform, but also they had to contend with a variety of domestic objections to the responses Europe required. To counterbalance these obstacles was the threat of Communism, and that was the proximate incentive for immediate action. There was also a mix of idealism and realism that transcended the sense of crisis in 1948. After World War II, the United States believed that they could help create the peaceful and prosperous world that the United Nations (UN) failed to secure. A United States of Europe, no matter how distant its realization, was expected to become a political and economic partner of the United States.

The United States faced many stumbling blocks on the road to achieving these goals. These problems ranged from visceral fears of isolationists worrying about the loss of national sovereignty to the military services concerned with the potential drain on their stocks to UN adherents convinced that a military alliance would subvert the UN's charter. Throughout 1948, the Truman administration had to cope with these three constituencies and at the same time deal with its own ambivalence about the strength of Europe's commitments. Together the events of that year produced a series of conflicts that were only partly concealed from public gaze. Given the stakes involved, it was only appropriate that the negotiations took more than a year to be completed.

In preparing this book, I have drawn on a number of my own books. Foremost have been the monographs and essays produced over the past generation. These began with a study of the military assistance program (A *Community of Interests: NATO and the Military Assistance Program, 1948–1951*) for the office of the secretary of defense in 1980 from which I extracted material on the beginnings of that program in chapter 8. I have reworked and transposed passages from my essays on the North Atlantic Treaty Organization's (NATO) formative years (*The United States and NATO: The Formative Years*), and they are scattered throughout the book. European conferences in Norway in 1983 and Germany in 1985 provided an opportunity to examine the relationship between the Western Union and NATO. By-products of those conferences are "An Unequal Triad: The United States,

Preface

This book has long been in the making. Immediately after finishing a doctoral dissertation on the foreign policies of the Jeffersonian era, I came to Washington in 1951 as a historian in the Historian's Office of the Office of the Secretary of Defense. One of my assignments in that office was to examine the impact of the new North Atlantic Treaty on the equally new Department of Defense. It struck me that by signing that treaty, the United States was breaking a long tradition of non-entanglement with the Old World that began in 1800 when the Franco-U.S. treaty of 1778 ended in mutual dissatisfaction. Why the United States waited almost 150 years before it was ready to engage in another entangling alliance—this time with ten European countries—is a question that intrigued me then—and now. The origins of this transformation are the subject of this book.

Throughout 1948 and into the spring of 1949, negotiations between the United States and Canada on the one side and Britain, France, and the Low Countries on the other finally produced a treaty that both sides could accept. For Europeans, the vital issue was engaging the United States in a Western European alliance or enlarging the alliance in a way that would satisfy U.S. reservations. Europeans had to demonstrate to the United States that they were worthy of U.S. assistance through their willingness to collaborate with each other. This meant resolving both the long-standing mutual suspicions between France and Britain and their working together to ensure that a reformed Germany would not threaten the peace of Europe again. The Europeans had to make accommodations for the place of the Low Countries and possibly other European nations in any alliance with the United States.

Contents

Dedicated to students in my NATO history classes at
Kent State University, 1984–1993, and
Georgetown University, 1995–2006

Western Union, and NATO," in *Western Security: The Formative Years*, ed. Olav Riste, and Norbert Wiggershaus and Roland G. Foerster, *The Western Security Community*.

I have benefited from the work of former students in my NATO history classes at both Kent State and Georgetown Universities. My thanks particularly for the seminal study by Sidney R. Snyder, "The Role of the International Working Group in the Creation of the North Atlantic Treaty, December 1947–April 1949," and for the insights of E. Timothy Smith on Italy's ambiguous position in the treaty negotiations in *The United States, Italy, and NATO, 1947–1952* and his sensitive treatment of NATO opponents in *Opposition Beyond the Water's Edge: Liberal Internationalists, Pacifists, and Containment*. George T. Mazuzan, *Warren R. Austin at the U.N., 1946-1953* is the most authoritative work on the U.S. representative at the UN in 1948 and 1949. Additionally, I have profited from the master's theses of two former students: Richard F. Grimmett, "Isolationist Opposition to NATO, 1949–1951," and Robert P. Batchelor, "The Delicate Balance: The Brussels Pact, NATO, and the United States, 1948–1951."

Two friends in particular deserve mention in this preface. Steve Rearden has been cheering me on for the past thirty years, and I continue to be grateful for his support. More recently, Stanley Kober, an international security specialist with a historical sensibility more acute among European than U.S. scholars, has helped me with his insights. My wife, Janice, has a feel for *le mot juste* that has served me particularly well in this project.

I am grateful for the support Pentagon librarians Yolanda Miller, Debbie Reed, and Barbara Risser have given me in the course of my research for this book. Similarly, I have benefited from the special attention Georgetown University librarians Kristina Bobé, Timothy Cash, and Rachel Donelson have given me in the microform room of the Lauinger Library. Susan McEachern has given me the benefit of her expertise at every stage of this project as editorial director for History, International Studies, and Geography with Rowman & Littlefield. It has made a difference.

Of all the help I have received, none has been more important than that of Morris Honick, former chief, Historical Section, SHAPE. Living in Casteau since his retirement, he has spent considerable time consulting on my behalf with Western European Union archivists and sending me copies of significant Western Union documents. Through his intervention, I had an opportunity to meet with Arnaud Jacomet, head, the Secretariat of the Western European Union; Tomas Galano, head of Western European Union Archives in Brussels; and Felipe Leitao, principal archivist. I am pleased to acknowledge the special contributions of Morris Honick on the title page of this book.

1

Introduction: The Isolationist Tradition, 1800–1947

A case may be made that World War II freed the United States from its obsession of a dangerous Europe preying on its innocence and entangling the nation in its coils. The conviction that the United States possessed the blessings of liberty denied to the Old World was based on its interpretation of its colonial history. The British colonies may have owed their existence to the economic ambitions and imperial visions of the mother country, but in Boston from the time of John Winthrop's "City Upon a Hill," the colonists saw themselves liberated in a vast new world separated by an ocean from the troubles and evils of the Old World. And ten years prior to that, in Plymouth, William Bradford envisioned himself as a Joshua and a Moses leading the new children of Israel across a large Red Sea to the "Promised Land." Over a century, Britain's mercantile system unwittingly encouraged a sense of political, social, and economic freedom to flourish in its colonies. By the middle of the eighteenth century when Britain had defeated its rivals and turned its attention once again to the colonies, it was too late for the British government to scale back the freedoms it had allowed, and revolution followed. Rather than appreciate the benefits the British Empire had given to colonists in the forms of trading privileges and protection with its powerful navy, the new republic saw only subjection in what it called foreign wars serving the dynastic interests of the British monarchy.

As a small insecure nation in 1800 it was reasonable for the United States to steer clear from the quarrels of monarchical Europe as much as possible. Although the French alliance of 1778 had helped to win the Revolutionary War, it subsequently became a burden as the young nation found itself caught up in the Anglo-French wars of the 1790s. In that decade the Anglophile Hamiltonians contended with the Francophile Jeffersonians to maintain neutrality in those European struggles. Not until the end of the War of 1812 was the United States free to expand across the continent without fear of serious opposition from Britain, France, or Spain. The Monroe Doctrine (1823) symbolized successful detachment from the threat of European intervention.

ISOLATIONISM REDUX

By the end of the nineteenth century, the nation was equal in resources to any European rival, ready to compete for global advantage but still wary of a European entanglement with any power, including the increasingly friendly Great Britain. When the United States entered World War I, it was as an "associated" power, not an "ally," of Britain and France despite a common opposition to German militarism. The idea of alliance was as uncomfortable to Woodrow Wilson as it was to most of the country.

The experience at the Versailles peace conference in 1919 confirmed America's suspicions of Europe and reaffirmed its opposition to alliances. The victorious Anglo-French allies acquired territories from the defeated Germans and made a mockery of Wilson's efforts to use U.S. power as a means of ending, once and for all, the power politics that led to war in the past. The League of Nations, the fourteenth point in Wilson's war aims, had been designed to remove the causes of future wars. It was an elaborate structure prepared to include all the nations of the world bound in a collective security system. Should any member attack another, it would risk the condemnation of all the others. But in 1919, the United States rejected the League, because it perceived the Treaty of Versailles with its division of Germany's overseas territories to have been a betrayal of the idealistic reasons of the United States for participating in the European war against the kaiser.

Isolationism deepened in the 1930s. As the Great Depression devastated the world's economies, Americans either ignored the rise of Fascism in Europe and Japanese militarism in Asia or felt that the demise of foreign democracies was no concern of the United States. The apparent lessons of World War I were manifested in neutrality laws during the administration of Franklin D. Roosevelt. Instead of helping victims of increasingly aggressive Fascist powers, such as Spain and Czechoslovakia, Congress, which had closed the nation's doors to most immigrants, was convinced that partiality for any side would risk the nation's involvement in foreign wars. The competing menace of Soviet Communism, which rivaled if not surpassed Nazism in some eyes, was more proof in the wisdom of abstaining from entanglements with the Old World. Only after Japan's invasion of China in 1937 and the Anglo-French appeasement of Adolf Hitler in 1938 over the status of Czechoslovakia's Sudetenland did the nation awaken to the potential consequences of a Europe under the domination of Nazi Germany and East Asia dominated by militaristic Japan.

The awakening did not come easily. When the Germans invaded Poland in September 1939, there was still a substantial constituency in the United States for abstaining from the conflict. When France fell in 1940, and Britain was fighting a lonely battle against a Germany in control of the European continent, the president himself was slow, or at least quite cautious, about educating the U.S. public to the dangers befalling European nations. A Nazi-Communist pact the year before had made the Soviet Union complicit in the destruction of democracy in Europe, and when the Germans invaded Russia in 1941, a beleaguered Britain represented the only democracy surviving in Europe. An energized Roosevelt employed all the weapons an able president possessed to win over Congress and the nation in supporting Britain, first in 1940 through supplying badly needed destroyers in exchange for British bases in the Atlantic and Caribbean and then pushing Congress to create a much more ambitious lend-lease program in 1941. Moreover, the United States violated its neutrality by escorting ships carrying weapons and supplies to Britain. At the same time Roosevelt was challenging Japanese aggression in Asia by restricting supplies of raw materials essential for the Japanese war machine. These actions were taken in the face of a potent and well-organized isolationist opposition dedicated to keeping the United States out of war by reminding the nation of how Europe betrayed the United States in World War I. Bipartisan interventionists, spearheaded by prominent Republican leaders, won the battle of public opinion. It took the Japanese attack on Pearl Harbor to silence isolationist voices.

THE WORLD WAR II "ALLIANCE"

After the United States entered the war against the Axis powers, the enthusiasm that animated the United States in 1917 was replicated a generation later. Isolationist sentiment was suppressed as the nation mobilized for unconditional surrender. The emotions that united the United States encompassed all the nations on the allied side, including the Soviet Communists; the United States put aside the memory of Communist behavior in 1939 and European behavior in general in 1919. Once again the United States was ready to look to a world that would rid itself of the scourge of war. But there was a major difference between the two world wars. In 1917, U.S. power and resources may have been equal—or superior—to those of any of the belligerents, but the leadership of the war was in the hands of the Allies. After 1941 there was no question about the dominance of the United States; its vast resources made it the dominant partner in the coalition that defeated the Axis powers, even though the Soviets endured greater sacrifices in the contest than their partners.

The failed League of Nations, rejected by the United States, was revived under the name of the United Nations, with some significant differences. The Roosevelt administration, unlike Wilson's, ensured U.S. leadership from the outset by embedding the organization in the United States, and Republicans would be as closely identified with it as Democrats. Yet leadership in creating the UN was only a partial step toward breaking with the past. The sacrifices of national sovereignty required by the UN charter were actually milder than those envisioned in the League of Nations covenant. The United States assumed the burden of creating a collective security organization based on the assumption that the victors of World War II would be harmonious peacekeepers. To ensure this harmony, the United States, along with Britain, France, China, and the Soviet Union, would have veto power in the Security Council that would insulate them from the judgments of the other fifty members of the original UN. Neither the United States nor its adversary, the Soviet Union, would trust its fate to a General Assembly of the UN or to each other.

The isolationist tradition was not yet buried. While the U.S.-British relationship in the war was touted as a grand alliance, it represented a personal alliance between Roosevelt and Winston Churchill, not a national alliance enshrined in a treaty. The combined chiefs of staff were not a permanent fixture. When the war ended, the Truman administration made it clear that no permanent entanglements had been made among any of the wartime allies. The lend-lease program with the Soviet Union was abruptly terminated, and Britain was informed that the wartime links would no longer apply. More significantly, through the McMahon Act of 1946, the United States emphasized that there would be no sharing of the atom bomb with former allies.

It was hardly surprising that the voices of isolationism would be heard again after the war. Soviet Communism had emerged as a challenge to the United States as early as the Yalta Conference, when the allies made plans for dividing a defeated Germany into occupational zones and determined the future of Poland. It was an uneasy arrangement, given the different understandings held by the United States and the Soviet Union over a prospective peace treaty with Germany and the governance of a reconstructed Poland. Critics claimed that Communism under Soviet auspices had been promoted by U.S. concessions to the former ally and argued that defeating Nazi Germany had only led to the rise of an even greater danger of Soviet Communism spreading through a destroyed Europe. The possibility of the United States turning its back on the outside world was once again in vogue. Winning the war had only produced another great enemy.

In reality an isolationist revival was remote in 1945. Movement toward a permanent abandonment of the tradition of nonentanglement with Europe was inevitable. The alternative would have been to turn the Old World over to Communism and invite an expanded Soviet Union to penetrate the West. France and Germany had large Communist parties, with their citizenry giving Communists credit for victory over the Nazis. Suspicions of Communist subversion in the United States and charges of U.S. weakness in allowing the Soviets to use the periodic meetings of their foreign ministers to keep the Soviet-occupied parts of Germany and the new regimes in Eastern Europe in the Soviet orbit were common. The Truman administration seemed to be rudderless in 1945 and 1946 in dealing with Joseph Stalin. The Soviets rebuffed half-hearted attempts of the United States to come to terms with them; Communism, as they saw it, would inevitably replace capitalistic democratic governments of the West, and the Soviets seemed ready to hasten that process by their efforts to intimidate Turkey and by supporting a civil war in Greece.

THE TRUMAN DOCTRINE

The drift in foreign relations came to an end in 1947 when the president replaced Secretary of State James F. Byrnes with General George C. Marshall and endorsed the concept of *containment* as a response to Soviet expansionism. This change did not signify acceptance of binding agreements with European nations. It did mean that the United States was prepared to recognize that the survival of Western democracies threatened by Communist internal subversion or external aggression was vital to the security of the United States itself. The United States was the only bulwark against the daunting power of the Soviet Union. To give direction to this policy, the Truman administration drew on the advice of a Soviet specialist in Moscow, George F. Kennan, whose seminal "long telegram" in 1946 circulated throughout the government with its message outlining the treatment of relations with the Soviet Union. It was later encapsulated in his "X" article in the summer issue of *Foreign Affairs*.[1] As a scholarly and perceptive student of Communism, Kennan propounded the thesis that only firm containment would control the dynamic ideology of the Soviet system. Conventional diplomacy was irrelevant to the relationship between the two nations. So was the UN. Hostility was inherent in the nature of the two societies. The only way to cope with this challenge was by patient containment of Soviet expansionism, anticipating the day when its economic failures and its lack of internal cohesion would lead to its demise.

Kennan's lengthy analysis of Soviet behavior was a product of his experience as an expert in the pathology of Soviet behavior. In 1925, a year after graduating from Princeton, he entered the U.S. Foreign Service, where he became one of the few specialists in Soviet affairs. Kennan accompanied

William C. Bullitt, the first U.S. ambassador to the Soviet Union, to Moscow in 1933, where he served most of the decade. He returned in 1944 as minister-counselor. Kennan possessed a keen mind and a gift for writing thoughtful commentaries. It was these qualities that attracted the attention of Secretary of the Navy James V. Forrestal in 1946. His containment recommendations won him an appointment as head of the State Department's policy planning staff.

The first implication of Kennan's hypothesis was that a divided world could not be bridged by the UN. But because the nation at large did not seem to share Kennan's views, the Truman administration's policymakers used the plight of Britain and civil war in Greece to force the United States to come to grips with reality. Britain's inability to afford continuous support of the Greek government against Communist opposition became the occasion for the United States to assume the British burden in the Mediterranean. In March 1947 the president announced the Truman Doctrine, promising economic and military support to the beleaguered countries of Greece and Turkey, who at that time were combating Soviet pressures on their borders. But the Truman Doctrine promised much more: to support as well "free peoples who are resisting attempted subjugation by armed minorities or by outside pressures."[2]

Although Kennan recognized that the doctrine was more sweeping than anything he had envisioned, the Truman administration understood the need for jarring the U.S. public out of its complacency. Its leaders also knew that military aid alone was insufficient; Europe needed massive economic aid to encourage its recovery and its ability to resist the lure of Communism. In June 1947 the Marshall Plan satisfied many U.S. worries about the excessive dependence on arms to deal with Soviet expansion. The plan promised massive economic aid to countries that would show their worthiness by demonstrating a willingness to help themselves and to break down economic barriers with other beneficiaries of U.S. support. Unlike the loans made after World War I, there would be no demand for repayment. Instead, the recipients were expected to integrate and revive their economies; the argument was based on the assumption that a reformed Europe would be strong enough to resist Communist pressure. It was recognized that a demoralized Europe mired in poverty was vulnerable to the promises of Communism. This was the reasoning behind the secretary of state's commencement address at Harvard University in June 1947.

THE MARSHALL PLAN

In many ways, the Marshall Plan reflected a combination of U.S. idealism and enlightened self-interest. Short-term handouts had failed in the past, and loans were not repaid. But a prosperous Europe was expected to be a partner that would not only contribute to the economic well-being of the United States but become an ally against Soviet penetration, because the European beneficiaries would adopt variations of the U.S. model of society. It is noteworthy that none of the expectations of the United States involved entangling political or military alliance. The objective was European integration, not U.S. integration with Europe.

U.S. leaders may or may not have perceived that the approaches they were making were moving toward a full break with the isolationist past; but the steps they were taking were definitely leading toward that goal. The Europeans knew this and made it clear that a binding U.S. military commitment was indispensable if the aims of the Marshall Plan were to be fulfilled. As long as Western Europe lacked a sense of security, economic aid would not suffice to build their confidence. In the postwar world, their military resources could not withstand a Soviet invasion. They believed that U.S. power was the only deterrent that would inhibit Soviet aggression, and this required a much deeper change in the involvement of the United States with Europe than either the Truman Doctrine or the Marshall Plan.

The Marshall Plan, according to its framers—undersecretaries of state William L. Clayton and Dean G. Acheson—was to be an extension of the purposes of the Truman Doctrine. Clayton, head of the world's largest cotton brokerage and an ardent internationalist, was undersecretary for economic affairs. Acheson, a prominent Washington lawyer, had been an assistant secretary of state in World War II. Charles Bohlen, a veteran diplomat with expertise in Soviet affairs like Kennan, deserved some of the credit: he drafted the essence of the final version.[3] If the United States were to provide effective support of the military efforts of embattled nations, as it had rallied to the defense of Greece and Turkey, it was necessary that the economic base of the beneficiaries be strong enough to take advantage of the military assistance. In this context, the Marshall Plan represented a significant underpinning of the Truman Doctrine. Indeed, embedded in the Truman Doctrine was the recognition that "the seeds of totalitarian regimes are nurtured in misery and want," and that "our help should be primarily through economic and financial aid which is essential to economic stability and orderly political processes."[4] In essence, if the chaos of Greece and Turkey was not to be replicated in France or in Italy, where large Communist parties were flourishing, the United States must help Europeans create economic conditions that would permit them to cope with the promises of Communism. In the president's mind, the Truman Doctrine and the Marshall Plan were "two halves of the same walnut."[5]

Truman had succeeded Roosevelt after his death in March 1945. As a Missouri senator, he had been identified with his patron, Thomas J. Pendergast, the legendary corrupt mayor of Kansas City. Although no taint of corruption

was attached to his name, Truman was considered a run-of-the-mill politi-
cian until his service during World II as chairman of the special committee
to investigate the national defense program. His visibility in that position
won him nomination as vice president in 1944, but he entered the White
House with little knowledge about foreign affairs. But after a year of seeming indecision over the direction of U.S. foreign relations, Truman emerged
as a forceful leader committed to both the containment of Communism
and reconstruction of Europe. The Truman Doctrine and the Marshall Plan
were not his doing, but as president he knew where the buck stopped. Truman gladly took responsibility for both programs.

The complementary features of the two initiatives were not evident to all
observers. Such influential observers as Walter Lippmann initially found ir-
reconcilable differences between the Truman Doctrine and the Marshall
Plan. The suddenness of the Truman message to Congress suggested to him
almost a hasty reflex action driven by the exigencies of the moment rather
than a carefully worked out plan within the larger frame of foreign policy.[6]
Military aid to Greece and Turkey was primarily a stopgap military exercise,
plugging leaks in a corner of Europe. The Truman Doctrine in this context
was a major strike in the burgeoning Cold War, despite the president's reference to economic rehabilitation.

The Marshall Plan, according to Lippmann, was a more mature expression of the assistance the United States gave Europe after World War I without the stigma associated with unpaid loans. The United States recognized
that its own welfare rested on the revival of Europe. To ensure success, the
administration required European beneficiaries to give evidence of their
own efforts toward recovery. Equally important was a demonstration of Europe's progress by reducing trade barriers that had prevailed before World
War II and moving toward economic integration of the continent or at least
that part of Europe outside Soviet control.

Critics from the Left, however, such as Henry Wallace, former vice president under Roosevelt and secretary of commerce under Truman, applauded
U.S. support for the principles of self-help, mutual aid, and yet identified
the corrupting influence of the Truman Doctrine on the Marshall Plan.
Given the primary functions of the Truman Doctrine, the European Recovery Program (ERP) in practice would result in the militarization of the social, economic, and political affairs of the recipients. As Wallace claimed,
"we will help you if you have our kind of government and subordinate your
economy to ours."[7] Wallace, vice president in Roosevelt's third term, had
opened himself to the charge of being an apologist for the Soviet Union, a
position that cost him his Cabinet post as secretary of commerce in September 1946.

From the Right, Edwin Borchard of the Yale Law School, who was a vigorous isolationist spokesman in the 1930s, worried about the enormous

costs the Marshall Plan would impose on the United States. Asserting that economic aid was based on "the unsound political plan of Potsdam," he felt that "so long as that basis stands any American money raised . . . will be the sheerest palliative and can serve no purpose of recovery." Moreover, it would serve to finance state socialism, a conclusion Borchard believed should clinch his case.[8]

But opponents of European economic aid lost some of their natural constituencies. The administration's care in assuring that the Marshall Plan would not be another species of the UN's ongoing agencies mollified liberals who had been alienated by the Truman Doctrine. Although the *Christian Century* admitted that the Marshall Plan was a gamble, the journal asserted that it was also "a great venture in statesmanship."[9] Even the acerbic *Nation* agreed that the plan "offers a new hope." Liberal journals were able to take comfort from Lippmann's clear distinction between "the Truman line and the Marshall line"—one unilateral, the other in harmony with the UN.[10] For Joseph Jones, who helped draft both documents, the links between the two were obvious and beneficial to Europeans and Americans alike. The two halves of the same walnut signified U.S. acceptance of responsibility as a world leader, and as such was the central feature of a "national conversion" that would forever change the nature of U.S.-foreign relations with the Old World.[11]

If there were lingering doubts about the conjunction between the Marshall Plan and the UN, the endorsement of leaders of the American Association for the United Nations (AAUN) should have resolved them. Clark M. Eichelberger, as its national director, offered a blessing by association: "The Marshall Plan must not be considered disassociated from the United Nations. Its success means stability for the nations of Europe, and the United Nations must derive strength from stable members." Although the majority of the Philadelphia branch of the UN council would have preferred that the plan be administered by the UN, that organization's letter to the Senate Committee on Foreign Affairs observed that "It is important to point out that there was a significant minority in favor of having the United States administer aid alone."[12] The majority's objections were a minor caveat. U.S. friends of the UN had put their imprimatur on the Marshall Plan.

Congress gave its approval, too, but only after agonizing debates about spending so much money on possibly unreliable and ungrateful beneficiaries. On 2 December 1947, members of the House of Representatives Rules Committee wondered about the lasting effectiveness of foreign aid as well as the potential impact on the domestic economy. In the Senate, Republican Robert Taft of Ohio, the foremost skeptic about European entanglements before and after World War II, managed to cut the proposed three-year program to a single year, with a proportionate reduction of funds.[13] It took the impending breakdown of the four-powers Council of Foreign Ministers meeting in London for Congress to come to terms with the interim aid bill on 15 December. The bill became Public Law 389 of the Foreign Aid Act of 1947 two days later.[14] Flying back to Washington immediately after the adjournment of the London conference, Marshall lent his weight to the act in a radio report on 19 December. He made it clear to the U.S. public that the East-West conflict would be fought out over the ERP rather than over the a doomed peace conference on the future of Germany.[15] This modest success was a signal for the full aid program to proceed in full force.

For the most part, Europeans recognized the opportunity offered by the Marshall Plan and proceeded to meet it. Under the leadership of the British and French foreign ministers, they sought to demonstrate that Europeans could overcome the economic barriers that had bedeviled interstate relations in the past and to show that they could utilize the massive aid envisioned in the ERP to serve the unity as well as the recovery of Europe. Sixteen nations from the East, as well as from the West, met in Paris in July 1947 and established the Committee of European Economic Cooperation (CEEC), chaired by British delegate Oliver Franks, to implement themes laid out in Secretary Marshall's address.[16]

Before any funds were raised, the Marshall Plan deepened a conflict with the Soviet Union that had already been underway. The Soviets had been invited to join the program and indeed were represented in Paris by a large delegation. Rather than reducing East-West tensions, the Soviets withdrew from discussions of the plan, charging that it represented a U.S. plot to control the destiny of all Europe. According to Foreign Minister Ernest Bevin's account to Prime Minister Clement Attlee, Soviet Foreign Minister Vyacheslav Molotov walked out angrily, "uttering threats." Bevin then confided to U.S. Ambassador to France Jefferson Caffery that "I am glad that the cards have been laid on the table and that the responsibility will be laid at Moscow's door." Here was an open breach between East and West and arguably the beginning of the Cold War. Bevin was reputed to have whispered to his private secretary, "This really is the birth of the Western bloc."[17]

In a sense, the Soviet withdrawal from the discussions in Paris over a European response to the Marshall address came as a relief to Kennan and Bohlen. The United States recognized that Soviet participation would kill the Marshall Plan in Congress. But in light of their familiarity with Communist behavior, neither diplomat felt that the Soviets could accept U.S. verification of the uses to which the funds would be put. When Poland and Czechoslovakia showed an interest in participating, the Kremlin intervened. It was obvious, as Bohlen anticipated, that if the countries in the Communist orbit should participate in the recovery program, its control over Eastern Europe would be in jeopardy.[18] This judgment was reasonable. Embarking on its campaign against the Marshall Plan, the Soviets not only forced Eastern Europe to join their opposition but also encouraged strikes and demonstrations by their Communist friends in France and Italy in protest of "American hegemonic intentions." The Soviets had some hopes, too, that France's worries about the potential success of Germany's economic recovery would be at the expense of their interests, and so would Foreign Minister Georges Bidault's support of the new CEEC.[19]

Bidault had won acclaim as a leader of the French underground in World War II and subsequently as foreign minister from March 1947 to July 1948. A member of the center-left Catholic party, the *Mouvement Républicain Populaire* (MRP), he walked a fine line between suspicion of a revived German militarism and a lively fear of Communism at home and abroad. His decision for a close association with Britain and the United States against a perceived Soviet threat earned him initial plaudits but ultimately led to his defeat in the summer of 1948. His countrymen felt that his embrace of the Anglo-Americans led to neglect of the German menace.

Understandably, Soviet expectations were buoyed by France's earlier concern that the Anglo-U.S. merger of their zones in Germany could lead to too hasty reconstruction of a potentially dangerous Germany.[20] The Soviets were to be disappointed when France agreed unofficially to trizonal fusion at the same time that it lent its support to the Marshall Plan in July 1948.[21] Before Marshall returned home from London in December 1947, he and his British and French counterparts implied that the fusion of the French zone with the other two would be "an evolutionary development," but one that could be resolved in the near future.[22]

BEVIN-BIDAULT COLLABORATION

Certainly, the vehement Soviet reaction to the Marshall Plan accelerated the Cold War, even if it did not ignite it. The Kennan warnings, along with Churchill's Iron Curtain speech at Fulton, Missouri, in 1946, when he accused the Soviets of sealing off Eastern Europe from the West, were clear preludes, and the Truman Doctrine laid down a challenge in no uncertain terms. The key element that determined East-West relations in 1947 continued to revolve around the German question. The victors of World War II had established the Council of Foreign Ministers at Potsdam in 1945 primarily to settle the future of Germany. Failing to evoke any interest from Molotov in a twenty-five-year security treaty, U.S. Secretary of State Byrnes moved to facilitate the revival and reorganization of Germany by merging the economies of the British and U.S. sectors of Germany in 1946. The British, beset with their economic troubles, agreed, and by the end of the year, a bizonia, linking the British and U.S. sectors, was in place. But the nub of the Soviet problem then and in 1947 appeared to be the issue of German reparations, particularly with respect to its own claims.[23]

When the ministers of the four powers met in Moscow in March 1947, it was apparent that their cooperation was coming to an end. But still hoping for economic unification of all Germany, advisers to Secretary of State Marshall, who had replaced Byrnes in January 1947, looked for a way to solve the reparations issue. They recommended taking reparations from current production as inducement to unify the four zones. Up to this point, the Soviets had been taking their reparations out of capital equipment.[24] Because this change meant that the financial burden would fall on the U.S. taxpayer, it was a significant concession but not significant enough. Stalin seemed uninterested in coming to an agreement on economic unity. The Moscow conference convinced the United States that by delaying German recovery the Soviets anticipated the resulting fear and disillusionment to bring Western Europe into the Communist orbit. Still, hopes for a peace conference were not fully dashed; the political aspects were left to the deputies to the foreign ministers to handle.[25]

The failure of the Moscow conference made the U.S. effort to restore Europe's economic life all the more imperative. The Marshall Plan was a measure of U.S. leadership. While not directly impinging on the status of Germany, it was obvious that Germany was central to the success of the program. In fact, before the end of the year, President Truman asked for funds for the economic revival of Germany as an integral part of the Marshall Plan.[26] The need to deal with Germany enabled Bidault and Bevin to move ahead with plans for cooperation in merging the French zone with the Anglo-U.S. sectors. When the last attempts to resolve the German question collapsed in London in December, the question of reparations was far less important than the larger issue of whether Germany would fall to the East or to the West.

As East-West relations worsened, Anglo-French ties grew closer as a means of engaging U.S. support and coping with Soviet hostility. The effort did not begin with the Bevin proposal to Marshall after the failure of the London meeting of the Council of Foreign Ministers. The signing of the anti-German Treaty of Dunkirk on 4 March 1947, a fifty-year pact designed to calm French passions about a resurgent German nationalism, initiated a new spirit of Anglo-French collaboration. This Anglo-French pact assured the nervous French that in the event of a German attack, the other ally would "provide all the military and other support and assistance in its power." (France's psychological wounds over its surrender to Nazi Germany in 1940 had not yet healed.) Britain's action helped to move France's leadership to a gradual recognition in 1947 that the Soviets rather than the Germans were the primary obstacle to a new order in Europe.

The transition did not come easily. France, plagued with Communist agitation and lingering mistrust of its British ally, could not come to a quick decision on the Dunkirk treaty. Jean Chauvel, head of the foreign office at the Quai d'Orsay, and René Massigli, ambassador to London, did not want to move too fast for fear of producing a meaningless paper agreement.[27] They were also worried about hostile Communist reactions, not only on the street but also in the caretaker government in Paris.

Bevin, too, had reasons for caution; he reportedly told Bidault that "we can't carry on a conversation between two great Powers, with a third great Power in the cupboard with a listening apparatus."[28] From the British perspective, the immediate purpose of the Anglo-French treaty was to bolster French opposition to Soviet influence as well as to underscore the potential danger of German revanchism. Massigli agreed but felt that Britain was mistaken in fearing that the French government would not resist temptations to forge closer ties with Moscow and accommodate the Soviets on the future of Germany.[29]

Soviet behavior at the Moscow conference in March and in Paris in July over the implementation of the Marshall Plan quickened the pace of collaboration between Bevin and Bidault over the six months before the London conference of foreign ministers. The Marshall Plan was a vehicle for many of their conversations, and inevitably they included questions about the role the United States might play in political as well as economic support of Western Europe. Ideally, Bevin, who looked to Britain's Labour government as a "middle way" between Soviet Communism and U.S. capitalism, would have preferred an Anglo-French collaboration to produce a Western European middle way.[30] But even as Bidault pondered over the possibility of a Western European defense pact, he raised the question of engaging the United States in the process.[31]

Although old issues, such as French pressures to increase coal deliveries from the Ruhr, surfaced in the conversations, as well as occasional references to an Anglo-French "third force" mediating between the United States and the Soviet Union, few illusions remained. Without minimizing the dangers from Soviet policies, neither minister regarded dependence on the United States as the first choice. Exercising statecraft to manipulate both superpowers to advance the position of Western Europe was an ideal that died hard. Indeed, it was to resurface periodically over the next two generations. Moreover, the Anglo-French discussions had to take into account the abiding British sense of a special relationship with the United States. In the words of Bevin's private secretary, "Europe under American water cans handled by British gardeners blossoms into a happy Western garden of Eden."[32] More critical to the success of Anglo-French discussions was Bidault's confession at a dinner in New York on October 7 that "he had burned his boats as regards to the Russians." He said he had "tried to follow a middle path for two years. . . . Russian moves had shown that they were determined to have two worlds rather than one."[33]

Both foreign ministers recognized that there had to be a military as well as a political and economic dimension to U.S. support. Following the

French general staff's advice, Bidault asked Marshall in October about a U.S. contribution to European security.[34] He received no satisfactory answer. And there was not full trust in its French ally on the part of Britain. Intimate though the conversations were, the French foreign minister still had to convince Bevin that French Communists were no longer an obstacle to Western unity and that French military representatives would be trustworthy. He succeeded, and on 2 December when Marshall asked for the best means of steadying the French, Bevin's response was quick—immediate passage of the interim aid bill.[35] Neither of these meetings evoked a response from the secretary of state about the United States joining any Western European defense program, but the Europeans felt a path was opening.

The path expanded when Bevin and Bidault were prepared to take advantage of implications in Secretary Marshall's speech to the Pilgrim Society in London on 12 December. Although there was no mention of U.S. interest in participating in a European organization, Marshall emphasized the beneficial effects that the ERP would have on the regeneration of Europe.[36] This was sufficient encouragement for the allies to agree that Franco-British staff talks should be held, with the hope of including the United States in the future. With his cabinet's support, on 19 December Bidault instructed General Pierre Billotte, then a member of the French delegation to the UN, to begin talks with the United States and Britain on negotiating a military agreement. The general reported that they were surprised but pleased at the French initiative.[37]

The allies moved quickly to facilitate an "engagement" with the United States. While Bevin gave Sir Ivone Kirkpatrick, British High Commissioner in Germany, the responsibility for providing a blueprint of a Western European military alliance, Bidault proposed a treaty with Belgium on 23 December. The proposal was couched in bilateral terms, along the lines of the Anglo-French Dunkirk Treaty concluded earlier in the year, with the idea of using the anti-German language to avoid open offense to Russia.[38] The two allies were then poised to take the next step of bringing the United States into this new Western European entity.

HICKERSON'S REACTIONS

Nominally, the breakdown of the London conference resulted from the West's unwillingness to meet Soviet Foreign Minister Molotov's demands for $10 billion in reparations at 1938 values. The larger issues were Soviet opposition to the Marshall Plan, the economic recovery of Western Europe, and the Anglo-U.S. bizonal arrangement to revive their West German zones. The meeting ended without resolution when "a dead silence" greeted Bevin's request for "suggestions as to the time and place of the next meeting." As the ministers went to the bar afterwards for a drink, Molotov was heard to remark, "This is awful."[39]

No participant in the proceedings of the foreign ministers was more in agreement with Molotov's remark than the State Department's Director of the Office of European Affairs, John D. Hickerson, even if his reasons differed from those of the Soviet foreign minister. A "tough minded West Texan," in Theodore C. Achilles's admiring words, he was also a dedicated internationalist and an experienced bureaucratic operator. Entering the U.S. Foreign Service in 1928, he occupied a variety of positions, drawing favorable attention in each of them. During World War II, he had served on the U.S.-Canadian Board of Defense and in 1945 was adviser at the Conference of International Organizations in San Francisco that framed the UN charter. In London, this veteran diplomat was familiar with many of the players at that ill-fated gathering.[40] Achilles, a U.S. Foreign Service officer since 1931, was director of the office of Western Europe Affairs and an acolyte of Hickerson. His devotion to the Atlantic alliance may have been even more avid than his superior's. Achilles spent his retirement years as a leader of the Atlantic Council of the United States, an organization devoted to the advancement of the Atlantic community.

Hickerson had listened to the words of Secretary Marshall in his Pilgrim Society address in London a few days before the termination of the meetings and shared Marshall's sentiments about "the great surge of American public opinion in support of the effort to alleviate the sufferings and hardships of the peoples on this side of the Atlantic" that World War II had inflicted. He particularly appreciated Marshall's emphasis on the "natural growth in the case of two peoples enjoying a common heritage and having a common outlook on the fundamentals of human society."[41] He was even more enthusiastic about the conversation at a private dinner Foreign Secretary Bevin had with Marshall at his flat in Carlton Terrace on 15 December, when Bevin spoke of his conviction that given little opportunity for dealing with the Soviet Union in the foreseeable future, the salvation of the West lay in the formation of some form of union supported by the United States and Canada to permit Western Europe to cope with the Communist challenge. Massigli observed sardonically that Bevin articulated his views "with remarkable imprecision." But Hickerson and Achilles were captivated by the foreign minister's language. According to Hickerson, Bevin used many of the same words that he repeated in his speech to the House of Commons a few weeks later. Achilles claimed that "these words were engraved on Jack's memory as they are on mine."[42]

Over the next few days Bevin elaborated on this theme, when at Marshall's request, Hickerson visited Bevin at the foreign office. On one level, Bevin referred to a "spiritual federation of the West" that was obviously not a formal alliance. At the same time he envisioned two "security arrangements,"

a smaller, tighter one embracing treaties with France and the Benelux countries and a larger and looser treaty with other European countries. Both
would have treaty commitments from the United States and Canada.[43]

The concept of a Western association, if not alliance, was in the air in the
fall of 1947, outside the confines of Anglo-French conversations. Canadian
statesmen were at the forefront of concerns about Atlantic links in which
their country would occupy a key role mediating between the United States
and Europe. Escott Reid, deputy undersecretary of state for external affairs,
speaking at the annual Conference of the Canadian Institute of Public Affairs in August, recommended a regional security organization within the
UN charter that could take measures of collective self-defense until the Security Council acted. He suggested that "this may be the first public statement advocating a collective defen[s]e organization of the [W]estern
world."[44] Reid was heartened to note that Hamilton Fish Armstrong, editor
of *Foreign Affairs*, had made a similar proposal, specifically adding a proto-
col to the UN charter. But it was Canadian Prime Minister Louis St. Laurent,
addressing the UN General Assembly on 18 September, who is credited
with first proposing "an association of peace-loving states" that would pursue the goals of the charter. Given the realities of the Soviet Union's veto
power in the Security Council, the association would operate under the auspices of an amended charter.[45]

Reactions from the secretary of state and his principal adviser on European affairs differed markedly; Marshall was a cool and stiff former army
chief of staff, celebrated as one of the architects of victory in World War II.
The fact that he "seldom looked like anything but a soldier" was an important factor in the president's choice in placing a military man in charge of
the State Department. He would have the toughness to face the Soviets that
his predecessors, Edward R. Stettinius, Jr., and Byrnes, had lacked. His
wartime experience included summit conferences involving political as well
as military matters. Senator Truman paid him the ultimate compliment in
1944 of being the greatest living American at a time, as historian Robert Ferrell pointed out, when "another great American was alive at 1600 Pennsylvania Avenue." Acheson, not easily impressed by his fellow man, was
moved to observe that "the moment General Marshall entered a room,
everyone in it felt his presence. . . . His figure conveyed intensity, which his
voice, low, staccato, and incisive, reinforced. . . . It compelled respect. . . .
There was no military glamour about him and nothing of the martinet. Yet
to all of us he was always 'General Marshall.' The title fitted him as though
he was baptized with it. . . . I should never have dreamed of addressing him
as 'Mr. Secretary'; and I have never heard anyone but Mrs. Marshall call him
'George.'"[46]

Given this persona, it was hardly surprising that Marshall's support of the
proposals of his European counterparts was carefully qualified. He was not

one to be carried away by enthusiasm, particularly when it emanated from his European counterparts. His Pilgrim Society speech on 12 December concentrated on the effect that material aid of the Marshall Plan would have on European unity but included no specific promise of U.S. participation beyond general approval of Bevin's path. As the U.S. charge d'affaires in London reported, Marshall "had no criticism of Mr. Bevin's general idea. But he thought there should be an understanding as soon as possible on their immediate objectives," which involved the "material regeneration" of Europe. When Bevin asked if he could share the substance of the dinner conversation with the French, the State Department responded that there was no objection to showing Bidault its "expurgated" contents as long as the French understood that Marshall "had not definitely approved any particular course of action and had hoped to receive specific British proposals before making any final commitment." Undersecretary of State Robert A. Lovett noted that since "the British have already shown the memo of conversation to the French, I suppose we should not refuse. If, however, we agree, I think we should make it clear that Bevin was speaking without the authority of his Cabinet, and as he put it, was thinking out loud."[47]

Hickerson looked at the Bevin initiatives from a different perspective. Well versed as he was in European matters and not given to emotional outbursts, he was nonetheless upset by the failure of the foreign ministers in London to reach a peace agreement with the Soviets over Germany and more importantly by the consequent condition of ongoing hostility between East and West. Bevin and Bidault had found a ready partner in this seasoned diplomat, although he was not at the level of authority they would have preferred.

Returning to Washington by ship, Hickerson had the opportunity suggest to a shipmate, John Foster Dulles, Senator Arthur H. Vandenberg's representative at the conference and putative secretary of state (should the Republicans win the White House in 1948), that Marshall's response was not good enough. Hickerson insisted that only U.S. acceptance of a military alliance could create sufficient confidence in Europe to restore the political and economic health of Western Europe.[48]

Hickerson could appreciate Marshall's caution and his assumption that the new "union" must be wholly European. The Marshall Plan, after all, was only six months old, and Europeans were bickering over who was to get U.S. aid, and Congress was hesitant to authorize, let alone appropriate, funds.[49] Yet the imperative was clear, and he and Achilles would be the engine in the state department to break the long tradition of nonentanglement in the military and political affairs of Europe.

Dulles did not need much convincing. At Marshall's suggestion, as Kennan noted, he had gone to Paris on 4 December to reassure the nervous French that the secretary of state's presence in London did not signify any diminution of U.S. concern for France's interests. He returned to London shaken by the sense of desperation he had found in Paris and convinced that the country beset by Communist-inspired strikes required immediate political reassurance of U.S. commitment.[50]

No statesman in U.S. history, aside from John Quincy Adams, had been more carefully groomed for a primary role in the shaping of foreign relations than this grandson of John W. Foster, secretary of state under Benjamin Harrison and nephew of Robert Lansing, secretary of state under Wilson. With both Republican and Democratic credentials in his family, Dulles was no narrow political partisan but an active follower of the internationalist faction in the Republican Party. As a Princeton undergraduate with the right connections, he served as secretary to the Chinese delegation to the Hague Conference of 1907. He was a participant in the peace negotiations at Versailles in 1919 and then went on to a distinguished career in international law with the prestigious firm of Sullivan and Cromwell. Dulles was also heir to the Presbyterian legacy of his clergyman father and devoted much of his time to serving the interests of the Federal Council of Churches in America. By World War II he was an influential adviser to the internationalist wing of the Republican Party.[51]

As early as January 1947, Dulles had delivered a major address in New York in which he urged the reconstruction of Europe along the lines of the federal union. He urged that "Americans ought to be able to give them precious assistance. . . . We have, more than any other people, experience in using the federal formula, and in developing its manifold possibilities." There was no further connection with the United States in that speech.[52] But by November before he joined Marshall in London for the foreign ministers meeting, he testified on the interim aid bill for Europe that we "should not forget that today the United States, in Germany, is a western European government. Our exhortations to other western European nations will sound hollow if we ourselves fail to do what we expect of others. We ought to set the example." His message specifically concerned the economic reconstruction of Germany but that the intimate involvement of the United States as a Western European government could lead to a political commitment as well.[53]

Dulles's views had been cleared with Governor Thomas E. Dewey and Senator Vandenberg, two of the most important leaders of the Republican Party. Around the country there were editorials and congressional voices looking to a European federation as a solution to the German problems. Democrats and Republican alike also identified political federation as a response to Western Europe's debilitating disunity. In March, Democratic Senators J. William Fulbright of Arkansas and Elbert Thomas of Utah presented concurrent resolutions to the Senate and House stating that "the Congress favors the creation of a United States of Europe within the framework of the United Nations."[54]

Although the Arkansas senator was an architect of the Greek-Turkish aid package as well as a vigorous advocate of the UN, Vandenberg was not happy with the open-ended commitments the Truman Doctrine would impose, and he was pessimistic about the ability of the UN to maintain collective security. The lack of a viable alternative turned his attention toward European federation. The Marshall Plan was a beginning but not a sufficient means of restoring stability to Western Europe. He urged quick action while the situation in Europe was still fluid. With the London conference of foreign ministers still in session, Fulbright, speaking at the University of Toronto in early December, warned that "the continent, in its present fragmentary form, is a large power vacuum which Russia is trying to fill. Let us be under no illusions. If Russia obtains control of Western Europe, the control of Africa, the Near East, and the Middle East will fall into her lap like a ripe plum."[55]

The particular historical precedent fitting the current situation in the minds of U.S. foreign-policy elites, liberal and conservative alike, seemed to be the United States under the Articles of Confederation in the 1780s, when the founding fathers introduced the federal constitution as the solution to their problems. The popularity of historian Carl Van Doren's *The Great Rehearsal*, a recounting of the making of the U.S. Constitution, lay in the contemporary message it offered to its readers when it appeared in the fall of 1947. Van Doren himself prompted the comparison, as he noted in his preface, that the meeting "might be, though of course no one of them ever used the term, a rehearsal for the federal government of the future."[56] The vehicle for change in his book would be the UN, not a U.S. membership in a Western European alliance.

But what Hickerson had wanted, and Dulles agreed to in confidence, was just that—a U.S. association with Europe that would be a huge step beyond just oral support for European unity. The United States had to be a part of this process. The model that influenced Hickerson and Achilles was the work of the U.S. journalist Clarence K. Streit, whose book *Union Now* had urged the joining of the Anglo-U.S. democracies in 1939, at a time when the survival of Britain was at stake. After the war he expanded its scope to include some fifteen Atlantic democracies, including the self-governing dominions of the British Commonwealth. Like Van Doren's recommendations, the new union would be modeled on the U.S. federal union of 1787.[57]

Neither Van Doren nor Streit was a model Marshall had in mind. They were far too ambitious for his taste. Nor did his European counterparts look to an ideal United States of Europe for their immediate salvation. They had their own more narrow objectives when they proposed a relationship with the United States that would build their economic revival on a military guarantee of their security. This was Bevin's and Bidault's goal.

The thoughtful British journalist Barbara Ward placed the events of 1947 in the perspective of a sea change in the United States' outlook on the world as she looked ahead to 1948. Writing in the *New York Times Sunday Magazine* on 28 December, she called the new year "the Decisive Year for Us." It will be in 1948, she predicted, that the United States will take on "our world responsibility" that the events of 1947 set in motion. Ward asserted that "a liberal world order will either pivot on the United States or it will be neither liberal or ordered." The Truman Doctrine and Marshall Plan particularly were earnests of future commitments that "have crystallized the forces making for responsibility and action which had been gathering force ever since the end of the first World War."[58]

Hickerson had no doubts about the meaning of the failed conference of foreign ministers in London. When he returned to Washington on 24 December, he approached Achilles at his desk about 3 PM on the afternoon before New Year's Day. It was the custom of Washington's Metropolitan Club to hold open house for its members over the holiday. Drinks were free. Hickerson was "full of fishhouse punch and an idea for a North Atlantic Treaty." According to Achilles, he exclaimed, "I don't care if entangling alliances have been considered worse than original sin since George Washington's time. We've got to have a peace time military alliance with Western Europe. And we've got to get it ratified. It's your baby. Get going."[59] Although Achilles was convinced that martinis, not the Club's punch, stoked Hickerson's outburst, he fully agreed with the sentiments.

NOTES

1. George F. Kennan, *Memoirs, 1925–1950* (Boston: Little, Brown and Co., 1967); excerpts from the *Long Telegram*, February 22, 1946, 592–98.

2. President's Message to the Congress, March 12, 1947, in *Public Papers of the Presidents of the United States 1947* (Washington, DC: Office of the Federal Register), 178–79.

3. Charles E. Bohlen, *Witness to History, 1929–1969* (New York: Norton, 1969), 264.

4. President's Message to the Congress, March 12, 1947, 180.

5. Cited in Joseph M. Jones, *The Fifteen Weeks (February 21–June 4, 1947)* (New York: Viking Press, 1955), 233.

6. Walter Lippmann, *The Cold War: A Study in U.S. Foreign Policy* (New York: Harper & Row, 1947), 54–55.

7. Henry A. Wallace, "My Alternative to the Marshall Plan," *The New Republic* 118, no. 3 (January 12, 1948): 13–14.

8. Edwin Borchard, "Intervention—The Truman Doctrine and the Marshall Plan," *American Journal of International Law* 41, no. 4 (October 1947): 887.

9. *Christian Century* 64, no. 31 (July 30, 1947): 920.

10. *The Nation*, 164, no. 25 (June 21, 1947), 730; Lippmann, *Cold War*, 52.

11. Jones, *Fifteen Weeks*, 262.

12. Teichel Berger testimonial in *Hearings* on U.S. assistance to European Recovery Program, Senate Committee on European Relations, part 3, February 5, 1948, 936; Ltr Francis Fussell to Senator Vandenberg, in *Hearings* on U.S. Assistance to European Economic Recovery, Senate Committee on Foreign Relations, part 2, January 28, 1948, 926; Ltr Francis Fussell to Senator Vandenberg, in *Hearings* on U.S. Assistance to European Economic Recovery, Senate Committee on Foreign Relations, part 3, February 5, 1948, 1429.

13. *New York Times*, December 4, 1947.

14. *Statutes-at-Large*, Public Law 389, December 17, 1947.

15. The London Meeting of the Council of Foreign Ministers, November 25–December 18, 1947, December 19; Department of State *Bulletin* 27, no. 443 (December 1947): 1247.

16. Jefferson Caffery to Secretary of State, June 20, 1947, *Foreign Relations of the United States* (hereafter cited as *FRUS*) *1947*, III: 333.

17. Caffery to Secretary of State, June 19, July 1, 1947, 302–3.

18. Bohlen, *Witness to History*, 2.

19. Undersecretary Robert Lovett to Secretary of State, August 3, 1947, *FRUS*, 1947, IV: 1015, on French Communist suspicions of American intentions.

20. Heike Bungert, "French-American Relations, 1945–1948," *Diplomatic History* 28, no. 3 (Summer 1994): 342–43.

21. Bungert, "French-American Relations," 349.

22. Memo of conversation by Ambassador Lewis W. Douglas, December 17, 1947, *FRUS*, 1947, II: 813–14.

23. Frank Ninkovich, *Germany and the United States: The Transformation of the German Question since 1945*, updated edition (New York: Twayne/Macmillan, 1995), 56. All Western efforts to allay Soviet suspicions of American motives were "met by indifferent silence" by Soviet Foreign Minister Molotov.

24. Philip Zelikow, "George C. Marshall and the Moscow CFM Meeting of 1947," *Diplomacy and Statecraft* 8, no. 2 (July 1997):105–7.

25. *Facts on File Yearbook, 1947*, 7, no. 339: 126.

26. *New York Times*, December 8, 1947.

27. Jean Chauvel, *Commentaire: d'Alger a Berne, 1944–1952* (Paris: Fayard, 1972), 189–91; René Massigli, *Une comedie des erreurs, 1943–1946* (Paris: Plon, 1978), 91.

28. Quoted in Anne Deighton, *The Impossible Peace: Britain, the Division of Germany and the Cold War* (Oxford: Clarendon Press, 1990), 163.

29. Massigli, *Comedie*, 92.

30. Geoffrey Warner, "Britain and Europe in 1948: The View from the Cabinet" in *Power in Europe: Great Britain, France, Italy and Germany in a Postwar Europe*, ed. Josef Becker and Franz Knipping (Berlin: Walter de Gruyter, 1986), 34–35.

31. Herbert Feis, *From Trust to Terror: The Onset of the Cold War, 1945–1950* (New York: Norton, 1970), 285–86.

32. Quoted in Deighton, *The Impossible Peace*, 190.

33. Deighton, *The Imposssible Peace*, 204.

34. George-Henri Soutou, "France," in *The Origins of the Cold War in Europe: International Perspectives*, ed. David Reynolds (New Haven: Yale University Press, 1994), 105.

35. Alan Bullock, *Ernest Bevin: Foreign Secretary, 1945-1950* (Oxford: Oxford University Press, 1985), 495-96.

36. George C. Marshall, "Peace and Understanding—The Desire of All Mankind," Address to Pilgrims Society, London, December 12, 1947, Department of State *Bulletin*, 17 (December 21, 1947): 1201-3.

37. Soutou, "France," 108; Pierre Billotte, *Le passé au future* (Paris: Editions Stock, 1979), 58.

38. Massigli, *Comedie*, 105.

39. *Facts on File Yearbook, 1947*, 7, no. 373: 397.

40. Theodore C. Achilles, *Fingerprints on History: The NATO Memoirs of Theodore C. Achilles*, edited by Lawrence S. Kaplan and Sidney B. Snyder (Kent, OH: Lyman L. Lemnitzer Center for NATO and European Community Affairs, Kent State University, 1992), 11, 13.

41. Marshall, "Peace and Understanding," 1201-3.

42. Achilles, *Footprints on History*, 12; Massigli, *Comedie*, 105.

43. Escott Reid, *Time of Fear and Hope: The Making of the North Atlantic Treaty, 1947-1949* (Toronto: McClelland and Stewart, 1977), 37.

44. Reid, *Time of Fear and Hope*, 30-31.

45. Reid, *Time of Fear and Hope*, 32.

46. Robert H. Ferrell, *George Marshall* in *The American Secretaries of State and Their Diplomacy 15*, eds., Robert H. Ferrell and Samuel F. Bemis (New York: Cooper Union Press, 1966), 3; Dean Acheson, *Sketches from Life of Men I Have Known* (New York: Popular Library, 1962), 123.

47. Telegram, Chargé in London to Secretary of State, December 22, 1947, *FRUS, 1948*, III: 1; tel 5350 to U.S. Embassy in London, December 24, 1947, 840.00/12-2247, Record Group (hereafter RG) 59, National Archives and Records Administration (hereafter NARA), not printed but summarized in footnote on p. 3; memo, Lovett to Bohlen, December 23, 1947, 840.00/3-3018, box 5643, RG 59, NARA.

48. Achilles, *Fingerprints on History*, 12-13

49. Reid, *Time of Fear and Hope*, 37.

50. Kennan, *Memoirs*, 420.

51. Richard Immerman, *John Foster Dulles: Piety, Pragmatism, and Power in U.S. Foreign Policy* (Wilmington, DE: SR Books, 1999), 1-15.

52. John Foster Dulles, "Europe Must Federate or Perish," in *Vital Speeches of the Day* 13, no. 8, (February 17, 1947): 236.

53. Interim Aid for Europe, Senate Committee on Foreign Relations, *Hearings*, November 19, 1947, 80th Cong, 1st sess., 241.

54. Senate Congressional Resolution 10, 80th Cong., *Congressional Record* 93 (March 21, 1947): 2347.

55. Quoted in Randall B. Woods, *Fulbright: A Biography* (New York: Cambridge University Press, 1955), 141.

56. Carl Van Doren, *The Great Rehearsal: The Story of the Making and Ratifying of the Constitution of the United States* (New York: Viking, 1948), 10.

57. Clarence Streit, *A Proposal for a Federal Union of the Democracies of the North Atlantic* (New York: Harper and Bros., 1939).

58. Barbara Ward, "The New Year, the Decisive Year for U.S.," *New York Times Magazine*, December 28, 1947, 5ff.

59. Quoted in Achilles, *Fingerprints on History*, 11.

2

"The Speech": 22 January 1948

SPIRITUAL FEDERATION

The signals announcing the impending union of Western Europe were as mixed as the transatlantic weather on New Year's Day of 1948. A fierce winter storm almost shut down New York, while London was enjoying spring-like temperatures.[1] The year 1947 had ended with the expectation that the "spiritual federation of the West" would materialize early in the new year. This did not occur. Indeed, Britain and the United States held different assumptions about the meaning of federation, and neither gave much credence to the spiritual character of federation.

The obstacles were formidable. From the U.S. perspective, the administration's first priority was *not* providing military aid, let alone joining a Western federation, but securing congressional approval for the Marshall Plan. And at the State Department and the Pentagon, there was no consensus about the U.S. role in Europe's defense.

France's position was even less promising. The most supportive French diplomats wondered about the implications of a spiritual federation and looked quizzically at its composition even as they admired its imprecision. Their doubts did not end with the public presentation of this idea before the House of Commons on 22 January.[2] France's preoccupation was still centered on the dangers of a German revival, even as Georges Bidault worked to redirect the nation's attention to the Soviet danger. Ernest Bevin's unified Europe offered no solutions to their concerns.

As for Britain, its military leaders were not yet convinced that France was a reliable military partner and continued to resist commitment of British troops to Europe in the event of war. Historian John Baylis noted that despite Bevin's initiative, the foreign office was not at all clear about the meaning of spiritual federation.[3] Bevin further confused the issue by keeping alive the notion of Western Europe as a "third force" between the United States and the Soviet Union.[4]

Although the spiritual aspect of Western unity was nebulous, it had its uses. The Soviet danger was not simply from the threat of its military power. Rather, it was the genuine possibility that Communist parties in critical countries, such as France and Italy, would assume office. The challenge was ideological, benefiting as it did from positive roles in the resistance against the Nazis in World War II. In 1986, historian Robin Edmonds observed that the Soviet threat as perceived in London and Washington was as much psychological as military: "Bevin's phrase 'spiritual federation' may have an odd ring today, but at that time it corresponded to a deeply felt fear of what the Communist parties of Western Europe might be able to achieve, politically and industrially, in response to the Kremlin's directives."[5] In 1948, the phrase invoked the shared religious values of the West that could compete with the ideological challenge of Communism.

UNDERSTANDING BEVIN

To "employ a sprat to catch a mackerel" is a phrase that has captured the popular imagination, at least among the community of British scholars. It suggests that Foreign Minister Bevin shrewdly, and with calculation, intended to lure the United States into an alliance with Western Europe controlled by Britain. The image of a united Europe breaking down old barriers and developing its own resources to the best of its ability reflected the demands that the Marshall Plan imposed on Europeans and to which they responded through economic cooperation. In this scenario, Bevin emerges as a wily magician manipulating the United States and Europe alike.

French colleagues seemed to embrace this view, noting, as René Massigli did, the purposeful imprecision of his presentation to George Marshall in December 1947. When Bevin finally delivered his speech before the House of Commons, Massigli made a point of emphasizing the differences between his clear statements to Jean Chauvel and the Quai d'Orsay and the vagueness of his public pronouncements.[6] To make matters worse to French colleagues was the accentuation of an anti-Soviet tone that embarrassed Bidault. Bevin's perceived failure to recognize the German danger encouraged a Gaullist attack against the foreign minister, accusing him of joining Britain in the demand that a rejuvenated Europe be built around a unified Germany.[7]

This perception of Bevin as a Machiavellian puppet master was furthered by the care he took to remove a paragraph on the third force from a memorandum to the foreign office on 4 January, when he sent the substance of the document to the U.S. State Department a week later.[8] Obviously, he did not want the United States to know that his appeal for U.S. aid was in support of a goal that the United States might not appreciate. Marshall, according to Dean Acheson's impression, seemed to underscore the element of deviousness in Bevin's character. He felt that Bevin had let him down at the London meeting in December, when he failed to follow through with a motion to adjourn the conference, presumably because he did not want to be out in front in a confrontation with the Soviets. In Marshall's mind, the foreign secretary was an unreliable partner.[9]

But did Bevin's vagueness about the nature of European unity, his seeming placement of a present Soviet danger ahead of a German military revival, or his downplaying an apparently wistful hope of an independent Europe signify guile behind his grand design for a Western Union? Acheson himself certainly did not think so.[10] What Acheson saw was a man completely at odds with the image of the cultivated, immaculately dressed British statesman and in fact at odds with Acheson's own appearance and breeding. He could not have been more different from his predecessors, Anthony Eden and the Earl of Halifax. Born in rural West England, his mother was a domestic servant, and his father was unknown; he was orphaned at age eight and his formal schooling ended at eleven. But ambition and a love of reading lifted him to the summit of the British Labour Party as head of the Trade Union Congress. Winston Churchill appointed him Labour Minister in his war cabinet in 1940. From this perch, Clement Attlee picked him as foreign secretary despite absence of experience in the field. Notwithstanding his inexperience, Bevin was a success in his office. Bluff, irrepressible "Ernie" earned the respect and affection of his U.S. counterpart.[11] Paul-Henri Spaak, Belgium's premier and foreign minister in 1948, shared this affection. He observed that "despite his lack of conventional training, he succeeded absolutely, thus proving once again that for a minister technical accomplishment is far from indispensable. What matters is sound judgment, a sense of responsibility, a will to act—and to act decisively—and a fighting spirit."[12]

Rather than displaying a calculating temperament, Bevin had a quick temper, which was not always under control, and if not a quick mind, one that clearly grasped the essence of Europe's plight after World War II. Such was Acheson's judgment.[13] If he confused his French associates with imprecise language, it may have been because he was not sure himself just how to proceed. Initially his views were vague and ill defined. The French ambassador Massigli may have perceived his January 1948 speeches as anti-Soviet, but as late as February Bevin himself tried to avoid the implication that the projected Western Union was purposely anti-Soviet in its conception. His behavior after the London meeting appeared eccentric rather than sinister, "swinging from optimism to despair and always tempered by caution, hope, and even a 'born again' patience." At a Labour Party conference in May 1947, Bevin claimed that "I have cultivated for the first time in my life, as all my colleagues will agree, a remarkable patience. I must have been born again."[14]

Gladwyn Jebb, Assistant Undersecretary of State for Foreign Affairs, was as close to Bevin as any of his advisers. Jebb had been in the diplomatic service since 1924 and had attended all the major World War II conferences. His position as deputy to Bevin on the Conference of Foreign Ministers in 1946 led him to think that the foreign secretary had come to the notion of a Western Union in the winter of 1947–1948, after the obvious failure of a unified Europe. And Jebb shared Bevin's hope that Stalin would not object; he had raised no objections to the Franco-British Treaty of Dunkirk. The next step, then, was an association of other Western nations, with the Low Countries serving as the nucleus. Germany would ultimately be welcomed, once its democratic future was assured. In this context, the foreign secretary included the United States with its resources but without specific commitments. Jebb was convinced that in the early stages of Bevin's plans he did not "actually propose a multilateral treaty, still less a multilateral defensive pact." As he worked his way toward the dramatic speech of 22 January, he knew that tying the United States directly into a Western Union would have alienated the Senate and recognized as well that in repudiating dismemberment of Germany, he was not proposing reunification of Germany, just a future reunification of Europe. "Altogether," Jebb noted that Bevin's address to the House of Commons "was a very clever speech. The secretary of state knew perfectly well what he was after, but he had to achieve his end by stages, gaining as many allies as he could in the process."[15]

TOWARD "THE SPEECH"

Jebb's observations could be used to confirm the Machiavellian judgment of Bevin's approach to European unity. But they also could serve to identify a keen mind in slow motion. The foreign secretary knew what he wanted: a united West supported by U.S. power. His steps to achieve this result did not follow a straight line, arguably because he was not sure how to reach his goal or even exactly the form that goal should take. France and the Low Countries would be vital cogs to be joined eventually by other like-minded Western nations. How Germany would be involved in the short run or how the British Commonwealth would contribute was not clear. And no clarity was possible in January, when France had problems with Britain's position on German economic recovery and when Britain had difficulties with France's seeming intransigence over the economic revival of West Germany. Nor could the U.S. role be fully explored when Bevin himself had not given up on Europe as a third force and when he knew that U.S. attention was directed to the U.S. Senate's acceptance of the Marshall Plan. Was his ultimate intention to produce a specific military alliance in which the United States would be embedded in Western Europe? It is unlikely that his thoughts had progressed to that point five weeks after the collapse of the foreign ministers' meeting.

Before the end of December, the foreign office had been looking into the possibilities of permitting individual and collective defense without involving a veto in the Security Council under Article 51 of the UN charter. Early in January, Jebb proposed that Bevin open private talks with the State Department about a security arrangement under the cover of Article 51. Bevin's response was positive, but he did not want to get into details. In the words of Nicholas Henderson, Bevin's private secretary, "He believed that the essential thing over this, as over the European Recovery Program (ERP), was to unleash an idea and back it with vigour from the start, letting the final mould be determined in subsequent discussions."[16]

On 13 January, the British ambassador to the United States, Lord Inverchapel, summarized the first steps Bevin wanted to take: It was "some sort" of union in Western Europe, formal or informal, that would be backed by the "Americas and the Dominions." He did specify the states that would initiate this union, again mentioning the spiritual forces behind it. They included Scandinavia, the Low Countries, France, Italy, Greece, and even possibly Portugal. Spain and Germany, "without whom no Western system can be complete," should be added and included "as soon as circumstances permit." Ready for consolidation as Western Europe might be, Bevin made a point of noting that union need not take the form of a formal alliance, "though we have an alliance with France and may conclude one with other countries." But he did assert the need for British leadership and recommended as a first step an Anglo-French extension to Belgium of the Dunkirk pact.[17]

The initial U.S. reaction to his memorandum did not meet Bevin's expectations. George Kennan as director of the State Department's Policy Planning Staff had serious objections to Bevin's proposals. Not only did he fail to see the offer to the Benelux countries on the Dunkirk model as useful, he disliked the ideas of a military union as a starting point. It was too negative. This approach could alienate the Scandinavian countries and certainly have no appeal to Germans, given the language of the Dunkirk treaty. Moreover, if a union were to have meaning, it would need a federal framework lacking in the Bevin proposal.[18]

As director of the Office of European Affairs, John Hickerson had to repress his own convictions about a U.S. connection. He, too, was dubious about the Dunkirk connection and suggested the Inter-American Treaty of Reciprocal Assistance, signed at Rio de Janeiro on 2 September 1947, as a working model. Its link to the Monroe Doctrine would appeal to the U.S. public. Article 3 in that pact agreed that an armed attack by any state against any state in the Americas would be considered "an attack against all the American States," which would invoke the inherent right of collective defense recognized by Article 51 of the UN charter. The Rio pact had the advantage of conforming to both traditional hemispheric solidarity and the UN charter. Consistent with Bevin's sentiments, Hickerson added that the United States must join the Europeans for such a treaty to be really effective.[19]

But Marshall's official reply to Inverchapel was much more circumspect, and Hickerson's conversation with the British ambassador on 21 January reflected the secretary's caution. Although it was understood that no regional defense organization would be complete without U.S. membership, the State Department's consideration would have to take into account its association both with the UN charter and with the understanding that the organization was to be a product of European initiative. Inverchapel took this response as positive and concluded that Marshall did not rule out U.S. participation in a second stage.[20]

REACTIONS TO THE SPEECH

Refreshed from several weeks of rest on the Isle of Wight, the foreign secretary returned to London to address the House of Commons on 22 January with a speech that had been in the making since the breakdown of the Conference of Foreign Ministers in London five weeks before. The details were kept secret before it was unveiled, in accordance with parliamentary tradition of the unveiling of a major policy. But as *New York Times* correspondent Herbert L. Matthews was given to understand, the speech was going to be one of those high-water marks to which historians look back—a turning point in British history, according to one high-placed authority.[21]

This was Bevin's intention, and he made the most of the opportunity, covering every sensitive issue—some lightly, others in generalities, and a few with specifics. The most specific was the instruction to representatives in the Benelux capitals to negotiate a security pact with Britain and France along lines of the Treaty of Dunkirk. In fact, this instruction was dispatched the day before the speech, noting that the French were in agreement with this decision.[22] Ultimately other "historic members of European civilization" would be invited to join the union, including in the near future the new Italy, and in the more distant future, even a regenerated Germany. To the United States, he gave high praise for its generous Marshall Plan, which included an implicit assumption that the ERP then debated in the Senate would be advanced by the speech. As for France and Germany, recognition was paid to the reorganization of the three Western sectors into a future Trizonia in which currency reform would be a priority. The Soviet Union received blame for the regrettable division of Europe. Bevin asserted that "anything which the British Government does now will not be directed against the Soviet Union, but we are entitled to organize the kindred souls of the West, just as they have organized kindred souls in the East." But the primary message of the speech was to tell the world that Britain had abandoned its isolation from Europe and would take the leadership in creating a union of Western democracies.[23]

There were seemingly Delphic elements in the speech. In one sentence he stated that "We are not now proposing a form of political union with France." Yet a few sentences later, he spoke about those consultations with Benelux representatives about binding treaties "making with France an important nucleus in western Europe." The distinction between military and political union here was blurred. As noted previously, when he spoke of the Communist adversary (no actions directed at the Soviet Union), he apparently did not recognize that his speech was setting in motion just the kind of conflict he wished to avoid. Compare this language with the final words of his speech: "We shall not be diverted, by threats, propaganda, or fifth-column methods, from our aim of uniting by trade, social, cultural, and all other contacts those nations of Europe and the world who are ready and able to [cooperate]."[24]

Even more open to possible misunderstanding was Bevin's approval of "American policy, which like the policy of all great countries, must have regard to American interests." But just what were those interests? He came close to an answer with his observation that "the United States power and resources . . . will be needed if we are to create a solid, stable, and healthy world." Whether or not this meant military aid to the Western Union or an entangling association with the new European order was not clear—and purposely so. It certainly had none of the clarity Hickerson and Theodore Achilles had recognized was necessary if there were to be a successful Western Union. But it is unlikely that the foreign secretary was being disingenuous in his approach. Deviousness was not his style. Henderson's judgment was that Bevin would float an idea and back it vigorously at the start and then let "the final mould be determined in subsequent discussions."[25]

The speech was greeted enthusiastically in Britain, with Conservatives joining in the congratulations. Churchill, as a member of the Conservative Party, graciously welcomed "everything that was said by the Foreign Secretary about the more intimate relations we are to seek with France." The former prime minister could not refrain, however, from adding his satisfaction in seeing that "not only the British but also the American Government have adopted to a very large extent the views which I expressed at Fulton [Missouri] nearly two years ago and have, indeed, gone in many ways far beyond them." The influential *Economist* was convinced that Bevin had "set the faltering pulse of Western Europe beating more strongly . . . [and] headed British foreign policy in a new direction." Bevin himself was exhilarated by the reaction his speech inspired. When one of the two Communist members of the House of Commons accused the foreign minister of selling out, Bevin responded in good humor, "I was once accused by a Communist newspaper of selling out, and the courts gave me 7,000 pounds damages. Perhaps the House will be interested to hear I never got the order."[26]

If the speech's main target was the United States, Bevin was justified in sounding jubilant. The State Department issued as statement heartily endorsing his proposals as reinforcing the efforts of the two nations for peace. Equally if not more important than the administration's imprimatur was the boost it gave for passage of the ERP. John Foster Dulles, as Republican foreign policy adviser, agreed that the ERP was "more than ever imperative" in light of Britain's plans for Western unity.[27]

Bevin seized this response as an opportunity to raise the issue of a defense agreement that would give Europeans an incentive to commit themselves to a defense system. While he recognized the difficulty the United States might have in committing its forces to the European continent, he felt that if the two nations joined "in a general commitment to go war with an aggressor, it is probable that the potential victims will feel sufficiently reassured to refuse to embark on a fatal policy of appeasement." The urgent need for a commitment was spelled out in the British ambassador's letter to Undersecretary of State Robert Lovett on 27 January, reporting that Bevin wanted early talks between U.S. and British representatives to "clear their minds before the French at the forthcoming talks on Germany."[28]

THE ERP AS A CATALYST

It was obvious from this communication that the British foreign minister was ready to set the "final mould," referred to by Henderson, in place. It also appeared that the vague role for the United States implied in his speech was not at all vague. Certainly, his U.S. colleagues recognized what Bevin wanted and were not prepared to grant it. Undersecretary Lovett, who became the chief spokesman for U.S. policy throughout the rest of the year, understood Bevin's expectations. Although Hickerson was receptive to the invitation, Marshall and Lovett balked. Any agreement involving the use of armed force, as Lovett emphasized in his response to the British ambassador, would have to respect "certain procedures within the executive branches as well as the appropriate congressional committees." Too little time was available before the tripartite discussions on Germany were to begin in London on 19 February. But the main response was that Europe must take the first steps before engaging the United States.[29] Only after the United States knew exactly what Europeans were prepared to do for themselves would the administration take any action.

"Show us what you're prepared to do for yourselves and each other and then we'll think about what we might do" was the U.S. theme for the next few months, according to Achilles, and remained so even after the Western Union took shape in March. Hickerson laid down two ground rules. First was the requirement that the Senate Foreign Relations Committee be fully involved in the process, with its advice playing as important a function as its consent. Second was the need for bipartisan approval, a vital prerequisite in a presidential election year with a Republican congress and a Republican chairman of the Senate Foreign Relations Committee.[30]

Henderson blamed a schism in the State Department—between those who wanted U.S. participation in a Western security system and those who did not—for the sudden coldness that followed Marshall's warm initial response to the speech. The principal skeptics were the State Department Counselor, Charles Bohlen, and the head of the Policy Planning Staff, Kennan, both Soviet experts whose advice carried weight with the congenitally cautious Lovett. The undersecretary managed to have all papers relating to European unification cleared by Bohlen before reaching his office. Hickerson and Achilles were effectively marginalized—at least for the time being.[31]

The domestic political environment was as important to the administration's response to Bevin's initiative as any internal division of opinion in the State Department, and this fact of life was enough by itself for the United States to hesitate. The success of the ERP was by no means assured on 22 January. On that day Herbert Hoover urged Congress to scrap the program in favor of a $3 billion fund for world destitution relief and a $1 billion loan to revive Europe's industries. The former president's words carried particular weight, because, as the *New York Times* observed, "he has no political ambitions, because he has reached the age where partisan considerations cannot be foremost in this thinking, and because he has had wide experience in administering foreign relief." But the editorial regretted Hoover's limiting aid to basic categories of food and steel and omitting the moral element in the limited commitment of his proposal.[32]

The ERP sponsors were quick to respond. President Harry S. Truman weighed in with a rejection, but more important at this point, Arthur H. Vandenberg, the Republican chairman of the Senate Foreign Relations Committee to whom Hoover's letter was addressed, insisted that the Marshall Plan required a four-year commitment to ensure the revival as well as the future unity of Europe.[33] Secretary Marshall, addressing delegates of the National Farm Institute conference in Des Moines, Iowa, on 13 February, also appealed for support of the ERP on the grounds that "this is far more than a mere economic transaction. It represents a tremendous effort for constructive leadership. If adopted, it will rank, I think, as one of the great historical undertakings in the annals of world civilization."[34]

The Hoover intervention was not an isolated instance of Republican opposition. Less than a week before Bevin's address, Robert A. Taft, the most influential Republican skeptic in the Senate—and a candidate for the party's presidential nomination—had attacked the program for being too large and for failing to have an administrator independent of the State Department.[35] From another quarter, the Progressive Citizens of America, supporters of former Vice President Henry A. Wallace issued a seventy-four-point program urging abandonment of both the Truman Doctrine and the Marshall Plan as provocations to the Soviet Union. Opposition to the ERP would be one of the planks of the platform on which Wallace would run for president in 1948. To replace the Marshall Plan, he proposed a $50 billion "lend-lease program for peace" under UN auspices.[36] The State Department also had to contend with some reservations from Democrats on the Senate Foreign Relations Committee. Senator Tom Connally of Texas fretted that Western Europe's industrial production above prewar levels would be at the expense of the U.S. taxpayer. Senator Walter George of Georgia was unhappy with the uncertainties about which agency would be responsible for administering the program.[37]

The opposition made some headway in forcing concessions from Vandenberg's Foreign Relations Committee, which had begun hearings on the ERP on January 8. In the committee's report on 26 February, the $6.8 billion that the State Department had requested for the first fifteen months of the program was whittled down to $5.3 billion, and the covered period reduced from fifteen to twelve months. While the committee felt that in light of such imponderables as crop failures or political disturbances the initial figure should be regarded as a minimum rather than a maximum, it "considered it wise, however, to reduce the amount." Without admitting political considerations, the committee judged that the reduced figure would give the administration sufficient time to evaluate the results of the program. Vandenberg, recognizing the pressures from the opposition, cut his losses by proclaiming victory: "The timetable of foreign aid is just as important as the fund totals." There was nothing "sacrosanct" about the administration's appropriations request, and the administration's witnesses had put excessive emphasis on the cost of the first year's operations.[38]

Vandenberg was the key player in shepherding the ERP through the Senate, as columnist James Reston pointed out in an appreciative article on the senator's role. The Republican-controlled Congress had the power to paralyze the administration's foreign policy and chose not to do so, in large measure because of Vandenberg's position: "The Senator from Michigan has been walking the knife-edge for months between the broad objectives of the administration's policy, which he approves, and the reluctant halfway policies of his colleagues, who were neither isolationist nor internationalist, but somewhere in between, at sea." The genius of his leadership, Reston claimed, is his ability to understand and even sympathize with both sides. If anyone has a suggestion to improve the bill, "he would come down to his office and hear him out at any hour of any day or night." Without fully satisfying any critic, he was able to move the ERP bill toward completion without sacrificing its core principles.[39]

It helped the administration's case that Vandenberg had some special allies within the Republican camp. Charles P. Taft, a Cincinnati lawyer and younger brother of the senator from Ohio, presented the endorsement of the Federal Council of the Churches of Christ in America and added his own personal support as well. Unlike the senator, he did not think the proposed expenditures excessive or the time frame for the assistance too long. When he called on him for testimony, Vandenberg assumed that he was not speaking for the Taft family. "Well, I am not sure," Taft responded with a smile, "but that the Taft family might agree with some of the other statements, too, Senator." Charles Taft did recommend establishing a separate agency for the ERP but with the State Department serving as a coordinating office.[40]

The careful compromises crafted by Vandenberg had the effect he had sought. Even Senator Taft came around to endorsing a "reasonable" aid program, although he still felt that the administration was not following a true bipartisan policy. The Republican House Speaker Joseph W. Martin, Jr., of Massachusetts put his own spin on the acceptance of the ERP. He urged voters to elect a Republican president and a Republican Congress to guarantee the success of the Marshall Plan.[41] In this political environment the Foreign Relations Committee agreed unanimously on 17 February to an appropriation of $5.3 billion for a twelve-month period, beginning on 1 April 1948 and using $3 billion from current treasury surplus funds to cover the first year of the ERP. The committee had already invested authority for administering the program in an independent agency, with an agreement added by Vandenberg making aid contingent on "the continuity of cooperation among the countries participating in the program."[42]

Had Vandenberg conceded too much for the sake of consensus? Pundit Arthur Krock wondered if the outcome of negotiations was really a victory for the administration. He noted the unusually vigorous State Department campaign for the original budget, conducted "with the zeal of true converts" but which ended in retreat. He also noted its strong objections to an independent administrator of the ERP, quoting Marshall's comment that "there cannot be two Secretaries of State."[43]

Yet this is exactly what the administration settled for. Or was it? In the long run, neither of these concessions stood in the way of the Marshall Plan's implementation.

From the European perspective, there was an obvious link between the ERP and European unification and—even more significant—U.S. participation in that process. Testifying on the foreign assistance bill just two days before Bevin's speech, Dulles stressed the importance of European political unity that would benefit from the passage of the ERP.[44] As a confidant of Governor Thomas E. Dewey—once again a presidential candidate—Dulles had the governor's ear. This was apparent when Dewey delivered a Lincoln Day speech in Boston commending aid to Europe as a means of speeding the establishment of a federation of free nations. If U.S. economic assistance were not given, he was convinced that the ERP "could be another disastrous adventure."[45] This was the first major speech the governor made since he announced his candidacy for the Republican presidential nomination, and it could accelerate both congressional passage and European unification. Bevin's speech struck a responsive chord with an important constituency.

FRANCE DIT: ATTENDEZ DONC

The official U.S. reaction to Bevin's speech, however, was a setback for the British government, even if it was not wholly unexpected. But Marshall's caution and the ERP debates notwithstanding, there was sufficient empathy with Bevin's program in Washington to give encouragement both to transatlantic advocates of Western Union and to those, such as Hickerson and Achilles, who wanted something more from the United States. A critical obstacle in the way of implementing Bevin's proposals in the winter of 1948 was the stance of Britain's French ally. There was fragility about the Anglo-French alliance that Bidault had been unable to strengthen. True, the Dunkirk pact was a symbol of a new relationship; the Soviet treatment of the Marshall Plan demonstrated the nature of Communist hostility to the West; and the breakdown of the London meeting of the Council of Foreign Ministers made Anglo-French military conversations a necessity. Moreover, Bidault was in tune with Bevin about the importance of addressing the need for European unity and the role the United States might play in its achievement.

While France barely survived crippling Communist strikes against the direction Bidault was leading the country, Gaullist spokesmen were berating the foreign minister for his supine deference to British leadership. After the Bevin speech, Gaston Palewski, Charles de Gaulle's private secretary, asserted that European federation should take form "under the inspiration of France since no other country was so well fitted to be the disinterested leader of the European states." He asked "Why has France remained silent? Why has France proposed nothing? Why did not Mr. Bidault say something? He had the best of opportunities at the moment of the closing of the conference of London, but Mr. Bidault lacked the necessary presence of mind or perhaps he did not wish to anticipate the conclusions of the party of which Mr. Attlee [the British prime minister] is the Pope and Mr. Leon Blum [the French premier in 1947] is the High Priest."[46]

Bidault was the victim of France's circumstances, in a position where he was an inevitable scapegoat for the nation's insecurities vis-à-vis the Anglo-Saxon allies. There was little he could do to avoid the embarrassment of being upstaged by his partner in London. Massigli suggested that he was blindsided by the anti-Soviet tone of the speech and was continually frustrated by the vagueness of Bevin's pronouncements. If he was not a puppet of the British, as Palewski charged, he was forced into the position of being a junior partner of his British counterpart.[47] The influential French economist Jean Monnet felt that "there was something pathetic" about Bidault's position. "It was not his fault," Monnet asserted, "if France was weaker than her international partners." Bidault had done all he could to maintain France's interests in these circumstances.[48]

The apparent Anglo-French solidarity based on the Dunkirk treaty deepened in the wake of Soviet rejection of the Marshall Plan in the summer and culminated after the London Conference in December in a joint recognition that political unity must accompany economic recovery, which in turn required a U.S. commitment. All these events took place in 1947 under the guidance of Bidault.

But France's embrace of a British-crafted federation was always skittish and susceptible to dissonant forces. Granted that Communist agitation had failed to shake the government, and Gaullist opposition had diminished with the departure of de Gaulle himself from the political scene. Still, the financial crisis that required the devaluation of the franc on January 25 roiled relations with Britain. Just one day after Bevin's address to Parliament, France warned that it would withdraw from the International Monetary Fund (IMF) unless the board of governors approved the French project for convertible currencies in France and a free market in gold. Worried about inflation, France was intent on stabilizing its currency—and not incidentally making the U.S. dollar more available. Without waiting for a response or for the results of Britain's chancellor of the exchequer's urgent trip to Paris for conversations with Finance Minister Andre Mayer, Premier Robert Schuman announced the devaluation of the franc and intended to go ahead with its financial program irrespective of the opposition of the IMF and of its British ally. Britain was concerned that the currency change would damage its own economy, an argument that failed to impress the French. Its economists feared that France's economy would be wrecked within six months, with its gold reserves dangerously low, while a British financial crunch would not come until much later.[49]

The flare-up over the franc coming as it did in the wake of Bevin's speech was a factor, but not the only factor, in France's cool response. Initially, after the London foreign ministers' meeting in December 1947, Bidault expected to take the initiative to line up a federated Europe with a speech in Brussels. A small dinner party organized for the two foreign ministers after its conclusion was the setting for Churchill to endorse, as Cyrus Sulzberger noted, the concept of a federated Europe, "long one of Mr. Churchill's pet schemes."[50] But the uncertain political climate in Paris required the French to turn over the leadership of the plan to the British. The French were then miffed not only over the vagueness of Bevin's language but also by his failure to follow up France's interest in extending political association to embrace a common economic front.

Nevertheless, the substance of Bevin's speech should have conformed— and did conform—with French interests. The French welcomed a system of bilateral pacts to be negotiated with the Benelux countries, the Scandinavian bloc, and Italy as well, by both Britain and France, based on the model of the Dunkirk treaty. Moreover, inclusion of Italy suggested the desirability of a Franco-Italian customs union as part of the economic reconstruction to be reinforced by political association.

What disturbed the French and what made Bidault's position so vulnerable was the German factor in the projected federated Europe. Where would West Germany fit into the picture? Even as the Foreign Ministers Conference in London came to a close in December, plans were made for a meeting over Germany in London in the middle or end of January, to which Bidault was agreeable. He was less satisfied with Bevin's intention of putting the role of the Ruhr low on the list of matters to be discussed despite France's belief that the key to the problem was the administration of the Ruhr, and that once it was resolved, the other matters would fall into place. Still, it could be part of what he called "a general package."[51] In fact, Britain was being put on notice that Germany remained a primary object of France's concerns no matter how serious its recognition of the Communist menace was. General Jean-Pierre Koenig, a confidant of de Gaulle, made a point of observing that no French government could survive without progress on the Ruhr, because it would be attacked by the Socialist Left and the Gaullist Right.[52] As at the end of World War I, it seemed vital to many French leaders that the industrial Ruhr remain out of German hands.

Creation of a trizonia with full French membership, anticipated from the beginning of the bizonal merger, could not take place until the German problem was solved. But just as the Bevin speech was germinating, the U.S. and British commanders in Germany early in January, Generals Lucius D. Clay and Sir Brian Robertson, meeting in Frankfurt on 6 January, agreed to grant new powers to German members of the Bizonal German Economic Council that had been created in 1947. Not only would German membership be doubled, but the council would be given full control of customs as well as the right to levy taxes.[53] This arrangement was made without France's contribution—or even knowledge—and immediately aroused French anxieties. The feelings of French diplomats in London and Frankfurt were initially soothed when they were informed that negotiations with the Germans were of an "oral character" and that no firm agreement would be made without final approval from Britain and the United States.[54]

Their superiors in Paris, however, were outraged. Without knowing details, Massigli, who had previously seemed receptive to U.S. explanations, was instructed to express the foreign ministry's shock over this act of betrayal.[55] Armand Bérard, the Minister Counselor of the French embassy in Washington, who received similar instructions, noted that France saw this move as an embryonic government, presaging the future constitution of Western Germany.[56]

U.S. and British diplomats were also surprised. According to the U.S. political advisor for Germany, Robert Murphy, Clay had not informed the War Department of the proposals to the Germans for reorganization of the bizonal agencies.[57] Nor had the proposals been committed to paper. Informally, the French officials on the scene at Frankfurt felt that the excitement in Paris was exaggerated and unfounded but recognized that when Bidault returned to Paris after the London meetings, he had been promised that the French would be consulted on all matters of importance concerning Germany. Instead they were faced with what Bidault called a "fait accompli."[58]

When he visited the Riviera for a brief holiday in early January, Bidault had been confident that French aims with respect to German powers in the Bizonia and an international status for the Ruhr were acceptable to the Anglo-U.S. partners. Above all, future economic and financial plans would have to consider the need to avoid a centralized German government. Prosperity for Germany was certainly vital for the future of a united Europe but only in the context of a decentralized government sustained by the creation of strong federal states. Such were the instructions given to General Koenig for talks in Berlin. The French government spoke as if its primary concern was that a centralized government centered in Berlin would fall under the domination of the Soviets. In reality, its underlying worry was over the possibility that a revived Germany could once again threaten the security of the nation. There would be no Trizonia until French caveats were satisfied.[59]

Clay's reaction to France's criticism was not apologetic. Coming to his post as military governor of the U.S. zone without any predisposition in favor of German recovery, he quickly learned that there could be no European recovery without a vital German contribution, including ending the dismantling of industry. This West Point–educated general may have known little about Germany, but in the words of his admiring civilian counterpart, Murphy, he had the technical skills "to interpret ambiguous regulations, avoid paper roadblocks, to persuade obstinate officials—these universally political talents were bred in Clay's bones and nurtured in childhood." Murphy was much impressed with Clay's lineage as a great-grandnephew of the Kentucky statesman Henry Clay.[60]

This sterling heritage did not guarantee empathy with an ally's sensibilities or appreciation of the coeval functions of the State Department. Tact was not one of Clay's virtues. He saw the rebuilding of western Germany as the only response to the Soviets attaching Eastern Germany into the Eastern European economic system. Without openly precluding the establishment of eventual economic and political unity of Germany, Britain and the United States were prepared to move forward with the economic rehabilitation of Western Germany under a democratic government, whatever its formal name might be. Clay, pretending to be surprised at French opposition, felt that delay could no longer be tolerated and that France should agree to trizonal fusion immediately. Even after Murphy warned him of the need to make some kind of gesture to the French to avoid the charge of a fait accompli, Clay professed that his instructions were to "effect German reorganization as promptly and efficiently as possible," and he would continue to follow them.[61]

Compromise was inevitable among France, Britain, and the United States. Britain had made a French alliance a cornerstone of its future, while the United States recognized French sensitivities as well as the importance of a French participation in a trizonal policy. As meetings on the organization of the West German economy began in London on 20 February 1948, concessions were underway. The Saar question was effectively resolved when France was given full control over Saar's coal production, effectively separating the Saar region from Germany and integrating it into the French economy. The result would be what the United States considered "de facto separation" from Germany.[62]

The future of the Ruhr was more difficult to resolve, but there was movement toward controlling production and distribution of resources without establishing a separate state or formally internationalizing either the territory or its coal mines before West Germany had acquired a constitution.[63] These measures were taken to encourage France to join Bizonia as soon as possible. They were still insufficient. France maintained that no Trizonia could be established until substantial agreement was reached over international control of Ruhr production and the creation of a Germany with limited authority.[64] Frustrated by France's resistance, U.S. ambassador to Britain, Lewis Douglas, suggested that France might be persuaded to change its position if its share of the ERP depended on its willingness to merge its zone with Britain and the United States.[65]

Despite mutual irritations, progress had been made at the London meeting on the Ruhr issues. The United States was willing to concede that access to Ruhr products "should not be exclusively controlled by Germany." Furthermore, long-term Allies' control of the Ruhr was reasonable, as long as it would not be so punitive that it would increase Soviet bargaining power in Germany. As the conference came to a close, Douglas judged that the traditional fear of Germany still governed French public opinion and that if the French could be satisfied with some formula for tripartite consultation to deal with the threat of future German aggression, they would not have to inject their insecurity into all other matters, including the creation of a Trizonia. He realized it was important to put France on an equal basis with the United States and Britain to meet future goals. The French delegates responded favorably to this approach, even though no conclusion had been reached when the conference adjourned on March 5.[66]

BENELUX SUSPICIONS

Even as the German problem strained the Anglo-French alliance, Bevin and Bidault continued to collaborate in their plans for a treaty that would embrace the Benelux and ultimately other European nations in a binding political and military alliance. Early in January, the French had pressed Britain to join them in obtaining a treaty with Belgium, and both nations felt that their proposal would be warmly received. There was a sense of complacency in Bevin's instructions to British diplomats, who with their French counterparts in The Hague, Brussels, and Luxembourg undertook negotiations along the lines of the Dunkirk pact. These instructions, in fact, were delivered a day before Bevin made his historic speech before Parliament.[67] The allies had sent enough signals in advance and received sufficient encouragement to expect a rapid response.

The speech immediately won "a hearty endorsement" from Belgian Foreign Minister Spaak. As a Socialist prime minister in the 1930s and foreign minister of the Belgian government-in-exile during World War II, Spaak had been an ardent supporter of European unity. In his memoirs, Spaak was unrestrained in his admiration for this new breed of statesman represented by Bevin. He was convinced that Bevin's speech in the House of Commons was "a historic event, for it marked the beginning of a new European policy and heralded a future Atlantic policy." He was particularly impressed with Bevin's disregarding "the advice of his over-cautious civil servants" and striking out on his own. "At all events, never before had Britain been so outspoken in proclaiming her readiness to help promote the unity of Western Europe, nor has she ever shown such courage since. For one moment in her political history Britain was enthusiastic, and, may I say, lucid, about Europe."[68]

Although there was no equivalent display of sentiment about the Bevin speech in the Netherlands, the official silence did not indicate disapproval. It reflected, according to the U.S. Embassy in The Hague, a "difference [in] national temperament rather than difference [of] opinion."[69] The Dutch presumably were less effusive than the Belgians.

Spaak's appreciation of Bevin's performance included thoughts about connections with France and Britain from the outset that neither the British nor the French negotiators may have anticipated. Two weeks before the Bevin address, the Belgian foreign minister confided to a U.S. lecturer from the National War College that among the benefits of an association with the French and British would be their recognition of the importance of the Belgian Congo if the Soviets troops should overrun Western Europe in the initial phase of a Russian-U.S. conflict. European governments would then have to move to Africa.[70]

Admiration for Bevin's performance notwithstanding, the Belgians and Dutch were discontented with the inferior roles that the two larger allies had assigned to the Benelux partners. One manifestation of their discontent was resentment over their exclusion from the tripartite conference on the future of Germany in the London conversations that followed the Bevin address. They felt justified in believing that they had an important stake in the outcome of the larger allies' plans for Bizonia and Trizonia. The Belgian and Dutch foreign offices demanded representation at the London meetings and were not satisfied with the initial response that evaded the question whether political as well as economic issues would be discussed. Not until a few days before the conference was scheduled to begin was Spaak able to extract an understanding from British Minister of State Hector McNeil that its purpose was to discuss economic questions and that Benelux representatives would have an opportunity "to give reasons why they desired voice on other questions." The Dutch foreign ministry felt that McNeil had been reasonably explicit about arranging for Benelux ambassadors in London to sit in at discussions on every subject.

But a week later, on the eve of the London meeting, the Belgian ambassador in London recognized that McNeil's recommendations had not been followed up and that the most Benelux countries could count on at the moment was an assurance that they would be informed on policies regarding Germany. This was not enough.[71] The disposition of German coal and steel products was of vital concern to its Benelux neighbors, particularly when they were carried down the Rhine to Rotterdam.

When the French seemed ready to allow the Benelux partners to present their views but not participate in discussions, Belgium regarded the proposal as ridiculous and observed that if this represented Bevin's ideas of a Western Union, it was making a poor start. The State Department agreed with the Benelux position, and despite anticipated French opposition, the

United States supported direct Benelux participation in discussions of long-range questions at every stage of the conference with the exception of operational matters involving just the occupying powers.[72]

The combined U.S.-Benelux pressure succeeded in putting the Benelux concerns on the agenda at the first meeting of the three-power talks on Germany. They agreed to be represented by a single delegation headed by the Netherlands ambassador, assisted by his Belgian and Luxembourg counterparts, as well as by one high ranking officer from each country's foreign office.[73]

While the issue of consultation over Germany's future was an obstacle to the fulfillment of Bevin and Bidault's plans for a Western Union, this was more easily solved than the terms of the prospective treaty joining the five nations. From the outset, France had settled on the Dunkirk model, because it was a bilateral arrangement and identified Germany as a future threat. Even before Bevin spoke to the parliament, Spaak asserted that unless it was a device to conceal a defense system aimed at the Soviet Union, invoking the German menace was meaningless given Germany's present status. Moreover, it made more sense to him to promote regional rather than bilateral pacts, which would satisfy U.S. interests and be more clearly aimed at Soviet expansion. Despite British willingness to remove the anti-German element in a treaty, France was adamant. Unlike the Benelux partners who wanted clarity about the Communist danger, France claimed to be worried about antagonizing the Soviets.[74]

On 30 January, the Benelux foreign ministers issued a communiqué accepting the Anglo-French invitation but with important reservations. After welcoming it "with lively satisfaction," it asked for clarifications "in a spirit of constructive cooperation in the framework of the Charter of the United Nations." "Constructive cooperation" was a euphemism for a voice in future deliberations of Britain, France, and the United States on Germany's future. But their most significant caveat was an assurance that the pact would be tied to the UN.[75]

The Dunkirk model was the major stumbling block. The Benelux powers rejected the French argument that by identifying Germany as a target, the new union would avoid offending the Soviets. Spaak thought that this was a childish subterfuge too transparent to deceive the Russians. The Dunkirk formula, he felt, would be just as offensive to them, because it would be obvious that the perceived threat came from the Soviet Union, not from a rearmed Germany. Moreover, a series of bilateral treaties would not be as effective as the regional arrangement proposed by the Benelux partners. Spaak added that the Dutch were even more stubborn than the Belgians on this subject. He was also unhappy that Bevin was going along with the French and abandoning the approach taken in his 22 January address, which had clearly identified the adversary as the Soviet Union.[76]

France's demands placed the U.S. and Britain in an uncomfortable position. The United States neither favored a bilateral approach nor approved of the anti-German message in the Dunkirk treaty, a point the U.S. ambassador to Belgium emphasized.[77] The U.S. position was close to the Benelux proposal, namely, favoring a regional pact using the Rio pact model under UN auspices or at least linked up with the UN. The Rio pact fitted the concept of a regional association envisioned by the Marshall Plan and so would find Congressional approval more easily than bilateral pacts that retained an anti-German element.

Although Britain was irritated by France's pressure, it felt forced to accede to the Dunkirk model when the offer of a formal partnership was tendered to the Benelux nations on 18 February. The British did point to a difficulty with a regional pact under the UN charter because of the Soviet veto power on the Security Council, but it was unlikely that this was their primary worry. Deference to the concerns of its most important European ally was imperative. A broadened Dunkirk agreement seemed to have been the most acceptable compromise at the time.[78]

The U.S. reaction to a five-power pact, whether or not it was modeled on Dunkirk or Rio, posed a problem for the British. Although Bevin and his advisers understood the domestic constraints on U.S. policy with respect to a military guarantee to the Western Union, they were "conscious of a risk of getting into a vicious circle," as Ambassador Inverchapel told Lovett. Without assurance of U.S. involvement, Britain was unlikely to succeed in "making the Western Union a going concern." But U.S. willingness to take such a step hung on the assumption that the Western Union was a going concern.[79] Despite all the correspondence—transatlantic and intra-European—that followed the speech, no firm resolution had been concluded in February about the terms of the pact that would formally create a Western Union.

THE SOVIET UNION AS DEUS EX MACHINA

Benelux's grudging and qualified acceptance of the Anglo-French invitation portended a long delay before the differences would be settled. It was not simply a contest between the advocates of the Dunkirk pact against the Rio pact. There was also a danger of antagonizing the Soviets, as the French saw it, without any military guarantee from the United States.[80] The solution to these dilemmas came from the East—from Soviet intervention in Prague and the fears they inspired in the West.

Tension between East and West independent of the impending Western Union that had been building since Bizonia had become a reality. Bizonia seemed to the Soviets to be a prelude to West German sovereignty.[81] On 23 January, one day after Bevin announced plans for a meeting of the Western allies to discuss Germany's future, Soviet officials stopped a British passenger train en route to Berlin and detained the train for twelve hours when the British refused to allow inspection of the cars.[82] This action was a harbinger of things to come as the Soviets felt pressure arising from the creation of the Bizonia, from the announcement of a German role in the Marshall Plan, and from the proposals to grant West Germans more authority in economic planning. When the Soviets heard of the conference in London on Germany to which they were not invited, they railed against it as a violation of the Potsdam agreements. Ambassador Murphy considered the stoppage of Berlin-bound trains to be a test of Western determination to stay the course at its most vulnerable location.[83]

Was the coup in Prague then an escalation of increasing Soviet hostility to the Western allies' actions in Germany, leading to the blockade of Berlin later in the year? Was it a signal to the West of its anger over the creation of an obviously anti-Soviet union of Western states? Or even more ominously, was it the beginning of a developing military campaign against the West? The British, French, and Benelux allies may have been uncertain about where Soviet rhetoric would lead, but there was no uncertainty about their reaction to Soviet orchestration of the ousting of the pro-Western government of President Eduard Benes in Czechoslovakia and its replacement by a Communist regime favorable to Moscow. Secretary of Defense James V. Forrestal described the shock he felt when a violent Communist coup d'etat seized power in Prague after "action committees" roamed the countryside, intimidating all opposition. The suppression of democracy in Czechoslovakia was all the more disturbing to the United States because of its history of intimate relations between the two since its founding in World War I.[84]

When the news of Benes's bowing to Soviet pressure for a Communist-controlled government became public, James Reston of the *New York Times* was convinced that the Europe's security problem was now equal to its economic problem. He felt that the fate of the Czechs was a warning that Europeans by themselves could not contain internal subversion, and that without a U.S. commitment the rest of Europe would suffer the same experience.[85]

The Communist coup d'etat in Prague on 24 February suddenly concentrated all minds in Europe and the United States on the importance of unity in the face of an immediate threat from the Soviet adversary. It helped to clarify hitherto murky issues that plagued relations among the Western allies as they worked their way toward a formal treaty. Czechoslovakia's fate reminded the French government that the Russians were more of a problem than the Germans, even though Bidault himself needed no reminders. For him, mention of Germany in a treaty was just for domestic reasons. But in Massigli's judgment, Germany remained a threat: when Slavs press westward, Germans do likewise.[86] Nevertheless, the seeming French obsession with the Dunkirk treaty had dissipated. Bidault confessed he was no longer concerned about sticking with that formula. Nor was he bothered about offending the Soviets by concluding a military alliance. After Prague, the issue was how to deter Soviet aggression.[87]

Britain and the United States felt the fall-out from the coup almost as severely as France. Congressional debate over ERP legislation was advanced in Washington as was advocacy for an early conclusion of a defense pact under the UN charter (or at least under Article 51 of that charter) that would evade a potential Soviet veto on the Security Council. The need for immediate action was shared by Bevin as well, who feared that Europe was "now in a critical period of 6 to 8 weeks which . . . would decide the fate of Europe."[88] The Benelux powers would now receive concessions that had been in doubt before the Prague coup. The scene was set for fulfilling the promise of the speech.

NOTES

1. *New York Times, Times of London,* January 2, 1948.

2. René Massigli, *Une comédie des erreurs, 1943–1946* (Paris: Plon, 1978), 107–8.

3. John Baylis, "Britain and the Formation of NATO," in *The Origins of NATO,* ed. Joseph Smith (Exeter: University of Exeter Press, 1990), 11.

4. John Baylis, *The Diplomacy of Pragmatism: Britain and the Formation of NATO* (Kent, OH: Kent State University Press, 1993), 66; quotation in Robin Edmonds, *Setting the Mold: The United States and Britain, 1945–50* (Oxford: Clarendon Press, 1986), 172.

5. Edmonds, *Setting the Mold,* 173.

6. Massigli, *Comédie,* 10.

7. Tel James C. H. Bonbright, Chargé d'Affaires, Paris, to Secretary of State, February 26, 1948, no. 285, Sub: Speech of Gaston Palewski concerning the German problem in the political reorganization of Europe, p. 4, 840.00/2–2648, RG 59, NARA (hereafter cited as Palewski speech).

8. Baylis, *Diplomacy of Pragmatism,* 66; the document submitted by British Ambassador Inverchapel to Secretary of State, January 13, 1948, "Summary of a Memorandum Summarizing Mr. Bevin's Views on the Formation of a Western Union," *FRUS,* 1948, III: 4–6.

9. Dean Acheson, *Sketches from Life of Men I Have Known* (New York: Popular Library, 1962), 9.

10. Acheson, *Sketches from Life,* 31.

11. Acheson, *Sketches from Life,* 11–12.

12. Paul-Henri Spaak, *The Continuing Battle: Memoirs of a European, 1936–1966,* trans. Henry Fox (Boston: Little, Brown and Co., 1971), 143.

13. Acheson, *Sketches from Life,* 13.

14. Massigli, *Comédie,* 107; quoted in Sean Greenwood, *The Alternative Alliance: Anglo-French Relations before the Coming of NATO* (London: Minerva Press, 1996), 182.

15. Lord Gladwyn, *Memoirs of Lord Gladwyn* (New York: Weybright & Talley 1972), 210–211.

16. Nicholas Henderson, *The Birth of NATO* (Boulder, CO: Westview Press, 1963), 2–3.

17. Tel British Ambassador Lord Inverchapel to Secretary of State, January 13, 1948, *FRUS*, 1948 III, see Massigli, *Comédie*, 10.

18. Memorandum by Director of Policy Planning Staff (George F. Kennan) to Secretary of State, January 20, 1948, *FRUS*, 1948, III: 7–8.

19. Memorandum by Director of the Office of European Affairs (John Hickerson) to Secretary of State, January 19, 1948, *FRUS*, 1948, III: 7–8.

20. Memorandum of Conversation, by Director of the Office of European Affairs (Hickerson), January 21, 1948, *FRUS*, 1948, III: 9–12.

21. Herbert L. Matthews, *New York Times*, January 22, 1948.

22. Tel American Ambassador (Jefferson Caffery) to Secretary of State, Paris, January 22, 1948, no. 372, 840.00/1–2248, RG 59, NARA.

23. Margaret Carlyle, ed., *Documents in International Affairs, 1947–48* (London: Oxford University Press, 1952), 208, 211; quoted in Baylis, *Diplomacy of Pragmatism*, 67.

24. Carlyle, *Documents*, 211.

25. Carlyle, *Documents*, 216; Henderson, *Birth of NATO*, 2.

26. *Parliamentary Debates*, House of Commons, January 23, 1948, 5th series, vol. 446, 1947–48: 551, 554, 394; *Economist* article quoted in Baylis, *Diplomacy of Pragmatism*, 67.

27. *New York Times*, January 24, 1948.

28. Tel British Ambassador (Inverchapel) to Undersecretary of State (Robert Lovett), January 27, 1948, *FRUS*, 1948, III: 15.

29. Tel Lovett to Inverchapel, February 2, 1948, *FRUS*, 1948, III: 17–18.

30. Theodore C. Achilles, *Fingerprints on History: The NATO Memoirs of Theodore C. Achilles*, edited by Lawrence S. Kaplan and Sidney B. Snyder (Kent, OH: Lyman L. Lemnitzer Center for NATO and European Community Affairs, Kent State University, 1992), 13.

31. Henderson, *Birth of NATO*, 9.

32. Editorial, *New York Times*, January 23, 1948, 22.

33. Editorial, *New York Times*, January 23, 1948, 22.

34. Department of State *Bulletin*, February 22, 1948, address, "Survival of Democracy Dependent on Survival of ERP," 18, no. 45: 231.

35. *New York Times*, January 19, 1948.

36. Wallace testimony, in *Hearings on Foreign Policy for a Post-War Recovery Program*, House Committee on Foreign Affairs, February 19, 1948, 80th Cong., 2nd sess., part 2, 1598–1600.

37. Tom Connally, questions to Ambassador Lewis Douglas, in *Hearings on ERP*, Senate Committee on Foreign Relations, January 10, 1948, 80th Cong., 2nd sess., part 2, 170–71; Walter George, questions to Douglas, in *Hearings on ERP*, Senate Committee on Foreign Relations, January 10, 1948, 80th Cong., 2nd sess., part 2, 173–75.

38. Senate Committee on Foreign Relations, *Report*, no. 935, on European Recovery Program, February 26, 1948, 80th Cong., 2nd sess., 653.

39. James Reston, "Policies Affecting GOP But Not Its Basic Aims," The Week in Review, *New York Times*, February 8, 1948, E3.

40. Arthur Vandenberg exchange with Charles Taft, in *Hearings on ERP*, Senate Committee on Foreign Relations, January 31, 1948, 80th Cong., 2nd sess., part 3, 1149.

41. *Facts on File Yearbook 1948*, no. 380: 47.

42. *New York Times*, February 13, 1948; *New York Times*, February 18, 1948, 1.

43. Arthur Krock, *New York Times*, February 12, 1948, 22.

44. *Hearings*, on ERP, Senate Committee on Foreign Relations, January 20, 1948, 80th Cong., 2nd sess., 588.

45. Thomas E. Dewey, "Steps to Permanent Peace," Lincoln Day address to Middlesex Club, Boston, February 12 ,1948, *Vital Speeches of the Day*, March 1, 1948, 14, 295.

46. Palewski speech, 4.

47. Massigli, *Comedie*, 107–8.

48. Jean Monnet, *Memoirs*, trans. Richard Mayne (Garden City, NY: Doubleday & Co., 1978), 174–75.

49. *New York Times*, January 24, 1948; *New York Times*, January 25, 1948.

50. C .L. Sulzberger, "Franc Snag Delays Pact Plan," *New York Times*, January 25, 1948, 32.

51. Memorandum of conversation by Ambassador to UK (Lewis Douglas), December 17, 1947, subject: Post-Conference Discussions with the British and French, *FRUS*, 1947, II: 811.

52. Ann Tusa and John Tusa, *The Berlin Blockade* (London: Hodder and Staughton, 1988), 92–93.

53. Tel U.S. Political Adviser for Germany (Robert Murphy) to Secretary of State, January 9, 1948, *FRUS*, 1948, II: 20.

54. Tel U.S. Ambassador to France (Caffery) to Secretary of State, January 10, 1948, *FRUS*, 1948, no. 162, II, 20–21.

55. Tel U.S. ambassador to France (Caffery) to Secretary of State, January 10, 1948, FRUS, 1948, no. 162, II: 21.

56. Armand Bérard, *Un ambassadeur souvient: Washington et Bonn, 1945–1955* (Paris: Plon, 1978), 136ff.

57. Tel Murphy to Secretary of State, January 9, 1948, *FRUS*, 1948, no. 47, II: 19.

58. Tel Murphy to Secretary of State, January 15, 1948, *FRUS*, 1948, no. 107, II: 26–27.

59. Vincent Auriol, *Journal du Septennat, 1947–1954* (Paris: A.Colin, 1970), II: 22, 26; John W. Young, *France, the Cold War and the Western Alliance: French Foreign Policy and Post-War Europe* (New York: St. Martin's Press, 1990), 715.

60. Robert D. Murphy, *Diplomat among Warriors* (Garden City, NY: Doubleday, 1964), 289.

61. Tel Robert Murphy to Secretary of State, January 28, 1948, *FRUS*, 1948, no. 225, II: 43.

62. Economic Agreement between the United States, the United Kingdom, and France regarding the Saar, February 20, 1948, *FRUS*, 1948, II: 73–75; *New York Times*, February 21, 1948.

63. *New York Times*, February 26, 1948.

64. Lovett Memorandum of Conversation with Ambassador Henri Bonnet, February 17, 1948, *FRUS*, 1948, II: 70.

65. Tel Douglas to Secretary of State, March 1, 1948, *FRUS*, 1948, no. 787, II: 107.

66. Tel Douglas to Secretary of State, March 2, 1948, *FRUS*, 1948, no. 807, II: 110–11.

67. Tel Caffery to Secretary of State, January 22, 1948, no. 372, 840.00/1–2248, RG 59, NARA.

68. Spaak, *The Continuing Battle*, 143.

69. Tel Bonsal (The Hague) to Secretary of State, January 16, 1948, 840.00/1–2258, RG 59, NARA.

70. Tel Millard (Brussels) to Secretary of State, January 8, 1948, no. 49, 840.00/1–848, NARA.

71. Tel Millard to Secretary of State, February 7, 1948, no. 273, 840.00/2–748. RG 59, NARA; tel Baruch (The Hague) to Secretary of State, February 7, 1948, no. 86, 840.00/2–748, RG 59, NARA; tel Millard (Brussels) to Secretary of State, February 14, 1948, *FRUS*, 1948, no. 331, II:65.

72. Tel Secretary of State to Embassy in UK, February 16, 1948, *FRUS*, 1948, II: 66.

73. Tel Douglas to Secretary of State, February 26, 1948, FRUS, 1948, no. 745, II: 91 RG 59, NARA.

74. Tel Millard to Secretary of State, January 17, 1948, no. 110, 840.00/1–1748, NARA; John Young, *Britain, France, and the Unity of Europe* (Leicester: Leicester University Press, 1984), 83.

75. *New York Times*, February 1, 1948, 26.

76. Tel Millard to Secretary of State, February 19, 1948, no. 371, 840.00/2–1948, RG 59, NARA.

77. Tel Millard to Secretary of State, February 18, 1948, no.426, 840.00/2–1948, RG 59, NARA.

78. Tel Millard to Secretary of State, February 19, 1948, no. 365, 840.00/2–1948, RG 59, NARA.

79. Ltr Inverchapel to Lovett, February 6, 1948, *FRUS*, 1948, III: 19.

80. Tel Caffery to the Secretary of State, February 22, 1948, *FRUS*, 1948, no. 980, II: 29; Young, *France, the Cold War, and the Western Alliance*, 178.

81. See John Gimbel, *The American Occupation of Germany: Politics and the Military, 1945–49* (Stanford, Calif: Stanford University Press, 1968), 205–6.

82. Daniel Harrington, "The Berlin Blockade Revisited," *International History Review* 6, no. 1 (February 1984), 93.

83. Tusa and Tusa, *Berlin Blockade*, 312.

84. Walter Millis, ed., *The Forrestal Diaries* (New York: Viking Press, 1951), 382.

85. James Reston, *New York Times*, February 27, 1948.

86. Tel Caffery to Secretary of State, March 2, 1948, *FRUS*, 1948, no. 1110, III: 34–35; Massigli, *Comedie*, 111.

87. Henderson, *Birth of NATO*, 10–11; Reston, Commentary, *New York Times*, February 27, 1948, 1–2.

88. Quoted in Baylis, *Diplomacy of Pragmatism*, 71.

3

The Brussels Pact: 17 March 1948

THE ALMOST PERFECT STORM

The coup in Czechoslovakia in February 1948 coincided with a series of events that appeared to be a prelude to a Communist takeover of Western Europe. In February, Italian Communists, having failed to overthrow the government of Alcide de Gasperi in December 1947, were poised to win power at the polls in the April elections. The Soviet Union was pressuring Norway to sign a nonaggression pact that could force that country into the Soviet orbit. Communist presence in the Mediterranean and at the approaches to the Atlantic was a sobering prospect for the United States, arguably more than for Europeans. And the evidence of Soviet aggressive action in Germany to counter the development of bizonia became more ominous when General Lucius Clay, the U.S. military commander in Germany, sounded an alarm in Washington warning that a Soviet invasion "may come with dramatic suddenness."[1]

Each of these worries of itself might have been sufficient to push the United States into a new relationship with Western Europe, but one event more than any other—the suicide or murder of Czechoslovakia's foreign minister, Jan Masaryk—traumatized the nation to the extent, it seemed, of involving the administration in an entangling alliance of the sort John Hickerson and Theodore Achilles had been urging since the failure of the London foreign ministers meeting in December. Masaryrk symbolized the nation's democratic traditions, and his death by defenestration just two weeks after the Communist coup in Prague triggered an outpouring of sorrow over the destruction of a country with deep roots in U.S. history. The Czechoslovak republic was born during World War I when the two exiled leaders in the United States, Masaryk's father, Tomas, and Eduard Benes, carved a new republic out of the dying Austro-Hungarian Empire. Given a government shaped in large measure by the U.S. experience, it was hardly a surprise that Czechoslovakia would have a special place in the hearts of the U.S. citizenry. In 1938, when the Munich agreement made the republic a victim of Nazi aggression and Western weakness, the United States was shamed. After Germany's defeat, Benes returned to Prague from his refuge in Chicago to become president, and with Masaryk as his foreign minister, tried to maintain a democratic presence amid a Soviet-dominated Eastern Europe.

Benes's removal from office in February energized the West, which was made all the more sensitive to the coup because of the keen memories of 1938. It was understandable that Anthony Eden, who resigned as foreign minister in protest of Britain's appeasement of Adolf Hitler at Munich, warned in a speech to his parliamentary constituency that the events of 1948 must remind the world of repercussions far beyond Czechoslovakia.[2] Just ten years before, the same two men—Benes and Masaryk—had been driven into exile after the Nazis took over the country. Western guilt over their fate and the fate of their country played a part in the U.S. reaction to the February coup.

Benes died a few months after resigning, aware of his failure to avert the Communist seizure of power. In Masaryk's case, death was the result of suicide, out of hopelessness, as some of his friends and admirers believed, or the result of murder as many in the West feared and evidence from Soviet archives later confirmed. Disillusionment with the Soviet Union followed from this tragic event. From his Harvard College house, Ray Cline, a future deputy director of the CIA, would never forget the impact of Masaryk's death on a distinguished teacher, Francis O. Matthiessen. Friends had told him that his adviser, a devoted believer in the Soviet Union as the wave of the future, committed suicide in the wake of the disaster in Prague. He jumped to his death from the top of a Boston hotel; Cline ascribed it to depression not only over the death of a great man but also over the loss of faith in his Communist beliefs. "The God that failed" led the professor to his own death.[3]

Masaryk's putative leap from the bathroom window of his third floor apartment in the Foreign Ministry building evoked memories of 1618, when a group of Protestant noblemen ignited the Thirty Years' War by throwing commissioners of the Austrian Empire out of a Prague palace window. For days after Masaryk's death on 10 March, the world not only mourned the loss of an esteemed leader but seemed convinced that the Soviets were behind the tragedy. The head of the Czechoslovak mission to the

UN, in defiance of the new Communist regime, asked for a Security Council investigation of how the Soviet Union installed a Communist dictatorship in Prague. On the same day, Secretary George Marshall claimed that Masaryk's death "indicates plainly what is going on." It was a reign of terror that could intimidate other vulnerable nations in Europe.[4]

General Charles de Gaulle, leader of the Free French in World War II and president of the provisional government in 1945, left office in disgust with the French party system in 1946 to organize his own *Rassemblement du Peuple Francais* in 1947. But he was a fierce critic of Communism as well as of the Fourth Republic and saw the loss of Czechoslovakia as a fire bell in the night. He warned France and Europe that Russia was aimed at world domination. Communist dissidents in every European country were creating crises and divisions to prepare the way for overthrowing legitimate governments. De Gaulle asked for U.S. military aid to keep Europe free and felt that the present French government was too weak to cope with the situation. But because of the message that the Prague coup sent to Europe, the Robert Schuman cabinet had managed to survive. At the last moment thirty-nine conservative deputies decided to abstain rather then reject a vote of confidence.[5]

Masaryk's death seemed to have been the last straw. It hastened the passage of the ERP, accelerated the integration of West Germany into the West, and facilitated the creation of the Brussels Pact. It also moved the United States toward the goal of an Atlantic alliance that Hickerson and Achilles had been championing since New Year's Eve. As Armand Bérard, the French ambassador to the United States, recalled, the "Czech affair" was the starting point of the North Atlantic Treaty.[6]

Yet there was a considerable temporal distance between Bérard's *point de depart* and its completion over a year later. The rising fear of Communism on the march everywhere in Europe in the winter of 1948 had led to an expectation that the United States, so vital to European security, would become an integral part of a new Western defense system. The Pentagon conversations of the United States, Britain, and Canada immediately after the signing of the Brussels Treaty promised exactly that, even though the promise was kept secret and the Western alliance would go under an "Atlantic" name. But in the spring of 1948, the momentum for embedding the United States in Europe had stalled, and Europeans as well as their U.S. friends had reason to wonder if the hopes embodied in the Brussels Pact would be realized. The storm that had gathered strength from so many sources appeared to have passed without producing a transatlantic union or even a comprehensive West European Union, even though it did produce a five-nation pact.

THE ITALIAN DISTRACTION

Of the many critical areas in Europe sensitized by the Czech crisis, Italy's position was arguably the most pressing. Italians had been in the forefront of Communism, in fact the brains of the twentieth-century Marxism since Antonin Gramsci founded the party in 1921. Although Gramsci had passed from the scene before World War II, his partner and fellow theoretician, Palmiro Togliatti, continued his legacy when he returned from the Soviet Union in 1944. Under his leadership, the Communist Party took much of the credit for the defeat of the Fascists, and its partisans enjoyed more prestige than any other resistance force. Joining with Leftist parties, Togliatti had served in coalition governments after the end of the war.

But with the rise of the Christian Democratic Party under de Gasperi, the Communists were ousted from the government in 1947. This led to a powerful opposition combination of the splintered Socialist Party and the Communist Party, which waged an active campaign against the Marshall Plan. When riots, strikes, and intimidation failed, the Communists counted on their supporters taking power at the polls. The parliamentary elections in April 1948 would be a test of Communist success.

The United States and its British ally were worried about the potential loss of Italy to Communism and its consequences for security in the Mediterranean. The Italian peace treaty of 1944 called for withdrawal of U.S. troops from Italy by the end of 1947. It is worth noting that the first document (1/1) of the newly created National Security Council (NSC) recommended that if Communists seized all or part of Italy before the scheduled departure date, the United States should suspend withdrawal and reconsider terms of the treaty with Italy.[7]

Linking Communist subversion in Italy to the civil war in Greece, Harry S. Truman's administration was determined to prevent the fall of Italy, not only for the sake of Western control of the Mediterranean but also for the message a Communist Italy would send to other Western nations.[8] When President Truman announced the troop withdrawal on 13 December 1947, he informed de Gasperi that "If . . . it becomes apparent that the freedom and independence of Italy upon which the peace settlement is based are being threatened directly or indirectly, the United States . . . will be obliged to consider what measures would be appropriate for the maintenance of peace and security."[9]

The United States responded to the challenge but not always to good effect. Ambassador James Dunn and others in the State Department recognized that if intervention was too blatant it could backfire. Communists could then point to the de Gasperi government as a U.S. stooge. Moreover, by encouraging Vatican involvement, the administration could be charged with collusion with the Catholic Church, particularly when the Pope was urging the U.S. Catholic hierarchy to give its backing to U.S. initiatives.[10] In taking this step, the church had to overcome its doubts about the loyalty of the center-Left government of de Gasperi to its values. The Defense Department unwittingly contributed to Togliatti's campaign by sending a thousand marines to reinforce the Sixth Fleet stationed in Naples in January 1948. This apparent interference in Italian politics embarrassed the de Gasperi government. Collaboration between Washington and Rome had been conducted quietly up to this time. U.S. ships visiting Italy, for example, were always admitted only after the express consent of the Italian government.[11]

The situation was now too serious for Washington to maintain the discretion it had previously displayed. The new Central Intelligence Agency (CIA) and National Military Establishment (NME)—both created in 1947 to unify the disparate intelligence operations of the military services with those of state and cognate departments—were restless over the relative inaction of the administration. In light of the importance of Italy to Europe's security, and by extension to the United States as well, the NSC on 10 February issued NSC 1/2 that expanded the more cautions recommendations of 1/1 by urging the use of all available political, economic, and even military resources, if necessary, to ensure the preservation of an independent democratic and anti-Communist nation.[12] The document responded to the fear of the Communist pattern of strikes and political agitation preliminary to winning the parliamentary elections in April. No further strikes or attempts at insurrection were expected until election had secured a victory for the democratic coalition and perhaps not until Congress has passed the ERP and alleviated the economic plight in the country. If shut out of power, the Kremlin might then order an armed insurrection.[13]

On 19 February, the U.S. Joint Chiefs of Staff (JCS) objected to an aggressive policy in Italy. They were worried about both the difficulty of providing sufficient military supplies and equipment to an Italian force before the April election and the jeopardy this diversion of aid might place the anti-Communist offensive in, as it was scheduled for the spring by the Greek government.[14]

The Czech coup swept away these hesitations. On 1 March, Secretary of the Army Kenneth Royall informed Marshall that the JCS would carry out the NSC recommendations and transfers of at least limited quantities of military materiel to Italy. In view of recent developments in Europe, the army was ordering the immediate shipment of the required nonsurplus supplies.[15] Nevertheless, the chairman of the JCS warned that no matter how dangerous the Italian situation was, the forces necessary for implementation of recommendations were dangerously low. Partial mobilization might solve the manpower problem but "neither limited nor general mobilization will result in appreciable augmentation of our combat strength for at least one year after mobilization is actually initiated."[16]

This warning was disregarded as Election Day grew closer. On the same day, 10 March 1948, that the JCS withdrew its reservations, the NSC recommended further measures to prevent a victory of the Communist-dominated People's Bloc. Success at the polls might present the Soviets with bases in Sicily or southern Italy. In a second revised version of NSC 1/1, the administration wanted to make sure that no economic aid under ERP would be forthcoming if the successor government included parties hostile to U.S. interests. To facilitate de Gasperi's coalition, a campaign would be initiated in the United States. The State Department hoped that the British and French allies would press for immediate inclusion of Italy in the negotiations for the Western Union. The language of panic escalated each time from NSC 1/1 on 14 November 1947 to NSC 1/2 on 10 February and again to NSC 1/3 on 8 March 1948. It even affected the normally cool head of George Kennan who speculated from Manila that the Italian government should outlaw the Communist Party before the elections, even at the risk of igniting a civil war. Should that ensue, the United States could then undercut the insurgents by reoccupying Italian military bases.[17]

Kennan's military solution was not the administration's. Propaganda and funding were used instead. To cope with the extensive Soviet financial support for the People's Bloc, the NSC had recommended covert funding of the anti-Communist coalition by the CIA. Secretary of Defense James Forrestal would see to it that funds for military purposes would be dispatched. This money was to be laundered through a tax-exempt group in New York as well as through a Swiss bank.[18] Pressure was exerted on Italian immigrants when the Justice Department announced its intention to expel Communist party members living in the United States, a threat that carried special weight in southern Italy where remittances from relatives abroad were vital for economic survival. This pressure was intensified by propaganda efforts to publicize the importance of the ERP role in Italy as well as to expose the truth about life under Communism. Special arrangements were made to show the Hollywood film *Ninotchka* in Italian theaters. Probably more effective were the activities of Italian American leaders in the United States, dispatching letters to friends and relatives in the Old Country to influence the upcoming election. The Czech coup was a symbol of what might happen to Italy if the Communists won at the polls.[19] The result was a resounding victory for the de Gasperi coalition on 18 April 1948.

Italy was as much on the minds of the framers of the future Brussels Pact as it was in Washington. It was not just the United States that wanted consideration of Italy as a member of the Western Union, which would grow out of the Brussels treaty. France was most eager to engage Italy at the economic as well as the military level. On 4 March, Georges Bidault announced that he would go to Turin at the invitation of Italian Foreign Minister Carlo Sforza, to negotiate a customs union. He hoped that a by-product of the new Franco-Italian solidarity would be a strengthened anti-Communist coalition in the forthcoming election.[20] Belgium's Foreign Minister Paul-Henri Spaak looked forward to including Italy in an economic conference after the signing of the Brussels Pact.[21]

Membership in the new Western Union itself was desirable, and Italy was always listed as one of the Western European countries that an extended Brussels Pact would embrace. Secretary Marshall had made a point of asking the U.S. Embassy in Brussels to find out views of the ministers gathered in Brussels on admitting Italy into their prospective organization in the immediate future. He raised the question again a week later with Ambassador Dunn in Rome by asking if early inclusion in the association would serve the democratic cause in Italy. He was convinced that after the Czech debacle, U.S. public opinion would support strong measures to strengthen non-Communist elements, and he knew that Ernest Bevin and Bidault shared his concern for Italy.[22] The consensus, though, was to hold off immediate action, if only because it might have an adverse effect on the election. This was also de Gasperi's judgment.[23] But after the pact was signed, the allies recognized that an Italy outside the pact would be under greater Communist threat than any other Western power and so it became a major topic at the first meeting of the Anglo-U.S.-Canadian security conversations.[24] The Italian issue remained alive as negotiations moved slowly toward an Atlantic alliance.

NORWAY UNDER THE GUN

At the same time that Italy was facing an internal Communist threat, Norway presented still another challenge to the West. Shortly before the Prague coup inflamed the West, the Norwegian defense minister anxiously approached U.S. military attachés to ask what assistance could be expected if the Soviets should strike Norway. It seemed likely that Oslo would follow Finland as a recipient of Stalin's invitation to sign a nonaggression treaty.[25]

The British, in particular, were exercised over what might result from Soviet pressure on the Norwegians. Formally, Britain urged the United States to help thwart a Soviet effort to intimidate Norway by including them in a regional Atlantic mutual assistance pact to which Norway and other Atlantic nations could participate under Article 51 of the UN charter. Bevin proposed the creation of three systems within which the West could be protected. First would be the new Western Union backed by the United States; second, an enlargement of the Benelux area to embrace an "Atlantic security, with which the United States would be even more closely concerned" and under which Norway would be covered; and third, building a Mediterranean security system to provide for Italy.[26]

Informally, the foreign office had warned the U.S. Embassy a few days before the unveiling of the Brussels Pact that after the Czech coup and pre-election Communist demonstrations in Italy, "Norway may be next scheduled to be called to Canossa, where the Holy Roman emperor bowed to the authority of the pope in 1077." The prospect of opening the Soviets to the Atlantic, under terms of a treaty dictated to the Norwegians, was deeply troubling to the British, and they felt is should be equally unsettling to the United States. In this context, British Ambassador Lord Inverchapel was hoping that back-channel Anglo-U.S. talks could result in some sort of joint action to strengthen both Atlantic and Mediterranean defenses.[27] Inverchapel's prospects were buoyed by Marshall's apparent agreement to proceed immediately to a joint discussion "on the establishment of an Atlantic security system."[28] Whether intentional or not, Marshall's brief response prompted the Pentagon talks on Atlantic security that followed the signing of the Brussels Pact.[29]

The subtext of British concerns centered on the experience of Finland, the Scandinavian neighbor closest to the Soviet Union. Just two weeks before the treaty was concluded, Stalin had invited Finland to sign a mutual assistance pact against potential German aggression. It would be similar to friendship treaties the Soviets had already made with Romania and Hungary. Given a cabinet with a strong Communist-Leftist bloc, it was hardly surprising that the Finns accepted the invitation. While hoping for language that would not violate its neutrality, Finland accepted a ten-year mutual defense pact on 6 April, which non-Communist leaders felt was "the best possible one Finland could obtain under the present circumstances."[30]

The Finnish-Soviet treaty provided that the Russians would be the judge of when their troops should move into Finland to protect that country. The image of Canossa seemed appropriate here, particularly when Hertta Kuusinen, a leading Finnish Communist, claimed that "The road Czechoslovakia has taken is the road for us."[31] Yet, the possibility of the United States seeking to bring Finland into a prospective Western alliance may have had a moderating effect on the Kremlin's attitude toward its neighbor. Donald Maclean, one of Britain's representatives at a secret Pentagon meeting in March and a longtime Communist mole, may have warned his masters of this possibility. In any case, the Finnish delegates in Moscow were relieved to find that Stalin was willing to accept an obligation that Finns consult with Moscow in the event of a foreign threat. The price of neutrality might have been much higher.[32]

Finland's Scandinavian neighbors were acutely aware of the implications of accommodating Soviet wishes, and Norway, which like Finland but unlike Sweden and Denmark bordered on the Soviet Union, remembered its fate in World War II. With the recent past in mind Ambassador to the United States, Wilhelm de Morgenstierne asserted, "We shall fight with everything we have against any attempt by foreign or domestic enemies to destroy our freedom, independence and democratic institutions. Once more we shall prefer to die on our feet than live on our knees."[33]

When these bold words were uttered in April, the crisis seemed less urgent after the United States and Britain had sent out signals to the Soviets that were obviously heeded. Nevertheless, Scandinavia's role in a future network of defense arrangements was not yet clear. Sweden's preference for neutrality, influenced by its successful avoidance of World War II, remained firm, even though the Soviets could threaten that country as well as its neighbors. Denmark's response to a Soviet overture would be negative but still troubling to the United States. Its foreign minister pointed out that joining Benelux or Norway would not stop Soviet aggression. Only "a clean declaration" from the United States would inhibit an aggressive act.[34] Propelled by the storm that seemed to be coming from all directions, the United States was moving rapidly in this direction by the time the North Atlantic Treaty was signed.

CLAY'S WAKE-UP CALL

The storm clouds over Germany had been gathering since the formation of Bizonia. Soviet opposition was painfully visible. Propagandists in Eastern Europe railed against what was assumed to be Western sponsorship of a West German government, which by its existence would be a revanchist if not a neo-Nazi regime. Echoes of these charges had been heard in France's reactions to Anglo-American proposals for the Ruhr and in its insistence on a firm anti-German statement in the proposed Brussels Pact. But it was the exposed position of Berlin, some 110 miles inside the Soviet zone of Germany, that presented Communists with the best opportunity to take advantage of their opposition to the West's currency reform and to its plans for consolidating the British and American zones and eventually the French zone in Germany. The Soviets themselves seemed prepared to escalate tensions when they stopped a British train en route to Berlin on 23 January.[35]

In January, interference in the traffic between West Germany and Berlin was short-lived, but it presaged increasing pressure on the Western allies. Soviet propaganda increased in February with serious new charges that Western delegations intended to disrupt the harmony of the quadripartite administration of Berlin. Moreover, the Soviets claimed that the Western powers intended to use their presence in Berlin to interfere in the affairs of the Soviet zone.[36] Without documenting a particular reason for his concerns, General Clay dispatched a telegram to the army general staff on 5 March that alarmed Washington: "For many months, based on logical analysis, I have felt and held that war is unlikely for at least ten years." But he went on to observe that "within the last few weeks, I have felt a subtle change in Soviet attitude which I cannot define but which now gives me a feeling that it may come with dramatic suddenness." He repeated that he had no evidence "other than to describe it as a feeling of a new tenseness in every Soviet individual with whom we have official relations."[37]

If there were still traces of complacency in the Pentagon and State Department over Soviet behavior in Germany, Clay's troubling words were enough to dispel them. He was not alone in his fears. Two days before, on 5 March, Clay's civilian counterpart in Germany, Robert Murphy, also observed a change in the atmosphere. Murphy claimed that in the first weeks after the breakdown of the London conference, relations had been relatively friendly at the quadripartite headquarters in Berlin, and agreements were reached even if there were only minor matters. The mood soured in the last week of January when the Soviets detained the British train en route to Berlin for twelve hours. Thereafter, Murphy noted, they would seize on any statement and any question on the agenda to accuse the Western delegates of subverting the Soviet's position in the city and in its occupation zone. The purpose of their tactics, he surmised, was to goad the West into a rash action that could justify Soviet terminating the four-power arrangements in Berlin.[38]

The United States and Britain continued to talk of quadripartite cooperation in currency reform for all Germany, but they were just going through the motions. In practice, the United States recognized that a quadripartite currency would deprive the West of a vital monetary tool for achieving an effective economy and administration in the western zones. Even though bizonal currency reform would sanction an East-West partition of Germany, it would also ensure a much needed economic stability hitherto lacking in the country.[39]

Were the increasing Soviet provocations intended to be the spur that would divide Germany in a way that would protect their zone? If so, Clay played into their hands on 12 March by halting the dissolution of Germany's trusts, with the exception of I. G. Farbenindustrie.[40] The process of decartelization of Germany's heavy industry had been an important component of the regeneration of the country. By reversing such a basic policy, U.S. behavior could be seen as proof of the West's coddling ex-Nazis. At the least, it could stoke Europe's fears of a revival of the elements in Germany that produced Nazism. It could also give the Soviets the excuse they needed to end cooperative participation in the control of Berlin.

The Allied Control Council in Berlin was moribund. Clay wanted to accept the inevitable when he gave up on the prospects of future cooperation. The signing of the Brussels Pact, while not directly linked to the actions in Berlin, was accompanied three days later by an ostentatious abrupt departure of the entire Soviet delegation from the four-power council. The reason that Marshal Vassily D. Sokolovsky, the Soviet chairman at that meeting, gave the order for this action was the allies' rejection of Soviet representation at the three-power conference on Germany then being held in London. The Soviets wanted, at the least, information on decisions taken at the conference.[41]

When they did return at the end of the month, it was with the intention of exercising greater control over travel to Berlin. The Soviet deputy military governor for Germany spelled out new regulations to Clay, including that effective 1 April the identification of all passengers, as well as baggage and freight, on military trains would be subject to check.[42] Refusal would result in stopping all trains at the zonal border. Although Clay had made an effort to calm German fears a week before by saying that the issue was political not military and that the Soviets had never threatened use of force, the situation in Berlin did not warrant these assurances. The Soviet noose around Berlin was steadily tightening.[43]

Ambassador Murphy claimed that the United States was reluctant to issue new money in its plans for currency reform and did not do so until the Allied Control Council had dissolved. The new currency was finally put into circulation in all three Western zones on 20 June. The Berlin blockade then was in place. The Soviets had thrown down the gauntlet, and the West took it up with the massive airlift that preserved the Western presence in Berlin. The Kremlin had given enough warnings about its attitude toward currency reform and the steps it would take to thwart it. That the Soviet reaction was essentially a defensive stance against a potentially revived and hostile West Germany was not unreasonable, but it was open to question.[44] That the action they took centered on the vulnerable Western outpost in Berlin deep inside the Soviet zone was less open to question. The outcome was the addition of the Berlin problem to the many pressure points that were in place as the Brussels Pact came into being.

THE CLOUDS BURST OVER BRUSSELS

The Benelux partners and the Anglo-French allies reacted to the crises breaking around them in Italy, Norway, and Germany by accelerating the pace of their negotiations for a binding union. Many of the earlier reservations on the part of the Benelux countries either disappeared or were relegated to the background in the first two weeks of March. Meeting in Brussels three days after the Prague coup, the Benelux premiers and foreign ministers pressed for a speedy conclusion of the treaty.[45]

While Germany and the German threat remained a source of difficulty for French diplomatists, they were willing to look for ways of assuring the

French public about the impact of a reconstructed Germany inside a Western bloc. One path to building confidence would be a commitment to maintain U.S. troops in Germany until the Communist threat had ended. Bidault indicated on that same day that he was ready to abandon the Dunkirk model as long as explicit mention of Germany was included in the treaty.[46]

Once France had broken the logjam over the Dunkirk model, progress toward a five-power treaty moved rapidly. No longer was France disturbed about upsetting the Soviets with a pact obviously aimed at them. The Communist menace was close to home, and the fate of Czechoslovakia was a cautionary tale for a country with a large and determined Communist minority. It took only ten days after the five-power conference met in Brussels on 4 March for a text to become final.

The key elements were competing yet complementary drafts by the Benelux powers and the British within that ten-day period. The Benelux draft emphasized a mutual assistance based on the provenance of Article 51 of the UN charter, embracing the inherent right of individual and collective self-defense. Should one party be a victim of armed aggression, the others would come to its aid with all possible assistance. Equally strong was the reference to the economic dimension, wherein economic cooperation among themselves and with other nations in appropriate international organizations would be encouraged. The Benelux document was vague about language preventing possible German aggression in the future.

The British proposal, with French guidance, differed from the Benelux's because of the attention it gave to a German menace. Both proposals made obeisance to the importance of fashioning a unified strategy to create a workable organization. The British opposed the Benelux conception of an economic organization for the five countries that would duplicate the machinery for the sixteen countries involved in the ERP.[47] The Benelux powers were appeased by the British explanation that a consultative council could establish such secondary economic units as became necessary. They also were pleased with their success in thwarting Franco-British efforts to include a "military guarantee" of colonial territories outside of Europe.[48]

At the same time that differences were being ironed out for the Brussels signing, the allies were preparing a sixteen-nation economic conference in Paris that would link the economic recovery of the Western Union to the economic revival of Europe as a whole through the implementation of the Marshall Plan. Bevin was anxious to demonstrate that separate negotiations on Germany or on a European customs union, or a military pact in the Western Union all led to the same goal, namely, the economic revival and common defense of a united Western Europe.[49] This larger perspective facilitated the British effort to disengage the Western Union from the Benelux support for an economic organization that would coexist with the political and military consultative council.[50] All parties agreed to make the Western Union open to other like-minded nations, with Italy particularly in mind.

The final text of the treaty had all the foregoing matters in mind. The most important of the ten articles of the Brussels Pact should have been Article IV: "If any of the High Contracting Parties should be the object of an armed attack in Europe, the other High Contracting Parties will, in accordance with the provisions of Article 51 of the charter of the United Nations, afford the party so attacked all the military and other aid and assistance in their power." But how meaningful was this promise when all the parties recognized their inability to cope collectively as well as individually with the power of military might in the Soviet Union? Europe's answer was membership of the United States in this union. It was officially unstated. Privately, the pleas for the United States "to shed its fine scruples of non-intervention in the internal affairs of Europe, and participate actively in the elaboration of the union while there may be still time" was clear. This advice came from one of France's elder statesman, former premier Paul Reynaud, just two days before the signing of the treaty. Without U.S. participation, Reynaud claimed, the Western Union "would be a mere outline with no substance and dangerous as well, since it would encourage illusions of non-existing strength."[51]

The official delegates had to be more discreet, even though their message was unmistakable. According to British delegate Alexander Rendel, they all agreed that they had to avoid giving any indication that U.S. support was expected and that nothing should be put into a treaty that could conceivably be interpreted as a request for aid or membership. Weighing the risks of entering into a European treaty without guarantees from the United States, Bevin had few doubts, according to Gladwyn Jebb, two weeks before the Brussels Pact was signed: "It seemed pretty clear that the Americans would, in fact, come in the long run, and recent events have made this all more likely."[52]

President Truman seemed to reward their private hopes with a stirring address delivered in person to a joint session of the Congress on 17 March. While the potential of a united Europe burying its divided past was on the president's mind, the immediate dangers of Communism had been foremost. The new treaty now seemed so important that the president made a last-minute change in his plans for a St. Patrick's Day address in New York. The New York speech was to have been a relatively moderate censure of Soviet behavior. But after becoming aware of an emergency war plan prepared by the JCS, Truman felt he had to deal more vigorously with the problems of Europe. He then determined to make a dramatic address to the Congress underscoring his concern for Western Europe before flying up to New York for his scheduled speech on domestic affairs.[53]

Marshall would have preferred "a weak message" in "simple businesslike" language that would not sound belligerent. The president was more attentive to the insistence of adviser Clark Clifford that the tone of the message be blunt enough to justify legislation it asked for.[54] Truman followed Clifford's advice when he informed Congress that "At the very moment I am addressing you, the five nations of the European community, in Brussels, are signing a 50-year agreement for economic cooperation and common defense against aggression. . . . Its significance goes far beyond the actual terms of the agreement itself. It is a notable step in the direction of unity in Europe for the protections and preservation of its civilization. This development deserves our full support. I am confident that the United States will, by appropriate means, extend to the free nations the support which the situation requires. I am sure that the determination of the free countries of Europe to protect themselves will be matched by an equal determination on our part to help them protect themselves."[55]

To Spaak, the most ardent advocate of the Brussels Pact, there could be no doubt of the significance of the president's speech: "A new page in the annals of history was thus turned on 17 March 1984: the Monroe Doctrine was dropped; America's isolation was dead. The road ahead was clear and President Truman took it without hesitation."[56] Richard Coudenhove-Kalergi, the leading spokesman for European integration since World War I, was lyrical in his "good hopes of seeing in 1948 or 1949 the great day when all the bells of a free Europe will ring to greet the opening of a new and brighter page of history: the birthday of the United States of Europe." Coudenhove-Kalergi wrote these exultant words in a letter to the *New York Times* on 16 February in anticipation of what the Brussels treaty might yield.[57] The terrible storm of unhappy events in the winter of 1948 seemed to have produced a rainbow of hope as spring approached.

THE EUROPEANISTS TRIUMPHANT?

Cheering from the sidelines as the five-power union was being put in place were European ideologues, each pressing for his own version of European unification and willing to believe that the Western Union was a major stepping stone en route to the fulfillment of this goal. Ever since Bevin had made his seminal speech in January, the excitement over the prospects for some kind of union of Western Europe was rising. The boldest and most vocal of the Europeans was Coudenhove-Kalergi, whose own lineage, linking Flemish, Austrian, Greek, and Japanese traditions, made him an ideal vehicle for promoting the cause of European unification as secretary-general of the European Parliamentary Union.[58] Enthusiasts like him had been dismissed as dreamers before World War II. In the wake of a looming Soviet threat, the time for change seemed to have come at last.

The European supporters of a new order in Europe had U.S. counterparts who were equally devoted and just as articulate in their embrace of European unity. As early as January 1947, John Foster Dulles spoke to the issue of Europe's disunity as a factor inhibiting the revival of Germany.[59] The solution for Germany and Europe would be a movement toward political federation. Influential journalists, such as Dorothy Thompson and Walter Lippmann, took up the theme that was crystallized in the Senate resolution of J. William Fulbright of Arkansas and Elbert Thomas of Utah on 21 March 1947. This would have Congress favor "the creation of a United States of Europe within the framework of the United Nations." On the same day, Congressman Hale Boggs proposed a resolution in the House of Representatives in identical terms.[60]

Even though the resolution was not passed at the time because of Secretary Marshall's reservations, it reflected a growing consensus in Congress. There remains a question about just what the consensus meant.[61] Was it just moral or even military support of European unity, or did it mean U.S. participation in whatever form European unity might take? And just what was meant by European unity? There was no single definition of the word. The fact that terms such as *union, unity, unification*, or even *federation* and *confederation* were so interchangeable meant that each believer in a united Europe was free to see in the Brussels Pact his or her own vision realized. The submerging of national sovereignty under a larger political unit might be a litmus test of unity, but there still was the question of how much sovereignty would be yielded. It might mean anything from an economic act of cooperation, as in a customs union, to the fusing of several governments into a single central entity.

The question that Bevin, Bidault, Hickerson, and Achilles wanted answered was whether the United States would be a member of a European federation. From their perspective, only U.S. participation in the Western Union or in a larger organization would assure the survival of the West. Despite the excitement engendered by the events of February and March, the U.S. promoters of a United States of Europe did not have a place for the United States of America. Fulbright and Boggs, ardent as they were on behalf of European political integrations, were not advocating U.S. participation in the new union.

The most prominent U.S. propagandist for a Europe that would have the United States as a key partner was the journalist Clarence K. Streit, the sponsor of a federal union of Atlantic democracies. His was a lonely position in 1948 and drew fire from former U.S. isolationists, who, for their own reasons, welcomed European federation. They looked at the Marshall plan as a "means of persuading western nations," according to Congressman Hamilton Fish of New York, "to form a federation or union of democratic nations." Testifying before the House Foreign Affairs Committee two weeks earlier, Ray Sawyer, a national director of the American Veterans of World War II, was more specific: "As a condition for receiving aid from the United States, we should insist that the ultimate goal in western Europe be a United States of western Europe irrespective of what you may call it, a union similar to the Union of independent American States out of which grew the United States of America. United Europe can stand on its own feet as a powerful united states of Europe. Divided Europe can only repeat its own history."[62]

The isolationists' enthusiasm for a united Europe evoked Streit's scorn. He interpreted it as a device to lessen the U.S. economic burden in Europe. If Europeans could come together, it seemed reasonable that they would become more self-sufficient. Streit wrote a sarcastic letters to the *New York Times* in March 1948, claiming that Senator Burton K. Wheeler and his followers pushed for European union so that the United States "would escape responsibility, while enjoying the satisfaction of either seeing our federal principles adopted by others, or, in the event of failure, confirming the view that the British and Europeans are hopeless." Wheeler protested that he had been "one of the first public officials in this country" to urge a union of European states, but he also made it clear that the United States should be excluded from such a union "because the whole cause of democracy could be jeopardized by putting our kind of political life at the mercy of a number of states still in the kindergarten of what we call democracy."[63] Conceivably it was this sentiment rather than a Machiavellian isolationism that distressed Streit. The United States would not be a part of this European association.

Motives aside, was the isolationist position absenting the United States from a politically integrated Europe essentially different from the views of Fulbright, Thomas, or Boggs? At no time in this period was Fulbright championing U.S. membership. His campaign was to link the Marshall Plan and the ERP to political as well as economic integration of Europe. He tried to amend the Economic Administration Act to give it a political character. Fulbright's case rested on the assumption that revival of economic prosperity in Europe without political unification was "a mere palliative" not a "cure."[64] To counter the objection that the United States might appear to be dictating to the Europeans the terms of their aid, thereby interfering with national sovereignties, the Arkansas senator cited Dulles' belief that while they do not want to be kicked, they do need a "little push" to remind their citizens what the goal of aid should be.[65]

Although Fulbright won over some congressmen, he had to listen to the cautious advice of veteran Senator Alben Barkley of Kentucky, who observed that "While we may entertain the hope that there would be a merger or amalgamation of the nations of Europe into one country, we cannot by implication make that a condition upon which we make this aid available." The chairman of the Senate Foreign Relations Committee chimed in with his own reservations, believing that the insertion of specific reference to political integration "would be a maxim embarrassment for at least a few of the exposed European countries."[66] The consensus among supporters of a United States of Europe was the assumption that the Economic Cooperation Administration (ECA), created to administer the ERP, would move the Europeans in that direction without the need to add a Fulbright amendment. The passage of the ERP bill on 2 April was another by-product of the winter storm.[67]

U.S. membership in a European association entered the consciousness of European federalists as well as of such obvious opponents as the Gaullists. While an Atlantic approach to union inspired familiar fears from Gaullists, it also evoked expressions of concern from statesmen and political thinkers who did not share the anger and contempt associated with the Gaullist view of the United States. A serious European federalist such as the Dutch scholar and statesman Hendriks Brugmans showed no animosity toward the United States but felt it was "unlikely that the medium states of Europe are prepared to enter a federation where one power—America—is predominant." An Atlantic approach of this sort risked the loss of European identity. Moreover, Brugmans recognized that the U.S. experience with federalism did not provide a useful model for Europeans with their culturally distinct fatherlands. Any federal system that would unite Europeans would have to be "extremely different from those of the American type. . . . It would therefore be wholly unrealistic to put the European 'states' on the same footing as those that formed their 'more perfect union' in North America around 1780."[68]

Coudenhove-Kalergi, leader of European unification in prewar Europe and an experienced analyst of the divisive elements in all the many manifestations of European unification, could not have been unaware of ambiguities in the support the United States brought to his cause. Yet they seemed to pale in significance in light of the events in the winter of 1948. On the assumption that the United States was motivated both by its fears of a Communist expansion and by its tradition of enlightened self-interest, Coudenhove-Kalergi was convinced that he could exploit the U.S. obsession with Communism to accelerate its acceptance of his goals.[69]

Coudenhove-Kalergi had spent the war years in New York as a professor at New York University where he had an opportunity to mingle with and influence potential friends of the European unifications. It was in high spirits that he returned to the United States in January 1948 expecting to use the congressional debates over the ERP as the vehicle to win decisive U.S. assistance for his European Parliamentary Union. Because of the accelerating pace of U.S. public opinion since Dulles had made his seminal speech a year before and since Fulbright had offered his Senate resolution, it was not surprising that Coudenhove-Kalergi would anticipate a successful conclusion to his labors. In the United States, the critical potential constituencies seemed to have fallen into place—the White House, State Department, and both houses of Congress. Having credited himself with inspiring Fulbright's resolution on the creation of a United States of Europe, he felt no sense of presumption when he told a reporter in New York that he had come back to the United States to "coordinate the union of Europe with the Marshall Plan." This was intended as shorthand for the union of Europe with the United States.[70]

In Washington, Coudenhove-Kalergi recalled that "his proposals fell everywhere on fertile ground" after "thorough" conversations with President Truman and Secretary of State Marshall. He also spoke with the principal figures in the State Department, from Kennan to Hickerson, who were all pleased to hear of the progress of the European movement. They declared themselves ready to serve it in every way possible. Although Coudenhove-Kalergi did not take credit for Bevin's address to the House of Commons, he did regard it as a complementary promotion of his own efforts to establish the Brussels Pact and to ensure passage of the Foreign Assistance Act. Both these objectives he claimed were achieved during this 1948 visit to the United States.[71] When he returned to Europe in April, he left behind the American Committee for a Free and United Europe, which he had founded on 18 April, with Senator Fulbright as president and such luminaries as former head of the Office of Strategic Services General William Donavan, former President Herbert Hoover, Senator Wheeler, and Socialist leader Norman Thomas as members.[72]

This was an impressive array of political leaders from all parts of the political spectrum. Most notable were members of the old isolationist bloc whose advocacy reflected the views of Senator Wheeler rather than Senator Fulbright. But what meaning did this all-encompassing embrace of European unity have for those few in Washington and their counterparts in London and Paris who looked not just for U.S. cheers but rather for U.S. participation in a Western security alliance? It was essentially background music that may have reflected a changing public perception of the United States's role in Europe. In the same week that Coudenhove-Kalergi celebrated his new U.S. committee, a report of a public opinion survey of an accurate cross section of the total U.S. population conducted at the end of March and early April showed that by a ratio of more than eight to three, the public believed that the United States "should promise to back up England, France, and other countries of Western Europe with our armed forces, if they are attacked by some other country." An even larger majority would agree to help defend those countries if the actions would be "in line with the UN Charter." About the same proportion of those surveyed would support those Western European governments in danger of being overthrown by internal Communist subversion.[73]

THE "ULTRA-ULTRA SECRET" PENTAGON TALKS

The winds of change propelled by the winter storm of events did not yield the immediate results that Bevin, Bidault, and Spaak in Brussels or Dulles, Hickerson, and Achilles in Washington were seeking. Not that there was any doubt about a U.S. consensus over European unification. It was genuine and widespread. And it would include military aid to prevent Communist internal or external control of any Western democracy. The Czech crisis of February helped it ensure this sentiment. But the most that the public and Congress would accept at the time the Brussels Pact was crafted was aid after a disaster was in process. This was not enough. There was no question that the Brussels Pact signatories believed that the United States must be a partner in the new union if Soviet-controlled Communism was to be kept at bay. The founding fathers of the Western Union ultimately triumphed. The United States did join their union even if the language had to be altered and the time frame extended. But this was in 1949, not 1948.

There was partial success in the short run but at a heavy cost. Within a week after signing, the British and Canadians joined with the United States in six secret meetings at the Pentagon from 22 March to 1 April 1948. The object of these conversations was to produce precisely the kind of linkage between Europe and the United States that Hickerson and Achilles had anticipated in December 1947 and that Bevin and Bidault had labored for in the following months. As Achilles noted, the talks were held in the JCS War Room in the bowels of the Pentagon. The existence of these conversations was so secret that one driver of a JCS staff car transporting the participating dignitaries got lost trying to find the secret entrance in the basement.[74] Secrecy itself presented a problem for the future. None of the Western allies knew of these conversations. The French were conspicuously absent out of fear of continuing Communist influence on their government. Ironically, the British team included Maclean, the Communist mole, who presumably provided more information to the Soviets than any of the allies present.[75]

Hickerson was able to draw the conclusions he wanted from Marshall's reactions to his recommendations on 8 March that the president consider the possibility of U.S. participation in a North-Atlantic–Mediterranean regional defense arrangement based on Articles 51 and 52 of the UN charter. Hickerson was careful to embed this recommendation in a list of four less inflammatory subjects, along with a requirement that Western European governments be prepared to pool their resources to help maintain their freedoms. His message assumed the completion of the Brussels Pact, which would then set the stage for additional U.S. commitments.[76]

The secretary's response to the Hickerson memorandum was indirect and clear. He argued that the French presented a security problem; their codes were too unreliable to permit their involvement in the secretive negotiations in the Pentagon. His fear of Communist penetration was obvious, and it would have been deeper had the participants known about the Communist ties of British delegate Maclean. In retrospect, Achilles felt that the Soviets must be getting "a daily play-by-play account" of the negotiations.[77]

More central was the question the British and Canadians felt to be the "first order of business," namely, what was the U.S. commitment? The most the British could extract at this moment was only a presumption of full support, because no specific promise would be made without Senate approval. The delegates did agree to explore three possible defense pact possibilities—an extension of the Brussels pact, an Atlantic pact, and a worldwide arrangement under the UN charter. All of these options posed problems, even as the British and Canadians pressed for an Atlantic pact that would absorb the Brussels Pact and hence remove the regional restrictions implicit in it.[78]

A policy planning staff report opposed the idea of a U.S. membership in the Western Union on the same day that the second round of the Pentagon conversations was held. Nevertheless, preparations were made for an initial draft of the security pact for the North Atlantic area, which was framed by Achilles and Hickerson the following day at the third meeting. Western Union membership would be extended particularly to Italy and the Scandinavian countries, the two most threatened regions. In one fashion or another, they would have to be part of an enlarged Western Union.[79]

The draft was primarily the work of Achilles, an achievement he was justly proud of. Regrettably, Achilles admitted that he was unable to find any trace of this draft in the archives, although he had deposited it in a safe when he left Washington in 1950.[80] But it did not matter. The final product was much the product of the two diplomats who remembered how they had celebrated the new year wondering how George Washington would have greeted their plans for the nation. The Pentagon Paper was a U.S. document, with the British and Canadians occupying a supportive but subsidiary role. After all, it was a U.S. initiative that determined the need for a military alliance covering a wider scope than the Western Union, with the United States now as a major player. At the sixth and last meeting in the Pentagon on 1 April, Hickerson did caution the British that the paper "was only a concept of what is desired at a working level" and that the secretaries of state and defense along with congressional leaders had to give their approval. But the cautionary note seemed pro forma.[81]

That sixth session ended with a sense of accomplishment. The first paragraph of the final draft opened with the observation that the purpose of the paper was to implement President Truman's declaration of support for free nations of Europe that he made on 17 March.[82] It seemed that Bevin and Bidault finally had succeeded after all in bringing the United States into their Western Union.

What spoiled the perfection of the storm that produced a U.S. commitment to a security pact was a series of obstacles that postponed completion of a transatlantic treaty. First was the discomfort of leading members of the State Department. Before the Pentagon conversations had finished, Marshall had left the country to attend the International Conference of American States in Bogota, Colombia, on 30 March and did not return until 2 May.[83] Robert Lovett was acting secretary of state and was as cautious in his approach to the Europeans as Marshall would have been, even though Hickerson exploited Lovett's tentative approval of the Pentagon draft. He noted that Lovett "on the basis of insufficient study *considers* it desirable in principle."[84] As the Brussels Pact was being considered, Lovett had made it clear that the extent of U.S. involvement depended on Europeans fulfilling their promises.[85] This statement was a more accurate reading of Lovett's feeling, no matter how desirable a U.S. affiliation might have been in principle.

A second obstacle was the secrecy surrounding the six meetings. Not only were most of the allies unaware of the proceedings in the Pentagon, but France, a key partner, was deliberately excluded. There was bound to be negative repercussions from a country always sensitive to an Anglo-Saxon condominium that would reduce France to a second-class status in an enlarged alliance.

Not least of the hurdles the allies had to surmount was the judgment of the Senate, particularly its chairman of the Foreign Relations Committee, Arthur H. Vandenberg of Michigan. The Senate leader had been an isolationist who was converted in World War II to a believer in the UN as the ultimate peacekeeper. Supportive of European unification as he was, membership of the United States in a frankly military organization in a treaty relationship with European powers was arguably the most difficult challenge Hickerson and Achilles had to face. By contrast, the old isolationists, led by Senator Robert A. Taft of Ohio, were marginalized with a few articulate but essentially powerless followers. Nor would the vocal friends of European unity, such a Fulbright and Boggs, be automatic supporters of a U.S. presence in an anticipated United States of Europe.

Such were the issues that faced the State Department planners. Time and skilled diplomacy would be required to move the Atlantic security pact from the basement of the Pentagon to the light of Senate investigation and the heat of France's resentment—and then to the ultimate goal of an entangling alliance with Europe. At the end of the month, however, it was possible that the storm that promised rainbows in March would blow over in April without changing the climate of transatlantic relations.

NOTES

1. Quoted in Walter Millis, ed., *The Forrestal Diaries* (New York: The Viking Press, 1951), 387.

2. *New York Times*, February 29, 1948, 1.

3. Ray Cline, *Secrets, Spies and Scholars: Blueprint of the Essential CIA* (Washington, D.C.: Acropolis Books, 1976), 98.

4. Statement by Secretary of State George Marshall on the communist seizure of power in Czechoslovakia, March 10, 1948, Department of State *Bulletin*, 17, no. 435 (March 21, 1948): 381.

5. *New York Times*, February 29, 1948.

6. Armand Bérard, *Un ambassadeur souvient: Washington et Bonn, 1945–1955* (Paris: Plon, 1978), 180.

7. NSC 1/1, "The Position of the United States with Respect to Italy," November 14, 1947, *FRUS*, 1948, III: 726

8. E. Timothy Smith, *The United States, Italy, and NATO, 1947–1952* (New York: St. Martin's Press, 1991), 28–31.

9. *Public Papers of the Presidents of the United States 1947*, 510.

10. James E. Miller, "Taking Off the Gloves: The United States and the Italian Election of 1948, *Diplomatic History* 7, no. 1 (Winter 1983): 44.

11. Miller, "Taking Off the Gloves," 45.

12. Miller, "Taking Off the Gloves," 45.

13. NSC 1/2, "The Position of the United States with Respect to Italy," February 10, 1948, *FRUS*, 1948, III: 766–67.

14. Memorandum by JCS for Secretary of Defense, February 19, 1948, *FRUS*, 1948, III: 770–71.

15. Secretary of the Army to the Secretary of State, March 1, 1948, *FRUS*, 1948, III: 773.

16. Memorandum by JCS for Secretary of Defense, March 10, 1948, Sub: The Position of the United States with Respect to Italy in Light of the Possibility of Communist Participation in the Italian Government by Legal Means," *FRUS*, 1948, III: 783.

17. NSC 1/3, Report by the National Security Council, March 8, 1948, *FRUS*, 1948, III: 775–79; President to Secretary of Defense, March 10, 1948, *FRUS*, 1948, III: 781–82.

18. Director of the Policy Planning Staff to Secretary of State, March 15, 1948, *FRUS*, 1948, III: 848.

19. Miller, "Taking Off the Gloves," 48–49.

20. Miller, "Taking Off the Gloves," 50–51.

21. *New York Times*, March 5, 1948; *New York Times*, March 21, 1948.

22. Tel Chargé in Belgium (Millard) to Secretary of State, March 4, 1948, *FRUS*, 1948, no. 452, III: 37.

23. Tel Secretary of State to Embassy in Belgium, March 3, 1948, *FRUS*, 1948, no. 313, III: 35; tel Secretary of State to Embassy in Italy, March 11, 1948, *FRUS*, 1948, no. 660, III: 45–46; tel Ambassador in Italy (Dunn) to Secretary of State, March 16, 1948, *FRUS*, 1948, no. 1155, III: 53–54.

24. Minutes of the First Meeting of the United States–United Kingdom–Canada Security Conversations, March 2, 1948, *FRUS*, 1948, III: 60–61.

25. Olav Riste, "Was 1949 a Turning Point? Norway and the Western Powers 1947–1950," in *Western Security: The Formative Years*, ed. Olav Riste (Oslo: Norwegian University Press, 1985), 138–39.

26. Aide-Memoire, British Embassy to the Department of State, March 11, 1948, *FRUS*, 1948, III: 47.

27. Ltr, U.S. Embassy, London, to Hickerson, March 13, 1948, 840.00/3–1348, NARA.

28. Secretary of State to British Ambassador (Lord Inverchapel), March 12, 1948, *FRUS*, 1948 III: 48.

29. Escott Reid, *Time of Fear and Hope: The Making of the North Atlantic Treaty* (Toronto: McClelland and Stewart, 1977), 42–43; Olav Riste, *The Norwegian Intelligence Service* (Portland, OR: Frank Cass, 1999), 178.

30. *Facts on File Yearbook* 8, no. 388 (1948): 111.

31. Edwin James, *New York Times*, April 4, 1948, E3.

32. Vojtech Mastny, "The February 1948 Coup in Prague and the Origins of NATO," *Soudobe Dĕjiny* (Prague) 2 (1998): 247–56.

33. James, *New York Times*, E3.

34. Tel Ambassador in Denmark (Josiah Marvel) to Secretary of State, March 12, 1948, *FRUS*, 1948, no. 230, III: 51.

35. See chapter 2.

36. Tel U.S. Political Advisor for Germany (Robert Murphy) to Secretary of State, March 3, 1948, A-182, *FRUS*, 1948, II: 878; Avi Schlaim, *The United States and the Berlin Blockade, 1948–1949* (Berkeley: University of California Press, 1983), 113.

37. Quoted in Millis, ed., *The Forrestal Diaries*, 387.

38. Tel Murphy to Secretary of State, March 3, 1948, A-182, *FRUS*, 1948 II: 878–79.

39. Memo, Frank Wisner, deputy to Assistant Secretary of State for Occupied Areas, *FRUS*, 1948, II: 879–82

40. *New York Times*, March 13, 1948.

41. Schlaim, *The United States and the Berlin Blockade*, 113.

42. *New York Times*, March 30, 1948.

43. *New York Times*, March 26, 1948; *New York Times*, March 30, 1948; Eugene Davidson, *The Death and Life of Germany: An Account of the American Occupation* (New York: Alfred A. Knopf, 1959), 191.

44. Robert D. Murphy, *Diplomat among Warriors* (Garden City, NY: Doubleday, 1964), 313; Daniel Harrington, "The Berlin Blockade Revisited," *International History Review* 6, no. 1(February 1984): 945; Ann Tusa and John Tusa, *The Berlin Blockade* (London: Hodder and Stoughton, 1988), 95–96.

45. *New York Times*, March 1, 1948.

46. Tel Ambassador to UK (Douglas) to Secretary of State, March 2, 1948, *FRUS, 1948,* no. 1595, II: 111; tel Ambassador to France (Caffery) to Secretary of State, March 2, 1948, *FRUS, 1948,* no. 1110, III: 34–35.

47. *New York Times,* March 5, 1948; tel Galman (London) to Secretary of State, March 5, 1948, no. 954, 840.00.3/–1148, NARA.

48. Tel Millard to Secretary of State, March 10, 1948, no. 496, 840.00/3–1048 NARA.

49. *New York Times,* March 3, 1948.

50. Tel Millard to Secretary of State, March 9, 1948, no. 486, 840.00/3–948, NARA.

51. Tel Millard to Secretary of State, March 15, 1948, no.1349, 840,00/3–1548, NARA.

52. Memcon Gladwyn Jebb with Sir Orme Sargent, Sir Ivone Kirkpatrick, and Ernest Bevin, March 3, 1948, Foreign Office (hereafter cited as FO) 371 73050, Public Records Office (hereafter cited as PRO).

53. Special Message to the Congress on the Threat of the Freedom of Europe March 17, 1948, *Public Papers of the Presidents, 1948,* 182–86; St. Patrick's Day Address, March 17, 1948 *Public Papers of the Presidents, 1948,* 186–90.

54. Daniel Yergin, *Shattered Peace: The Origins of the Cold War and the National Security State* (Boston: Houghton Mifflin, 1977), 353.

55. Special Message, March 17, 1948, *Public Papers of the Presidents, 1948,* 184.

56. Paul-Henri Spaak, *The Continuing Battle: Memoirs of a European, 1936–1966,* trans. Henry Fox (Boston: Little, Brown and Co., 1971), 150.

57. Richard Coudenhove-Kalergi, letter to editor, *New York Times,* February 16, 1948, 20.

58. Warren F. Kuehl, *Biographical Dictionary of Internationalists* (Westport, CT: Greenwood Press, 1983), 172–74.

59. See chapter 1.

60. *Congressional Record,* 80th Cong., 1st sess., 1947, 93: 2437.

61. Altieri Spinelli, *The Eurocrats: Conflict and Crisis in the European Community* (Baltimore: Johns Hopkins University Press, 1966), 10–17, presents the various approaches to European unification.

62. Ray Sawyer, *Hearings on ERP,* January 21, 1948, House Committee on Foreign Affairs, 678; February 5, 1948, HR, 80th Cong., 2nd sess., 1388–99.

63. Clarence K. Street, letter to editor, *New York Times,* March 9, 1948; Burton K. Wheeler, response to letter to the editor, *New York Times,* March 17, 1948, 24; Wheeler's further comments in *Congressional Record,* 80th Cong., 2nd sess., 93: appendix A1689.

64. *Congressional Record,* 80th Cong., 2nd sess., March 1, 1948, 93: 1914; *Congressional Record,* 80th Cong., 2nd sess., March 3, 1948, 2030.

65. *Congressional Record,* 80th Cong., 2nd sess., March 3, 1948, 2034.

66. *Congressional Record,* 80th Cong., 2nd sess., March 3, 1948, 2037.

67. *Facts on File Yearbook 1948* 8, no. 387, 104.

68. Quoted in Elliot R. Goodman, *The Fate of the Atlantic Community* (New York: Praeger, 1975), 9–10.

69. Note Richard Coudenhove-Kalergi's pamphlet, "How to Successfully Fight the Propaganda of the Cominform," February 2, 1948, Office of European Affairs, 840.00/2–1648, box 5649, RG 59, NARA.

70. Richard Coudenhove-Kalergi, *Kampf um Europa: Aus Meinem Leben* (Zurich: Atlantis Verlag, 1949), 277; *New York Times,* January 2, 1948.

71. Coudenhove-Kalergi, *Kampf um Europa,* 277.

72. Coudenhove-Kalergi, *Kampf um Europa,* 280; the committee was formally organized on April 23, 1948, *New York Times,* April 24, 1948.

73. Memo, S. Shephard Jones to Charles Bohlen, April 12, 1948, 840.00/4-1348, RG 59, NARA.

74. Theodore Achilles, "Fingerprints on History," 14; the section on the Pentagon conversations owes a special debt to the manuscript of Sidney W. Snyder, "The Role of the International Working Group in the Creation of the North Atlantic Treaty" (Ph.D. dissertation, Kent State University, 1992), 66ff.

75. That Maclean was a secret agent of Moscow in Washington from 1944 to 1948 in a position to know the most intimate details of Anglo-American military planning has been recognized since his defection to the Soviet Union. Whether the Soviets processed the information is still open to question; see Sheila Kerr, "The Secret Hotline to Moscow: Donald Maclean and the Berlin Crisis of 1948," in *Britain and the First Cold War,* ed., Anne Deighton (New York: St. Martin's Press, 1989), 71–87.

76. Memo by the Director of the Office of European Affairs (John Hickerson) to Secretary of State, March 8, 1948, *FRUS,* 1947, III: 40–41; memo by Secretary of State to President Harry S. Truman, March 12, 1948, *FRUS,* 1947, III: 49.

77. Achilles, *Fingerprints on History,* 15.

78. Minutes of the First Meeting of the United States–United Kingdom–Canada Security Conversations, Washington, D.C., March 22, 1948, *FRUS,* 1948, III: 59–61.

79. Report by Policy Planning Staff Concerning Western Union and Related Problems, March 22, 1948, *FRUS,* 1948, III: 62; minutes of the Third Meeting, March 24, 1948, *FRUS,* 1948, III: 66–67.

80. Achilles, *Fingerprints on History,* 15.

81. Minutes of the Sixth Meeting, April 1, 1948, *FRUS,* 1948, III: 72.

82. Minutes of the Sixth Meeting, April 1, 1948 *FRUS,* 1948, III: 72.

83. Robert H. Ferrell, *George Marshall as Secretary of State, 1947–1949,* in *The American Secretaries of State and Their Diplomacy,* XV, ed. Robert H. Ferrell and Samuel F. Bemis (New York: Cooper Square Publishers, 1966), 172, 178.

84. Minutes of the Fifth Meeting, March 31, 1948, *FRUS,* 1948, III: 71.

85. Memo of Conversation by Hickerson, February 7, 1948—Inverchapel, Lovett, *FRUS,* 1948.

4

The Vandenberg
Resolution: 11 June 1948

THE STATE DEPARTMENT CONFLICTED

While the storm of unsettling events in the winter of 1948 had swayed U.S. public opinion and congressional attitudes down the road toward entanglement with Europe, it had not blown away the misgivings of the State Department. Notwithstanding the convictions of John Hickerson and Theodore Achilles and the conclusions of the sessions in the Pentagon, U.S. leaders had not committed the United States to a European alliance. Their behavior in the spring, both in the administration and the Congress, did not promise an early response to the hopes of the framers of the Brussels Pact.

Given the prominence of Hickerson and Achilles, the State Department should have been the U.S. agency most receptive to the cries of the Europeans. Certainly, its position in the Pentagon conversations suggested as much. But those were secret conversations, barely acknowledged by senior members of the department. If their outcome projected an Atlantic alliance, it would only be in a future that was not visible in the spring of 1948.

Some of the difficulties the proponents of an alliance would meet were reflected in the reactions of State Department officials to Richard Coudenhove-Kalergi's visit in February. These differed markedly from the memories that the veteran propagandist for European unity had of his encounters with U.S. officials. Looking at the effect of that visit on Washington policymakers offers a cautionary tale about the prospective U.S. role in Europe in the winter of 1948. It became obvious that Coudenhove-Kalergi chose not to look too deeply into the background of the officials he met. He emerged as a willing prisoner of his own dreams and of statesmen's words. That the preamble of the "Marshall-Plan-Gesetz" seemed to link the promise of European unity to U.S. economic aid ignored the fact that a preamble, no matter how stirring, carried in itself no legal significance.[1] For Coudenhove-Kalergi to believe that Harry S Truman or George Marshall hung on his words, let alone were converted by them, was a species of self-delusion. Although the Austrian nobleman was a recognized voice of a new Europe and a positive influence on such legislators as Senator J. William Fulbright, he was, for men of power in Europe and the United States, just a symbol of a constituency that had to be attended to and possibly even mobilized. But he and his movement ranked far behind more urgent matters in their scale of priorities.

The State Department's response to his request for a meeting with the secretary of state in February was revealing of the administration's attitude toward European unity as a political movement. In seeking an audience with Marshall through Charles Bohlen, Counselor of the State Department, Coudenhove-Kalergi claimed that failure to meet the secretary could damage his work in Europe because "nobody there would understand why I have not seen the Secretary during my prolonged visit to the United States."[2] Bohlen was not much impressed. As he informed Hickerson, "Coudenhove-Kalergi has been on my neck. I saw him when he was down here. You will note that he wants me to try to get him in to see the secretary. Could you let me have an estimate of his standing in Europe and whether his advocacy of European federation is taken sufficiently seriously abroad to justify recommendation that the secretary see him or is it more of a personal gambit?"[3] Hickerson responded that Coudenhove-Kalergi's position as secretary-general of the European Parliamentary Union was important enough, in light of Ernest Bevin's speech and the "widespread support in this country for some kind of federation," that his request should be accepted. "If he does not see the Secretary for a *few minutes* it might indicate that we have less interest in sponsoring a European federation than is the case."[4]

Such was the actual setting for the meeting between Count Coudenhove-Kalergi and Secretary Marshall and is considerably different from the impression given in the European's memoirs. Bohlen's recommendations to Marshall's staff contained a caveat: "I don't think it needs to be 15 minutes unless the Secretary is interested."[5] The suggestion of fifteen minutes evokes an image of busy officials handling a crank, if not a bore, to whom they paid attention only because of potentially unfavorable repercussions if they failed to go through the motions of civility. In any event, the interview did not delay Marshall's escape to his Virginia farm for the weekend. Coudenhove-Kalergi was unaware of the reluctant reception he was given. Before leaving Washington, he managed to give the secretary an autographed copy of one his books, which he considered sufficient proof of his influence over U.S. foreign policy.[6]

U.S. counterparts of Coudenhove-Kalergi would have received similar treatment unless they were too well placed to ignore either as power brokers or as popular icons. The State Department regarded the influential journalist Dorothy Thompson as a gratuitous irritant in introducing a pan-European weekly magazine in the United States to promote the concept of European unification. No matter how noble its motivation, the plan could be interpreted as another U.S. interference in a purely European problem that would invite resentment abroad among friends as well as enemies. The foreign policy establishment regarded Coudenhove-Kalergi and Thompson as well-meaning amateurs whose goals were either unrealistic or disturbing to U.S. interests. An unsatisfied Thompson received a letter of encouragement from the secretary of state but with the proviso that the circulation of the new magazine be limited to U.S. subscribers.[7]

There was clearly a disjunction between the intentions of the European bureau's Hickerson and Achilles and those of Department of State's leadership—Marshall and Robert Lovett—as well as George Kennan's policy planning staff. In varying degrees, they were opposed to any binding commitments that would limit the nation's freedom of action, despite Hickerson and Achilles's efforts to change their minds. Moreover, the Senate, an acknowledged vital partner in any decision for future entanglement, was left out of the secret negotiations and would have to be carefully wooed if that body and its leader, Arthur H. Vandenberg, were to accept the direction the security talks in the Pentagon had been heading.

But what was peculiarly striking in the State Department's reactions to Coudenhove-Kalergi and Thompson's importunities was the chilly reception it gave to any attempt to associate U.S. foreign policy with the advancement of European integration. These supporters of European unity did not ask for or expect a U.S. entanglement, yet their views were brushed aside, even as Hickerson, Achilles, and Ambassador Lewis Douglas were working with the British and Canadians to make an Atlantic security treaty with the United States occupying a dominant role. Granted, a loose interpretation of Hickerson's endorsement of Coudenhove-Kalergi's meeting with the secretary of state might suggest that his "few minutes" could pave the way for a closer tie with the European leader's organization. Still, this would be a stretch of imagination. Hickerson, presumably sensitive to the prevailing views of his superiors, was simply avoiding any possible embarrassment to the State Department by speaking up for Coudenhove-Kalergi. Obviously, he was not prepared to challenge Bohlen at this time on the issue of public support for European unity let alone to urge U.S. participation in a European defense organization.

This colloquy took place in February, before the president spoke in favor of a Brussels pact. But the rejection of Thompson's proposal took place in April after the creation of the Western Union and after the passage of the

Economic Administration Act—and, even more significantly, after the recommendations in the Pentagon conversations for a "Collective Defense Agreement for the North Atlantic Area." The absence of coordination in the Truman administration following the signing of the Brussels Pact made the path toward U.S. participation in a European defense organization all the more tortuous.

THE HAGUE DIVERSION—MAY 1948

Coudenhove-Kalergi could not get out of his mind that his visit to Washington in February accelerated if not inspired the Truman administration's embrace of the Brussels Pact as well as Congress's passage of the Foreign Assistance Act of 1948. His success in establishing a committee in support of European unification was to him proof enough of his influence over the administration's foreign policies. But most of the distinguished members of the U.S. committees, such as former President Herbert Hoover and General William Donovan, the former head of the World War II Office of Strategic Services, were either out of office or as in the case of Fulbright and Supreme Court Justice Owen Roberts, were outside the foreign policy establishment.

The old campaigner for European unification erred both in the estimation of his own role in the events of the day and in conflating his conception of a united Europe with the objectives of the new Western Union. Coudenhove-Kalergi's European Parliamentary Union had a vision of a Europe united in a federation that would be based on more than a defense system for its survival. His vision of cultural unity was closer to that outlined by Winston Churchill in his speech at the University of Zurich in 1946, when he proclaimed that the remedy for the plight of a divided Europe was "to recreate the European family, or as much of it as we can, and to provide it with structure under which it can dwell in peace, safety, and freedom. We must build a United States of Europe."[8] It was Churchill, not Coudenhove-Kalergi, who led like-minded Europeans in a campaign that embraced not only his newly founded United Europe Movement in the United Kingdom but also counterparts in France, Italy, and the Low Countries. Under the directorship of Churchill's son-in-law, Duncan Sandys, a Congress of Europe was held in The Hague in May 1948.[9]

For three days, from May 7 to 10, more than 750 delegates from every country outside of Soviet control, including Alcide de Gasperi from Italy, Paul-Henri Spaak from Belgium, and an array of French leaders representing a spectrum of political positions—from the technocrat Jean Monnet to the Christian democrat Robert Schuman and the socialist Leon Blum. Resolutions about European unity flowed from the many commissions of the Hague Congress with a consensus over the need for European powers to relinquish some of their sovereign rights in aid of economic and political unity of the continent. The outcome of these deliberations did not lead to a recommendation for a fully federal government for Europe, but it did recommend an assembly composed for representatives of all European nations, which presumably would complete the task of economic and political integration.[10] The Council of Europe in 1949 was the fruit of these labors.

Inevitably, the prestige of Churchill put Coudenhove-Kalergi in the shade. The count's European Parliamentary Union became just one of many groups promoting European unity as the British hero of World War II dominated the scene in Zurich. Ironically, the British delegation to The Hague Congress, the largest at the meetings, was uncomfortable with the proceedings. That the leadership of the European movement was in the hands of the Conservatives was a major factor in Labour's opposition to a strong federalist approach to a European Assembly. Prime Minister Clement Attlee admitted that "a federation of Europe" was a desirable goal. But he was not prepared "to call a constituent assembly right off."[11]

David Linebaugh, the U.S. attaché at the embassy in London, had outlined the British divisions over the European movement in great detail a month before the congress assembled at The Hague. He found divisions even within the Conservative Party over the wisdom of European Union; the majority opinion in the party "believes that federation is impractical and unnecessary, and might result in reducing the British standard of living." As for the Labour Party, it did all that it could to discourage its members from attending the congress. The party's formal position had been presented at a Conference of Socialist Parties on the ERP, held in London in March. To keep the initiative for European union "in Socialist hands and away from Mr. Churchill, the party appeared willing to support the principle but not the auspices."[12]

As a result of the British government's ambivalence, the State Department had doubts about the official U.S. position on the congress. On April 11, after a conversation with Churchill, Ambassador Douglas thought it might be a good idea to send an unofficial observer, given "our interest in western European unity." The Council of Foreign Relations or the Foreign Policy Association might be suitable candidates.

Two days later he had second thoughts. Because most of the Socialist governments apparently were boycotting the meeting, the Attlee government instructed Labour members of parliament (MP) not to attend. Under these circumstances, even an unofficial government observer might be undesirable. Douglas wondered if a U.S. member of the Inter-Parliamentary Union might serve to show "our interest without involving the administration." Even this step was too much. When Sandys, chairman of the organizing committee for The Hague meeting invited Marshall to send a message to the meeting, the secretary of state could not bring himself to make even that gesture: Douglas was instructed to tell Sandys that the secretary "welcomes any concrete progress toward greater unity of thought and action between free nations of Western Europe, but that he does not consider it appropriate to send message [of support] to meeting."[13]

The brief U.S. debate over The Hague meetings hardly mattered. The congress did win applause from U.S. supporters and a benediction from the *New York Times*. It appeared to have been a great success. Some Labour members did show up, as did Socialists from most Western European countries. Germans attended the congress and received hope of future integration into a united states of Europe. There was even a representation from exiled citizens from countries beyond the Iron Curtain who were welcomed but denied a vote. As Churchill noted, "When you consider how much unites us together, think how far it outweighs the differences."[14] Coudenhove-Kalergi, celebrating the creation of a U.S. committee in support of his conception of a united Europe, predicted in April that the Hague Congress would call for a parliamentary conference in Interlaken, Switzerland, in September to draft a final constitution for the United States of Europe.[15]

But once the cheers died down and the self-congratulations of the delegates wore off, the resolutions went into a black hole. While a Council of Europe did come into being, it was toothless and essentially meaningless. What Marshall wanted from the Hague Congress was encapsulated in the word *effort*, substituted in his response to Sandys's invitation for *progress*, which was scratched out of the cable.[16] There was plenty of effort made in The Hague but little progress. Movement toward European unity would only develop from NATO, which emerged from the Brussels Pact and from the Organization for European Economic Cooperation (OEEC) that emerged from the Marshall Plan.

Despite the cautious official U.S. approach to the Hague Congress, the administration's position of support without explicit ties to European integration was closer to its aspirations than the Western Union's hopes of bringing the United States into its organization. All public signals suggested approval of European federation. In addition to such well-known friends as Fulbright and Hale Boggs, Governor Thomas A. Dewey of New York, a Republican presidential aspirant, came out boldly in favor of a federated Europe. Speaking on the campaign trail in Lincoln, Nebraska, on 8 April, he asserted that "what is needed to restore stability in the world is a unified Europe—a strong third power devoted to the cause of peace. What is needed is a 'United States of Europe.'"[17] Given the absence of any U.S. obligation to participate in the United States of Europe, the United States could appear as a benevolent patron discreetly in the background and yet available for guidance when needed. The *New York Times* pundit Anne O'Hare McCormick applauded the passion for unity expressed by Europeans at The Hague. She saw them seeking "not a Union of the West but a Union of the Free" to which the United States should give its blessing. Europe's vision as seen in Zurich looked far beyond the five-power Western Union.[18]

Wittingly or not, Coudenhove-Kalergi had conflated the drive toward a federated Europe with the activities of the Brussels Pact powers and the new Economic Cooperation Administration (ECA) created to bring the Marshall Plan to life, as if those two actions were instruments of his—and Churchill's—grand design for a united Europe. Certainly, the spirit of the Hague Congress lifted the hopes of the editorial writers of the *New York Times*. Their rhapsodies over Churchill's eloquence clearly linked the appeals at The Hague directly to the Brussels Pact and the Marshall Plan. The editorial went on to urge the United States to learn from the isolationism of the 1930s and make "common cause with these allies by the only method that might have spelled success in 1939 and which alone can spell success today. That is a hard and fast alliance with them."[19] In a few paragraphs, the editorial managed to equate the vague promises of a federated Europe with the formation of the Brussels Pact and the need for a U.S. military alliance. It is no small wonder that the emerging Western Union powers were unsure of U.S. intentions.

THE WESTERN UNION IN DISARRAY

It was not that the Brussels Pact framers relaxed their pressures after the signing of the pact. On the day of its creation, Bevin and Georges Bidault asked for the next step in their relations with the United States—preliminary discussions with their ambassadors in Washington. Rather, it was the combination of hesitation and vagueness of the replies they received that disconcerted them. The only response that Marshall made at the moment was to meet with the British and French ambassadors.[20] But this was just a formality, a psychological gesture before departure for Bogota and the more immediate matter of inter-American solidarity.

Britain, with the most intimate connections with the United States, was arguably the most troubled by the outcome of the Pentagon talks. The other members of the Western Union, unaware of the recommendations for an Atlantic security pact, had lower expectations. True, the secret conversations did not resolve the territorial scope of the prospective alliance or determine its membership. Nor did it deal with the terms of mutual aid; the British preferred the clear language of Article 4 of the Brussels treaty, while the United States and Canada looked to the Rio model, which did not specify a precise response to an attack on one of its members. But the British hoped that once the decision for an alliance was made, sufficient momentum would be built up to subsume those questions under the new alliance.[21] In the long run, as Nicholas Henderson, the second secretary at the British Embassy, observed in the summer of 1948, the proposals Hickerson had hatched in the Pentagon were to be "an unseen presence, like some navigational device . . . to keep the negotiations on a steady course throughout the many months ahead."[22]

In the short run, the British diplomats were distressed by the apparent stasis in April 1948. Nothing seemed to have been done to implement the promises of March. Bevin had gone out of his way to express agreement with the U.S. idea of a conference to discuss defense arrangements for the North Atlantic area. Failing to act, he insisted, would put all parties at risk.[23] But when Ambassador Lord Inverchapel reported British acceptance of the Pentagon proposals to Lovett, the undersecretary of state was pessimistic about their prospects. All he could see were the obstacles in the way—opposition within his own department, rumblings of discontent in the Pentagon, and—most significantly—inevitable outcry from isolationists in the Congress, a branch of government completely ignorant of the program plotted in the Pentagon conversation. Moreover, any public disclosure of the Anglo–U.S.–Canadian discussions for a military alliance could upset the delicate negotiations in the Congress over funding for the newly authorized Foreign Assistance Act of 1948. With the presidential campaign already underway, presidential leadership could not be expected.[24] In light of these U.S. preoccupations, Bevin had already informed Prime Minister Attlee that it was doubtful that the United States was ready to "pronounce in favour of a treaty binding the [United States] for the first time in history to accept positive obligations in the way of defen[se] of her natural associates and friends."[25]

British frustration over the apparently stalled Anglo-U.S. plans for an Atlantic security pact was a logical consequence of the secrecy that had enshrouded the negotiations. The principal members of the Western Union knew nothing about them. France was excluded partly out of concern that continuing Communist influence on the government would compromise the proceedings. This concern was all the more persuasive because of a suspicion that Moscow had broken French codes. The irony, of course, lay in the fact that a prominent British representative at the talks was Donald Maclean. Maclean was the first secretary of the British Embassy in Washington and a member of the spy network that had supplied the Soviet Union with critical U.S. atomic power information as well as details of the planning and organization of the North Atlantic Treaty. As Canadian Deputy Undersecretary of State for External Affairs Escott Reid observed, he was "in a position to send the Soviet government a play-by-play account of discussions up to the end of August 1948."[26]

There was a penalty to be paid for this omission in the confusion that pervaded the Western Union in the month following the signing of the treaty. For example, Spaak complicated planning by noting that military conversations should begin immediately between the U.S. military and the five Western Union members.[27] But two days later, Spaak told Lovett that he saw no immediate danger of a Soviet attack. While he believed that the Western Union should increase its defense potential, he speculated that an alliance with the United States was not yet needed; it would create danger for those European countries left out of the organization. With Hickerson and Achilles sitting silently by his side, the acting secretary could only reaffirm U.S. support of the five-power treaty and lamely respond that the only question was how best to do it.[28] The Dutch were also uneasy about the state of Western Union–United States relations. Their foreign minister knew that the British had conversations with their U.S. counterparts and wanted to make clear that Britain was not the designated spokesman for the other members of the Western Union.[29] The Benelux countries intended to resist the tendency of the British and French to dominate the Western Union.[30]

It was France that seemed most at sea over where the United States was heading. Both Spaak and Bevin had been aware of Bidault's nervousness and apparent indecision over what course the West should take. On the day the Brussels Pact was signed, he was in a funk, according to Spaak, fearing that war would begin within a week. He found Bidault's "wavering, shifting and excessively nervous attitude" difficult to understand.[31] Bevin recognized, too, the insecurity of his French partner and worried about Bidault's disposition to hold back on defense preparations on the grounds that there was little that the Western Union could do in the face of the overwhelming superiority of the Soviet adversary, unless the United States had committed itself to prompt support. Ambassador Douglas told Bevin that this was just the sort of attitude that would prevent a U.S. commitment. Whatever steps the United States would take had to be conditioned on Western Europe's determination to defend itself.[32]

The French continued to be suspicious of both U.S. and British behavior. When Ambassador Armand Bérard heard about the U.S. decision to create a seventy-group air force, he jumped to the conclusion that the United States would strike the Soviet Union in the event of war and not even attempt to defend Western Europe. Once again, the French were asking about a "guarantee," rather than just "support." In response, Achilles promised that talks with the Western Union members would begin shortly but gave no hint of what had transpired the month before in the Pentagon.[33]

The U.S. answers did not satisfy the French. The authoritative Paris newspaper *Le Monde* underscored what it considered to be U.S. "uncertainties." It worried about U.S. indecision over the size of its army, over the types of armament, and over popular opposition to a military draft as well as over conflict between the Congress that emphasized air power and the administration that preferred a more evenly balanced defense program. Not least was the worry that if war erupted, the United States might offer weapons to Germany, and that would be unacceptable to France.[34]

Arguably, it was the German question that was at the heart of Bidault's suspicions about the European policies of the United States. While the first session of the London conference on Germany did yield concessions to France on decentralization and a Ruhr authority that essentially internationalized this critical area, Bidault did not receive the credit he felt was his due. President Vincent Auriol and his fellow Socialists protested Bidault's actions and suspected that the second session of the London conference would witness the revival of the German menace and provoke war with the Soviet Union.[35] Actually, Bidault won more concessions in this session that ended on 7 June; a military security board to ensure Germany's long-term disarmament was established. Still, he had to agree to the early formation of a West German government. He feared that Britain and the United States would set up a German government on their own if France dissented. As France's ambassador to Britain, René Massigli, noted, refusing to ratify this accord would be equivalent to France renouncing its commanding role on the continent. No Franco-German political cooperation would be possible if U.S. and Soviet propagandists posed simultaneously as defenders of the German people against a paranoid France.[36]

The foreign minister lost his office as a result of the London accords, but his successor, Schuman, like Bidault a member of the liberal Catholic *Mouvement Républicain Populaire*, patched up relations with the Anglo-Saxon powers in time for new negotiations between the Western Union and the United States. There was no alternative to rapprochement with the allies; dependence on U.S. aid was a reality that could not be evaded.[37]

Britain, too, despite better knowledge of the ultimate intentions of the United States, was not immune to the jitters that afflicted the French. It manifested in an ambivalence toward the Western Union that was displayed in discomfort over the prospect of transferring sovereignty to that body. Benelux representatives felt that the British were reluctant to give the Western Union effective powers and cited their preference to limit the role of the secretariat.[38] While Bevin did not want to give the United States the impression that Britain would not fight if attacked, he was pessimistic about chances of survival. Unlike 1940, the country could not hold out for two years while the United States dithered over active participation in its defense.[39]

WESTERN UNION INITIATIVES

Lovett's pessimism, combined with Bevin's, forced the British to give up bilateral initiatives in mid-April, at least temporarily, and instead to use the

Western Union as an instrument to push the United States along the path of alliance. But first the Europeans had to come to a consensus. Although anxious to have the five foreign ministers form a controlling body, Bidault was opposed to designating London as its headquarters for fear that his countrymen would interpret this decision as France becoming "an annex of the British empire." But he was willing to have London as headquarters for military affairs as long as economic affairs would be located elsewhere.[40]

The idea of establishing a Consultative Council to demonstrate progress the Western Union was making in defending themselves was known to the State Department before it was officially announced. Admitting that its organization was still in "somewhat of a state of flux," the Head of the Western department of the foreign office told Douglas in strict confidence to anticipate an early resolution of all differences that could stand in the way of its creation.[41] The Consultative Council would be the Western Union's response to U.S. pressure for action. The United States should have been prepared to join in discussions for the coordination of production and supply of weaponry.[42] This would be a major step toward the entanglement all the members wanted.

With a flourish, the Western Union issued a communiqué on 17 April announcing the formation of a permanent consultative council of foreign ministers that would meet at least once every three months. It would be composed of diplomatic representatives of each of the signatories of the Brussels Pact who would comprise the permanent organ of the council and meet at least once a month. A permanent military committee would sit in London and function under the authority of the council. Of lesser importance at this juncture were economic, social, and cultural questions—issues that would be taken up by special committees.

The Benelux partners were pleased with these arrangements, according to Jean Chauvel of the foreign ministry. Their worries about Bevin and Bidault going behind their backs were unfounded. And as evidence of British and French good faith, the chief of the secretariat would be a member of the Benelux countries. So, one month after the Western Union came into being, all the partners were satisfied that it was prepared to go into action.[43]

The subtext of the communiqué, however, had little to do with the nature or composition of the Consultative Council. Rather, it provided the occasion for the allies to demand that the United States begin serious negotiations for the defense of Europe. In brief, the Brussels powers claimed they had shown their good faith in getting together to fight their own battles. This assurance responded to Lovett's repeated demands of some proof of their determination before talks could get underway. Now, the British and French ambassadors in Washington could say that "despite the difficulties that confront the U.S. Administration, we urge strongly that if a favorable opportunity is not to be missed and if a fresh impetus is not to be given to

the cause of Communism, it is essential to initiate without delay the conversations contemplated by the Government of the United States."

The Western Union powers, however, undercut their military promises
when no action followed the pronouncement that exploratory military staff
conferences would be in place within two weeks after the pact was signed.[45]
It required more than a month before the British could announce that they
had invited the Western Union defense ministers to meet in London to discuss a joint defense program. The *Manchester Guardian* made a point of noting that the danger to Europe was not U.S. unwillingness to stand by their
side but that the United States would not be strong enough at first to prevent the continent from being occupied. For this reason, Europeans must
"hold this fort until the United States can bring its enormous potential
power to bear on the enemy."[46]

The five defense ministers and their chiefs of staff finally met in London
on 30 April, six days after the first session of the Consultative Council, and
came to an agreement on the structure and procedure of the permanent
military committee. The first assignment of the permanent military committee a week later was to survey the effectiveness of existing equipment,
project what requirements could be met by their own production and, most
importantly, what needed to be asked of the United States to fill the gaps.[47]
Given the primacy of the British role on the committee, Chauvel was anxious to have a U.S. observer present. The French were not pleased with the
prospect of the British acting as the main channel of information on the
participants' military views and decisions. A U.S. presence would minimize
the risk of leaks and serve as a more efficient agent of information. It would
also limit Britain's influence on the committee.[48] The Benelux representatives agreed with the French on this issue but for a different reason. They
felt that the British tended to limit the role of the permanent organization
and secretariat, which could stunt the organization's growth.[49]

A danger for all the allies was the possibility of the new organization serving as a Potemkin village, concealing the lack of genuine progress toward
collective self defense. As the French military representative observed, "a
four story edifice was set up. On the top floor are the National Defense Ministers; the third floor has the Chiefs of Staff; the second floor, the Ambassador's Committee at London with a permanent Secretariat and a Dutch
secretary; the first floor, committee of special military representative at London and an English secretary."[50] The machinery was in place, but what
would the Western Union do with it?

The initial actions of the defense ministers and chiefs of staff on 30 April
were as incoherent as they were confused. In response to U.S. queries, the
French representative was ready to pool military resources and agreed to
standardization of equipment. But he discredited this readiness by noting
that logically its implementation would require a clear defense plan that

was impossible to achieve until a decision was reached over holding the line at the Elbe or at the Rhine. The British representatives, on the other hand, were concerned not with Western Union future planning but rather with the importance of not letting the partners know current Anglo-U.S. defense plans. Yet as reported to Ambassador Douglas, "defense ministers and military men set themselves resolutely to tasks with few words and meetings were in fact highly satisfactory."[51] Or so they claimed.

British concerns about security, particularly keeping Anglo-U.S. negotiations from their Western Union allies, were paramount in the spring of 1948. They were also understandable. The United States and Britain had drawn up emergency plans for evacuating the continent in the event of war in the next eighteen months; the U.S. plan was called Halfmoon, the British, Doublequick. The major difference between them was over the timing of a strategic withdrawal, with the British striving to prevent it from being part of a formal plan. It was not only that the British were "almost pathologically predisposed to avoid another Dunkirk," as historian Martin Folly judged, but that knowledge of Anglo-U.S. thinking along these lines would undermine Europe's willingness to resist a Soviet attack. Consequently, the Western Union partners were not to be informed about either plan. Should an invasion take place, much of the burden would fall on Western Europeans, and informing them of evacuation plans would sap their morale.[52] The need for secrecy, however, obviously hobbled progress of the Western Union military committees.

The immediate interest of the allies was in securing U.S. assistance to fill gaps in equipment and provisions. But being shut off from the Anglo-U.S. negotiations, they had little chance of fulfilling the requirement presented by NSC 1/9, that Europe present a coordinated defense system with all means available to its members and then supply the United States with an inventory of deficiencies.[53] Recognizing this problem, Bevin proposed to solve it by informing the allies of the U.S. intention, which was expressed in the Pentagon conversations, to enter into an Atlantic security organization. Even if there were problems about including other countries into such an arrangement, the combination of the United States, Canada, and the five Brussels Pact members could be enough to deter any Soviet miscalculation as well as encourage democratic forces everywhere. Knowledge of U.S. acceptance of a definite commitment to Europe's security would do more than the presence of U.S. forces in Germany to give assurance to Italy and Scandinavia that United States was ready and able to defend them. Even more important would be its effect on France; it would relieve the French people of the doubts expressed in the London meetings about pursuing a joint policy in Germany with the United States and Britain. This solution would be to open negotiations "in the near future" for a North Atlantic pact.[54]

LOVETT'S PROBLEMS

If the British were unhappy over the U.S. delay in acting on the recommendations of the Pentagon paper, consider the anxiety of other Western Union members left out of the British, U.S., and Canadian talks. When the allies presented a joint message on the necessity of U.S. aid or an effective defense of Western Europe, Lovett vigorously asserted that the United States had no intention of backing away from the promises made at the time of the signing of the Brussels Pact. It was at this time, 20 April, that he had raised the issue of Europe having to come up with defense plans of its own.[55] From Bogota, Marshall pitched in with his own effort to remove the Western Union's obvious sense of frustration. He explained to Bevin and Bidault: "It is vital, I feel . . . that any assurances from this country on this matter have maximum country-wide support and backing of the Congress. As you know, this is a complicated matter but Mr. Lovett advises me he is making good progress in the preparations for Washington conversations with Bonnet, Inverchapel and a Benelux representative. I hope to be able by next week to suggest a definite date."

Eventually these talks did take place but not "next week." Yet there was certainly evidence that Congress, the State Department, and the new NSC were giving serious thought to the concerns of the Europeans. There had been significant informal discussions involving the military as well as the executive and legislative branches about seeking an amendment tying military assistance to economic aid in a broadened ERP, as Title VI of the Foreign Assistance Act. To deflect further entanglement with the Western Union, Representative John Vorys of Ohio offered this amendment. The conference committee of the House and Senate deleted it, and the president denied that he had intended to revive a military lend-lease program for Western European democracies.[56]

A military ERP was not to be considered one of the "appropriate means" the president had cited in his 17 March statement of support of the defense of the West. It might have jeopardized the economic program by raising alarm among congressional advocates of the UN as the nation's appropriate instrument in aid of Western democracies. A too-hasty mix of military and economic aid could have damaged the fragile fabric of European-U.S. relations if the Brussels Pact countries were perceived as being more interested in military than in economic aid.

The deletion of Title VI from the foreign aid bill did not stop rumors of a mammoth multi-billion-dollar military assistance program from circulating in the press and on Capitol Hill. Some of the rumors were so wild that Marx Leva, special assistant to the secretary of defense, was convinced that Congress would accept a $750 million military aid program. He suggested that the submission of a military assistance bill, separate from the ERP, would be raised again with Lovett and Bohlen. It might be more popular in the Senate than an economic aid bill. At a meeting at the Bureau of the Budget on 5 May, State Department and Defense Department representatives agreed to work on legislation for a limited interim program along the lines of the aborted Title VI. The subject, however, died at the desks of Secretaries Marshall and James Forrestal.[57]

Failure to add a military component to the ERP did not dampen the administration's interest in helping Europe without making the kind of commitments the Europeans wanted. Two documents emerged from the new NSC to which the State Department had referred the problem. One was NSC 1/7 on 30 March, a general report on the "Position of the United States with respect to Soviet-directed World Communism" that recommended a counteroffensive to "strengthen the will to resist of anti-communist forces throughout the world." First priority would be assigned to Europe, and a strong endorsement would be given to the Western Union, along with formulas to be worked out for "military action by the United States in the event of unprovoked armed attack against the nations in the Western Union or against other selected non-Communist nations."[58]

Even more pointed was NSC 1/9, 13 April, "The Position of the United States with respect to Support for Western Union and Other Related Countries," a document presumably responding to Western Union's requests. It proposed an extension of the Western Union to include the Scandinavian countries, and possibly Italy, to encourage their joining the five-power union and negotiate for a larger "Collective Defense Agreement for the North Atlantic Area." The president then would make a statement saying that any aggression in the North Atlantic area would be considered an attack against the United States.[59]

The potential roles of other European nations were a constant preoccupation of U.S. planners and intruded into most of their deliberations. If Italy was left out for the time being, it was largely because the outcome of the elections in that country had not been determined until late in April. Of lesser importance were the military restrictions in the Italian peace treaty, which Ambassador James Dunn felt might be overcome by modifying the military clauses of the treaty through the application of the right of self defense under Article 51 of the UN charter.[60]

The Scandinavian countries, on the other hand, were freer to participate and certainly were anxious for U.S. military aid. Norway doubted if it would join the Western Union without Denmark and Sweden. But if faced with an emergency, it would go with the West alone. Sweden, with its history of neutrality in World War II, preferred to maintain a neutral stance despite warnings from the United States that its attitude might invite a Soviet attack and signal to the United States that it did not want help.[61] Sweden's argument was that for all practical purposes its geographical position stood in the way of future membership in the Western Union. What galled Marshall were Sweden's attempts to win over Norway and Denmark to its policy of neutrality between the blocs.[62] For its part, the Brussels Pact members gave lip service to adding new members. Their priority in the spring of 1948 was entangling the United States in Europe rather than extending the scope of the Western Union.

Although the Western Union recognized that NSC 1/7 and 1/9 were intended to demonstrate backing of defense efforts by the United States, these documents had in common the distancing of the United States from the one obligation that the Europeans wanted, namely, U.S. membership in the Western Union or in the larger North Atlantic community. NSC 1/7 was more elliptical with respect to its connection with the United States, and NSC 1/9 specifically stated that "The United States should not now participate as a member in Western Union."[63] It was just as well that caveats appeared in both documents, given the judgment of Republican Congressional leaders on 12 April—the day before NSC 1/9 was issued—that the Senate would not ratify any treaty obligating the United States to go to war to defend any Western European nation.[64] The only acceptable commitment would be the Rio pact formula, which promised assistance without the guarantee of a declaration of war. In the event of aggression there was no pledge to say precisely what would be the U.S. reaction.

Undersecretary Lovett had to cope with Europe's dissatisfaction with anything less than a treaty. A presidential declaration that an attack against a Brussels Pact member would be considered an attack against the United States was not good enough. Bevin had made it clear a few days earlier that any declaration not having the imprimatur of the Senate would leave the Western Union in doubt about just what would be done by the United States in the event of conflict, what countries beyond the five members of the Western Union would be covered, and what obligations the Europeans should have. In brief, Britain saw no substitute for a treaty promising Western Europe that a North Atlantic defense system was in the offing.[65]

The objections of Bevin and his European colleagues were just one part of Lovett's problem in putting together an alliance that would shatter the U.S. tradition of nonentanglement. The burden fell on him because Marshall was away in Bogota attending the meetings of the new Organization of American States (OAS) during the critical month of April. Lovett only gradually came to the conclusion that separated him from Marshall in this period, namely, that an Atlantic alliance wider than the Western Union was a necessity for the security of the United States. It took some time before he was prepared to adopt the views of Hickerson, Achilles, and John Foster Dulles. During the Pentagon conversations, Hickerson was careful to note that Lovett be informed but not be fully knowledgeable about the contents of the Pentagon paper.[66]

As a new convert to the principles of a North Atlantic alliance, Lovett had to cope with the challenges noted by Inverchapel in his report to Bevin.[67] These began with opposition within the State Department itself. Kennan, director of the policy planning staff, and Bohlen, counselor of the department, veteran experts in Kremlinology, both ranked higher in the departmental hierarchy than Hickerson and Achilles and were vigorous in their objections to an entangling treaty. Kennan felt that a formal alliance was superfluous, because the Soviet Union could not be in any doubt where the United States would stand if it attacked the countries of the Western Union. The presence of U.S. troops in the territory between Russia and Western Europe should be "an adequate guarantee" if it attacked the countries of the Western Union. His main point was that there was little that the United States could do at this moment to stop a Soviet advance, if it were attempted. Hence, the direction of the nation should not be toward an alliance but massive aid and military staff talks with the Soviet Union.[68]

When Kennan returned to Washington from an Asian tour after the Brussels Pact had been signed, he consulted with Bohlen about the problems flowing from the Western Union's expectations of a positive U.S. response to their needs. He found that he and Bohlen agreed with the opponents of a military alliance, although not always for the same reasons. Bohlen was convinced that the matter should be dropped, because the Senate would never ratify a military alliance. He recommended instead that "we get Congress to approve a massive military assistance program and let it go at that." If this failed, his fallback position, according to Achilles, was a bilateral agreement of some sort between the United States and Canada on one side and the parties to the Brussels Pact on the other. "He more or less fought a rearguard action against the treaty all the way through." In effect, Bohlen was less flexible than Kennan. Achilles credited Hickerson with getting Lovett to transfer Bohlen to Paris, thereby removing an influential obstacle to negotiations for a treaty.[69]

The JCS agreed with Kennan and Bohlen over the dangers of an alliance. It seems that they did not take the prospect seriously. Major General Alfred M. Gruenther, director of the joint staff, represented the secretary of defense but made no substantive contribution to the proceedings. He admitted as much in a letter to Admiral William D. Leahy, President Franklin Roosevelt's chief of staff, after attending the first two sessions: "This far I have managed to say practically nothing. I consider my role to be that of an observer."[70] The Pentagon paper was the product of the State Department's most zealous supporters of an Atlantic alliance, composed without input from the military.

When the JCS realized the implications of the talks, it was military aid that was most disturbing to them. Military aid sounded like sanction for a raid on their own severely strained supplies. Following the Brussels meeting,

European countries outside the Western Union as well as the five members lined up with their requests and had to be turned down or postponed on the grounds, as the Danes were told, that "a piecemeal approach would not provide a satisfactory solution."[71] But this was hardly the end of the matter.

The JCS were particularly uncomfortable with NSC document 1/7. What attracted their special attention was its call for formulas to be worked out for military action in the event of unprovoked armed attack against Western European countries. Although the JCS endorsed the document's stand on compulsory military service, they looked askance at the recommendation that machine tools be provided for European arms industries and were distressed by the specific point that military equipment would be included in the "counteroffensive." The mention of machine tools triggered a concern that supplying Europeans with them might interfere with U.S. needs or be subject to capture by Soviet forces.[72] Secretary of Defense Forrestal emphasized to the NSC "the extreme importance of keeping our military capabilities abreast of our military commitments."[73]

Beyond the impulse to protect their own stocks, the JCS fretted about the general weakness of European forces. They assumed, as did their Western Union counterparts, that the Western powers individually or collectively could not stop the Soviets should they wish to march to the Atlantic or to the Channel in 1948. U.S. membership in their alliance would place the military in a hopeless position.

THE ODD COUPLE: LOVETT AND VANDENBERG

An even more important consideration for Lovett was the negative reaction from the isolationist faction in the Congress. This was inevitable once the substance of the Pentagon paper was leaked. Representative John Taber of New York, chairman of the powerful House Appropriations Committee, was proud of his role of watchdog of the U.S. Treasury. He cast a jaundiced eye on the ERP and would be quick to expose waste in any military assistance that would be given to Western European countries. Two months after the passage of the Foreign Assistance Act, Taber's Republican majority slashed more than $2 billion from the ERP in the face of Marshall's warning that this action might have serious political repercussions in Europe. Most of the deleted funds were restored by the Senate a week later.[74] It would be reasonable to assume that the House leadership would be as insistent on a voice in any agreement the Senate might make on aid to Western Europe as it was over funding the ERP.

The Senate, however, was the key congressional player in foreign relations, at least in fashioning policy. Here the isolationists of the 1930s, led by Robert A. Taft, were no longer central to passage of legislation, but their opposition could not be ignored. The leader in matters of foreign relations in the eightieth Congress was Vandenberg of Michigan, a powerful figure behind the administration's European policies but a formidable isolationist prior to Pearl Harbor. World War II had converted him to the cause of internationalism and to the role of the UN for its implementation. Soviet-led Communism in his judgment was both perverting the functions of the UN through its abuses of its veto power on the Security Council and threatening Western democracy in general. On these grounds, he was sympathetic to Europe's efforts to defend itself and to the economic assistance that the United States could offer.

Mentored though he was by John Foster Dulles, the Republican shadow secretary of state, Vandenberg had not accepted Dulles's position on a political relationship with Western Europe. The approach that Dulles, Hickerson, and Achilles had in mind would lead to a traditional military alliance, which meant, he feared, a return to the balance-of-power politics of prewar Europe. For Vandenberg, the preeminence of the UN was indispensable to the international order.

Vandenberg was not an easy man to deal with. A newspaper publisher from Grand Rapids, Michigan, he had been a leading figure in the Senate since his election in 1928. His abilities and ambitions propelled him into presidential politics; he was a candidate in 1940 as an isolationist and did not discourage candidacy in 1948 as an internationalist. But his first priority was to protect the achievements he made in the eightieth Congress, notably the ERP, along with a carefully calibrated commitment to the security of Western Europe. He was more interested in inserting a "Vandenberg plank" into the foreign affairs platform of the party than he was in seeking the Republican presidential nomination. As the Republican national convention approached, Vandenberg's hat was still in the ring, but barely.[75]

Vandenberg's personality was larger than life. He had all the qualities associated with the stereotypical senator. As journalist Don Cook noted, "there was a large balding head, a bulky torso that overflowed deep leather chairs, a love of attention, an air of self-importance, a pompous manner, a constant cloud of cigar smoke, a mellifluous speaking style of loud and florid phrases."[76] Dean Acheson in his acerbic way saw him as a hurricane: "Its center was filled with a large mass of cumulonimbus cloud, often called Arthur Vandenberg, producing heavy word fall." He had "the rare capacity for instant indignation, often before he understood an issue, or even that there was one."[77] At the same time, both Cook and Acheson admired much about Vandenberg. Cook saw him as an honest man, wanting to do the right things for his country and for the world. As for Acheson, he came to respect the senator's ability to listen and learn, even as his ego had to be massaged in the process. Acheson ultimately judged that "without Vandenberg

in the Senate from 1943 [to] 1951, the history of the postwar period might
have been very different."[78]

Undersecretary Lovett turned out to be the perfect foil for the senator. His
personality was the polar opposite. His disposition was low key, unpreten-
tious, and comfortable with a backstage position. A friend and colleague of
W. Averell Harriman and Acheson, he moved from Yale to Wall Street and
then to Washington as assistant secretary of war under Henry Stimson in
the Roosevelt years and undersecretary of state under Secretary Marshall. In
all his posts, he combined a patrician charm with administrative abilities of
high order, both qualities that would serve him well in dealing with a prima
donna like Vandenberg. Biographers Walter Isascson and Evan Thomas
numbered him among the "wise men" of the political establishment. "His
greatest strength," they judged, "was in getting others, particularly congressmen, to do what had already been decided."[79]

Lovett needed all these virtues to cope with Vandenberg's forceful personality. While Vandenberg appeared to be a loyal member of the opposition compared with Taft and his followers in the Senate, he was sensitive to
the fact that 1948 was an election year in which he would play an important part. In this context, Lovett found him unwilling to accept a unilateral
declaration announcing that President Truman was prepared to negotiate a
military alliance with the Brussels Pact powers. According to Achilles, when
Lovett raised this idea with Vandenberg, he "got a resounding 'No.'" "Why,"
asked Vandenberg, should Truman get all the credit?" He proposed instead
that the Senate be involved in the preparation for a new transatlantic relationship.[80]

Lovett welcomed this counterproposal. He, like Hickerson and Achilles,
had predicated negotiations with caveats about the importance of the Senate's consent to any arrangement between the United States and the Western Union. Hickerson had included Vandenberg's blessing specifically in
the last meeting of the tripartite security conversations at the Pentagon.
There was a bonus for Lovett in bringing the issue to the Senate. It would
deflect pressures from the Western Union powers for immediate negotiations on an alliance. Senate deliberations would inevitably slow the pace
and give time for the administration itself to reach a consensus on what
kind of treaty it wanted.[81]

The wooing of Vandenberg was just beginning. Lovett became accus-
tomed to spending his cocktail hours visiting Vandenberg at his apartment,
500 G in the Wardman Park Hotel, skillfully stroking the senator's ego by
agreeing with the changes and revisions his host insisted on. It often
seemed that Vandenberg was less interested in fundamental changes in
Lovett's proposals than in inserting a term or a paragraph that would represent his stamp of approval. More often his changes simplified the wordy
language of the State Department; verbose as he was in his oratory, he in-

sisted on brevity of written proposals. He wanted a draft resolution that would fit into one page and in twenty minutes time was able to shrink a three-page resolution to one page. The document would then be Vandenberg's, or more accurately, "one-page Vandenberg." The senator, according to Achilles, typed the final draft himself, "although he had to use very narrow margins and almost ran off the bottom of the page."[82]

THE VANDENBERG RESOLUTION

The draft resolution was the end product of long discussions in April. The senator had no problem with military assistance to the Western Union powers. He also agreed that in the short term, assurances had to be given to Europeans that the United States would come to their aid in the event of attack, but it would have to be done in a way that protected other vulnerable nations besides those of the Western Union. At a key meeting on 11 April, Lovett tried to convince Vandenberg to apply the Rio treaty to the North Atlantic area, with only partial success. The Rio treaty had involved Latin America where there had been a long history of special associations that could not be replicated with Europe. Cool to the idea of a formal guarantee, the senator was open to working out a procedure based on firm evidence of the Europeans building defense machinery based on self-help and mutual aid. He could accept a presidential call for a conference that would discuss pooling of military supplies and standardization of equipment. But the proposal for military guarantee was "doubtful and perhaps dangerous at this time."[83] The Senate would never allow incidents in Europe to automatically commit the nation to war.

It was at this meeting that Vandenberg raised the most promising and at the same time the most troublesome approach to an alliance with Western Europe. He brought up the possibility of energizing the role of the UN as an instrument to maintain international peace. He regarded himself one of its founding fathers, having helped to draft Article 51 as a member of the U.S. delegation at the San Francisco conference in 1945. This involved the inherent right of individual and collective self-defense in the event of an armed attack and could be the cornerstone of a new commitment to Western Europe. Vandenberg noted that many of his Conservative colleagues subsequently had prepared a resolution to prevent further Soviet abuse of the veto that would have required a rewriting of the UN charter. He found their approach unacceptable and had it pigeonholed in the Foreign Relations Committee. If their resolution would remove the veto only in case of armed aggression but retain all the charter provisions for peaceful settlement of international disputes, it would mean that the UN "would allow others to tell us when we must go to war."[84]

While the chairman was dismissive of the views of Republican Senators Homer Capehart of Indiana or Kenneth Wherry of Nebraska, he was still sensitive to the mood of the Senate. He was also predisposed to have the UN serve as a means of taking the sting out of the military character of a potential alliance. No U.S. obligation to the Western Union could be made that would violate the charter of the UN. And no resolution would come out of the Foreign Relations Committee that did not give prominence to its conformity with the charter.[85]

Lovett and the State Department could live with this, if it were couched in language permitting a regional defense agreement along the lines of the Rio treaty. A mechanism had to be found to facilitate the linkage between the UN charter and U.S. association with the Western Union, and Dean Rusk's office of UN Affairs performed this operation.[86] In light of the importance of this issue and the delicacy of its implementation, the State Department produced a resolution in remarkably short time, less than six weeks. Inevitably, the document needed fine tuning, along with commentary by Marshall, Kennan, and Dulles as advisers to Vandenberg, as well as of course by the senator himself. The secretary of state, still in Bogota and always cautious, listened to the advice of General Matthew B. Ridgway, Army member of the U.S. delegation to the Conference of American States. Ridgway objected to a clause in paragraph 2 that would publicly express U.S. willingness to participate in military conversations with representatives of the Western Union.[87]

Kennan offered minor revisions that were incorporated into the final resolution. His gloss did not conceal his considered judgment that no alliance was necessary and that a unilateral declaration of support for the defense of Europe should suffice to give Europe the sense of security it demanded. Even this should have been superfluous. "What in the world," he complained, "did they think we were doing in Europe these four or five years? Did they suppose we had labored to free Europe from the clutches of Hitler merely to abandon it to those of Stalin?" Instead of the "mixture of arid legalism that so often passes, in the halls of our domestic-political life, for statesmanship," he wanted realistic staff talks to see what could be done to coordinate military measures in the event of war. But he confessed that "there was little he could do affect the course of events."[88]

Achilles produced the final draft, pared down to a single page as demanded by Vandenberg with few of the generalities of verbiage that so annoyed Kennan. The resolution met the senator's requirement that it open with the Senate reaffirming the policy of the United States to achieve international peace and security under the provenance of the UN charter. But the key paragraphs—two, three, and four—were the work of Achilles, with one addition by Vandenberg. There was no call for an alliance, but a loose construction of the resolution opened the way for just such a result, as long as the arrangements met the terms of the charter. And Vandenberg's addition of "by constitutional process" to U.S. association with regional and collective arrangements for individual and collective self-defense assured the nation that "association of the United States" would not involve bypassing the Congress if war broke out in Europe.[89]

The resolution sailed through hearings before the Senate Foreign Relations Committee. It passed unanimously on 19 May.[90] Vandenberg and Lovett had touched every base. The senator was anxious to get the resolution through the Senate ahead of the Republican National Convention, scheduled to open on 20 June. He was, after all, a potential presidential nominee at the convention.

There were dissenters. Walter George, an influential Democrat from Georgia, doubted the wisdom of the resolution. He worried about overextending U.S. commitments, even if he would not vote against the resolution in the Foreign Relations Committee.[91] The more vociferous critics were on the Senate floor on 11 June. A few rabid dissidents on the Right, such as George Malone of Nevada, railed against European wiles and the entanglements that would follow passage of Senate Resolution 239. In effect he believed that the Vandenberg Resolution "guaranteed that a future Senate will ratify such treaties."[92] There was opposition on the Left as well. Senator Fulbright wanted to add "political unity" to the second paragraph, strengthening the call for developing individual and collective self-defense. When the vote was taken on 11 June, three of the four naysayers were from the Left—Republican William Langer of North Dakota and Democrats Claude Pepper of Florida and Glenn Taylor of Idaho. Senate Resolution 239 passed by a vote of 64 to 4. Neither Taft nor Fulbright cast a negative vote; they were among the abstainers.[93]

Vandenberg managed to keep critics at bay both in the Foreign Relations Committee and in the Senate debate. The title of the resolution itself reflected Vandenberg's priorities—"The United Nations and Collective Security Resolution." Appropriately, it has come down in history as "the Vandenberg Resolution" and was so dubbed from the day of its passage. Achilles claimed that the senator did his bipartisan best to label it as simply a resolution of the Foreign Relations Committee. But modesty did not fit Vandenberg, no matter how sincere he may have been in disclaiming credit. Achilles noted that "he could not have been displeased when the press and everyone else preferred to call it by his name."[94]

While it was unlikely that Vandenberg would have been chosen to be the Republican nominee in 1948, he was certainly not an active campaigner. Governor Kim Sigler of Michigan announced on 19 June that the senator was available, but Vandenberg had signaled earlier that he did not want his presidential candidacy to distract his attention from U.S. aid to defensive alliances. His primary concern was to ensure that the Republican Party platform contain a plan encouraging the development of a collective security system under the auspices of the UN.[95]

TOWARD AN ATLANTIC ALLIANCE

Even a knowledgeable observer may be excused for failing to read into the Vandenberg Resolution a U.S. commitment to a transatlantic alliance. The Senate, supported by a similar resolution from the House of Representatives, was now prepared to "associate" with a regional defense organization of European states. But was this really an advance from Truman's promises to the Brussels Pact powers on 17 March? The Senate committee report itself noted that the defense arrangements under consideration were "not to be confused with military alliances." Nor could any future commitments be "open-ended or unlimited."[96] They would have to be consistent with the requirements of self-defense and cooperation in the spirit of the Marshall Plan, and any treaty obligation would require Senate ratification. Moreover, the Vandenberg insistence on placing all actions under the rubric of the UN charter was the most visible element of the resolution.

A collective agreement conforming to the UN charter was not what Bevin and Bidault or Hickerson and Achilles had in mind when they conceived a military alliance with the Western Union. Article 53, covering regional associations, would directly engage the veto power of the Soviet Union as a member of the Security Council to which a regional association would report. But the resolution identified only Article 51, which did not require approval from the Security Council. The language of the Vandenberg Resolution was Delphic enough to further the objectives of Hickerson and Achilles.

The constant pressure from the Europeans may have been counterproductive in pressuring Lovett and Marshall, but the introduction of a Canadian view by Foreign Minister Louis St. Laurent on 29 April was a promise of association clearer than that given by the United States. This was the first public declaration of support for a collective security arrangement by any Western leader, U.S. or European.[97] St. Laurent's speeches energized British negotiators and even encouraged Kennan to accept progress toward a North Atlantic alliance, at least to the extent that "we should be equally careful not to encourage the project to a point where we arouse false hopes but also not to throw so much cold water on it as to put ourselves in the position of obstructionists."[98] But three days after the Vandenberg Resolution was passed, Kennan emphasized, with the concurrence of Marshall, that political conversation with Europe "should be entirely exploratory and directed toward ascertaining the area of agreement among us concerning the requirements of the situation and the probable effects of the various possible courses of action."[99] British and French pressures notwithstanding, the Soviet extension of the Berlin blockade notwithstanding, and the wishes of Hickerson and Achilles notwithstanding, the State Department's emphasis was on the word "exploratory" with the recognition that results of exploration would have to await the presidential election in the fall.

Despite the brakes that the State Department leadership wished to place on a transatlantic alliance, the revised NSC 1/9, first delivered as NSC 9/2 a week after the Senate acted on the Vandenberg Resolution and then delivered as NSC 9/3 on 28 June, loosened those brakes and placed the nation firmly on the path of political and military entanglement with Western Europe. Actually, its contents had been communicated to all the members of the Western Union on 23 June. They now knew that, in line with the Vandenberg Resolution's recommendations, the United States was ready to explore with them the future of U.S. association with the defense of Europe.[100] Whether the credit for the ultimate acceptance of the abandonment by the United States of its tradition of nonentanglement belongs to Vandenberg or to the president for his role in the bipartisan actions, or to Hickerson and Achilles for their behind-the-scenes advocacy—or as Escott Reid believed[101]—to the British for their pressures on the United States, was less important than the events they set in motion.

NOTES

1. Richard Coudenhove-Kalergi, *Kampf um Europa* (Zurich: Atlantis Verlag, 1949), 278, details his interpretation of the Foreign Assistance Act.

2. Coudenhove-Kalergi to Charles Bohlen, February 16, 1948, 840.00/2–1648, RG 59, NARA.

3. Bohlen to John Hickerson, February 18, 1948, 840.00/2–1648, RG 59, NARA.

4. An appointment was arranged for 11:30 a.m. on February 26, Hickerson to Bohlen, February, 20, 1948, 840.00/2–1648, RG 59, NARA; Bohlen to General Carter, George Marshall's aide, February 21, 1948, 840.00/2–1648, RG 59, NARA; Bohlen to Hickerson, February 24, 1948, 840.00/2–1648, RG 59, NARA.

5. Bohlen to Carter, February 21, 1948, 840.00/2–1648, RG 59, NARA.

6. Memorandum, Marshall to Carter, March 3, 1948, 840.00/2–1648, NARA.

7. Marshall to Dorothy Thompson, March 26, 1948, 840.00/3–248, RG 59, NARA.

8. *New York Times*, September 20, 1946, 2.

9. Arnold J. Zurcher, *The Struggle to Unite Europe, 1940–1958* (New York: New York University Press, 1958), 25–26.

10. *New York Times*, May 8–11, 1948.

11. See Clement Atlee's comments in *New York Times*, May 10, 1948, 14.

12. Tel David Linebaugh to Secretary of State, May 11, 1948, no. 824, sub: United Europe Movement, 840.00/4–148, RG 59, NARA.

13. Tel Douglas to Secretary of State, April 17, 1948, no. 1599, 840.00/4–1748, RG 59. NARA; April 19, 1948, no. 1605, 840.00/4–1948; tel Marshall to Embassy in UK, May 4, 1948, no.1598, 840.00/14–3048, RG 59, NARA.

14. Winston Churchill, speech in The Hague, May 7, 1948, in *Vital Speeches of the Day*, May 15, 1948, 14: 450–52.

15. "New Group Backs Federated Europe," *New York Times*, April 24, 1948, 3.

16. Marshall to Embassy in UK, May 4, 1948, no. 1598, 840.00/4–3048.

17. See Thomas E. Dewey, quoted in *New York Times*, April 9, 1948, 3.

18. Anne O'Hare McCormick, "An Unofficical Call for a Union of the Free," *New York Times*, May 8, 1948.

19. Editorial, *New York Times*, May 9, 1948, 8E.

20. Joint Message by George Bidault and Ernest Bevin to Secretary of State, March 17, 1948, *FRUS*, 1948, III: 55–56; tel Secretary of State to Embassy in France, March 25, 1948, *FRUS*, 1948, no. 965, III: 68.

21. John Baylis, *The Diplomacy of Pragmatism: Britain and the Formation of NATO, 1942–1949* (Kent, OH: Kent State University Press, 1993), 15–16.

22. Sir Nicholas Henderson, *Birth of NATO* (Boulder, CO: Westview Press, 1983), 33.

23. Paraphrase of a telegram from Bevin of April 9, 1948, Regarding Recent Talks on North Atlantic Security Arrangements, nd, *FRUS*, 1948, III: 79–80.

24. Henderson, *Birth of NATO*, 21.

25. Quoted in Baylis, *The Diplomacy of Pragmatism*, 17.

26. Escott Reid, *Time of Fear and Hope: The Making of the North Atlantic Treaty* (Toronto: McClelland and Stewart, 1977), 71; Theodore C. Achilles, *Fingerprints on History : The NATO Memoirs of Theodore C. Achilles*, edited by Lawrence S. Kaplan and Sidney R. Snyder (Kent, OH: Lyman L. Lemnitzer Center for NATO and European Community Studies, Kent State University, 1992), 15.

27. Tel Millard to Secretary of State, April 3, 1948, no.667, 840.00/4–348, RG 59, NARA.

28. Memorandum of conversation by Theordore Achilles, April 5, 1948, *FRUS*, 1948, III: 76.

29. Memorandum of conversation by Baruch with Jonkheer O. Reuchlin, April 6, 1948, 840.00/4–648, RG 59, NARA.

30. Tel Caffery to Secretary of State, April 13, 1948, no. 1930, 840.00/4–1348, RG 59, NARA.

31. Tel Millard to Secretary of State, March 28, 1948, no. 627, 840.00/3–2248, RG 59, NARA.

32. Tel Douglas to Secretary of State, April 16, 1948, *FRUS*, 1948, no. 1584, III: 89.

33. Memorandum of conversation, Achilles with Armand Berard, Minister, French Embassy, April 15, 1948, 840.00/4–1548, RG 59, NARA.

34. Quoted in tel Caffery to Secretary of State, April 28, 1948, no. 2239, 840.00/4–2848, RG 59, NARA.

35. John W. Young, *Britain, France, and the Unity of Europe* (Leicester: Leicester University Press, 1984), 93.

36. John W. Young, *France, the Cold War, and the Western Alliance, 1944–49: French Foreign Policy and Post-war Europe* (New York: St. Martin's Press, 1990), 195.

37. Young, *Britain, France, and the Unity of Europe*, 94–95; Young, *France, The Cold War, and the Western Alliance*, 183.

38. Tel Douglas to Secretary of State, April 28, 1948, no. 1798, 840.00/4–2848, RG 59, NARA.

39. Paraphrase of a telegram from Bevin of April 9, 1948, regarding recent talks on North Atlantic security arrangements, nd, *FRUS*, 1948, III: 79–80.

40. Tel Caffery to Secretary of State, April 8, 1948, no. 1833, 840.00/5–848, RG 59, NARA.

41. Tel Douglas to Secretary of State, April 7, 1948, no. 1246, 840.00/4–748, RG 59, NARA.

42. Tel Douglas to Secretary of State, April 16, 1948, *FRUS*, 1948, no. 1584, III: 89.

43. Tel Caffery to Secretary of State, April 18, 1948, no. 2059, 840.00/4–1948, RG 59, NARA.

44. Henderson, *Birth of NATO*, 23.

45. *New York Times*, March 19, 1948.

46. *New York Times*, April 27, 1948, 6.

47. Communique on Consultative Council, April 24, 1948, in tel Douglas to Secretary of State, May 3, 1948, no.118, 840.00/4–2748; tel Douglas to Secretary of State, May 4, 1948, no. 1912, 840.00/5–448, RG 59, NARA.

48. Tel Caffery to Secretary of State, May 8, 1948, no. 2475, 840.00/5–848, RG 59, NARA.

49. Tel Douglas to Secretary of State, April 28, 1948, no. 1798, 840/00/4–2848, RG59, NARA.

50. Tel Caffery to Secretary of State, May 5, 1948, no. 2394, 840.00/5–548, RG59, NARA.

51. Tel Douglas to Secretary of State, May 4, 1948, no. 1918, 840.00/5–448, RG 59, NARA.

52. Martin H. Folly, "The British Military and the Making of the North Atlantic Treaty," in Joseph Smith, ed., *The Origins of NATO* (Exeter, UK : University of Exeter Press, 1990), 35.

53. British Embassy to State Department, nd, sub: Substance of Message from Mr. Bevin of May 14th on North Atlantic Security, *FRUS*, III: 122–23.

54. Henderson, *Birth of NATO*, 23.

55. Tel Acting Secretary of State to Secretary of State of Bogota, April 26, 1948, *FRUS*, 1948, III: 96–97; tel Secretary of State to French Minister of Foreign Affairs, April 21, 1948, *FRUS*, 1948, III: 99.

56. *New York Times*, April 29, 1948; *New York Times*, May 1, 1948.

57. Steven L. Rearden, *History of the Office of Secretary of Defense: The Formative Years* (Washington, D.C.: Historical Office, Office of the Secretary of Defense), I: 490–91.

58. NSC 7, March 30, 1948, in *FRUS*, 1948, I: 548–49.

59. NSC 9, The Position of the United States with Respect to Support for Western Union and Other Related Countries, *FRUS*, 1948, III: 86.

60. Tel James Dunn to Secretary of State, April 24, 1948, no. 1930, 840.00/4–2448, RG 59, NARA.

61. Tel Acting Secretary of State to Embassy in Denmark, April 5, 1948, *FRUS*, 1948, no. 204, III: 75; tel Ambassador to Norway (Bay) to Secretary of State, April 9, 1948, *FRUS*, 1948, no. 224, III: 81.

62. Memorandum of Conversation by Ambassador in Sweden (Herbert L. Matthews), May 5, 1948, *FRUS*, 1948, III: 114; American Embassy in Ottawa to Andrew B. Foster, Division of Commonwealth Affairs, April 13, 1948, 840.00/4–1348; informal letter noting Sweden minister to Canada's justification of its neutrality in Europe; memorandum by Secretary of State to President Truman, June 3, 1948, sub: Swedish Neutrality Policy, *FRUS* 48, III: 134.

63. Rearden, *History of the Office of Secretary of Defense*, 490–91; NSC 7 in *FRUS*, 1948, I: 548–49.

64. *New York Times*, April 13, 1948.

65. Paraphrase of a telegram from Bevin of April 9th regarding recent talks on North Atlantic security arrangements, nd, *FRUS*, 1948, III: 79–80.

66. Minutes of the Fifth Meeting of the United States-United Kingdom-Canada Security Conversations, March 31, 1948, *FRUS*, 1948, III: 71.

67. Henderson, *Birth of NATO*, 21.

68. Memorandum by George Kennan to Marshall and Lovett, April 29, 1948, *FRUS*, 1948, III: 108–9.

69. Achilles, *Fingerprints on History*, 20–21.

70. Quoted in Alex Danchev, *Oliver Franks: Founding Father* (Oxford: Oxford Oxford University Press, 1993), 92.

71. Tel Acting Secretary of State to Embassy in Denmark, April 5, 1948, *FRUS*, 1948, no. 204, III: 75.

72. NSC 1/7, *FRUS*, 1948, part 2, I: 549.

73. Memorandum, James Forrestal to National Security Council (NSC), April 17, 1948, *FRUS*, 1948, I: 563.

74. *New York Times*, June 4, 1948; *New York Times*, June 13, 1948.

75. *New York Times*, June 17, 1948; *New York Times*, June 20, 1948.

76. Don Cook, *Forging the Alliance: NATO: 1945–1950* (London: Secker & Warburg), 157.

77. Dean Acheson, *Present at the Creation: My Years in the State Department* (New York: W. W. Norton & Co., 1969), 71.

78. Cook, *Forging the Alliance*, 157–58; Dean Acheson, *Sketches from Life of Men I Have Known* (New York: Popular Library, 1962), 110.

79. Walter Isaacson and Evan Thomas, *The Wise Men: Six Friends and the World They Made: Acheson, Bohlen, Harriman, Kennan, Lovett, McCloy* (New York: Simon and Schuster, 1986), 418.

80. Achilles, *Fingerprints on History*, 16; Reid, *Time of Fear and Hope*, 89.

81. Minutes of the Sixth Meeting of the United States–United Kingdom Canada Security Conversations, April 1, 1948, *FRUS*, 1948, III: 72; Cook, *Forging the Alliance*, 161–62.

82. Memorandum of conversation by Lovett, April 27, 1948, *FRUS*, 1948 III: 107; Cook, *Forging the Alliance*, 162.

83. Memorandum of conversation by Lovett, April 11, 1948, *FRUS*, 1948, III: 82.

84. Arthur H. Vandenberg, Jr., ed., *The Private Papers of Senator Vandenberg* (Boston: Houghton Mifflin Company, 1952), 404.

85. Memorandum of conversation by Lovett, April 11, 1948, *FRUS*, III: 82–84.

86. Tel Acting Secretary of State to Secretary of State at Bogota, April 20, 1948, 1948, *FRUS*, no. 93, III: 96.

87. Tel Secretary of State to Acting Secretary of State, April 23, 1948, *FRUS*, 1948, no. 89, III: 103.

88. Memorandum by Kennan to Marshall and Lovett, April 29, 1948, *FRUS*, 1948, III: 109; Kennan, *Memoirs*, 431–32.

89. S. 239, as printed in *Congressional Record*, 80th Cong., 2nd sess., June 11, 1948, 94: 7791.

90. The Vandenberg Resolution and the North Atlantic Treaty, *Hearings* in Executive Session before Senate Committee on Foreign Relations, 80th Cong., 2nd sess., on Senate Resolution 239, May 19, 1948, 66.

91. *Hearings*, Executive Session, 65.

92. *Congressional Record*, 80th Cong., 2nd sess., June 11, 1948, 94:7809.

93. *Congressional Record*, 80th Cong., 2nd sess., June 11, 1948, 94:7846.

94. Achilles, *Footprints on History*, 17.

95. *New York Times*, June 20, 1948.

96. *Senate Report 1361*, May 19, 1948, 80th Cong., 2nd sess., 5–6.

97. Reid, *Time of Fear and Hope*, 77.

98. Memorandum by Kennan for Marshall and Lovett, May 24, 1948, *FRUS*, 1948, III: 128.

99. Memorandum of Conversation by the Secretary of State, June 14, 1948, *FRUS*, 1948, III: 137.

100. Tel Secretary of State to the Embassy in France, June 23, 1948, *FRUS*, 1948, no. 2251, III: 139.

101. Reid believed that Vandenberg—and Americans in general—received "undeserved credit" for initiating negotiations that resulted in the North Atlantic Treaty. Rather, it should go to the British government that opened the way in March; Reid, *Time of Fear and Hope*, 91. British scholars give primacy to Bevin and his advisers. This emphasis is exemplified in Martin H. Folly, "Breaking the Vicious Circle; Britain, the United States, and the Genesis of the North Atlantic Treaty," *Diplomatic History* 12, no. 1 (Winter 1988): 59–77.

5

The "Exploratory" Talks:
July–September 1948

ARRIÈRES-PENSÉES—JUNE 1948

The European partners knew what they wanted from the forthcoming talks with the United States and Canada. The Brussels Pact powers anticipated the entanglement of the United States either in their alliance or in a widened version of the Western Union in return for their efforts in collective self-defense. To underscore the seriousness of their commitment they set in motion the Western Union Defense Organization (WUDO) with headquarters in London, which was intended to move along a parallel track with the political talks in Washington.

Canada's participation was initially more appreciated by Europeans than by the United States, although its importance to the United States increased when its geographic location became a ploy in wooing congressional support for an Atlantic pact. Ernest Bevin enthusiastically supported the State Department's sounding out Canada's interest in participating in a meeting with the Brussels powers.[1]

For the United States, the outcome was less clear cut. From its perspective, the talks would cautiously extend the nation's commitments to the Europeans but only after the Western Union clearly demonstrated its willingness to integrate the resources of its members and be prepared to defend itself to the best of its ability in advance of U.S. political and military support.

Given U.S. ambivalence over prospective talks, Britain and France envisioned problems in their relations with the United States in June that might have doomed the negotiations before they had even begun. Anglo-U.S. connections had suffered serious strains over the differing positions the two powers took after Britain abandoned Palestine in May 1948. Britain had long chafed over U.S. criticism of its policy toward Jewish immigration and resisted as long as it could the establishment of Israel. When Israel declared its independence on 14 May, the United States gave de facto recognition of the provisional government. Britain not only failed to follow suit but used its influence within the UN and with its European partners to stall recognition on the assumption that the shelf life of the new state would be brief, as the Arab world acted to invade and destroy the fledgling nation. Britain made nominal efforts at peacekeeping, but its voice was on the side of the Palestinian Arabs and its funds and troops were the backbone of Transjordan's Arab Legion.

Bevin raised the specter of the Soviets profiting from division between the allies. A week after the expiration of Britain's mandate in Palestine, he emphasized to Ambassador Lewis Douglas that his country's policy in the Middle East safeguarded Western interests threatened by the Soviets.[2] The implication was that the U.S. bias in favor of Israel served Soviet interests. Bevin was particularly concerned about the possibility of the United States ending its embargo on arms for Israel to compensate for Britain's continuing flow of supplies to the Arabs. Bevin had some justification for his concerns. Styles Bridges of New Hampshire, chairman of the Senate Appropriations Committee, called for a repeal of the arms embargo on arms to Israel on 21 May and wondered if U.S. economic aid to Britain facilitated its military support to the Arabs.[3]

Britain's hostility to Israel found an echo in some quarters of the State Department and among the principal U.S. diplomats in Europe and the Middle East. They were not only embarrassed by what they considered the administration's surrender to pro-Israel pressure in its precipitate recognition of the new state but also worried about the damage to U.S. interests in the Middle East. Not least among the State Department's concerns was that the Soviets would take advantage of an Anglo-U.S. split.[4] Certainly, the hasty Soviet recognition of Israel was an example of its campaign to divide the allies. In London, Ambassador Douglas felt that the "crevasse widening between [U.S.] and Britain" was "seriously jeopardizing foundation-stone of [U.S.] policy in Europe—partnership with a friendly and well-disposed Britain." It would be folly, he was convinced, if the impetuous recognition of Israel was followed by lifting the embargo on arms to the Middle East.[5]

Sharp as they were, Anglo-U.S. differences over the Middle East were less troublesome than Anglo-French differences over Germany. French suspicions of German ambitions and British apparent willingness to place German revival above French interests continued to roil relations even as Georges Bidault accepted the London Accords of 2 June at the conclusion of the conference on Germany.[6] The accords did not appease French fears about a revived Germany. While Bidault managed to secure internationalization of the Ruhr, the price France had to pay was the fusion of the occupation zones and the issuance of a new currency. There was not much choice. Bidault realized that Britain and France would go forward on a bizonal basis no matter what position France took. The French National Assembly approved the accords on 17 June by a narrow margin, with reservations that tied the future of the accords to assurances against the revival of German nationalism.[7]

An early consequence of this decision was the qualified agreement of the French military governor, General Jean-Pierre Koenig, with his British and U.S. colleagues to help create a West German government with its seat in Frankfurt. To demonstrate their resolve, the three military governors flew to Frankfurt on 30 June to meet with presidents of the eleven states of West Germany and formally transmit the decisions of the London conference. Koenig, however, would not sign off on plans to draft a constitution for a federal republic until the allies agreed to a French interpretation of the London Accords.[8]

The price for France's cooperation proved to be too high for Bidault personally; he was forced out of the foreign ministry in July. The London Accords became a factor in intensifying the usual instability of the French government. Two failed attempts to form a stable government were made before the ministry of Henri Queille was formed on 10 September. Robert Schuman served as foreign minister throughout the turbulent summer.[9]

IMPACT OF THE BERLIN BLOCKADE

The Berlin blockade entered a new and more dangerous phase as a result of the currency reform in the western zone. Although General Lucius Clay noted that the changes effective on 20 June would not apply to Berlin, Marshal Vassily Sokolovsky called the reform illegal and blamed it for completing the division of Germany.[10] The Soviets then suspended passenger traffic on all roads to and from Berlin, including the Autobahn. Rather than knuckle under to Soviet action, the three Western commanders announced the introduction of the new currency to the Western sectors of Berlin.[11] They concluded that the issue in Berlin was not over currency but over the larger Soviet aim of driving the West out of Berlin.

The U.S. response, endorsed heartily by the British and warily by the French, was the Berlin airlift of critical supplies to the beleaguered city. General Clay on his own initiative had directed Major General Curtis Le May on 14 June to assign every available aircraft to carry those supplies. Secretary of State George Marshall reinforced this decision by stating publicly the U.S. intention to use air transport to supply civilian needs.[12] Land routes may have been blocked but not air routes, possibly because the Soviets assumed that airlifts, no matter how massive, could not succeed in lifting the blockade.[13]

Allied counteraction involved the risk of war, but intelligence estimates concluded that the Soviets did not want war. Yet there was always a danger of unintended consequences in an accidental shooting down of an Allied aircraft. This was a possibility that contributed to France's ambivalence over its solidarity with Britain and the United States. The French saw too many risks ahead in challenging the Soviets.[14] To calm the French, President Harry S Truman and Secretary of Defense James V. Forrestal warned Clay not to make any statement that referred to the possibility of war over Berlin.[15] Still, French fears were not frivolous The Soviet blockade of Berlin and the U.S. response with an airlift did produce a crisis that might have resulted in war. The crisis served to sideline Anglo-U.S. friction over Israel as Britain, the United States, and France faced a more serious problem in Europe.

FRANCE JOINS ITS ALLIES—WITH RESERVATIONS

Considering the political disarray in France in the summer of 1948, it is not surprising that French leaders expressed doubts about the policies they were reluctantly endorsing. Was it wise, they asked, for the allies to hold on to their precarious position on Berlin? To "die for Berlin" had little appeal to France at any time.[16] Soviet reaction was much on the minds of France's leaders. Even before the full blockade had begun, France's president, Vincent Auriol, had wondered if plans for the currency reforms would be excessively provocative to the Soviets.[17] The blockade then was just the action he had anticipated. At the Quai d'Orsay, the chief of the central European division confided his misgivings about the West's position on Berlin to Ambassador Jefferson Caffery. He was convinced that the allies had made a serious error in their commitment to the defense of West Berlin and in their insistence on remaining there at all costs. The physical location of Berlin gave every advantage to the Soviet adversary in confronting the West.[18] This was the voice of a supporter of the London Accords. Naturally, the Gaullist and Communist opposition was more vociferous in their condemnation of France's policies.

Although the sense of chaos in France and a concomitant hostility to Britain and the United States may have been real, it was also misleading with respect to the development of a transatlantic alliance. France's foreign ministry was led by two pro-Western figures in this period: Bidault, who had guided the nation into the Western Union in close collaboration with Britain, and Schuman, an Alsatian raised in imperial Germany and devoted to rapprochement with a regenerated Germany. Like Bidault he was a member of the moderate Catholic party. "A lean man," Dean Acheson observed, "slightly stooped, his long, serious, even ascetic face gives an appearance of baffled solemnity, enhanced by the bald dome and his habit of sinking chin in collar to peer over the top of his spectacles."[19] Even though he was strikingly different from Bevin in appearance, temperament, and manner, he worked more congenially with the British foreign secretary than the more mercurial Bidault had been able to do. Consequently, the foreign ministry was a center of stability amid the chaos in the National Assembly. Under its guidance, the nation had accepted the London Accords with its promise of a West German government; linked France to the bizonal currencies; and despite recurring reservations, joined with Britain and the United States in identifying the Soviets as the main threat to the future of Western Europe.

The French military was also a factor in aligning the country with Britain and the United States. As Minister of Armed Forces Pierre-Henri Teitgen pointed out, "The French nation, notwithstanding appearances, in fact recognized that at present there is no purely German danger and that they [the French military leaders] were quite ready to accept the American view that the only real present danger was from Soviet Russia." He claimed that much of the opposition to the London agreements stemmed from fear of the Soviets interpreting them as a provocative gesture. But if war should come, the U.S. connection was all the more necessary.[20]

The French carefully segregated threats to their security—and to their partners—into three categories: first and always foremost, the "eventual" threat of a resurgent Germany; second, the "actual" threat of a menacing Soviet Union; and most urgently, the "immediate" threat of Soviet aggression in Germany. With exquisite logic, they recommended meeting these threats "on three places: conception, preparation and execution." Under conception they identified an immediate inclusion of France in the Washington-based U.S.-UK military commission, an important objective even if it required a leap of logic, because the Combined Chief of Staff of World War II no longer existed. Preparation was simply the dispatch of a U.S. representative to the Western Union's military committee in London. And execution required a unified military command in Germany.[21] France then was prepared to participate in the Washington exploratory talks that would tie the United States to the defense of the West. The Berlin blockade tested France's resolve, and it passed the test. As the time for the meetings in Washington approached, all the Western allies could find in the Berlin airlift a symbol of their progress toward unity.

THE AMBASSADORS GATHER

When the time came for action, it almost seemed as if the United States had to be dragged into the talks with the Europeans for fear that the talks would lead to more entangling relations than the Vandenberg Resolution had advised. On 28 June, the NSC recommended the implementation of the resolution "without seeking [a] commitment more formal than that given in the President's March 17 message and the Senate Resolution at least until there has been more time for the development and practical implementation of the Brussels Treaty system." The NSC also hoped that the Brussels Pact countries would engage in military talks that would involve a military assistance program based on the concept of mutual aid.[22] No action could be expected, however, until January 1949 when the new Congress would convene.

Only after this less-than-enthusiastic endorsement was made were talks to begin. These formally began on 6 July, a hot and muggy day, as might have been expected in Washington in that month. The temperature reached 95°F as the ambassadors gathered.[23] Secrecy was considered vital even though it was impossible to conceal the fact, as Nicholas Henderson noted, that talks were being held.[24] The State Department was leery of having the British Foreign Office send Gladwyn Jebb, assistant undersecretary of state for foreign affairs, to the first meeting even though Lester Pearson, Canadian undersecretary for external relations, was coming down from Ottawa. Robert Lovett felt that a visit from a Canadian neighbor could be considered routine but not the sudden appearance of a senior British diplomat. Jebb's presence could provoke too many inquiries.[25] Among the penalties for secrecy was confinement of the ambassadors in a stifling hot room. But at least they had to suffer for only three days from 6 to 9 July when the lower-level working party was left to work out the many details as well as tackle unresolved issues from 12 July to 9 September.

Secrecy was vital to the success of the talks, given the rhetoric that would flow out of Washington as the presidential conventions in the summer of 1948 were getting underway. Should there be leaks from the conversations of the Ambassadors' Committee and its working group, the Dixiecrats and the antimilitary Progressive Party, both splitting from the mainstream Democrats, surely would be more likely to pounce on the administration for some kind of sell-out than would the consensus-minded majority in the Republican and Democratic parties.[26]

John Hickerson drafted a press statement at the end of the first meeting, saying that the sessions would be informal and discussions would not be disclosed. The members agreed that "in no circumstances would they give interviews or give out any information whatsoever until the report had been made to the governments." Speaking of the working group, he noted with only slight exaggeration that "we extracted a blood-sealed oath from all those there that they just wouldn't talk." And nobody did. When James Reston, the well-connected Washington bureau chief of the *New York Times* approached Hickerson saying, "Look, the *Times* is in a sort of special category. You just have to tell me some of this stuff, for the background." Hickerson responded, "Now Scotty, Scotty, Scotty, I'm just not talking."[27] Nor did anyone else. The only article Reston wrote for his paper on Western Europe that summer was published three days before the first meeting of the Ambassadors' Committee, and while he expressed concerns about Western Europe's apparent slackening of efforts toward integration he also emphasized the bipartisan nature of the nation's foreign policies.[28]

Although the exploratory talks in Washington remained under wraps, the U.S. and Canadian decision on 20 July to participate in joint military planning with the five members of the Western Union opened a Pandora's box of speculation. The announcement was made in a one-sentence communiqué from the British Foreign Office, and both the U.S. Embassy and the Canada House in London purposely omitted names of officers who would serve as non-members. But the cloak of secrecy was discarded, though "timorously," as Clifton Daniel of the *New York Times* pointed out. Timorously or not, the announcement opened the way for Daniel to assert that "the United States for the first time in the long history of isolationism was associating itself with a group of European powers, however tentatively, for the purposes of military planning in peacetime."[29]

Despite all the precautions taken in Washington, the cat was out of the bag. If the purpose of keeping the proceedings of the Washington talks and the Pentagon talks from the eyes of the Soviet adversary, the whole exercise was futile, because the Soviet agent Donald Maclean was present at almost all sessions through his position in the British Embassy in Washington; presumably there was little that Moscow did not know about what went on behind closed doors. A case can be made that knowledge of what the allies were up to may have reduced Soviet paranoia, at least with respect to the West's aggressive intentions. More likely, as journalist Don Cook suggested, Maclean's reports were pigeonholed and ignored by his masters.[30]

THE CAST OF CHARACTERS

The limits of secrecy were only one of the issues that might have compromised the exploratory talks. The sheer number of diplomats present presented a problem, although the quality of the diplomats representing the seven participating nations was high. Lovett was the key figure in all the proceedings, although Secretary Marshall formally opened the first session. He had a talented group of aides with him. Hickerson and Theodore Achilles participated from the beginning. George Kennan was absent for the first meeting, but Charles Bohlen was there. It was a testament to Hickerson's leadership in the movement toward an Atlantic alliance that he was next in line to Lovett in the exploratory talks, although Bohlen as counselor to the department outranked him. Given Hickerson's doubts about where Kennan and Bohlen stood on the wisdom of a treaty, the British wanted them present from the start, if only to inhibit their carping from the outside.[31]

The undersecretary of state represented the United States in the Ambassadors' Committee and at the insistence of his colleagues continued to serve as chair rather than rotate the position. Modestly, Lovett wanted to be considered more as master of ceremonies rather than chairman. But if his manner was appealing, his caution about where the talks were heading had not changed. No military representative was at the meetings, despite General Alfred Gruenther's active involvement in the Pentagon conversations; there would be no premature signal to the Europeans that the United States had committed a military decision in their favor. Lovett set the tone for the ambassadorial gathering.

The other ambassadors composed a distinguished group, each flanked by senior staff members. Sir Oliver Franks, an Oxford don with a background in moral philosophy, was a happy choice to represent Britain. He was not cut from the same cloth as his predecessor, "a dyed-in the wool professional, the amiably erratic Lord Inverchapel (Archibald Clark Kerr)," as historian Alex Danchev called him.[32] Inverchapel was sixty-six years old and on his last assignment before retirement. Franks was only forty-three but already enjoyed a reputation as a man of principle who could relate easily to the U.S. establishment. He knew the United States, and at one point in his life had been tempted to follow an academic career at the University of Chicago. He took office in May 1948 in time to play a leading role in nurturing transatlantic ties. His service presiding over the implementation of the Marshall Plan's European organization stood him in good stead in Washington. And his vision of a North Atlantic pact, rather than including the United States in an enlarged Brussels Pact, fitted the image that Hickerson and Achilles had of the future of the West. Although not participating as an ambassador, Jebb exerted his influence from London as one of the architects of the Atlantic alliance.

Canada had its equivalent of Jebb in Pearson, undersecretary of state for external relations, with Hume Wrong as ambassador in Washington. Belgium and the Netherlands had a strong presence in Baron Robert Silvercruys and Eelco van Kleffens, respectively. Silvercruys, with long experience in the ways of Washington, was adept in coming to the point whenever possible. Van Kleffens, as Henderson saw him, "was invariably sensitive and sensible. He had no axe to grind either for himself or his government and he always sought to contribute by clear analysis and timely suggestion to the success of the negotiations." Hugues Le Gallais, the Luxembourg ambassador, was absent from the ambassadorial meetings but participated in the working group set up by the Ambassadors' Committee.[33]

Isolated from the others by France's demands for special treatment and ignorant of what had transpired at the Pentagon talks, the French ambassador Henri Bonnet was out of step with his colleagues. Where the other diplomats were in every way diplomatic, expressing their differences in muted tones and understatement, Bonnet was blunt to the point of rudeness. "M. Bonnet, of course, was not inhibited by any Anglo-Saxon notions of team spirit," Henderson claimed. "He was there to state the French case, and nothing but it. This he did with remarkable tenacity and tactlessness from the beginning to the end of the negotiations." Franks felt that he would have been more effective if he refrained from the "language of conditions," which gave the impression of intransigence. This was not the way business was conducted in this gathering. He added that when Bonnet spoke of conditions, it was as if he were putting a pistol to his head, making an agreed solution all the harder to reach. For his part, Bonnet felt that he was talking to a wall when he addressed his colleagues.[34] This lack of communication between the French and their allies would plague the working group as well as the Ambassadors' Committee.

A VIENNESE MINUET?

Veteran journalist Cook's sprightly account of the first five days wrote off the ambassadors' performance as a chase around in circles on a high plateau, "rather like a Viennese minuet with the dancers approaching each other, bowing, touching hands, retreating, turning, circling and then approaching to bow again and prepare to start the dance." In brief, the meetings were a charade. Nothing substantial was accomplished, and issues that might have been substantial were relegated to the working group of mid-level diplomas to deal with, if not to solve.[35]

The way the topics were handled lends credibility to Cook's image. In sequence they included estimates of Soviet intentions, defense measures taken by the Brussels Pact powers, security relations with other Western European countries, and discussion on the nature of the U.S. association with Europe in conformity with the prescriptions of the Vandenberg Resolution. The first three were essentially window dressing; there was little to be said that made a difference. It was the fourth that absorbed the European partners—just what kind of association was the United States prepared to make—and here Lovett refused to offer any answer. He was there, he pointed out, to hear the views of the ambassadors. Henderson, then a young second secretary in the British embassy in Washington, was not present at any of the first five meetings of the Ambassadors' Committee, but he perceived that the U.S. attitude "was that of some modern Minerva, ready to lend its shield to the good cause of European democracy, but not prepared to promise to descend into the earthly European arena and become involved itself should trouble occur."[36]

Yet the charge of irrelevance was overblown. Many of the questions that were finally answered in the North Atlantic Treaty were raised in the Ambassadors' Committee. One of them, posed by Lovett at the first meeting, was the warning that "military lend-lease," which had been a possibility in the spring, would be ruled out categorically. There would be no aid given that would not require evidence of self-help and mutual assistance. The OEEC that emerged from the Marshall Plan would be the model. The Senate would insist on some kind of reciprocation. Article 3 of the North Atlantic Treaty answered most of the questions identified in the first meeting of the Ambassadors' Committee.[37]

The allies could accept this admonition but were uncomfortable with reference to the Senate's assertion that the United States could not afford to "rebuild a firetrap." This term implied that the old system of alliances had produced World Wars I and II, and that the United States would not be a party to replicating those experiences. But this concern was irrelevant to the Europeans. Pearson noted that they would be the first victims in a firetrap, and the whole purpose of the talks was to take actions to prevent such an eventuality.[38]

A second and more crucial issue was the future of the Western Union as the European partner of the United States and Canada. Should it be enlarged, and if so, should new members enjoy equality in the union? Or should the Western Union give way to a larger entity? This was the substance of talks at the fourth meeting of the ambassadors. Van Kleffens emphasized that the Brussels Pact was not intended to be a "closed shop." He recognized the desirability, as well as the need, for an early association of other countries. But he wondered if it would not be wiser to let the Brussels members strengthen their own ties before bringing in new members. Silvercruys agreed with his Dutch colleague and suggested that enlargement would be more likely if the Europeans knew the nature of U.S. association with the Western Union. And van Kleffens added that while no other country was knocking at the Western Union door at this point, others "might be willing to join some other security system of a wider adherence."[39]

By mentioning a larger entity than the Western Union, van Kleffens eased the way for Franks to fill in the gaps by identifying Greenland, Iceland, Norway, and Denmark as logical additions, if not to the Western Union then to an Atlantic community bloc. He emphasized that the Western Hemisphere nation would want to know which countries on the Atlantic's eastern shores would be part of the security zone. Lovett then added that Portugal's Azores would be important. Germany, too, could be a possibility in the future and Italy in the present.[40]

While repeatedly saying that the United States was not making any proposals, Lovett's comments nonetheless pointed toward an enlargement of the Western Union before the United States would act. He cited the case of a hypothetical nation, "Neuralgia" at the fourth session, a country prepared to defend itself, if it received sufficient assistance. But if it was not a party to a group with which the United States was associated, it might either succumb to Soviet intimidation or ask for piecemeal U.S. military assistance. Neither alternative was acceptable; the answer had to be to link Neuralgia with the Western Union.[41]

None of these alternatives appealed to the Western Union partners. If they had to choose enlargement, they wanted it to be on their own terms. And if U.S. pressures could not be resisted, as few new countries as possible should be admitted and then as second-class citizens of an enlarged Western Union. Van Kleffens presented the most persuasive argument for a subordinate role for new members, while yielding ostensibly to the movement toward "some North Atlantic Pact" and disclaiming any expectation of the United States joining the Brussels Pact. He evoked the image of a "peach, the Brussels Pact [which] would be the hard kernel in the center and a North Atlantic Pact, the somewhat less hard mass around it."[42] In his scenario, the Western Union would remain the privileged partner of the United States.

Without endorsing the van Kleffens scenario, the United States continued to press for an increase in self-help among the European allies but at the same time recognized the inadequacy of the Western Union as the frame for new security arrangements. It was both too "European" for the United States to accept and too small to be a credible deterrent to Soviet aggression. Hickerson observed at the fifth meeting of the Ambassadors' Committee that "in one sense the Brussels Pact was not broad enough as to membership and in another sense was too broad as to obligation." The economic and cultural clauses of the pact were appropriate for the European members but broader than appropriate for countries not part of the Western Union. The United States could not become an overseas member of the Western Union.[43]

THE UNITED STATES AS QUESTION MARK

Whether or not the Brussels Pact might have been widened sufficiently to include the United States was not a subject of negotiation at the ambassadorial talks. What remained on the table was the need to enlarge the scope of the Western Union in Europe, if the defense of the West were to become a reality. Just which countries would be part of the Atlantic security zone, and under what conditions they would be admitted, were questions not resolved in those committee talks.

The foregoing issue was framed against the basic question asked by the Europeans: Exactly what would be the U.S. association with an enlarged Brussels Pact?

Everything hinged on the response to this query. All the partners expressed irritation over Lovett's hesitancy to present a U.S. position. Bonnet brushed aside arguments over expansion; he wanted to know the extent of U.S. involvement before the Western Union expanded. The other Brussels partners were more discreet in expressing their wishes, but on this issue Bonnet spoke for them all. Bonnet challenged Lovett for his repeated requests for evidence of European actions to defend themselves by saying that the Western Union had already said what it can do: "The Five Powers had already tried to do what they could from the point of view of mutual aid. . . . The Five were giving something to collective security, were risking the lives of their nations. When would the discussions get down to concrete points, not only in the military field, but as to the form of association which might be formed?"[44]

Lovett bobbed and weaved over this overt challenge. He cited the Rio Pact as a "take-off point," although not sufficient in itself. It was too closely identified with a long history of inter-American relations. Unlike the Western Union members, the Latin American partners could provide considerable assistance in the form of raw materials. Nevertheless, Pearson speculated about the possibilities of the Rio pact as a model for an Atlantic security arrangement. He found it particularly useful because it did not automatically equate "assistance" with an obligation to go to war. And each country could decide for itself just what kind of assistance should follow an attack on one of the allies. While the machinery for implementing such a pact would have to be worked out later, Canada was in favor of participating in an Atlantic organization for mutual assistance but with the caveat that it would not be effective without the membership of the United States.[45]

Before the fifth session adjourned, Lovett foresaw an expansion of the Brussels Pact taking place simultaneously with the evolution of some other collective security arrangement that would not exclude a North Atlantic Pact. Without explicitly identifying a U.S. presence in this community, he judged that from a U.S. perspective, a group that was primarily "Atlantic" would have a positive effect on the reception it would receive in the United States.[46]

One path toward this solution was the "two pillar" relationship in which an Atlantic treaty would embrace the Brussels powers as one pillar and the North American nations as the other. While Kennan had never been enthusiastic about an Atlantic alliance, he did respond to the concept of "two anchors," with the United States and Canada as equal partners with the Western Union, and "stepping stone" countries, such as Norway and Denmark, serving as a bridge over the Atlantic for military aid to the members of the alliance. The ancillary countries' security would be guaranteed against attack in return for military facilities, such as air bases, turned over to members of the Atlantic pact.[47]

This approach had considerable appeal for Bohlen—a more resolute opponent of an alliance with Europe than Kennan—who recognized the importance of five stepping-stone countries: Norway because of Spitsbergen, Denmark because of Greenland, Portugal because of the Azores. Iceland—and even Ireland—had claims on the alliance which the core countries could not deny if they wanted U.S. participation. Following the logic of a two-pillar relationship, the United States revived the issue of enlargement, raised in connection with the Western Union at the fourth meeting of the Ambassadors' Committee. In the fifth session, it was connected with a larger but still vague Atlantic association. As Bohlen observed at that meeting on 9 August, "without the Azores, Iceland and Greenland, help could not be got to Europe in significant quantities at all." He was obviously in agreement with Lovett's statement the day before that "Greenland and Iceland were more important than some countries in Western Europe to the security of the United States and Canada."[48]

Most of the European partners were uncomfortable with this Atlantic emphasis for fear that it would not entangle the United States sufficiently in the defense of Europe. They had an advocate in Hickerson, who also opposed Kennan's ideas, although for different reasons. Hickerson wanted a widening of the Western Union to include Italy and other beneficiaries of the Marshall Plan. Kennan would assign the stepping-stone countries to a subsidiary role, while Hickerson would have them as full members by enlarging the Western Union. This conflict remained unsettled when the security talks ended.[49]

Hickerson and Achilles had reason to be confused, as well as pessimistic, about the proceedings of the Ambassadors' Committee. When Bonnet agreed with Kennan and Bohlen over undue apprehension over the prospect of a Russian invasion of Western Europe, they wondered if Bonnet, in inadvertent collaboration with Kennan and Bohlen, would derail efforts to secure a treaty. Bonnet made the point that if the Soviets went to war, it would be against the United States, not the Western Union members.[50]

Obstacles loomed everywhere Hickerson and Achilles looked, many of them seemingly insurmountable. Not least among them were the negative attitudes of two key players on the State Department team, Kennan and Bohlen. Kennan never understood why a military alliance with the Brussels Pact nations was a priority of the administration. Nor did he understand the excessive deference to the Senate on the part of Marshall and Lovett. He was unhappy both with the Vandenberg Resolution and with the State Department's part in producing it. His recommendation, "the dumbbell" concept, ideally would keep the two pillars separate in identity and membership but linked by acknowledgment on the North American side that military aid and even a unilateral guarantee of their security would be granted for the sake of the Western Union members' sense of security. A military alliance, he believed, was unnecessary, given the absence of any evidence that the Soviets intended military action against the United States.[51] Kennan's language in the Washington exploratory talks was much more nuanced than in his memoirs, but the skepticism about the value of treaties was still evident, even as he remained part of the State Department team.

Bohlen's position was clearer than Kennan's. He joined with Kennan in rejecting the thesis that the Communist Soviet Union was bent on world conquest. He wanted to put the genuine Soviet threat into a proper perspective. If it was primarily economic or political, the United States should react differently to a challenge that was not primarily military. In July 1948 he doubted that the situation called for a military union with the Europeans. He felt that the years of maximum danger—1945 to 1947—had passed. The United States, therefore, should be "careful not to adopt measures here which would be weakly provocative."[52]

Achilles was convinced, though, that Bohlen's opposition to a unified Europe was based on a conviction that the Senate would never ratify a military alliance. It is no small wonder then that he and Hickerson worked together to convince Lovett to transfer him to Paris: "We cooked up a new job for him, that of military supervisor of the military assistance program, which didn't exist yet but which we were confident Congress would approve."[53] Bohlen, however, did not leave Washington until the exploratory talks had concluded.

The Canadian delegation held a position on the nonmilitary aspects of a transatlantic alliance that it tried to insert at every opportunity. Whatever form the relationship would ultimately take, it should be more than a military alliance. The Canadians believed that the closer the North Atlantic community moved toward political and economic union, the greater the potential for the British and French to restrain the power of the United States. The alliance, as Deputy Undersecretary of State for External Affairs Escott Reid realized, could make "Canada a countervailing force against the United States; the alliance would call in Britain and Western Union to restore the balance in the United States." He felt that the nonmilitary provisions in an Atlantic pact should be even more extensive than those in the Brussels Pact. Secretary of State for External Affairs Louis St. Laurent specifically called for economic, social, and cultural cooperation, believing as he did, that the weakness in Western Europe was not primarily military. The problem was psychological, a weakness of the will, that had to be overcome.[54] The broader the appeal of the prospective Atlantic alliance, the more opportunity it would have to cope with the Communist challenge.

After the first meeting of the Ambassadors' Committee, Pearson noted that Lovett referred to a North Atlantic system that would not be merely negative, "that cooperation should be wider than merely military and should be closely related to the principles and purposes of the United Nations." Lovett, he exclaimed, was talking "Canadian."[55] But Lovett was only giving lip service to this goal. Other priorities prevailed. Yet Canada took a position that had to be taken into account before a final treaty could be made. Its range of concerns was broad and idealistic in their content.

French concerns by contrast were precise and narrowly focused on France's advantage. If Ambassador Bonnet's views also served those of his colleagues, it was often coincidental. What he wanted was simple: arms and supplies for the French military and a timetable for early delivery. He was impatient with generalities. He wanted no expansion of the Western Union, with specific application to Italy, and found Lovett's professed ignorance of the military capabilities of the Brussels Pact powers an unacceptable excuse for delaying U.S. aid.[56]

It was obvious to all participants that no conclusions were possible in the five meetings of the Ambassadors' Committee, and none was likely if there would be no change in the tenor of the discussions. Bonnet would continue to be confrontational, the Dutch and Belgian representatives indecisive, and Lovett evasive. Because the meetings were formal and fully recorded, the members of the committee and their staffs would not even try to come up with difficult compromises. How could they when their masters at home were able to see if there were any deviations from the instructions of the foreign offices.

The upshot of these uncertainties was an agreement to have a working party composed of mid-level officials come up with a schedule that would work out the problems emerging from the Ambassadors' Committee or at least produce a schedule indicating tasks to be grappled with so that future meeting of ambassadors could have a "more precise definition of the ultimate form." Such was Lovett's recommendation.

Had the leaders then thrown up their hands in failure by turning the agenda over to others to resolve? Belgian Ambassador Baron Silvercruys did not think so. Even though he had no "clear picture as to the sort of association which the United States and Canada were prepared to contemplate," he felt that there had been a useful explorations of some points of the agenda. Lovett implicitly agreed about the most important subject of exploration, namely, that the ambassadors had been seeking to find the right kind of organization that would permit the United States to accept membership.[57]

THE BAND OF BROTHERS

Hickerson and Achilles may have been minor players at the Ambassadors' Committee, but they were the stars of the international working group. Hickerson presided, with Achilles as his principal aide. Achilles chaired the drafting committee that essentially wrote the report that was the basis for the North Atlantic Treaty. In the hothouse atmosphere of a room without air conditioning, the working group shed their coats and rolled up their shirt sleeves. They worked as a team and became lifelong friends as a result of the exciting days cooped up in what seemed to be a tropical Washington. They met almost daily from July to September, long enough to "become a real band of brothers," as Achilles nostalgically noted. It was as if the working group had gone through combat together and came through victoriously with a draft treaty that was a basis on which to negotiate a North Atlantic Treaty. They conspired to evade rulings and judgments from their superiors. When Frederick Hoyer Millar, first secretary of the British Embassy and British member of the team, made a proposal that others felt was nonsense and told him so, he replied: "These were my instructions. All right. I will tell the Foreign Office I made my pitch and was shot down and try to get them changed." Here was the birth of the "NATO spirit" as Achilles saw it.[58]

Not surprisingly, the French did not share this spirit. Armand Bérard, Minister-Counselor of the French Embassy in Washington, displayed the same single-minded devotion to France's particular interests that Bonnet presented to his colleagues on the Ambassadors' Committee. "The French boggled at everything," as Achilles noted, and Bérard did not deviate from the pattern. That Bérard was odd man out only solidified the bonds of brotherhood among the other members of the working group. Henderson was more amused than annoyed with Bérard. He saw him, like Bonnet, as inclined to overlook the fact that the law of diminishing returns applied in argument as in economics. Bérard harped on French needs, oblivious of the dwindling appeal of his words. Exasperating as he could be, "he was never dull and was frequently entertaining."[59]

The U.S. and British members were the dominant forces in the working group; the views of Hoyer Millar were in harmony with Hickerson and Achilles's. He was joined by Henderson, the second secretary, who was a keen observer of the scene and of his colleague Hoyer Millar, who, he observed, "did not believe in getting worked up about anything, and he was not impressed when others did so." His was a moderating influence if not quite as detached as Henderson claimed. Thomas Stone was the senior member of the Canadian working group and was familiar both with the process of fraternal cooperation and with the special Canadian concern for the nonmilitary aspects of a future Atlantic pact. He made his argument with consistent good humor.[60]

The Benelux representatives were relatively quiet. Le Gallais of Luxembourg was the least visible and audible of the group, partly because he was still in Europe when the Ambassadors' Committee met. When he did participate in the working group "he was not obsessed with the burden," according to Henderson, "and did not allow his presence at the long afternoon meetings to interfere with the regular siesta habit which he had acquired during his long residence in the East." If asked for specific opinions, "with infinite sagacity and solemnity he would reply: 'I agree with the views of my Benelux colleagues.'" Roger Taymans, counselor of the Belgian embassy, appeared to watch the others impassively except on the occasion when the Belgian Congo became an issue. He was seconded by Roger Vaes, attaché at the embassy. Otto van Reuchlin, the Dutch member, was not much more aggressive than Taymans and was "always the perfect diplomat of the party He was formal, friendly and never embarrassed—not even by the Indonesian question."[61]

THE WORKING PARTY IN ACTION

In this congenial environment, Hickerson was usually able to have his way. The give-and-take nature of the informal brotherhood permitted each delegate to blow off steam as he promoted his country's interests. Bérard flatly wanted the new pact to include all France's colonial possessions. Van Reuchlin made his case for continued Dutch control over the East Indies but recognized U.S. unwillingness to supply aid to any nation that did not resolve its colonial problems. Indonesia was a sticking point that was not settled until 1949. Taymans weighed in with an effort to bring the Belgian Congo into an Atlantic pact on the grounds that it was a main supplier of uranium to the United States, a vital resource in the atomic defense of the West. If Italy could be considered a potential member, why not the Congo? Taymans was "normally an inscrutable and impassive watchdog," according to Henderson, until "he suddenly started barking loudly in an attempt to get the Belgian Congo included in the pact. He was quickly muzzled by the other representatives and retreated once again behind his sombre tortoise shell, never to re-emerge." Achilles resolved the issue by reassuring Belgium of the importance the defense of the Congo was to U.S. interests.[62]

The Canadian special interest was of a different order. From the outset of its involvement with the United States and the Western Union, its leaders had warned against an excessive emphasis on the military role of a projected Atlantic alliance. Hickerson and Achilles were in essential agreement with the Canadian position, as expressed in St. Laurent's speeches, that military considerations alone would not be sufficient to create "a true Atlantic Community." But the working group did not share the sense that social and economic factors should have prominence in a treaty. Bevin felt that such emphasis would duplicate the functions of other organizations specifically identified with coordinating Europe's economic problems.[63]

With the help of Hickerson and Achilles, the Canadians ultimately won some recognition of their efforts in Article 2 of the North Atlantic Treaty, which concluded with the admonition that the members "seek to eliminate conflict in their economic policies and will encourage economic collaboration between any or all of them." There was no mention of social policies. The language of Article 2 was the best that a consensus could offer. The Washington paper in September did include the promotion of "general welfare" as the end product of economic and social collaboration, but when Vandenberg and Tom Connally found out that the early version, supported by Hickerson and the Canadians, employed that phrase, they "reacted strongly," recalling that the phrase had created more difficulty in the framing of the U.S. Constitution than any other.[64]

CORE ISSUES

The foregoing issues were not the main business of the working group. Its obligation was to come up with a draft treaty that the respective governments would accept. To do this, the larger questions of where the United States would fit into the pact, of the role the Western Union powers would play, and of whether other European nations would become members of an enlarged Brussels Pact or join the new Atlantic security organization directly would have to be answered. Hickerson's openness to all ideas quieted many of his European colleagues' doubts about any hidden agenda he might have had. He and Achilles were frank about their conviction that a pact had to be made and that the United States had to be part of it, as long as there was no conflict with the UN charter and the U.S. Constitution.[65]

Hickerson and Achilles always had to contend with Kennan's perspective, which too frequently collided with theirs. So disturbing to them were Kennan's positions that in his memoirs Achilles refused to recognize his presence in the working group. He was particularly irritated by Kennan's claim to have been his department's representative and indeed, the chairman of the working group: "George was never on it," Achilles insisted, "and I don't think he ever attended a meeting."[66] The published record supports Kennan's position on the working group, if not in the role of chairman.

Wrangling with him over the composition of the future North Atlantic security organization complicated Hickerson's life. Kennan wanted to limit its members to the North Atlantic area, preferably on the basis of the "two anchors" approach, and would exclude Italy. As for the stepping-stone nations, such as Norway, they could join "on an associate basis"; their chiefs of staff, for example, would not attend the military conversations to implement the treaty. Kennan also thought of a third category for nations outside the fold, in which there would be fewer obligations but, as Jebb suggested, would involve arrangements to consult in a crisis on measures necessary to restore stability. Kennan welcomed this gloss on his proposition.[67]

The problem of enlarging the Brussels Pact and determining who should join the larger Atlantic association dominated the working group sessions, just as they had the Ambassadors' Committee. The nub of the matter was succinctly stated by Bérard, who asked if idea of a North Atlantic Pact could not be "accompanied by some arrangements directly with the Brussels Union countries." This idea fitted comfortably into Kennan's hopes of restricting the pact to the seven members represented at the talks, added by no more than two other countries. "No wonder [Hickerson] cast at Kennan a look usually reserved for those who at football kick a goal against their side."[68]

The two-pillar approach conflicted with Hickerson's requirements. He and his U.S. colleagues, excluding Kennan and Bohlen, wanted a wider Brussels Pact that would avoid the piecemeal requests for military equipment of the kind the French were anxious to raise. Britain and the United States could agree on the importance of the Scandinavian countries participating in an Atlantic alliance, but there was no consensus about others. Strategic value was obvious with respect to Portugal and even Spain, while Greece and Turkey were too far removed from the Atlantic region. All but the United States ruled out Italy.[69]

Francisco Franco's Fascist history made Spain's admittance impossible, despite Britain's emphasis on its strategic importance. Portugal was a more likely candidate given the position of stepping stone the Azores could play. Yet there were concerns about Antonio Salazar's close ties to Franco. In Scandinavia, Sweden was a spoiler. If it chose not to participate with Norway and Denmark in working with the proposed Atlantic security pact, the United States would consider its military requests only after the countries within the new bloc were taken care of.[70]

It was obvious that no conclusions about membership in the Atlantic alliance would be immediately forthcoming. The Brussels powers might welcome new members as a second pillar but not if it meant increasing their numbers and diluting the aid that the United States would give. Nor would the stepping-stone countries be satisfied with an inferior role in the Brussels Pact without any assurance that the Western Union would or could respond to an attack on their territories.

An even more delicate matter was over the way the allies would respond to an attack on one of their members. The Western Union had a ready response: simply apply Article IV of the Brussels Pact, which unequivocally stated that the parties "in accordance with the provisions of Article 51 of the Charter of the United Nations, afford the party so attacked all the military and other aid in their assistance." This binding commitment was unacceptable under the U.S. Constitution, as Bohlen underscored, because congressional action would have to be the prerequisite to the nation's going to war.

The Rio pact, which the United States pressed into service as its model, only provided that a military staff committee would meet to plan overall strategy in event of an attack, and the Brussels Pact obligated its members to wage war. Hickerson added that in light of the Senate's approval of the Rio pact, it would be prudent for a North Atlantic Treaty to follow its precedent.[71]

Instead of presenting consensus on Article 5 to the Ambassadors' Committee, the working group offered three versions: the U.S., using the language of the Rio pact; the European, seeking language as close as possible to Article IV of the Brussels Pact; and a third version, following the preference of the Canadian representative. The latter sought a compromise by stating that the party attacked "in the area covered by the treaty be considered an attack against itself, and should consequently, in accordance with its constitutional processes, assist in repelling the attack by all military, economic and other means in its power in the exercise of the right of individual or collective self-defense recognized by Article 51 of the Charter."[72] These were awkward locutions but no more so than the final language of the treaty itself.

THE FRENCH WILD CARD

It should have come as no surprise that France would ignite the most sparks in the course of the long hot summer in Washington. When Hickerson pointed out that only a version of the Rio pact would be acceptable to the Senate, Bérard typically ignored the warning and simply repeated the rigid French position that the treaty would have trouble in France if it did not provide for immediate military assistance. Bohlen speculated that France's absence from the secret Anglo–U.S.–Canadian talks of April may have been responsible for its representatives' ill-tempered and ill-informed arguments in the Ambassadors' Committee and in the working group. Because the French were unaware of the substance of the Pentagon meetings, they did not recognize or appreciate the importance of an Atlantic connection to U.S. membership in an alliance and to the aid the United States would provide to a new entity.[73]

Nor did the French appreciate that concessions were indeed made to them. As early as 14 July, Averell Harriman, U.S. special representative in Europe for the ECA, recommended sending a limited number of P-40s or P-51s to equip a selected unit of the French air force. He was thinking of the psychological value that token shipments could have on French morale, much as the delivery of one million rifles had on Britain in 1940. After months of patient explanation to the European allies that long-range assistance was the only appropriate path to military aid, the administration moved to accommodate France. Harriman "was frankly concerned over the possibility of a reversal of the upward trend of determination in Europe unless we give some concrete evidence of support, not in top secret circles, but openly to the people." The president subsequently approved a transfer of sufficient U.S. stocks in Germany to equip three divisions in that country.[74]

The British concurred in the U.S. decision, if only to ameliorate another French Cabinet crisis. "France is essential to the Western system," Bevin noted in a memorandum to his cabinet, and "her collapse would involve the collapse of the whole." John Russell of the Foreign Ministry's Western Department believed that the decision to supply U.S. military equipment to the French had an excellent effect on the French. But a colleague could not refrain from wondering if the United States had set a bad precedent by violating its own rule of coordinated requests: "This U.S. unilateral action may encourage other countries to attempt to beat the pistol."[75]

But would any concession have satisfied the French delegates? For that matter, would a French presence at the Pentagon talks in March have widened their tunnel vision? At an informal meeting at Lovett's home with the members of the Ambassadors' Committee on 20 August, Bonnet could not contain himself. He asserted that a long-term pact was irrelevant to France for the time being; it would not provide the protection immediately needed. More than supplies, tanks should be a priority and should be done through talks at the chiefs-of-staff level.

Bonnet delivered an equally blunt message from the Quai d'Orsay that laid down three conditions that would have to be met before France would enter a North Atlantic Treaty. Beyond immediate U.S. assistance in equipping French forces would be an assurance that in event of war with the Soviet Union, the United States would send reinforcements of ground troops to Europe in defense of France—again, immediately. And, third, it was about time for France to become a member of the Anglo-U.S. Combined Chiefs of Staff, which had been created in World War II. That this staff no longer existed was either unknown to him or unaccepted by him.[76]

The State Department was furious with the French. In a cable four days after the meeting in Lovett's home, Achilles told Caffery that "the French Are in Our Hair." They can get much of what they want "if only they have sense enough not to spoil it by asking for precise promises which we cannot possibly make. If they keep up their present tactics they will make it very difficult for us to do anything with them."[77]

The other allies were worried that Bonnet's outburst might jeopardize the interests of them all. Pearson saw the United States "becoming impatient with the negative attitude of the French. There is, I fear, a real danger of the whole project being wrecked."[78] Consequently, the allies pressured the French to behave more discreetly. Even before Achilles fired off his cable to Paris, Bevin had sent Jebb to Paris to get Jean Chauvel, the secretary-general of the foreign ministry, to lower the decibels and back off from the demands.

Fortunately, Schuman had replaced the excitable Bidault as foreign minister in July and was open to Jebb's distinction between immediate and long-term security problems. While the French maintained their opposition to enlarging the Brussels Treaty, they did accept much of the U.S. approach to an Atlantic pact. In new instructions to their ministers in Washington, they even toned down objections to including Iceland, Ireland, Portugal, and the Scandinavian countries in the pact. Ironically, as France seemed poised to relent on possible Italian membership, the controversy over Italy inspired Kennan to revive his doubts about extending the alliance to Italy and to present his argument to Lovett against Hickerson's views for resolution as the Washington talks were coming to a close.[79]

THE LURE OF EUROPEAN UNITY

The Washington exploratory talks were not the only conversations being held over the future of Western Europe in the summer of 1948. At The Hague and at Interlaken, Switzerland, the Brussels Pact powers engaged in extensive talks without U.S. participation. Only a week after the working group began its sessions, the Western Union's Consultative Council met in The Hague on 19 and 20 July to deal with common problems. Inevitably, one of them was the need to have the United States make substantial military aid as a condition for the Brussels Pact countries "to make the most of its potentialities."[80] This was language France could appreciate. It meant that the United States should provide immediate aid without making the demands on the Western Union that its members could not fulfill. The French members of the delegation, joined by the Belgians, pressed for a U.S. association with the Brussels powers to serve as a key to an Atlantic Pact and emphasized that "any 'guarantee' as general as the Rio Pact would not be considered sufficient."[81] The council used the occasion to express doubts about including Iceland and Greenland in a future Atlantic pact, out of concern that the Soviets might consider these additions preparation for offensive actions.[82]

The French agenda at The Hague turned out to be broader than their usual demands for special military aid to French forces. Although Bidault was tottering from his perch as foreign minister in the chaotic political climate in Paris in the summer of 1948, he had used the last week in office to push for a European parliament in which France would occupy a major role. Addressing the question of a European federation on 26 July, Bidault was implicitly coopting the United States when he stressed that "we have been expressly and very loyally warned by the United States themselves, that they would not continue their efforts unless European States, for their part, organized to form a large economic unit." By taking the leadership of the

Brussels Pact powers in creating a European federation, initially through the creation of a European Assembly, France would appear to respond to continuing U.S. demands for Europe to demonstrate to its own people as well as to the United States that it was working toward economic, political, and military unity.[83] Not least of the virtues in this proposal would be France's primacy in its implementation.

Bidault's plan was a counterpoint to apparent disarray at The Hague meeting of the Western Union powers. In that meeting Paul-Henri Spaak had seemed depressed about the lack of progress at the Washington talks, which he called confused and rambling. As for extending membership to other European nations in a projected Atlantic pact, he feared that the Soviets would regard the Scandinavian countries as a threat. Their vulnerable geographical positions would weaken rather than strengthen an alliance until the military potential of the Western Union was realized. This was a point that Bidault would take up a few days later, when he announced his proposal for a European assembly. Spaak also suspected that some of his colleagues even doubted whether the United States was in a position to respond to an attack, regardless of any pledge given. This was another theme articulated by the French. The idea of a European assembly was a happy diversion from the malaise affecting the Brussels powers.[84]

Chauvel greeted the Bidault initiative at the Quai d'Orsay as a coup for France and was pleased that Belgians enthusiastically endorsed it. So did Bidault's successor, Schuman. Chauvel also noted that the British were less enthusiastic about summoning a European assembly that might tie them to an unstable Europe.[85]

René Massigli, France's ambassador to Britain, characterized Britain's reactions more vividly—and more negatively in his memoirs. Noting that when Bevin's aides failed to prepare him for a shock, the foreign minister, forgetting the presence of a member of the French embassy, blurted out in a loud voice, "I have never heard such foolishness." In a footnote Massigli explained that this was a "diplomatic translation for much cruder language."[86]

In fact, Britain's reaction was even more negative than either diplomat admitted. The foreign office was angry over Bidault's leaking the proposal to the press and complained that if the parliaments of constituent nations would designate the members of the European parliament on the basis of proportional representation, the new body would contain a large bloc of Communist members. Moreover, what use would European assembly have if it did not represent an existing organization? Still, as one foreign office official remarked, it was obvious to the British that "the French action has rather put us on the spot."[87]

Almost as disturbing to the British as the proposal itself was the apparent support the United States gave to the prospect of a European assembly.

When France specifically asked the Brussels Pact members to consider a convocation, the State Department released the following statement: "We favor the taking by the Europeans themselves of any steps which promote the idea of European unity or which promote the study of practical measures and the taking of such measures."[88] Secretary Marshall then appended comments to the press release for the benefit of U.S. missions in Europe. These suggested that U.S. approval was more than a formality; he added that "While avoiding endorsement of French or any other specific proposal looking [for] unification of Europe we intend to encourage publicly and privately the progressively closer integration first of free Europe and eventually of as much of Europe as possible." He warned that partial measures were not enough, because "partial recovery will produce complacency and reduce European willingness to take bold measures" to help themselves. Unless the Europeans act together, they risk wasting U.S. effort to get them back on their feet. He equated preparation for a European assembly with Europe's intention to reduce its dependence on the United States.[89]

These sentiments mirrored those of the *New York Times*. Over a week before Marshall's press conference, one of the *Times's* editorials asserted that "the new French initiative is a happy augury that Europe is moving in the right direction, and the United States, in contrast to Russia, which is fighting such a development, can be depended upon to do all it can to pave the way for it."[90]

The official and unofficial reactions by the State Department and the leading newspaper of the United States confirmed fears that had been raised in Britain earlier over the impact of The Hague Congress in May. The dangers anticipated in the spring seemed to be realized in August, with the French continuing to bait their British ally. They undercut Britain's wish to have the Five Power Permanent Commission carefully examine the question of convening any kind of European Assembly. France jumped the gun by endorsing the proposals of the International Committee of the Movement for European Unity, thereby precluding any preliminary Western Union reaction. Only Belgian representatives were consulted. All the questions concerning the size, method of selection of delegates, not to mention the powers the assembly might be authorized, were swept aside in France's eagerness to have its way. Or so the British believed.[91]

France was far from being intimidated by the vigor of Britain's opposition. On 21 August, *Le Monde* exulted that the decision of the Council of Ministers on 18 August marked the day as one of the great dates in the history of Europe and evidence that France is launching "a new, active, and generous policy." It subsequently chided the Labour Party, which should have been joining other Socialists in the movement toward a federal Europe, for the "shabby" political reason that it did not want accept the leadership of the Conservative Winston Churchill.[92]

Under other circumstances, the French government might have refrained from giving its blessing to the veteran European propagandists for a federal Europe, Richard Coudenhove-Kalergi and his European Parliamentary Union. But in the heady mood of the moment, Massigli informed the Brussels Pact allies that it accepted the program of the International Commission of the Movement for European Unity, organized by the European Parliamentary Union, as its own.[93] Coudenhove-Kalergi considered the congress that convened in Interlaken, Switzerland, on 1 to 4 September a long-delayed victory for his objectives. Only coincidentally did his expectations mesh with France's ambition to use them in their plans for assuming the leadership of Europe, unfettered by Anglo-U.S. interference.[94]

There was a U.S. presence at the Swiss meeting in the person of William C. Bullitt, vice president of the American Committee for a Free and United Europe, to share French hopes for a French-led Europe. His views appeared to reflect the earlier State Department communiqué on behalf of the French plan.[95] Coudenhove-Kalergi and his U.S. acolytes drew sustenance from the new life that France breathed into the European movement. Senator J. William Fulbright was in Europe that summer and let it be known that "the British government seems to be at the moment undecided about the matter and reluctant to take any positive step on the political level. I do not feel that they are doing enough and I believe that we should do our best to persuade them to take more positive leadership in this movement."[96] And even as the State Department was privately disavowing the public impression, Lovett "spontaneously declared his conviction," according to Ambassador Franks, that the European nations must set up some kind of federation or risk the loss of U.S. funds for economic and military aid.[97]

Despite close collaboration between Britain and the United States since the failure of the London meeting of foreign ministers in December 1947, there was a distinct chill in the air as the Washington talks came to an end in September, colder than over the differing views on Palestine in June. When Jebb informed Marshall that Britain was the only government "really doing concrete planning" for Western European integration, at least in the economic area, he was told that "we had seen very little evidence of it." The general impression in the press and the public was that the "UK was dragging its feet." In September 1948, Britain seemed to have replaced France as the primary obstacle to Western unity. According to former Undersecretary of State Sumner Welles, Britain had become "strangely addicted to politics of utter sterility," while pundit Walter Lippmann discovered the source of British obstructionism in its adoption of socialism.[98]

How important then was the idea of European federation in 1948? There was a sense of a lost opportunity on the part of leading British and U.S. statesmen. It is unlikely that French counterparts shared that feeling. Federation for them was a means to challenge the authority of the United States and to keep Germany embedded in a European framework under France's control. Looking back over the years, Jebb bemoaned the failure to create a genuine supranational European community in that year. Had he been at The Hague Congress in May, he wondered if he might not have dispelled British aloofness. He understood why the fears aroused in Europe and the United States after the Prague coup and the Berlin blockade had produced the Western Union and the Atlantic alliance: "But what should have accompanied this great reaction of the Western world was an increasing advance toward real European unity also." In other words, somebody should have advanced the theory of the two poles in the Western world and made it an "actual condition of consent of America to entering any definite alliance."[99]

This was precisely what Fulbright and other U.S. supporters of a united Europe had identified as their first priority. In testifying for the North Atlantic Treaty in 1949, John Foster Dulles went a step farther when he speculated in an exchange with Fulbright that "it is possible that the historian may judge that the Economic Recovery Act and the Atlantic Pact were the two things which prevented unity in Europe which in the long run may be more valuable than either of them." While U.S. friends of Coudenhove-Kalergi certainly would agree with Dulles, they might have gone along with Jebb's retrospective belief that the most promising road to federation lay at hand in the enlarging and strengthening of the Brussels Treaty Organization by making it into a parliamentary body with an international secretariat.[100] Such a future also would have fitted into Kennan's dumbbell combination of one unit at the European end, based on the Brussels Pact, and another unit at the North American end—the two being separate in identity and membership but linked by an acknowledgment that the security of Europe was vital to that of the United States and Canada. It would be accompanied by a readiness on the part of the North Americans to extend to the European participants whatever was necessary in the way of military supplies, forces, and joint strategic planning.[101]

But both Jebb and Kennan, full of the wisdom of hindsight, were writing twenty years after these events. Their projections did not meet the needs that U.S. and British planners felt were paramount at the time. The unity of Europe was certainly of great importance, as the Marshall Plan had made clear, but how important was the form of a supranational organization to the framers of the North Atlantic Treaty? What counted was close cooperation and coordination in military and economic areas that would contribute to an effective defense against Communist aggression. Congressional promotion of a U.S. contribution to European security employed the language, but not the substance, of European federation. In this context the idea of a United States of Europe was simply the State Department's rhetorical means of mobilizing U.S. public support for departing from the tradition of nonentanglement with Europe. It was the stuff of which political platforms were made.[102]

The crux of the problem as seen in Washington and the Western Union capitals was Europe's weakness in the face of superior Communist power. Only a U.S. presence in Europe—political, economic, and military—could cope with this challenge. If European federationists and their U.S. friends should press too hard for unification, their enthusiasm could divert the course of an alliance from its main channels. This was a perception shared, though often for different reasons, by British, French, and U.S. leaders. A generation later, Hickerson and Achilles confessed to giving only lip service to the idea of European unity, fearing its negative effect on Atlantic unity.[103] Most of the worries expressed by leaders of the future North Atlantic Treaty were alleviated by the end of the year. Coudenhove-Kalergi remained a visionary with little influence on matters of state; Fulbright's strictures contained nothing that had not been uttered before, to little effect; and Bullitt was dismissed as an ineffectual gadfly. It was a relief to the British that little notice was taken in the United States either of Bullitt or of the Committee for a Free and United Europe.[104]

The end result of the passion for establishing a European Assembly was the illusion of movement combined with the reality of stasis. Given the relative ease with which Britain managed to derail the drive toward federation, it is understandable if its leaders perceived the Franco-Belgian position in the summer of 1948 as essentially soft. Bevin claimed in November that Schuman was relieved to find a way out of the Franco-Belgian Consultative Assembly that France had celebrated in July; he worried that a unified Europe might have been achieved at the expense of relations with the United States and Britain.[105] The British foreign minister's attitude was not wholly cynical. While it is true that he wanted to "spike the guns" of those in the United States who felt that Britain was not moving fast enough, there is no reason to doubt that he and other Brussels Pact leaders ultimately saw a European assembly as a diversion from their appropriate preoccupation with economic recovery and military security.[106]

THE WASHINGTON PAPER—9 SEPTEMBER 1948

At no time was there an expectation that the Washington talks would be definitive. The adjective *exploratory* is sufficiently revealing of just what might develop from the conversations. No one was under any illusion that a treaty could be completed before the U.S. presidential election in November. But building on the labors of the working group, the drafting committee did produce a paper ready to be submitted to the home governments of the participating nations. After all the wrangling over issues dear to individual countries or to the Western Union bloc as a whole, the players all agreed that they had come up with a workable draft with elements of both the Brussels and Rio treaties prominently displayed. They included reference to collaboration in economic, social, and cultural fields (Article 3); continuous and effective self-help and mutual aid (Article 4); provision for mutual assistance in meeting an armed attack (Article 5); and delineation of areas in which Article 5 would be activated (Article 7).[107]

It did not matter that the scope of the alliance was not settled, that membership was far from complete, or that the critical Article 5 was given multiple interpretations. What did matter was the message tucked into a one-sentence paragraph in the memorandum, known as the Washington Paper, sent by the participants in the exploratory talks on 9 September 1948. It stated that "No alternative to a treaty appears to meet the essential requirements."[108] And the most essential requirement was the incorporation of the United States into a transatlantic security system.

Hickerson and Achilles had every right to celebrate this as their treaty. Their fingerprints were all over the fourteen articles that were the heart of the draft. Gone were the pretentious locutions of the Brussels Pact; the "High Contracting Parties" of the Brussels Treaty was shortened to "Parties of the North Atlantic Treaty." A preamble was postponed until the treaty was almost finished, to avoid wasting time arguing about its contents: "No applesauce until we've finished with the meat and potatoes" was Hickerson's preference, along with language that could be understood by an Omaha milkman, as Achilles liked to say.[109] More than six months lay ahead before the North Atlantic Treaty would become a reality, but its substance was in place by September 1948.

NOTES

1. Escott Reid, *Time of Fear and Hope: The Making of the North Atlantic Treaty, 1947–1949* (Toronto: McClelland and Stewart, 1977), 55.

2. *Facts on File Yearbook, 1948*, 8, no. 394 (May 16–22), 157.

3. Memorandum of conversation by Robert Lovett, May 21, 1948, with Sir John Balfour delivering Bevin's views, *FRUS*, 1948, V: 1019; *Congressional Record*, 80th Cong., 2nd sess., May 21, 1948, 94: 6280.

4. *New York Times*, May 23, 1948.

5. Tel Lewis Douglas to Secretary of State, May 22, 1948, *FRUS*, 1948, no. 2213, V: 1031.

6. Communiqué, June 7, 1948, *FRUS*, 1948, II: 313ff.

7. John W. Young, *France, the Cold War, and the Western Alliance, 1944–49: French Foreign Policy and Post-war Europe* (New York: St. Martin's Press, 1990), 195; Timothy P. Ireland, *Creating the Atlantic Alliance* (Westport, CT: Greenwood Press), 100; *Keesing's Contemporary Archives, 1948–1950*, vol. 7, July 3–10, 1948, 9376.

8. *New York Times*, July 1, 1948; Don Cook, *Forging the Alliance: NATO: 1945–1950* (London: Secker & Warburg), 154.

9. John W. Young, *Britain, France, and the Unity of Europe* (Leicester: Leicester University Press, 1984), 94–95; *Facts on File Yearbook 1948* 8, no. 410 (September 5–11), 293–94.

10. Editorial note, "Establishment of the Berlin Blockade," *FRUS*, 1948, II: 909.

11. Tel Robert Murphy to Secretary of State, June 23, 1948, *FRUS*, 1948, no. 1450, II; 914.

12. Department of State *Bulletin*, 19, July 11, 1948, 54.

13. Tel Secretary of the Army Kenneth Royall to Lucius Clay, June 28, 1948, *FRUS*, 1948, no. 2443, II: 931.

14. Cook, *Forging the Alliance*, 151.

15. Memorandum by Chief of Division of Central European Affairs (Jacob Beam) for Record, June 28, 1948, *FRUS*, 1948, II: 928.

16. Quoted in Young, *France, the Cold War, and the Western Alliance*, 199.

17. Vincent Auriol, *Septennat*, June 18, 1948, II: 265.

18. Tel Jefferson Caffery to Secretary of State, June 24, 1948, *FRUS*, 1948, no. 3360, II: 916–17.

19. Dean Acheson, *Sketches from Life of Men I Have Known* (New York: Popular Library, 1962), 33.

20. Memorandum of Conversation, Jean Teitgen to Pime-Henri de Lattre de Tassigny, Inspector General of French Armed Forces, General Revers, Chief of Staff, Ground Forces, General Lecheres, Chief of Staff, Air Corps, June 126, 948, 840.00/6-2648-2618, RG 59, NARA.

21. Tel Caffery to Secretary of State, June 29, 1948, *FRUS*, 1948, no. 3436, III: 142–43.

22. NSC 9/3, 28 June 1948—The Position of the United States with Respect to Support for Western Union and Other Related Countries, *FRUS*, 1948, III: 140–41.

23. Cook, *Forging the Alliance*, 171; *Washington Post*, July 6, 1948.

24. Sir Nicholas Henderson, *Birth of NATO* (Boulder, CO: Westview Press, 1983), 33.

25. Henderson, *Birth of NATO*, 34.

26. Minutes of the First Meeting of the Washington Exploratory Talks on Security, July 6 1948, *FRUS*, 1948, III: 151.

27. Oral History Interview with John D. Hickerson, by Richard D. McKinzie, November 10, 1972, 18, Harry S Truman Library, Independence, MO.

28. "News of the Week in Review," *New York Times*, July 4, 1948, 3.

29. Clifton Daniel, *New York Times*, July 21, 1948, 8.

30. Cook, *Forging the Alliance*, 130, 174.

31. Henderson, *Birth of the Alliance*, 75.

32. Alex Danchev, *Oliver Franks, Founding Father* (Oxford: Clarendon Press, 1993), 87.

33. Cook, *Forging the Alliance*, 175; Henderson, *Birth of NATO*, 42.

34. Henderson, *Birth of NATO*, 42; Reid, *Time of Fear and Hope*, 58.

35. Cook, *Forging the Alliance*, 173.

36. Cook, *Forging the Alliance*, 173; Henderson, *Birth of NATO*, 33, 36.

37. Minutes of the First Meeting of the Washington Exploratory Talks, July 6, 1948, *FRUS*, 1948, III: 151; Minutes of the Third Meeting of the Washington Exploratory Talks, July 7, 1948, *FRUS*, 1948, III: 156.

38. Minutes of the Fourth Meeting of the Washington Exploratory Talks, July 8, 1948, *FRUS*, 1948, III: 168.

39. Minutes of the Fourth Meeting, 166.

40. Minutes of the Fourth Meeting, 167, 169

41. Minutes of the Fourth Meeting, 167.

42. Minutes of the Fifth Meeting of the Washington Exploratory Talks, July 9, 1948, *FRUS*, 1948, III: 171.

43. Minutes of the Fifth Meeting, 178.

44. Minutes of the Fifth Meeting, 172.

45. Minutes of the Fifth Meeting, 175–76.

46. Minutes of the Fifth Meeting, 147.

47. Memorandum by Director of Policy Planning Staff (George Kennan) to Lovett, August 31, 1948, *FRUS*, 1948, III: 225.

48. Reid, *Time of Fear and Hope*, 195; Minutes of the Fourth Meeting, 165.

49. Kennan to Robert Lovett, August 31, 1948, with Annex A—Kennan draft, Annex B, Hickerson draft, 840.00/8–3148, RG 59, NARA. Kennan's memorandum was published in *FRUS*, 1948, III: 225 without annexes.

50. Minutes of Third Meeting, 158.

51. George F. Kennan, *Memoirs, 1925–1950* (Boston: Little, Brown and Co., 1967), 428–30.

52. Memorandum of the Third Meeting of the Working Group Participating in the Washington Exploratory Talks on Security, *FRUS*, 1948, III: 185–86.

53. Theodore C. Achilles, *Fingerprints on History: The NATO Memoirs of Theodore C. Achilles*, edited by Lawrence S. Kaplan and Sidney B. Snyder (Kent, OH: Lyman L. Lemnitzer Center for NATO and European Community Affairs, Kent State University, 1992), 21.

54. Reid, *Time of Fear and Hope*, 137–38.

55. John A. Munro and Alex Inglis, eds., *Mike: Memoirs of Lester B. Pearson*, 3 vols. (Toronto: University of Toronto Press, 1972), II: 50.

56. Minutes of the Fifth Meeting, July 9, 1948, *FRUS*, 1948, III: 173.

57. Minutes of the Fifth Meeting, 181–82.

58. Achilles, *Fingerprints on History*, 19.

59. Henderson, *Birth of NATO*, 57.

60. Henderson, *Birth of NATO*, 58; editorial note listing the regular participants in the fifteen meetings of the International Working Group, *FRUS*, 1948: III: 182.

61. Henderson, *Birth of NATO*, 57.

62. Henderson, *Birth of NATO*, 57; Theodore C. Achilles, "How Little Wisdom: Memoirs of an Irresponsible Memory," in Lyman L. Lemnitzer Center for NATO and European Union Studies, Kent State University, 433. Belgium was appeased by an Achilles-drafted letter from Marshall to Spaak assuring the importance of the protection of the Congo to the U.S.; letter of Roger Vaes, Belgian member of Working Group, to Sidney R. Snyder, June 12, 1991, in Snyder, "The Role of the International Working Group in the Creation of the North Atlantic Treaty" (Ph.D. dissertation, Kent State University, 1992), 158.

63. Achilles, "How Little Wisdom," 436–37; Memorandum of the Thirteenth Meeting of the Working Group, September 2, 1948, *FRUS*, 1948, III: 226.

64. Washington Exploratory Conversations on Security, September 9, 1948, (Washington Paper) as submitted to respective governments, *FRUS*, 1948, 246; Achilles, *Fingerprints on History*, 24–25.

65. Henderson, *Birth of NATO*, 59–60.

66. Kennan, *Memoirs*, 436; Achilles, *Fingerprints on History*, 21.

67. Memorandum of the Thirteenth Meeting of the Working Group, September 2, 1948, *FRUS*, 1948, III: 227.

68. Memorandum of Conversation by Charles Bohlen to George Marshall, August 6, 1948, *FRUS*, 1948, III: 207; Henderson, *Birth of NATO*, 59.

69. Memorandum of the Sixth Meeting of the Working Group, July 26, 1948, *FRUS*, 1948, III: 204.

70. NSC 28/1, September 3, 1948, The Position of the United States with Respect to Scandinavia, *FRUS*, 1948, III: 232–33.

71. Memorandum of the Ninth Meeting of the Working Group, August 9, 1948, *FRUS*, 1948, III: 211; memorandum of the Tenth Meeting of the Working Group, August 10, 1948, *FRUS*, 1948, III: 213.

72. Annex to Washington Paper—Outline of Provisions Which Might be Suitable for Inclusion in a North Atlantic Security Pact, September 9, 1948, *FRUS*, 1948, III: 247.

73. Memorandum of the Tenth Meeting of the Working Group, August 12, 1948, *FRUS*, 1948, III: 213; memorandum Bohlen to Lovett, July 29, 1948, 840.00/7–2948, RG 59, NARA.

74. Tel U.S. Special Representative in Europe under the Foreign Assistance Act of 1948 (Harriman) to Secretary of State, July 14, 1948, *FRUS*, 1948, III: 183–84; tel Lovett to Embassy in France, September 20, 1948, *FRUS*, 1948, no. 2737, III: 253.

75. Tel Frederick Hoyer Millar to Ivone Kirkpatrick, November 6, 1948, "Supply of U.S. Military Equipment to French Divisions," FO 371/73310 Public Record Office, Kew, UK.

76. Memorandum of Conversation by Lovett, August 20, 1948, *FRUS*, 1948, III: 218–19; Henderson, *Birth of NATO*, 52–53.

77. Tel Achilles to Caffery, August 24, 1948, RG 59, NARA.

78. Quoted in Reid, *Time of Fear and Hope*, 119.

79. Henderson, *Birth of NATO*, 53; letter, Kennan to Lovett, August 21, 1948, *FRUS*, 1948, III: 225 (see note 49).

80. Tel the Ambassador in the Netherlands (Herman B. Baruch) to the Secretary of State, July 21, 1948, *FRUS*, 1948, no.455, III: 195.

81. Tel Embassy in London to Office of European Affairs, A-1502, July 27, 1948, sub: Action Taken on Various Points on Agenda of Consultative Council of Five Foreign Ministers at The Hague, July 19–20, 1948, 84-.00/7–2748, RG 59, NARA.

82. Tel Baruch to Secretary of State, III: 194.

83. Tel Caffery to Secretary of State, enclosure of Bidault proposal for European federation, July 26, 1948, no. 1041, 840.00/7–2648, RG59, NARA.

84. Tel Alan G. Kirk (Brussels) to Secretary of State, no.1484, 840.00/7–2448.

85. Jean Chauvel, *Commentaire: d'Alger a Berne, 1944–1952* (Paris: Fayard, 1972), 210–11.

86. René Massigli, *Une comedie des erreurs, 1943–1946* (Paris: Plon, 1978), 156.

87. Tel Douglas to Secretary of State, July 27, 1948, no. 3393, 840.00/7-2748, RG 59, NARA.; Douglas to Secretary of State, no. 3772, 840.00/8-1948, RG 59, NARA.

88. State Department comment in Secretary of State to Caffery, *FRUS*, 1948, no. 3255, III: 222–23.

89. State Department comment, *FRUS*, 1948, IIII: 223.

90. Editorial, *New York Times*, August 19, 1948, 20.

91. Tel Caffery to Secretary of State, August 21, 1948, no. 4322, 840.00/8-2148, RG 59, NARA; Douglas to Secretary of State, September 10, 1948, no. 3014, 840.00/9-1048, RG 59, NARA.

92. Tel Caffery to Secretary of State, August 21, 1948, no. 4322, 840.00/8-2148, RG 59, NARA; tel Caffery to Secretary of State, August 26, 1948, no. 4421, 840.00/8-2618, RG 59, NARA.

93. Tel Caffery to Secretary of State, September 4, 1948, no. 4614 840.00/9-448. RG 59, NARA.

94. American Legation (Berne), September 30, 1948, no. 725, Report on Interlaken Congress of the European Parliamentary Union, September 1–4, 1948, 840.00/9-3048, RG59, NARA.

95. Tel T. R. Snow, British Legation, Berne, to Bevin, September 21, 1948, no. 218, FO 371 73098, PRO.

96. Ltr J. William Fulbright to Dr. Reginald Lang, October 2, 1948, J. William Fulbright Papers, University of Arkansas Library, Fayetteville.

97. Tel Oliver Franks reported this information to the Foreign Office, August 27, 1948, no. 4102, FO 371 73097, PRO.

98. Tel Marshall to Embassy in London, September 13, 1948, no. 3626, 840/00/9-1349, RG 59, NARA; Franks's comments on Summer Welles and Walter Lippmann, September 1, 1948, in FO 371/73097 PRO.

99. Gladwyn Jebb, *The Memoirs of Gladwyn Jebb* (New York: Weybright and Talley, 1972), 220.

100. North Atlantic Treaty Sentate *Hearings*, 81st Cong., 1st sess., March 4, 1949, 2: 368–69.

101. Kennan, *Memoirs*, 429; Canadian reservations about a "two-pillar concept that would make Canada the odd man out in the alliance," in Reid, *Time of Fear and Hope*, 132.

102. The Democratic Party platform of 1948 pledged "continued support of regional arrangements within the United Nations Charter, such as the Inter-American Regional Pact and the developing Western European Union." The Republicans in turn "welcome and encourage the sturdy progress toward unity in Western Europe." K. H. Porter and Bruce Johnson, comps., *National Party Platforms, 1840–1956* (Urbana, IL: University of Illinois Press, 1956), 432, 453.

103. Reid, *Time of Fear and Hope*, 134.

104. Tel Snow to Bevin, September 21, 1948, no 218, FO 371/73098, PRO; FO, Minutes, on "Formation in the U.S.A. of a Committee on a Free and United Europe" by Mr. William C. Bullitt who represented the Committee at the Interlaken Conference.

105. Memorandum by Secretary of State for Foreign Affairs, November 2, 1948, on North Atlantic Treaty and Western Union, Cabinet Papers (48) 29, PRO.

106. Memorandum by Secretary of State for Foreign Affairs, November 2, 1948, Cabinet Papers (48) 7, PRO.

107. Washington Paper, September 9, 1948, *FRUS*, 1948, III: 246–48. See note 72.

108. Washington Paper, September 9, 1948, *FRUS*, 1948, III: 242.

109. Achilles, *Fingerprints on History*, 21–22; note Achilles, "'The Omaha Milkman': The Role of the United States in the Negotiations," in Andre de Staercke et al., *NATO's Anxious Birth* (New York: St. Martin's Press, 1985), 30.

6

The Western Union Defense Organization: 1948–1949

THE POTEMKIN FACTOR

To celebrate the triumphal cruise of Russia's Empress Catherine II and her guest, the Holy Roman Emperor, Joseph II, Prince Gregory Potemkin, Russian military leader, political adviser, and former lover of the empress, offered the monarchs spectacles of thriving settlements and cheering villagers as they journeyed down the Dnieper River in 1787. At every stop along the way, dancing peasants along with their flocks of sheep and goats greeted the visitors as they proceeded toward the Crimea. These spontaneous demonstrations were intended to show how successful Potemkin had been in creating happy and prosperous communities along the riverbanks. But according to Potemkin's many enemies, these settlements as well as the livestock and the peasants who tended them were just façades—painted screens on pasteboards that were moved along the river as the empress proceeded south. The visitors simply saw the same villages and the same peasants every day.

Were the Brussels Pact members creating their own Potemkin village to satisfy the demands of the United States? Parallel with the diplomatic negotiations among the United States and Canada and their European colleagues, the Western Union made a heroic effort to show that a credible defense organization was in place before the North Atlantic Treaty was signed. A U.S. military delegation was present at every stage of WUDO's development. Was the United States hoodwinked into believing in the reality of Europe's successful pooling of military supplies, active steps toward standardization of weaponry, and coordination in the production of new equipment?

In the summer and fall of 1948, the generals saw for themselves just how little progress WUDO was making. They sensed that WUDO was as much a façade, if not a fraud, as the Potemkin villages of the 1780s. Yet the JCS signed off on WUDO as a viable entity, worthy of the support that the Europeans anticipated from the United States. As far as the Potemkin villages were concerned, there was every likelihood that the herds of cows and sheep were genuine. Nor was there a need to import crowds to see the Empress. No czar had visited the south since Peter the Great, so the opportunity to gawk at two monarchs was irresistible. There is a consensus today that identifies the Potemkin villages criticism as a fabrication of his enemies.

It is worth examining the argument that there were no Potemkin villages in 1948 and that there was more substance to WUDO's activities than has been credited in the past. Was it more than a vehicle to guarantee a U.S. entanglement in a European alliance? Was WUDO a legitimate organization?

THE JCS IN A QUANDARY

To appreciate the U.S. military establishment's problem with helping Western Europe defend itself requires recognition of the military sense of vulnerability in the late 1940s. In 1948, the armed forces felt themselves short of sufficient money and manpower to protect the national interest. Selective service had ended, and the swollen wartime budgets were just memories three years later. Nor was Congress willing to pass a universal military training (UMT) program that would have solved the manpower shortage and put pressure on the administration to increase the military budget. The military services' estimates, however, reflected their own individual needs rather than those of the fledgling NME, that was intended to serve as an umbrella sheltering the army, navy, and the newly created air force. The most the president would accept was $15 billion for the NME.[1]

More than any other single obstacle to achieving sufficient strength to cope with potential Soviet aggression and to buck up the limited defense capabilities of the Brussels Pact allies was the low ceiling that the president had set for the military budget in fiscal year 1950. Secretary of Defense James V. Forrestal had been stewing over this figure throughout 1948. In fact, he claimed that the ceiling was actually $14.4 billion. Funds for stockpiling, to the tune of $600 million, would be charged against the $15 billion ceiling. This figure was not sufficient to maintain the force level the NME hoped to attain by the end of 1948. In July, when Forrestal asked the NSC for guidance in formulating a budget, there was no reply then or in the months that followed. He needed to know if there had been an improvement in the international picture to warrant the reduction in military forces planned for the fiscal year 1949. And if it worsened between the spring and the fall of 1948, had there been any thought about increasing the forces? As he told George Marshall in October, he and the JCS considered asking the president to lift the ceiling to provide enough troops to take "effective action in the event of trouble."[2]

Given the misgivings the military had about the administration's budget limitations, it is all the more surprising that its leaders would accept new burdens of providing aid to the Western Union allies. Two implications in particular were bothersome about the dispatch of military aid to Europe. The first was that the United States would be pressed into accepting military obligations beyond its capacity to fulfill them, given the tight military budgets in place in 1948. A second concern was the danger that Europeans would be competing through a military aid program for the same resources that the JCS believed were vital for the viability of the U.S. armed forces. The allies might be inclined, as Senator Arthur H. Vandenberg warned, to come up with uncoordinated shopping lists, although his concern was less with European greediness than with the perception that the United States might look as if it were imitating the Soviets in creating its own satellites.[3]

But there were no reasonable alternatives. Besides, the movement for aid was already in play. The recommendations embedded in NSC 9/3 on 28 June set in motion not only the exploratory talks in Washington but also military talks in London.[4] To facilitate its implementation, the JCS reluctantly went along with NSC 14/1 issued three days later that opened the way for military assistance of all kinds to nations outside the Soviet bloc.[5] The Western Union members would have priority in its distribution.

The administration, well aware of the JCS reservations, tried to calm its fears that a transatlantic alliance would divert equipment and funds from the U.S. military services. Military aid would be provided only after materiel requirements for U.S. forces had been met. If the administration took up the Western Union invitation to participation the five-power military talks in London, its acceptance, as George Kennan underscored, would not signify any U.S. commitment more formal than that given by the president in March following the signing of the Brussels Pact.[6] Whatever course the discussions take, the U.S. negotiators would have to use the ERP model as their guide. Congress would not accept any language that smacked of the lend-lease programs of the World War II experience. This meant that evidence of a coordinated defense program had to be presented before any screening of estimates of U.S. supplementary assistance could begin. The JCS were also mollified by an understanding that reciprocal assistance from the beneficiaries would be expected. In any event, no commitment of any sort would be undertaken without full bipartisan clearance in the Senate, and no such action could take place until the next Congress convened in 1949.[7]

Nevertheless, the JCS wanted to hold Western Union requests at arm's length and continued to worry that European access to the Army's stockpile of equipment could impair the basic mission of the nation. Loose construction of the term *surplus stocks* could result in an irresponsible raid on their supplies. And while the appetite of the European allies was probably insatiable, their willingness to repay U.S. generosity in the form of strategic raw materials and specific base rights was suspect.

A turning point in the military's willingness to help the allies may have arrived when General Hoyt S.Vandenberg, Air Force Chief of Staff—and the senator's nephew—admitted that U.S. security might be better served by curtailing some of the military's requirements. It was a position in which the JCS ultimately concurred. General Omar Bradley, Army Chief of Staff, observed in September 1948 that "it would seem a great mistake to concentrate our entire resources on a United States armament program in the belief that such action alone will contribute most to our national security."[8]

Hoyt Vandenberg was nonetheless uncomfortable with a program that defined minimum military requirements as the amount needed to equip forces identified in the emergency war plan. Because budget limitations would probably prevent realization of even minimum force levels, he felt that it would be counterproductive to pile military assistance on top of the military's requirements. Such a policy would risk U.S. economic security and by extension military security. Because of the inadequacy of surplus stocks to meet European needs, the JCS recognized by the end of the year that a congressional appropriation would be required to satisfy both U.S. and European needs.[9]

Ultimately, it was pressure from Secretary of Defense Forrestal and the NSC more than a newfound faith in the defense efforts of Europeans that accounted for JCS cooperation with the Western Union. Reservations about the aid program were never fully allayed. Years later, General Lyman L. Lemnitzer, the future director of the Office of Military Assistance, recalled General J. Lawton Collins, Army Deputy Chief of Staff, only half jokingly greeting him with the comment, "Lem, I understand you're up there doling out all the equipment that you're going to take away from the army and give to European allies."[10]

THE WESTERN UNION MAKES PROMISES

It was certainly reasonable for the Brussels Pact partners to assume that the various NSC documents amounted to an assurance that the United States would be a key partner in a new Atlantic security pact. Yet it was also understandable if the European partners feared that the U.S. commitment would not be honored unless they clearly demonstrated their determination to integrate and coordinate their own defense structure. The last sentence of NSC 9 on 13 April indicated just what would be expected of the

Brussels Pact members: "Military conversations should be initiated in the immediate future with parties to the Five-Power Treaty, with a view initially to strengthening the collective security through coordinating military production and supply."[11]

U.S. displeasure over Ernest Bevin's initial response a day later signaled its skepticism about the future behavior of the allies. Both the British and French instinctively, it seemed, stressed their impotence in the face of Soviet power and so claimed that there was little they could do unless the United States delivered prompt support. Bevin made a point of saying that consequently "the French were disposed to hold back and go slow." It was obvious to Ambassador Lewis Douglas, however, that this was the British position as well. Douglas responded that "this was precisely the attitude which, among other things might deter the [United States] from making any commitment." Bevin backed down with an explanation that Britain would always stand up and fight if attacked. But he still left the message that his country was weaker than it had been in 1940 and "could not hope for a successful stand against the Soviet hordes for a protracted period while we were considering whether we would participate actively." This was a reminder of Britain's lonely war against the Nazis until Pearl Harbor allowed the United States to "participate actively."[12]

To quiet lingering U.S. suspicions about the seriousness of European intentions to build a credible defense, Bevin spent much of his time in advance of the Washington exploratory talks trying to convince the Truman administration of the progress the Western Union was making. The main purpose for establishing its Consultative Council seemed to have been to make arrangements for military talks that would be held "in the near future."[13]

The near future became "a very short time." As early as 30 April, the defense ministers and chiefs of staff of the Western Union assured the United States through Gladwyn Jebb, chairman of the Permanent Commission, that the five powers would pool their equipment and resources, standardize new production, harmonize their respective military forces military organizations, and prepare an inventory of total military resources now available. There was a fifth—and more important—assignment as well, which was to decide what the Western Union partners would do until U.S. help was available. Their answer was clear. Should the Soviets attack, they would fight as far east in Germany as possible, giving the United States sufficient time to apply their military power decisively in aid of Western Europe.[14]

These brave words matched their intentions, but in every instance they were accompanied by caveats. Waiting for U.S. action in support of their plans was implied in almost all their responses. They recognized that pooling was essential, but its effect might undermine economic recovery, which would require special measures from the United States to ameliorate this problem. Standardization was a priority but not practical without interfering with present production programs. Long-term standardization depended on U.S. intentions, because it was critical that it be linked to U.S. plans. Harmonizing their military formations was the one decision where the allies could act without U.S. help; the national chiefs of staff appointed a committee in London to identify a common command and compatible system of supply and communications.[15] But this, too, was not immediately translated into concrete results.

None of these caveats was articulated in the meeting of the defense ministers and chiefs of staff held at Carlton Gardens on 30 April. Rather, they simply pointed to the inventory that would be drawn up, essentially an assessment of needs for immediate defense and calculations of what was needed to fill the gaps. The secretariat responsible for carrying out the military committee's activities would be mainly British officers proposed by the ministry of defense.[16]

LEMNITZER IN LONDON

Whatever reservations the JCS continued to harbor, the Western Union's Military Committee reported sufficient activity to elicit a positive reaction from Secretary Forrestal. The promise in the spring to produce a strategic concept, to encourage standardization of equipment, and to take stock of actual and potential military resources of the five powers was reported to be in process. For example, arrangements to have flying and technical personnel trained in Britain flowed from a common air defense plan. Inventories of military resources were ready to be examined by the military committee. Three service advisory committees had already made progress.[17] Or so the military committee claimed.

The result was the JCS appointment of a seven-man joint mission headed by General Lemnitzer to attend London sessions of the Western Union's military committee on a "non-membership basis."[18] The JCS had given Lemnitzer detailed instructions on what he might and might not do in talking with Europeans about a coordinated military supply plan. He was further informed of limits to the extent U.S. troops in Europe would support the Western Union's strategic concept of fighting as far east in Germany as possible. And most particularly, he was cautioned against agreeing to military arrangements of any sort that might "unduly influence U.S. global strategy."[19]

The allies had to understand, however, that in the short run at least U.S. military support would be limited to those forces already in Europe. Both short- and long-term strategic concepts developed by the Western Union would have to be based on the assumption that additional U.S. troops would not be deployed to Europe except possibly in a later stage of a war. These cautionary notes, produced on 9 July, a week before the delegation arrived in London, reflected the continuing hesitations of the JCS.[20]

More instructions followed a week later, clarifying the line of authority. The army chief of staff would act as executive agent for the JCS in defining the mission of the representatives. U.S. participation was to focus particularly on drawing up a coordinated military supply plan, and its precedent clearly would be the ERP. The Pentagon wanted to be sure that reciprocal assistance would be expected of the allies. It wanted to be sure as well that the allies would not be under any illusion that there would be an allied military council for global strategy.[21] In this context, the U.S. delegation seemingly had little opportunity for flexibility, for give-and-take negotiations with the Europeans.

Secrecy was vital to the success of this mission. Dramatizing the low profile he and his team were to adopt, Lemnitzer was to enter London on 22 July in civilian clothes to conceal his identity from the press. Within a day, however, the London *Daily Express* noted his arrival under a headline reading "America May Arm 35 Divisions." Having gone undercover at the end of World War II to join Allen W. Dulles, director of the Office of Strategic Services intelligence network in Switzerland, he relished the clandestine role he believed he was playing in 1948. It must have reminded him of the exciting days of 1945 when he was involved in determining the surrender terms of the German forces in Italy. In any event, he refused to believe that his anonymity had been compromised even when he was confronted with the newspaper evidence.[22] In fact, the newspaper explicitly stated that "U.S. General Lyman Lemnitzer, in London to advise the Military Committee on Western Union, had suggested that they set up a permanent staff and pool all secrets and weapons. The United States will partly arm 35 divisions of cadres before more first rated divisions are set up."[23] Obviously from the moment of his arrival he was a central figure at the Horse Guards headquarters.

It would require considerable delicacy for the U.S. mission to give heart to the European military leaders without raising excessive hopes. For this task, as chairman of the U.S. delegation, General Lemnitzer seemed to have been an appropriate choice for infusing the allies with his optimism. Whether he could squelch excessive hopes was less likely.

Despite some delusions about the invisibility of his presence in London, he was not at all invisible within the ranks of senior officers. A West Point graduate, class of 1920, he had missed service in World War I and then spent the interwar years in the usual slow path toward promotion. His abilities as a teacher were recognized in his appointments as an instructor at West Point from 1926 to 1930 and again from 1934 to 1935. As World War II approached, he served as an instructor of tactics at the Command and

General Staff College at Fort Leavenworth, Kansas, from 1936 to 1939 and as a member of the prestigious Army War College in Carlisle, Pennsylvania, in 1940. These appointments reflected talents beyond his training in coast artillery that might have led to significant field commands when the United States went to war in 1941.

He did not achieve this goal until the Korean War a decade later. He did win his stars during the war—brigadier general in 1941 and major general before the war ended. But his success as a planner kept him in key staff positions in the headquarters of General Dwight D. Eisenhower and as liaison with British Field Marshal Sir Harold Alexander in Sicily and Italy. Not only were his skills as an organizer and with planning in play during the war but his unassuming manner facilitated easy relationships with British and U.S. military leaders. He was deputy commandant of the National War College when he was tapped to lead the U.S. military delegation to London in July 1948.[24]

Nearing the end of his first year at the War College, he was about to leave for a fishing trip in Alaska when Forrestal summoned him to the Pentagon without telling Lemnitzer the reason. Only after the secretary commented on Lemnitzer's successful relations with his European counterparts was he told of his selection for a top secret mission to London to represent the JCS in meetings of the military committee of the Western Union.[25]

It was a task he welcomed with enthusiasm. He had made many friends with Allied leaders during the war and looked forward to renew and deepen these connections. That he had no command of French or German did not inhibit or distort his relations with foreign leaders. Biographer L. James Binder noted a rare moment when the normally ebullient and easygoing Lemnitzer seemed out of sorts. The occasion was back-channel negotiations over terms for Germany's surrender where a photograph showed him frowning and ill at ease at a Swiss café. Lemnitzer's discomfort listening to British and German generals speak in German was obvious.[26]

The general's wartime experience made him a true believer in the importance of a European alliance. Lemnitzer heartily agreed that Western Europe needed United States aid to make possible its resistance to Soviet military might. He immediately became a central figure in proceedings of the Western Union's military committee when he was invited to preside over the opening of the first formal meeting on 22 July. He appreciated as well the committee's decision to allow the United States and Canada to express any views they wished without bearing the responsibility for reports to the Western Union's defense committee.[27]

Although Lemnitzer basked in the glow of a receptive audience, he did not hesitate to push the allies to create a military supply board as quickly as possible to distribute logistical services and facilities among all the allies. He took a particular interest in the prospects for standardization of equipment and urged that the allies emphasize the practical aspects of implementing production resulting from standardization rather than dwell on its theoretical fine points that had been wasting the time of the Army Standardization and Inventory Subcommittee. He applauded the military committee's intention to recommend reequipping of allied air forces with standardized planes and promised that the United States would come up with specific actions to further these efforts. For example, he hoped that the United States would assist in pilot training. Although his proposals were modest; he spoke of turning out some 150 pilots over a two-year period.[28]

In the course of his brief service as chairman of the U.S. delegation, lasting only six weeks, Lemnitzer took a proprietary interest in the proliferation of subordinate units growing out of WUDO, from a defense committee to a chiefs of staff committee to a commanders-in-chief committee. He made sure that the Pentagon was aware of the importance the United States should attach to work of the emerging WUDO. In fact, he recommended that the JCS adopt the elaborate security procedure known as METRIC, established by the Western Union. For a precedent he cited Anglo-U.S. security collaboration in World War II: "If U.S. is to participate in activities of Western Union Military Committee . . . it will be necessary for U.S. representative to have complete access to all committee information."[29] In making this recommendation, Lemnitzer not only underscored the importance of the Western Union but also intimated the potential of U.S. influence in all Western Union committees.

There is no evidence that these communications from a respected but still relatively junior general immediately won over senior Pentagon officials at this time. Indeed, before he left London, Lemnitzer had to contend with the possibility of the JCS withdrawing its representation from the military talks. No less a figure than Lt. General Albert C. Wedemeyer, spokesman for the JCS, hinted as much. His query seemed to reflect continuing doubts about the usefulness of this connection.[30]

Lemnitzer was emphatic in his rejection of the idea. He felt that the U.S. presence in London had done much to speed up the activities of the military committee, and its removal could inflict serious damage to the developing Western Union structures. "In addition," his cable continued, "and without attempting to forecast what U.S. attitude or alignment towards Brussels Powers may eventually take, I believe it would be unwise to abandon or neglect taking full advantage of the opportunity to observe and influence military planning." His successor, he was convinced, must be a major general as heads of all the delegations were of that rank. Any downgrading in rank would be seen by Europeans as a sign of "waning U.S. interest in the Western Union with consequent harmful effect on activities of the Military Committee."[31] Lemnitzer obviously won his case. When Major General A. Franklin Kibler replaced him in mid-August, the new delegate was able to continue the progress Lemnitzer felt he had made.

CAUTIOUS REACTIONS

Lemnitzer's enthusiasm for WUDO was not contagious. The obstacles to implementing the military committee's recommendations were daunting. How much aid the United States could or would provide may not have been on the table in London, but its limits were the subject of informal conversations with British military leaders in June. A sobering judgment rendered by Secretary Marshall recorded that a large proportion of equipment from existing U.S. and British resources would require rehabilitation before it could be usable. While ideally large shipments would be important for any sudden expansion of the armies of Western Union members, such shipments would have to be made piecemeal as part of a gradual buildup because of the need for both technical and tactical training in the use of this equipment before a large shipment could be made. Moreover, legislation and appropriation of funds to support any aid program made it unlikely that any shipment of supplies to the Western Union could be made before 1 July 1949, and "reasonable material strength" would probably have to wait until December 1952.[32]

Had the JCS and the secretary of defense known the contents of a report made by the military committee at the second meeting of Western Union's Consultative Council in The Hague on 19 and 20 July, they might have thrown up their hands over any prospect of successful collaboration with the Europeans. As the U.S and Canadian military observers began working with their Western Union counterparts, the military committee's chairman provided a dismal picture of the state of readiness. On the matter of stocks in place, he reported "serious shortages all around and a position of actual weakness at the moment." But the "weakness" was not just in stocks of supplies and equipment. When the discussion turned to military reorganization of Western Union's forces, there was no answer beyond noting that "very big increases would be required in the budgets of the five countries; this not only to meet present requirements, but also to enable a gradual build-up of the military forces toward a potential war footing."[33]

As for questions of standardization of arms and organization of armed forces, the military committee appeared ready to sidetrack them by concentrating on a particular activity. Considerable progress on standardization was attributed to the use of British types of aircraft by the five members, but how much progress on other weaponry was left vague. Even vaguer were predictions about the armies. But as the spokesman for the military committee promised, "The committee was now pressing on, and he understood that the Belgian and Netherlands governments in particular wanted early decisions on standardization of rifles and artillery." No mention was made of French interest in these decisions. The one question that seemed immediately manageable was the organization of command. It also seemed to be the most logical first step, because the newly appointed commander would make plans that would affect all other objectives.[34]

MONTY AS "COMMANDER-IN-CHIEF"

The idea of making the choice of a commander-in-chief a priority conformed with the thinking of the JCS, particularly as it dovetailed with the German question. Independent of Western Union deliberations, the U.S. and British chiefs of staff were considering command relationships in the event of war. A month before Lemnitzer was dispatched to London, they agreed on the Rhine as the initial defense position, and on 23 July the JCS recommended the appointment of a single commander-in-chief of French as well as British and U.S. forces. If the choice would be a U.S. citizen, they proposed General Lucius D. Clay, already in position in Germany. Clay would be responsible to the revived combined chiefs of staff, to which a French member would be added. Among other benefits it would give the French an equality that they had long demanded. Predictably, the British opposed this arrangement.[35]

When Clay's duties as military governor made his appointment impractical, the British proposed a link to the Western Union, because the Brussels Pact powers would be automatically engaged if a conflict broke out in Germany. The Western Union chiefs of staff committee, with an accredited U.S. representative, would be responsible for selecting a supreme allied commander. For subordinate commands, the British recommended a British air officer, in light of the Royal Air Forces' role in training the air forces of the Western Union countries. To satisfy a potential French objection, a French flag officer would be in charge of port facilities. The JCS, always wary about entanglement, agreed to the proposal as long as the Western Union chiefs of staff would report in turn to a combined chiefs of staff.[36] Nevertheless, the JCS wondered if the British support of Clay might be used to relieve Europeans of efforts they might otherwise make toward integrating their forces. The allies could be tempted to substitute U.S. troops for their own. The JCS wanted to make sure that the United States was brought under an integrated command only on the outbreak of war.[37]

Whether or not the United States was wary, this decision would be a step along a slippery slope to the embrace Europeans had been seeking for the past year. The reason for postponing the appointment of a supreme commander was, as French Defense Minister Paul Ramadier observed in September, that the United States was not in a position to take an active part in the command organization at present. It was obvious that the defense committee's hope was that this would be a temporary situation.[38] At least the United States might be persuaded to appoint a U.S. as chief assistant to

Field Marshal Bernard Law, the Viscount Montgomery of El Alamein. This was the Western Union's interim aim in December. Plans for integrating U.S. occupation forces in Germany with the five Western Union powers under operational control of Montgomery surfaced at the same time and may have raised the expectations of the Western Union leaders.[39]

Command relationships had been a subject of a meeting of the JCS and the secretary of defense in Newport, Rhode Island, in the summer of 1948, where the U.S. position was refined. They suggested a British or French allied commander-in-chief with a U.S. deputy. The president approved these plans on 23 August, and the Europeans welcomed them.[40] Still, Truman added, "It is in my opinion however that we must be very careful not to allow a foreign commander to use up our men before he goes into action."[41]

This was an apparent victory for Western Union leaders, in good part because the German front was the venue. But the prospect of a U.S. supreme commander did not survive the summer. The repeated requirement that the United States on European committees would be there only as observers on an unofficial basis spoiled the initial expectations. Instead, the WUDO created a committee of commanders-in-chief to serve until the United States was ready participate on an official basis.[42]

The appointment of a European commander revealed the limits of their success. The choice inevitably would be selected from British or French candidates, and equally inevitably, the process demonstrated the weakness of Europe's defense posture. There were more than enough potential commanders. Montgomery and Alexander from Britain and General Alphonse-Pierre Juin and General Jean-Marie de Lattre de Tassigny from France. General Juin was the first choice of the United States. He had headed French and Allied troops in Italy in 1944 and was chief of the combined general staff of the French armed forces in 1945. He turned down the offer, ostensibly because of his role of commander-in-chief of France's North African forces, a region where he had spent much of his career.

The choice then fell between two prima donnas: Montgomery and General de Lattre de Tassigny; both men, as biographer Nigel Hamilton observed, "vain, ambitious, theatrical, visionary and passionate" in their likes and dislikes.[43] They were also distinguished military leaders. De Lattre de Tassigny had been a division commander before Dunkirk and commander of the First French Army in the final year of the war. Montgomery, the hero of the Battle of El Alamein in North Africa, ended the war as commander of British forces in Germany. The two adversaries vied for the post of commander-in-chief of the Western Union forces.

The Western Union's defense committee solved part of the problem by deciding at the end of September that the land commander-in-chief would be French—de Lattre de Tassigny—the air commander-in-chief British—Montgomery. At the suggestion of the British defense minister, the naval adviser should be elevated to flag officer, Western Europe, a title gratifying to the French, because its mission would be much wider than just the support of Western Union defense. At this point the Dutch defense minister wanted some assurance that the French naval officer would be assisted by high ranking officers from the Netherlands and other member nations. Although he did not mention the commander-in-chief's nationality, he assumed that because of the assignment of a French general as the land commander, the nod would go to the British.[44] Montgomery was the victor in this contest and took office on 5 October. His headquarters, however, was to be in Fontainebleau, nearer to Paris than to London.[45]

This decision was appreciated by the British military establishment eager to be free from Montgomery's overbearing presence as chief of the imperial general staff. As he noted in his memoirs, "By now there were plenty of people anxious to see the back of me. When I recall those days I often think that Whitehall was my least happy theater of war."[46] His appointment as chairman of the commanders-in-chief committee did not make him much happier. Montgomery felt that his position was compromised by being chairman of a committee rather than supreme commander. That position, presumably to be filled by the United States, would become operative only if war broke out. He had other complaints. Theodore Achilles read one of his early secret telegrams from Fontainebleau, which stated that "My present instructions are to hold the line of the Rhine. Presently available forces might enable me to hold the tip of the Brittany Peninsula for three days. Please advise." There was no need for advice. This was the period when Montgomery was saying that all the Soviets needed to reach the Atlantic was an adequate supply of shoes.[47] No one would dispute this judgment.

De Lattre de Tassigny, as number two on the committee, held the land command. Conflict grew out of de Lattre de Tassigny's claim that as commander-in-chief of land forces, he would be responsible directly to the Western Union's defense ministers without reporting to Montgomery. Only in the matter of planning did he consider himself under Montgomery's authority. From de Lattre de Tassigny's point of view, he was in charge of the existing defense forces of the Western Union, while Montgomery could be superceded by a supreme commander in time of war. Montgomery disagreed, and the quarrel deepened over time.[48] With NATO in being, de Lattre de Tassigny presented the Western Union defense committee with an embarrassing situation when he asked for the defense committee's support for his position. The chiefs of staff threw up their hands and admitted that "the constant tension between those two personalities has not yet ceased." They hoped that if the relationship did not improve, the Atlantic Pact could provide an umbrella under which "we might find a chance of settling this problem of personalities."[49]

The differences between the two leaders were never simply personal; they reflected a French concern about placing military power in the hands of a figure whose national interests could be in conflict with France's. While Montgomery could share de Lattre de Tassigny's conviction that "there is no such thing as a battle for France, but for western Europe,"[50] he had no faith in French or other European generals conducting operations on their own. He disparaged the "enormous ignorance" of European high-ranking officers about "the organization needed to create armed forces adapted to modern warfare." Many of them had spent the war years in German prisoner-of-war camps.[51] Given this attitude, de Lattre de Tassigny felt that the continental allies needed assurances that the British could not supply. While a battle for the Rhine would be vital for France and the Benelux partners, the British would give priority to a battle across the Channel. "If an Englishman or even an American is supreme commander they cannot be assured of such a guarantee if sole responsibility [for defense] lies in his hands."[52] Only a European, preferably a Frenchman, could be entrusted with the defense of Continental Europe.

In less temperate terms, General de Gaulle made the same case against a British commander. In a news conference on 1 October 1948, he declared flatly that "Europe cannot be defended in London . . . the question must be taken up again with a France that will have the means to be a center of force and, consequently, of Western strategy."[53] The nub of de Gaulle's argument on 17 November was simply that French forces should not be commanded by a foreigner when the defense of French territory is at stake. He had a case in point in 1945 when his successful intervention assured a French zone of occupation in Germany against the wishes of the Anglo-U.S. allies.[54]

The linking of the United States with Britain as unreliable defenders of Western Europe, implied by de Lattre de Tassigny and expressed by de Gaulle, was not the official French position. General Charles Lechères of the French delegation to the Western Union's military committee raised the issue of the U.S. role in contesting Montgomery's assertion that he might assume the position of supreme commander in the event of war. General Lechères wanted to leave the way open for the appointment of a U.S. supreme commander at that point.[55]

The JCS, however, did not favor a U.S. supreme commander but were willing to consider a U.S. deputy to a supreme commander as long as it was understood that, as in the case of Western Europe air forces, the air commander would not exercise any control over strategic air forces. At the same time, the United States insisted on keeping the U.S. delegates at WUDO headquarters as "observers" present on a "non-member" status. This role was made explicit on 2 December, when the operations officer on the staff of the commander of the U.S. Air Force in Europe flew to Fontainebleau to attend the first meeting of the air section of Montgomery's headquarters.

His flight anticipated a close association despite his presence just as an "observer." It was expected that a small U.S. group would join Montgomery's headquarters on a permanent but still unofficial basis in early 1949.[56]

There was never a real resolution to the conflict over either who was in charge or what the precise U.S. role would be. The fact that it took a committee to house the commanders-in-chief suggested that few results could be expected of this relationship. When the consultative committee met on 25 October, three weeks after the appointment of Montgomery was announced, it was clear that "the exact boundaries of Field Marshal Montgomery's command had not yet been defined."[57]

Between October and the end of the year, Montgomery's committee did its best to appear productive. The French National Assembly provided a credit of $40 million to establish its headquarters in Fontainebleau on the outskirts of Paris. The assumption was that the commanders would be closer to the scene of conflict if war broke out. Had the committee remained in London, it is doubtful if the French would have been so supportive. But when the assembly provided funds, it was on the condition, as the Gaullists insisted, that French sovereignty would not be impaired, that the commanders-in-chief committee be subordinate to the committee of defense ministers, and, most importantly, that Montgomery be just chairman of a committee not a commander-in-chief that could give orders to the French.[58] The committee's assignment was to prepare detailed operational plans for common action in the event of war. While an executive commander of forces would not be in place in peacetime, the officers were prepared to assume operational control in wartime.[59] Or so they asserted. But unless a U.S. supreme commander took control, it was unlikely that a divided committee could cope with the Soviet challenge.

What they could accomplish, they did. It amounted to little. Coordination with General Clay in Germany was touted as a major achievement.[60] But the records of the WUDO show just how little progress was made on pooling and standardization. Although the pooling of resources was the obligation of the military supply board, nothing had been done by January 1949. There was no follow-up of recommendations for distribution of surplus equipment that had been made in September. If there was little action, the Western Union had an excuse: the military supply board "has just been set up."[61] This was the situation in January, and yet the board had been recommended three months before, on 27 September, at the first meeting of the committee of defense ministers.[62]

There is a question whether any of these delays mattered. Montgomery railed about the lack of support, but what could be expected of command by committee? The assumption at all times was that everything depended on the U.S. factor in defense planning. General Lecheres recommended to the chiefs of staff committee, just three days after the announcement of

Montgomery's appointment, that all strategic planning be made in conjunction with the United States. "It was the only way," he claimed, "that the Western Union would be able to make a really economic distribution of effort. If the Americans undertook to plan the defen[se] of North Africa, then additional French resources could be devoted to the battle in Western Europe." Air Marshal Arthur William Lord Tedder, Lechères' British counterpart on the chiefs of staff committee, agreed fully with Lecheres' argument, but because of U.S. sensibilities, "it would be undesirable to make direct reference to the necessity for American assistance in any general statement on the subject."[63]

One of the more telling expressions of European military thinking at the end of the year was the military supply board recommendation that the "U.S. be made aware forthwith of the broad position of deficits, production capabilities and mutual assistance in the WU community." The board indicated that its situation would inspire "an appreciation of the extent to which outside assistance will be required for the Defense forces of the Western Union."[64]

In most matters where the primary issues were related to the military, the British and French foreign ministers were the key players. While Belgium's Paul-Henri Spaak and the Netherlands' Dirk Stikker, and even Luxembourg's Josef Bech spoke out volubly on political, economic, and geographical questions, their military representatives deferred to the two larger powers when it came to recommendations for defense preparations. Only the Dutch defense minister claimed to have something to offer, but beyond expressing the need to coordinate actions with the ministries of finance, his contribution at the second meeting of the defense committee in January 1949 was merely to support the positions of his British and French counterparts.[65]

INITIATING THE MILITARY ASSISTANCE PROGRAM

Lemnitzer's role as a U.S. observer in London and energizer of WUDO did not end with his return to Washington as deputy commandant of the National War College. Four months later he was tapped to be director of the Pentagon's Office of Foreign Military Assistance. As a true believer in the cause, he could not have been more pleased. He relished the secrecy imposed on him as much as he did the hard work. When Forrestal brought him back to the Pentagon in January 1949, he cautioned Lemnitzer that his role would be "super top secret. You can't even breathe this—you can barely think about it." Assigned to a cubicle without windows or furniture, in the D-ring, he went to work with the enthusiasm aroused by his assignment to London six months before, claiming that he "had never worked so much alone in my whole service."[66]

Lemnitzer did not have to work alone for long. He acquired a lieutenant colonel as an assistant and then became part of a team on the Foreign Assistance Correlation Committee (FACC), consisting of able civilian administrators from the State Department and ECA.[67] These actions took place in early 1949. But between Lemnitzer's return to Washington and the end of the year, plans for aid were set in motion—slow motion. In August, military aid priorities were established, with the expectation that the Benelux countries, Canada, France, and Britain would have first priority in military assistance.[68]

While U.S. observers, always on nonmembership status, were attached to the Western Union supply board and the Western Union finance committee to monitor and promote the use of military aid, little progress was made in this period in formulating a defense program that would make use of the aid. Not that there was any disagreement over the need for vital material; it was how to go about arranging it.

The Europeans understood that the United States would screen only coordinated requests, with the further understanding that there would be reciprocal assistance from the potential beneficiaries "to the greatest extent practicable."[69] After the Western Union planned its coordinated defense system with means at hand and determined how their military potential might be increased, the United States would determine the assistance that might be needed. When all the conditions were met, the military would ask for appropriate legislation.

The Western Union's military committee was to deliver the supply plan on 15 November. Unable to meet this deadline, the Western Union chiefs of staff offered an interim list of estimated deficiencies so that some information at least would be available as the basis of congressional action.[70] In place of an overall defense plan, the military committee was able to provide the U.S. representative with only a general statement of policy in which it proclaimed the importance of holding the enemy as far east in Germany as possible and of defending the Brussels Pact countries against air attack. The Western Union chiefs, however, could not do much to implement these worthy objectives other than provide a summary of forces available for mobilization in 1949 and recommend manpower increases on the assumption that the necessary equipment could be obtained.[71]

When the time came for the Western Union to meet the U.S. deadline for specific information on which U.S. aid could be based, the Brussels Pact powers failed and failed badly. There was no breakdown of materiel, troop, and financial deficiencies that would have permitted the kind of detailed screening promised by November to activate a rational military aid program.[72] The JCS accepted instead another interim solution that called for the Western Union chiefs of staff to inform them by the end of November of steps taken to plan Western European defense with means then available as well as of the extent of outside assistance needed. The Western Union chiefs would also provide a progress report on the standardization of equipment, the coordination of production, and the pooling of resources.[73]

Even this deadline for a scaled down version of NSC 9/3 requirements was not met. The best the chiefs could manage was no more than a summary of forces available for mobilization in 1949 and as always depending on U.S. provision of the necessary equipment. Such movement as had begun to pool inventories and production resources was sluggish when it was visible at all. The national lists of deficiencies were incomplete and haphazardly screened.

There was little that the United States could do about the response, or lack of response, of the Western Union allies beyond accepting the results as the basis for its military aid program. Despite the unhappiness of U.S. political and military leaders, there seemed to have been no alternative. No matter how irritating their behavior or deceptive their claims, the Brussels Pact organization members were at the heart of the program. The Western Union was too important to U.S. planners at the end of 1948 for its shortcomings to stand in the way of the impending North Atlantic Treaty. Without the presence of U.S. support of the Western Union, Europe would be like a fireman's role in Greece—ad hoc action wherever trouble erupted—rather than based on the self-help and integration of the Marshall Plan approach.

The slow pace of military assistance planning was not wholly disturbing to the Truman administration. The evasive responses of Europe to U.S. requests were matched by inadequate coordination on the part of U.S. officials in the fall of 1948. But at least some thought had been given to these problems on both sides of the Atlantic, and this was sufficient in an election year, when no further foreign aid legislation could have been considered by the Congress. Furthermore, under the political arrangements worked out in November, substantial military aid would have to follow the creation of the new North Atlantic political alliance, the framework within which the military aid program would operate.[74]

WAS THERE A CONSPIRACY?

In his authoritative history of the Office of Secretary of Defense, Steven L. Rearden observed that "by the end of 1948, despite the Joint Chiefs cautions on certain issues, the United States had moved extremely close to a de facto alliance with the members of the Western Union."[75] The logic of a U.S. military presence side by side with the Brussels allies prevailed over formal objections to linking U.S. troops to the Western Union's defense planning. As long as an attack from the east would have to come through German territory, a central American role was unavoidable. In examining the variety of possibilities of a Soviet assault, both U.S. and European leaders had the Soviet zone of Germany constantly in mind. In January 1949, when French Defense Minister Ramadier suggested that an attack could also be made by German elements from the eastern zone, the United States had a clear answer, one that settled the question about U.S. troops' involvement with the Western Union's defense, namely, that the U.S. military governor in Germany would then join his forces with WUDO's. Even before the Western Union defense committee had considered this subject, Major General A. Franklin Kibler, speaking to the Western Union's military committee about the possibility of Soviet aggression through East Germany, asserted that "any revolutionary movement in Germany would be considered by the American military authorities in the same light as an open aggression."[76]

This centripetal movement came about at the very time both State Department and Department of Defense officials were deprecating the activities of the European allies. When they were not disparaging them, they were venting their exasperation over the transparent attempts to conceal the inadequacies of their efforts. Yet the record of correspondence between London and Washington and of the minutes of the Western Union committees reflect more collaboration, even possible conspiracy, between the United States and Europeans than conflict.

This situation was particularly evident in the role that General Kibler played on WUDO committees in the fall of 1948. As U.S. delegate to the Western Union's military committee, he was present in all its deliberations and was party to its failings and failures as well as to its slim list of accomplishments. In fact, he often seemed to serve as a coach to his European colleagues, pointing out what might or might not win the votes of suspicious U.S. congressmen. On the basic question of U.S. military assistance to the Western Union, Kibler was fully aware of the deficiencies in the first estimate of equipment to be sought from the United States. But while he knew perfectly well how important it was to have the Western Union present a long-term plan, he also knew that there was no time to wait for this solution. So, inadequate as the proposals of the military committee were, he found nevertheless that they "would afford the basis of a reasonable approach to the U.S. Government." As for their possible effect on Congress, he was prepared to guarantee that the Western Union was "making the best use of the means at present available." Hence, he predicted that the European powers had a "fair chance" to make a convincing case to the Congress.[77]

Few doubts about the military committee's ability to meet the NSC's requirements were reflected in Kibler's communications to the Pentagon. Little of the substance of the military committee's deliberations was evident in his notation that the chiefs of staff's "plan will be recommended to Defense Ministers as a basis for an interim approach to United States (it is hoped by

December 1948) for supplementary aid for equipping forces of 5 powers intend to raise in the next year or so."[78] Even when Kibler critized WUDO's practices, he tried to do so discreetly. In responding to JCS dissatisfaction with the piecemeal approach to supply problems, General Lechères complained that Kibler must understand the complexities and difficulties involved in tasks never attempted before. Kibler retreated in the face of this rebuttal. He explained that he did not "imply that the work accomplished was on the wrong lines." He just wanted to alert his European colleagues that the Congress would be unhappy with a report that did not include completed actions by the military supply board.[79]

The U.S. representative at WUDO committee meetings was not always complacent about the behavior of his committee colleagues. In the spring of 1949, when the supply plan turned out to be inaccurate as well as incomplete, Kibler recommended the establishment of a permanent interservice logistical organization as a prerequisite for U.S. aid.[80] He was no more pleased with new recommendations than he had been with the old. The trouble, he claimed, was that the military committee approached the problem from the wrong direction. He urged the Europeans to present lists that made their priorities clear. Then, armed with appropriate information, the military supply board "could come up with a firm production program within present budgetary limitations."[81] But however vehement Kibler may have been about the behavior of the military committee, he did not share these concerns with the JCS. It is no small wonder that his Western Union colleagues on the military committee agreed with him; they had an ally in their corner.

On specific items, Kibler occasionally dissented from the consensus of the chiefs of staff committee. At a meeting of the committee in August, Belgium's Etienne Baele pressed for an immediate decision on standardization in favor of the British .303 rifle, which Montgomery identified as the best field gun available. When Kibler demurred on the grounds that the United States had no intention of abandoning the .300 rifle, the chiefs of staff, at the suggestion of Chairman Tedder, agreed to accept the U.S. judgment that action be deferred. Despite the obvious tensions raised at this session, Kibler's report to the JCS contained only a barebones mention of his inquiry into British advocacy of the rifle.[82] Apparently, Kibler did not want to ruffle the sensibilities of his European colleagues, even at the risk of misleading his superiors in the Pentagon.

It is difficult to escape the conclusion that Pentagon complaints, particularly those of its agents on WUDO committees, against the behavior and policies of the Western Union needed to be taken with a grain of salt. The notion that the Europeans first enticed the United States into their web and then forced them to accept their meager efforts as genuine is not credible. It is obvious that U.S. involvement in WUDO's activities on every level was so intimate that a charge of deception would be meaningless. When the U.S. representatives were not guiding—or controlling—their Western Union counterparts on one issue or another, they were preparing them to win their cases in Washington, whether or not these had substance. And when they were critical of WUDO's minimal efforts at integration, these criticisms were muted in dispatches to the JCS. Kibler and his successor, Lt. General Clarence R. Huebner,[83] were more than passive observers at committee meetings and more than conduits of information from London and Paris to Washington. They were actors on the scene, both influencing their European colleagues and being influenced by them on every major issue.

There was a natural gap between what U.S. military representatives said at meetings and what they reported, or failed to report, in their dispatches. It was not that they were consciously attempting to deceive the JCS. They may not have been aware in many instances of a distinction between the impression they made on fellow members of a committee in London or Fontainebleau and the impression they made in Washington. The differences were more often in tone than in substance. Or they were omissions rather than commissions. Lengthy exchanges in committee meetings were not always accurately encapsulated in a cable. Nuances were missing in some cases, important commentaries in others. What could be discussed in extended sessions face-to-face as recorded in committee minutes in London was not always shared with the generals in the Pentagon. The language of the cables was that of detached observers, as prescribed in their instructions.

In sum, if there was a conspiracy to deceive, then U.S. military representatives abroad were collaborators in it. They were coopted by the exigencies of the times. And they behaved in the same spirit that animated Hickerson and Achilles when they drank toasts to the end of the isolationist tradition. There seemed to have been no choice. A dangerously weak Europe had to be shored up, and to effect this result required convincing congressmen that the principles of the Marshall Plan were working in the military sphere. Inevitably, the measures taken by Europeans to achieve a credible integrated defense system were insufficient. A successful defense of Western Europe by even the most vigorous pooling of efforts or merging of sovereignties was never within the bounds of reality. Change would come only through a major U.S. commitment of resources, and to achieve this was the primary goal of WUDO and its U.S. participants.

WUDO was more than a mythical Potemkin village created by the Western Union in collusion with U.S. military supporters. The activities of its committees were basically exercises to influence the one power that could breathe life into their movements. From the time the Western Union's military committee gathered in London in June, it seemed unable to do more than invent committees with impressive names and equally impressive missions but with no ability or will to live up to their descriptions or to carry out their objectives. Yet Western Europe's groping toward a new integrated defense structure in 1948 deserves greater attention than it has received.

Historians and policymakers have written off WUDO and the Western Union itself as temporary expedients facilitating the security conversations of that year, which led to the signing of the North Atlantic Treaty in 1949. Thereafter, the activities, and even its structure, were subsumed under NATO. There was an element of pathos in Bevin's attempts to rally his colleagues on the consultative council in the summer of 1950 as war in Korea threatened to undermine the concerns of the United States with Europe. He reminded them of the Western Union's potential to become the spokesman for the European component of NATO, only if the Western Union could translate its efforts into facts and prevent the United States from getting the impression "that the Brussels Treaty Powers were not doing their utmost."[84]

NATO has acknowledged only occasionally, and then usually elliptically, its debt to the work of WUDO's committees in 1948. Their names—military committee, military supply board, finance and economic committees—were directly appropriated by the successor organization. Montgomery's commanders-in-chief committee at Fontainebleau was a model for NATO's Supreme Headquarters, Allied Powers in Europe (SHAPE). It is not too much to claim that the Western Union provided the basic infrastructure of NATO. Indeed, it is fitting that the concept of *infrastructure*—installations crossing national borders needed to service multinational armed forces—was itself a symbol of the integration begun under Western Union's auspices. If they survived the birth of a successor organization, it was in part the reluctance of an established bureaucracy to liquidate itself. A more likely reason was Europe's recognition that a Western Union in place, no matter how minimal in strength, might provide a balance to the weight of the senior partner in NATO.

NOTES

1. The National Military Establishment, created under the National Security Act of 1947, became the Department of Defense in 1949. See Steven L. Rearden, *History of the Office of the Secretary of Defense: The Formative Years, 1947–1950* (Washington, D.C.: Historical Office, Office of the Secretary of Defense, 1984), I: 32; Kenneth W. Condit, *The History of the Joint Chiefs of Staff: The Joint Chiefs of Staff and National Policy* (Washington, D.C.: Historical Division, JCS, 1992), II: 99ff.

2. Jamess V. Forrestal to George Marshall, October 21, 1948, *FRUS*, 1948, I: 644.

3. Robert Lovett, memorandum of conversation, April 27, 1948, participants: Marshall, Vandenberg, Dulles, *FRUS*, 1948, III: 105.

4. Report by the National Security Council, NSC 9/2, June 28, 1948, The Position of the United States with Respect to Support for the Western Union and Other Related Free Countries, *FRUS*, 1948, III: 140–41.

5. NSC 14/1, July 1, 1948, note, Executive Secretary on the Position of the United States with respect to Providing Military Assistance to Nations of the Non-Soviet World, *FRUS*, 1948, III: 587–88.

6. George Kennan to Lovett, May 7, 1948, *FRUS*, 1948, III: 117.

7. Kennan to Lovett, 118.

8. Condit, *History of the JCS*, 223.

9. Condit, *History of the JCS*, 224.

10. Lyman Lemnitzer interview, March 21, 1974, 10–12, Historical Office, Office of the Secretary of Defense.

11. NSC 9, The Position of the United States with Respect to Support for Western Union and Other Related Free Countries, April 13, 1948, *FRUS*, 1948, III: 88.

12. Lewis Douglas to Marshall, April 16, 1948, *FRUS*, 1948, no. 1584, III: 89.

13. Joint Message from Ernest Bevin and George Bidault to Marshall, April 17, 1948, *FRUS*, 1948, III: 91.

14. Douglas to Marshall, May 14, 1948, no. 2128, enclosing letter from Jebb and Star-Busman, Secretary of the Brussels Treaty Permanent Commission, *FRUS*, 1948, III:, 124–25; see also Summary Record of Conference of Five Defense Ministers and Chiefs of Staff of Brussels Treaty Powers, London, April 30, 1948, vol. I, PRO Ref DG1/5/29, Western European Union (herafter cited as WEU) Archives, PRO, London.

15. Douglas to Marshall, May 14, 1948, *FRUS*, 1948, no. 2128, III: 124–25; Summary Record, April 30, 1948, appendix E, WEU, PRO Archives, London.

16. Summary Record, April 20, 1948, First Meeting, 6; Foreign Office to His Majesty's Representative at Paris, May 6, 1948, PRO DG 1/4/23, WEU Archives, PRO, London.

17. Douglas to Marshall, July 6, 1948, *FRUS*, 1948, no. 2949, III: 146–48.

18. Major General Ray T. Saddocks, Deputy Director of Plans & Operations memo for Army Chief of Staff, subject: Military Representation in Connection with the Work of the Five Power Military Committee in London, June 29, 1948, 091 P&O files, JCS 1868/7, RG 218, NARA. This memo suggests a limit of eleven officers.

19. Rearden, *History of OSD*, 468–69; Condit, *History of JCS*, 197.

20. Condit, *History of JCS*, 167–68.

21. Memorandum by Director of Joint Staff (Alfred Gruenther) to John Hickerson, July 16, 1948, *FRUS*, 1948, III: 189–93.

22. Lemnitzer interview, March 21, 1974, Historical Office, Office of the Secretary of Defense, Pentagon.

23. *London Daily Express*, June 23, 1948, recorded in U.S. delegation to the Western Union (hereafter cited as DELWU) 3, Lemnitzer to Albert Wedemeyer, director of Plans & Operations Division, Department of Army, Command and Control Support (hereafter cited as CCS) 092, Western Union, RG 218, NARA.

24. L. James Binder, *Lemnitzer: A Soldier for His Time* (Washington, D.C.: Brasseys, 1991), 157–58.

25. Binder, *Lemnitzer*, 157–58.

26. Binder, *Lemnitzer*, 137.

27. DELWU 4, Lemnitzer to Wedemeyer, July 23, 1948, CCS 092, Western Union, RG 218, NARA.

28. DELWU 11, Lemnitzer to Wedemeyer, August 1, 1948, CCS 092, Western Union, RG 218, NARA.

29. DELWU 5, Lemnitzer to Wedemeyer, July 26, 1948, CCS 092, Western Union, RG 218, NARA.

30. Wedemeyer to DELWU, WAR 8661, July 26, 1948, CCS 092, Western Union, RG 218, NARA; DELWU 9, Lemnitzer to Wedemeyer, July 21, 1948 CCS 092, Western Union, RG 218, NARA.

31. DELWU 9, Lemnitzer to Wedemeyer, July 31, 1948, CCS 092, Western Union, RG 218, NARA.

32. Marshall to Lovett, July 23, 1948, *FRUS*, 1948, III: 199–200.

33. Record of Second Meeting of the WU Consultative Council at The Hague, July 19–20, 1948, Report of Military Committee, METRIC Document no. 98, WEU Archives, PRO, London.

34. Record of Second Meeting of WU Consultative Council.

35. Condit, *History of JCS*, 197–98; Rearden, *History of OSD*, 466; Theodore Achilles pointed out that the French never believed that the U.S.-British combined chiefs of staff ceased to exist after the end of World War II, in Achilles, *Fingerprints on History: The NATO Memoirs of Theodore C. Achilles*, edited by Lawrence S. Kaplan and Sidney B. Snyder (Kent, OH: Lyman L. Lemnitzer Center for NATO and European Community Affairs, Kent State University, 1992), 29.

36. Condit, *History of JCS*, 198.

37. Wedemeyer to Commander in Chief, Europe (hereafter cited as CINCEUR, WAR X) 90305, October 6, 1948, Leahy File, RG 218, NARA.

38. M.D. (48) 24 Revised Minutes and Documents of First Meeting of Defense Ministers, Paris, September 27, 1948, 2, PRO Ref DG1/5/30, WEU Archives, PRO, London.

39. *New York Times*, December 14, 1948; *New York Times*, December 18, 1948.

40. Condit, *History of JCS*, 198.

41. Quoted in Rearden, *History of OSD*, 467.

42. F.P. (48) 26, Minutes and Documents of the First Meeting of the Defense Ministers, September 27, 1948, 7, PRO Ref. DG1/5/30, WEU Archives, PRO, London.

43. Nigel Hamilton, *Monty: The Field Marshal, 1944–1976* (London: Hamish Hamilton, 1978), 739.

44. M.D. (48), Minutes and Documents of First Meeting of Defense Ministers, Paris, September 27, 1948, 2–3, PRO Ref DG1/5/30, WEU Archives, PRO, London.

45. Report of Office of Intelligence Research, November 17, 1948, *FRUS*, 1948, no. 4769, III: 276; Achilles, *Fingerprints on History*, 17; as early as August, Marshall expressed his preference for Juin but "the probability is that the French would not put forward General Juin, but someone else less desirable." Marshall, memo for president, August 23, 1948, sub: Western Union Organization of Defensive Forces, in Leahy, memo for secretary of defense; November 24, 1948, sub: Developments with Respect to the Western Union, Confidential Document (hereafter cited as CD) 6-2-49, RG 218, NARA.

46. Viscount Montgomery, *The Memoirs of Field Marshal the Viscount Montgomery of Alamein* (London: Collins, 1958), 453.

47. Quoted in Achilles, *Fingerprints on History*, 17; Montgomery was always doubtful about WUDO's viability; see Hamilton, *Monty*, 731.

48. Hamilton, *Monty*, 732.

49. M.D. (49) 32, Report by the Western Union Chiefs of Staff Committee, November 17, 1949, Western Union Defense Committee: Command in Western Europe, PRO Ref DG1/5/34, vol. VI, WEU Archives, PRO, London.

50. De Lattre Papers, June 20, 1948, M. 110, quoted in Andre Kaspi, "Prelude to NATO: Two Examples of the Integration of Military Forces," in *NATO After Thirty Years*, ed. Lawrence S. Kaplan and Robert W. Clawson (Wilmington, DE: Scholarly Resources, 1981), 196.

51. Montgomery, *The Memoirs of Montgomery*, 509.

52. De Lattre Papers, April 4, 1949, M. 158, quoted in Kaspi, "Prelude to NATO," 196.

53. *New York Times*, October 2, 1948.

54. American Embassy, Paris, to Secretary of State, December 16, 1948, no. 1471, European transmitting translation of article on General de Gaulle's views on Western European defense, 840.00.001–1648. RG 218, NARA; see *New York Times*, October 2, 1948, for speculation that Juin shared de Gaulle's reasoning when he declined appointment as land commander.

55. DELWU 52, A. Franklin Kibler to Wedemeyer, October 7, 1948, CCS 092, Western Union, RG 218, NARA.

56. *New York Times*, December 4, 1948, 4.

57. M.D. (162), Record of the Third Meeting of the Consultative Council, Paris, October 25–26, 1948, WEU Archives, PRO, London.

58. Tel Jefferson Caffery to Marshall, December 28, 1948, no. 6484, 840.00/12–2848, RG 218, NARA.

59. F.C. (49) 29, WUDO, January 7, 1949, Western Union Chiefs of Staff Committee Report on Outside Assistance for Western Union Defense, 2 WEU Archives, PRO, London.

60. Leahy memo for Secretary of Defense, November 24, 1948, sub: Developments with Respect to Western Union, 3, CD6-2-49, RG 218, NARA; F.C. (48) 31, Report by Western Union Chiefs of Staff Committee, December 23, 1948, sub: Aggression in Germany, WEU Archives, PRO, London.

61. F.C. (48) 29, WUDO, January 7, 1949, WU Chiefs of Staff Committee Report, part II: Progress Made towards Improving the Military Potential of Western Union through the Pooling of Resources, Co-ordination of Production and Standardization, 2, WEU Archives, PRO, London.

62. F.P. (48) 24 revised, September 27, 1948, Minutes and Documents of the First Meeting of the Minister of Defense, Paris, 7–8, DG1/5/30, Western European Union Archives, PRO, London.

63. F.C. (48), October 6, 1948, Second Meeting, Chiefs of Staff Committee, DG1/6/36, WEU Archives, PRO, London.

64. M.D (49), January 17, 1949, Minutes of Meeting of the Ministers of Defense, Brussels, January 14, 1949, 30, PRO DG 1/5/31, vol. III, Western European Archives, PRO London.

65. M.D. (162), October 25–26, 1948, Record of the Third Meeting of the Consultative Council, Paris, Western European Union Archives, PRO, London; M.D. (49), January 17, 1949, Meeting of Western Union Defense Committee, Brussels, January 14, 1949, 5,7, PRO DG1/5/31, vol. III, WEU Archives, PRO, London.

66. Quoted in Binder, *Lemnitzer*, 163.

67. *FRUS*, 1949, I: 250n.

68. State-Army-Navy-Coordinating Committee (SANACC) 360/11, August 18, 1948, Report by the SANACC Subcommittee for Rearmament, sub: Military Aid Priorities, *FRUS*, 1948, I: 262.

69. Gruenther, director of the Joint Staff, memo to Hickerson, July 16, 1948, encl. Instructions for the U.S. Representatives Attending the London Western Union Talks, *FRUS*, 1948, III: 190

70. NSC 9/6, November 24, 1948, memorandum by JSC to Forrestal, sub: Developments with Respect to Western Union, *FRUS*, 1948, III: 291.

71. Memo, FC (48), app B to encl A of JCS 1868/58, November 23, 1948, sub: WU Defense Policy, CD6-2-46, RG 330, NARA.

72. Report, JCS 1868/58, February 11, 1949, sub: Military Aid Program, sub: WU Defense Policy, D6-2-46, RG 330, NARA.

73. See footnote 70.

74. F.C (48) 33, December 29, 1948, Western Union Chiefs of Staff Committee memorandum by French Minister of Defense, sub: Defence Efforts of the Five Powers, WEU Archives, PRO, London.

75. Rearden, *History of OSD*, 469.

76. M.D. (49),17 January 1949, First meeting, Defense Committee, Brussels, 8–9, DG 1/5/31 WEU Archives, PRO, London; M.C.(48), November 10, 1948, Fifth meeting, Military Committee, Brussels, 8–9 , DG 1/5/31 WEU Archives, PRO, London.

77. F.C. (48), October 28, 1948, Third meeting, Chiefs of Staff Committee, London, DG 1/6/36, WEU Archives, PRO, London.

78. DELWU 86, Kibler to Wedemeyer, October 28, 1948, CCS 092 Western Union, RG 218, NARA.

79. F.C. (48), December 14, 1948, Sixth meeting, Chiefs of Staff Committee, DG 1/6/36, WEU Archives, PRO, London.

80. M.C. (49), April 21, 1949, Seventeenth meeting, Military Committee, London, DG 1/6/39, WEU Archives, PRO, London.

81. M.C. (49), May 4, 1949, Nineteenth meeting, Military Committee, London, DG 1/6/39, WEU Archives, PRO, London.

82. F.C (48) 3, August 26, 1948, First meeting, Chiefs of Staff Committee, London, DG 1/6/26, WEU Archives, PRO, London; DELWU 92, Kibler to Wedemeyer. October 30, 1948, CCS 092, Western Union, RG 218, NARA.

83. General Clarence Huebner began service on the Chiefs of Staff Committee on December 13, 1948.

84. Records of the Ninth session of the Consultative Council, The Hague, August 1, 1950, DG 1/1/2, WEU Archives, PRO, London.

7

The Hiatus: September–
December 1948

WAITING FOR DEWEY

Once the ambassadors and working group had finished their work and sent off their draft of the North Atlantic Treaty on 9 September to their respective ministries, nothing of any significance was expected to happen until the U.S. presidential election in November. The impression in Europe and in the United States was that the final touches to the treaty would have to await the results of the contest between the Republican candidate, Thomas E. Dewey, and the Democratic incumbent, Harry S. Truman. Put in another way, the policymakers in Washington and in the capitals of the future allies felt that the completion of the treaty awaited the inevitable Republican victory.

Given the prominent role of Republican supporters of the new relationship with Western Europe, particularly Arthur H. Vandenberg and the secretary-of-state-in-waiting, John Foster Dulles, they confidently looked forward to this outcome. Even within the Truman administration, the leading negotiators were either neutral participants in the political process or Republicans, such as Robert Lovett, inheritors of the Roosevelt administration's wartime draft of Republicans Henry Stimson and Frank Knox as secretaries of war and navy, respectively. They should have no trouble applauding a Republican presidential succession.

Yet the notion of complete stasis between September and November can be overdrawn. There was considerable activity in the councils of the future allies, some of it facilitating the postelection drive toward completion of negotiations. But it was the election itself that provided the necessary momentum, even though the results were not what pundits had anticipated.

The assumption that Republicans not only would win the White House in 1948 but would carry out the mission to secure an Atlantic alliance more easily than their Democratic opponents was more apparent in November than in the spring and summer of 1948 before Dewey's nomination. Looking at the Republican Party platform, one can find some deference to the positions of the failed Robert A. Taft candidacy in its emphasizing "the prudent limits of our own economic welfare" and in insisting "on businesslike and efficient administration of all foreign aid." Two lines were given to the welcome and encouragement of "the sturdy progress toward unity in Western Europe." The Vandenberg spirit appeared in the longer passage in support of the UN charter that included assertion of the party's belief in collective security against aggression. The pursuit of the Atlantic alliance might have been more clearly articulated had it not been for the constraints imposed by the remants of the isolationist tradition.[1]

By contrast, the Democratic party had fewer inhibitions in this regard. Its foreign policy plank celebrated the party's success in waging war and establishing an international organization to maintain peace. It claimed that its "pledges were gloriously redeemed under Roosevelt and Truman." It also pledged continuing full financial support for foreign aid to Europe, as opposed to the Republican Eightieth Congress's "reluctance to provide funds to support this program, the greatest move for peace and recovery made since the end of World War II." Unlike the Republican foreign policy plan, the Democrats' plan specifically named the "developing Western European Union" in its promise of "continued support of regional arrangements within the United Nations Charter."[2]

Neither party mentioned the negotiations for an Atlantic alliance then in progress over the summer of 1948. These were enshrouded in secrecy and were too sensitive a subject for the party platforms to address. The most reasonable explanation for the complacency of Europeans over the coming election was the combination of the imprint of the Dewey wing of the Republican Party on prospective policies with the confident expectation, shared on both shores of the Atlantic, that Dewey would be the next occupant of the White House.

The political elites and the national's influential newspapers never doubted that Dewey would be the next president of the United States. Elmo Roper suspended polling early in September, given the overwhelming odds in Dewey's favor. As Clark Clifford, Truman's special counsel, noted, the Democrats did not have sufficient funds to conduct their own polls, while the Republicans saw no need for any more.[3] *Newsweek* queried fifty leading political journalists for its 11 October issue and confimed the conventional wisdom. The survey included the brightest lights of the day—liberal and conservative—James Reston and Arthur Krock of the *New York Times* and the most authoritative of pundits, Walter Lippmann of the *New York Herald-*

Tribune. The vote was unanimous; not one journalist predicted a Truman victory.[4] A week later, the *New York Times* pronounced a premortem judgment with its survey on 18 October pontificating that with 266 Electoral College votes needed for victory, Governor Dewey was sure of 333 from twenty-seven states, compared with Truman's 82 votes from nine states.[5] When that newspaper spoke, the presidential contest was considered finished before it officially began.

This survey did not mean that the newspaper world succumbed to Dewey's charismatic personality or to the special qualities of the Republican Party platform. Dewey's speaking style was soporific, and his speeches were bland. He never bothered to emphasize his success as governor or even to spend time on the campaign trail that Truman took to with such vigor. Republicans who knew him found him hard to take, according to Truman biographer Robert Donovan. "Dewey was an acquired taste. At forty-six, eighteen years Truman's junior, he was too egotistical, too lordly, too overbearing, too didactic, too cold to like easily."[6] On the eve of the election, the London press wrote obituaries of the Truman administration without cheering the expected Dewey victory. The Washington correspondent of the London *Times* called the campaign "a period of undistinguished and pointless argument." Such criticism did not matter. Dewey ran for the presidency as if he were the incumbent.[7] And in retrospect one can hardly blame him.

In September *U.S. News and World Report* ticked off the reasons why the Republicans felt that the campaign was all over except for counting the votes. First, they considered the breakup of the key strands in the Democratic Party. The Progressive Party with its candidate, Henry A. Wallace, would siphon off liberal and even labor votes. Wallace had been secretary of agriculture and later vice president under Roosevelt and, until September 1946, Truman's secretary of commerce. Fired for his opposition to the administration's anti-Communist positions, he attacked the Marshall Plan for its implicit hostility to the Soviet Union and urged a conciliatory policy toward Communists based on mutual disarmament. While not a major threat, the Progressives were given the potential of winning 2 to 4 percent of the votes that Truman might have expected, and these would be in the Northern industrial areas, which he could not afford to lose.

The Dixiecrat party, with South Carolina's governor Strom Thurmond as its candidate, represented a rather different breakaway. Formed to protest to the administration's civil rights program, its appeal was obviously to the solid Democratic South and was presumably a greater threat to Truman's election than were the northern Progressives. *U.S. News and World Report* speculated that even if the Dixiecrats took only a handful of electoral votes—Mississippi and Alabama, for example—the defection could lead to Republicans possibly winning four other Southern states.[8]

But the putative disintegration of the Democratic Party was not the only reason for Republican optimism. The list of obstacles to Truman's survival was long and daunting. The political machines of the big cities, usually a reliable bastion of guaranteed Democratic votes, was cracking up in such places as Chicago and New York. The labor vote itself seemed to be fracturing, with Wallace gathering much of it. Its leaders were generally concentrating on congressional seats rather than on the presidency. So desperate were the Democrats' chances for success in November that prominent figures such as California Congressman James Roosevelt sought to replace Truman with General Eisenhower, even though neither Roosevelt nor other Democrats knew or cared about his party affiliation.[9] It was hardly surprisng that in this environment the Democrats were running out of money for their campaign.

When Truman fired back, as he did with increasing vehemence in the weeks before the election, he targeted the Eightieth Congress as his nemesis, repeatedly calling it the worst Congress in the nation's history. This charge overshot the mark. It was the Eightieth Congress that approved the Marshall Plan, signed the Rio pact, and set the nation on the course of an alliance with Western Europe. As the *New York Times* editorialized, "It could be argued that the President received better support for much of his program from the Eightieth Congress, which was Republican, than he did from the Seventy-ninth, which was Democratic."[10]

To make matters worse for the Democrats, the contentious competition for the Republican nomination in the spring and summer of 1948 that pitted Senator Taft, the heir of the isolationist tradition, against Dewey seemed to evaporate in the fall. Republican unity was spurred on by the impending landslide in November. The ideological differences between the two men were not unbridgeable, according to Taft's most authoritative biographer. By September, Taft had observed that Dewey might turn out to be "more conservative than we true liberals."[11] Certainly, no one—Old Guard Republicans or the Vandenberg internationalists—should have been disturbed by the tone and content of Dewey's speeches. They were filled with platitudes intended to keep foreign policy out of the contest. He felt that he did not need to emphasize differences over relations with Western Europe with Truman to nail down his victory.

Rarely did Dewey's speeches cause any difficulties with future European allies. But when he strayed from the consensus about a Europe united against Communist penetration, as he did when he was too specific about the form of unity Europe might take, he ruffled British feathers. It was one thing to speak well in general terms of European federation, especially when it evoked memories of U.S. federation under the Constitution; it was a challenge, however, to the British conception of European unity to say on the stump in Albuquerque, New Mexico, that "divided into sixteen separate and weak nations, each one is an invitation to attack. But united in a strong federation of nations, they would be an enormous bulwark to peace."[12]

The British resented the implication that they would be failing U.S. expectations if they opposed a European federation of the kind that France had been advocating since the summer. Early in October in Paris, George Marshall had to listen to Ernest Bevin's unhappy reaction. He wanted Marshall to recognize the delicacy of the federal question in the Western Union. It conjured up a European parliament that would contain "at least a third communist representation and would provide a perfect Communist Trojan horse in any such group." While Britain had taken major steps toward unifying Western Europe through the Brussels Pact and in negotiations for an Atlantic Pact, it had to take into consideration its relations with the British Commonwealth. In brief, he warned Marshall that the United States would be nourishing "bad blood" between the two countries if the British people perceived that the price of U.S. aid was an unacceptable form of European federation, as Governor Dewey's speech in Albuquerque seemed to indicate.[13]

This was only a minor tempest. Marshall responded by placing Dewey's language in a larger context. Since Winston Churchill's widely publicized leadership in support of European federation had a considerable effect on U.S. public opinion, he felt that it was against this background that the governor was speaking.[14] Marshall was closer to the reality than Bevin on this point. It was unlikely that Dewey had an anti-British agenda in making this and other speeches on European federation. As the campaign was coming to a close, Dewey was reported as saying "Europe must federate or perish," without bringing British wrath down on his head.[15]

For the most part, relations with Europe were not a serious preoccupation in the speeches of either party. The Democrats claimed credit for the major developments of the postwar years, while the Republicans reminded their audiences that the Republican leaders were responsible for all the significant actions that took place in the Republican Eightieth Congress.

There was one instance, however, when both parties claimed to have inspired the idea of a bipartisan foreign policy. Dewey precipitated the controversy in a speech in Louisville on 12 October by claiming that he had "founded" the nonpartisan U.S. foreign policy. There were no doubts about his authorship—in his eyes: "We have abandoned partisanship to speak through a bipartisan foreign policy. That was the great objective when I first proposed to Secretary Hull during the election campaign four years ago that we have cooperation between our two parties to win the peace. That was the beginning of our bipartisan foreign policy. Due to the bipartisan foreign policy I founded, our unity has been saved." His accolade to bipartisanship and to himself for proposing it was accompanied by further comments that Republicans not only originated the concept but improved whatever initiatives the Democrats had made since World War II. He deplored deviations the Truman campaign had made from this bipartisan policy.[16]

Dewey's assertion of his authorship of the new tradition brought immediate contradiction from former Secretary of State Cordell Hull. The initiative was his in 1944, broached in an effort to keep the formation of a new world security organization out of the presidential campaign. While giving credit to Dewey and Dulles for carrying out the agreement for a bipartisan approach to the new UN, he objected to the implication "that his party had taken the initiative in reaching it, and thus should have the credit for it. I finally drew up a statement that the President made public, calling attention to the origin of the agreement and the role I had played in it."[17]

What inhibited partisan impulses over this contretemps was the insistence of both parties that bipartisanship still animated their behavior. Sure of his coming victory, Governor Dewey praised Republican behavior in the election year "by which we can speak in one voice in the crisis we face." Not that criticism was wholly absent. He chastised the inability of the Truman adminstration through its "clumsiness, weakness and wobbling" to take advantage of the benefits a bipartisan foreign policy had given to the nation.[18] But almost to the end of the campaign, the Republicans abstained from doing much more than complaining about the lack of credit Vandenberg or Dulles had received from the administration. Dewey essentially pledged to continue and improve on the cooperation that he had begun in World War II.

Despite expectations of an easy victory on 2 November, the Republicans could not resist the temptation to take advantage of a lapse in Truman's conduct toward the Soviets. While Truman's seemingly impulsive intention to send Chief Justice Fred Vinson to Moscow to discuss major East-West differences never materialized, it generated anxieties in Europe. A radio talk scheduled for 5 October to announce the mission was cancelled, largely because Marshall feared that it would torpedo a plan forged by the Western nations to arraign the Soviets in the UN over the Berlin blockade.[19]

Senator Vandenberg found the president groping for some way to "spectacularly associate himself" with the negotiations in Paris, even if the Vinson mission did not get off the ground. He felt that Truman needed "a shot in the arm" to energize a failing campaign in its last days.[20] Senator Taft jumped into the fray after the plan was discarded, asserting that the Vinson mission would undercut the U.S. position at the UN and discredit the efforts of Secretary Marshall.[21]

Dewey's reaction was more nuanced. He recognized that Truman's proposal would help Communism at home and abroad. But assuming the mantle of a statesman, Dewey admitted there were no easy answers to the question of how to secure peace. "But of one thing we can be sure," he noted in a speech in Cleveland a week before the election; "we shall not achieve peace by conducting these desperately important matters on a happy-thought basis or by jovially remarking that we like good old Joe." The "happy thought" was a swipe at the impulsive act of Truman to send Vinson to Moscow and the "good old Joe" image referred to the president's naïveté in dealing with the dictator. Dewey promised that his would be an administration that would work for peace "calmly and patiently, that would work day and night to build up the strength of the cause of freedom, and, while refusing to appease Russia, would extend the hand of friendship to every country."[22]

Dewey's attack over the aborted mission might have been stronger. The Vinson affair was made to order to condemn the behavior of an impetuous president who was unaware of the damage he could create for the UN meeting in Paris and insensitive to the implications of dragging the Supreme Court into the international arena for political advantage. But Dewey was also aware that excessive politicizing of the Vinson affair could increase uneasiness in Europe and make life needlessly difficult for him as president-elect. It was one thing to attack the sitting president for mishandling the Soviets and misunderstanding the dangers of Communism; it was quite another when as winner at the polls a few weeks later he would have to live with the fallout in Europe. Off the record, he told reporters: "If Harry Truman would just keep his hands off things for another few weeks! Particularly if he would keep his hands off foreign policy, about which he knows considerably less than nothing."[23] This relatively mild response to a major Truman gaffe reflected the confidence the Republican Party had in the outcome of the election.

ENTR'ACTE—SEPTEMBER–OCTOBER 1948

The momentum driving the allies toward the conclusion of an Atlantic alliance was stalled but not stopped in September and October 1948. That the pace slowed almost to a standstill was inevitable, as the presidential election in the United States dominated the news. For once, France's Henri Bonnet could speak for fellow ambassadors on 10 September at the seventh meeting of the Washington exploratory talks when he observed that the draft of the Washington Paper would offer a complete picture of the status of the negotiations, so that "nothing could be gained by discussion of the paper at this time."[24]

Given this attitude, whatever advances possible were made in a leisurely fashion, with the understanding that quick decisions would not accelerate the negotiating process. The baby steps taken by the British with the Washington Paper illustrated the situation. The Western Union's defense committee was expected to approve it on 8 October but not present it to the Cabinet for security reasons. The paper would then go to the Permanent

Commission of the Brussels Treaty on 12 October and then to the Western Union's foreign ministers at the Consultative Council on 26 October. After the British government gave its final approval, it would take soundings with the Scandinavians and other possible members of the new alliance. When Nicholas Henderson of the British embassy in Washington wondered if this schedule was too slow, Theodore Achilles assured him that not much could be done anyway before November.[25]

To underline this point, John Hickerson expressed discomfort with the recommendations from the Western Union's Consultative Council on 25–26 October to negotiate a final text of the treaty with the United States and Canada and to do so in Washington, "the most suitable place for the negotiations." Canada had already notified the United States on 13 October that it was ready to to enter into a treaty along the lines of the Washington Paper of 9 September.[26] But the implication in the instructions to be given to the heads of mission was that the definitive actions would be taken quickly. Hickerson disabused the Brussels Pact allies of any early expectation of results. As he pointed out, the U.S. representatives were not in a position to commit their government to any agreement until congressional leaders had been fully consulted. It was obvious that 29 October, just a few days before the election, was too early to make any promises.[27]

Hickerson's response should not have come as a surprise to the European allies. They knew that there had been no official interchanges with Washington on an Atlantic pact since September. Marshall himself had not discussed the subject with Robert Schuman at all, despite the secretary of state's presence in Paris throughout October. Marshall's spokesmen denied any knowledge of impending negotiations. Not until the inauguration of a new president in January could there be any official commitment beyond the general blessing of the Vandenberg Resolution.[28]

But were the allies, especially the French, as firm in their support for an Atlantic alliance as the October decision suggests? While Schuman was ready to say more clearly than Georges Bidault that NATO was a vital complement to the Brussels Pact and that the French government now accepted "without reservation the principle of a contractual collaboration with the United States," Defense Minister Paul Ramadier was more reserved. He feared the consequences of placing French foreign policy under foreign control. Ramadier was concerned, as René Massigli pointed out, about France becoming a client state of the United States.[29]

THE STEPPING-STONE STATES

While the Brussels Pact powers anxiously awaited the results of the presidential election, the long pause permitted both the United States and the

Europeans to consider more fully the enlargement of the new alliance and the reactions of the countries to be approached.

During the Washingon meetings in the summer, the Europeans did their best to avoid the subject and failed. Lovett had raised the possibility on 9 August of an expanded Brussels Pact at the fifth session of the Ambassadors's Committee that would emphasize the Atlantic character of the alliance as well as the significance of a bridge from the United States to Europe facilitating the supply of aid to the European allies. Hence, Denmark's Greenland, Norway's Spitsbergen, and Portugal's Azores became subjects for discussion against the wishes of the core nations. Progress foundered over George Kennan's recommendation for a two-pillar arrangement wherein the Scandinavian nations, Iceland, and Portugal would have a subsidary role in NATO as opposed to Hickerson's advocacy of full membership.[30] These conflicting approaches had to contend with the possibility of a separate Nordic defense organization that Sweden envisaged as a neutralist bloc between the United States and Russia.

The Washington Paper of 9 September had finessed the issue. It recognized that "a North Atlantic security system composed exclusively of the United States, Canada, and the present parties to the Brussels Treaty would not be fully effective" and that the new alliance would have to provide for the security of the stepping-stone nations. At the same time, the paper suggested different categories of membership, with full membership only for those nations capable of fulfilling the obligations undertaken by the United States, Canada, and the Western Union. Such countries as Norway or Portugal or Ireland "may not now be prepared to accept fully the requisite responsibilities" and so should be invited "to accede to the Pact with limited commitments, the exact nature of which would be determined in negotiation with them."[31]

Given the open-ended language of the Washington Paper, it was reasonable to assume that the subject of expanded membership would be further explored in the fall of 1948. The Scandinavian connection was a major area of diplomatic activity for the United States. A Scandinavian foreign ministers' conference in early September ended with an agreement to study defense problems but with no requirement to accept the Swedish neutrality position. U.S. military aid was critical to any resolution from the Norwegian and Danish points of view. Should defense arrangements fail to be settled by the beginning of 1949, Denmark hoped that Congress would be ready by that time to consider military aid to the Scandinavian countries. This certainly was an expectation all three northern nations anticipated. Sweden, the prime mover in putting together a Nordic bloc, would have been happy to have a unilateral military security guarantee from the United States.[32]

While Denmark's Foreign Minister Gustav Rasmussen saw this development as assuring Scandinavia's adherence to the western bloc, the U.S.

ambassador to Sweden, H. Freeman Matthews, was not at all convinced that this would be the outcome. Rather, it could give Sweden confidence in its ability to fashion a Nordic bloc that would enjoy U.S. military aid and even a security guarantee without having to join an alliance. "To give any such 'guarantee' even in the most tenuous form would be contrary to all we are working for here."[33]

The question of the involvement of Scandinavian countries in the prospective Atlantic alliance consumed the time and attention of U.S. diplomats in the fallow period between September and December. The exploratory talks of the Ambassadors' Committee and the international working group had made it clear that the Western allies would have to accept, no matter how reluctantly, a Scandinavian relationship. U.S. access to Norwegian and Danish territories was a prerequisite for aid to any of the members. It was frustrating, then, for both the United States and the Western Union to find divisions within Scandinavia on the subject. Denmark leaned toward neutrality if it could manage it, and Sweden had no doubt about its stance. They wanted U.S. aid without strings attached. This position was unacceptable to U.S. negotiators. When the Swedes asked privately if they would still be eligible for aid if they did not accept the treaty, they were told, as Achilles noted, "that would be possible only if there was anything left after the needs of members had been satisfied."[34]

As far as the State Department was officially concerned, Norway and Denmark should receive invitations to become full partners on the condition that their territories would be in the service of the alliance. "We do not favor one-way commitments," as Lovett observed on 17 November. If Sweden were attacked without becoming a party to the alliance, all that would be granted would be consultation. Isolating the Swedes might be the best way to change their minds about joining the alliance.[35]

Only Norway, with the vivid memory of its sufferings in World War II, was anxious to participate in an Atlantic association. It was Norway, after all, that raised the alarm with Britain and the United States less than a year before over Soviet overtures for a nonagression pact. Foreign Minister Halvard Lange was an ardent advocate for a U.S. connection despite Norway's vulnerability to a Soviet assault, a geographical situation that Denmark did not face. Because the Norwegians speculated that full membership might make Norway the first point of an attack, a U.S. obligation to come to their aid might produce the badly needed counterweight to Soviet pressure.[36] Still, Norway did agree to join a Scandinavian Defense Committee in mid-October, designed to support Sweden's intention to stay out of any Western alliance. If Norway did not withdraw from the committee, it was only because of the government's need to convince its public that it was doing all it could to work out a satisfactory alternative system of Scandinavian defense. When the effort failed, Norway ultimately tilted a wavering Denmark toward the West. In a speech to Minnesotans, Prime Minister Wilhelm Morgenstierne underscored Norway's stance in declaring that "Norwegians would rather die tomorrow on their feet than live a thousand years on their knees."[37]

No such dramatic language was heard in Iceland. In fact, if Iceland were to join the Atlantic alliance, the issue of a U.S. base that had been settled in 1946 would be raised again. Iceland's foreign minister implied a positive view of the alliance, but the government insisted on being consulted before the pact was made public He felt that it would be "highly advisable" to make such an announcement in the company of Norway and Denmark.[38]

The Scandinavian issue was not settled in this period. At the meeting of the Western Union's Consultative Council on 25–26 October for concluding plans for an Atlantic pact, the delegates noted that the Scandinavian countries had been approached about future membership. When they had asked "for more time to consider the matter," the Western Union Council members seemed relieved. They had no wish to increase the number of countries involved beyond the core seven. Steps to increase the number of members would only delay the final negotiations. An invitation to Italy, for example, would raise difficulties with Greece and Turkey. It went without saying that bringing in new partners would decrease the size of each member's share of U.S. military assistance.[39]

Given the importance that the United States placed on stepping-stone nations as air and naval bases for aid to Western Europe, Portugal should have been as acceptable as the Scandinavian countries. Its main service to the alliance would be the Azore Islands, some 2,400 miles west of Portugal in the Atlantic, over one-third of the way to the Americas. If this was not the case, the reason primarily was its Fascist government under dictator Antonio Salazar. The objections came primarily from northern Europeans and from Canada. Foreign Minister Norman Pearson expresssed his discontent over inviting Portugal to be a charter member of the alliance, even before the Washington talks began in July. He wondered about the anomaly of having Portugal join an organization dedicated to a democracy and free institutions. Britain's Gladwyn Jebb responded that it would be even more a problem to exclude Portugal in light of the Azores's future role. This of course was also the U.S. position. It prevailed, even though the Washington Paper in September suggested a special category for nations outside the Western Union whose territorial integrity if endangered would require a NATO response. Nothing came of this possibility, although Escott Reid in retrospect wondered why Portugal could not grant military bases in the Azores under a treaty with the United States, just as Spain had done with the submarine base in Rota.[40]

The primary sticking point with most of the allies was Portugal's unwillingness to participate unless Spain would also be a member. This was a more sensitive matter for the Europeans, particularly for the Dutch and Scandinavians, than for Britain and the United States. The British and French military as well as the U.S. military would prefer to have a reformed Spain participate, although they recognized the political impossibility of their allies accepting Francisco Franco as a partner.[41] What might have made this possible was the Communist threat, but this consideration was not strong enough to overcome the hostility of northern Europeans to bringing Fascist Spain, an Adolf Hitler ally in World War II, into the company of democratic nations.

From the U.S. perspective, Salazar's neutrality in World War II, his concern about Communism in general, and the pro-American stance of the average Portuguese citizen buttressed by immigrant connections in the United States made Portugal amenable to a NATO alliance under benevolent U.S. auspices. The undemocratic nature of the Salazar regime diminished in significance when compared with benefits the Azores would bring. To win over the ruling class fearful of Communism but also fearful of "the undermining influence of democratic contacts" required sophisticated diplomacy to succeed.[42] Europeans like Paul-Henri Spaak grudgingly accepted the U.S. argument, with the recognition that Portugal's traditional relationship with Britain would weaken Brussels Pact opposition.[43]

Achilles was proud of his role in reducing, if not removing, Portuguese suspicions that Britain and France had designs on its African colonies. He drafted a personal message from Truman to Salazar stating that the United States shared Portuguese reluctance to get entangled with an integrated Western Europe. As an oceanic country, the U.S. concern for Atlantic security was an important reason for the United States and Portugal, another oceanic country, to become involved in an alliance. Achilles felt that his argument succeeded, although no agreement was made in 1948.[44]

Spain's acceptability to the allies was another matter. To West Europeans, the Franco regime was anathema, rightly shunned by the UN that had called for withdrawal of ambassadors in 1946. It was unfit to be part of the West's democratic community. Spain's Fascism may have been less dangerous than Soviet Communism, but from a moral standpoint, it was equally repulsive.[45] Norway's independent newspaper, *Verdens Gang*, argued that "the viewpoint that Fascism is the most effective bulwark against Communism is basically false and vulgar."[46] The London *Observer* praised Bevin for standing up to the U.S. military lobby's efforts to bring Spain into the Western Union: "Even in terms of hard-boiled realism, such a policy would be an unforgivable blunder. It would give the death-blow to French morale, split Britain from top to bottom, and would greatly reduce the prospects of bringing Scandinavia and Italy into the Brussels alliance."[47]

The U.S. attitude toward Spain was more complicated. Although Franco's government reminded most U.S. citizens of his alliance with the Nazis in

World War II, there were many in Congress and in the press who could put aside these memories in the face of the Communist menace. Some of the pressure to bring Spain into an alliance came from the military and their allies in the Senate. Chad Gurney of South Dakota, chairman of the Armed Services Committee, and U.S. officers accompanying him on a visit to Spain were impressed with the morale of Franco's army, the ports and airfields Spain could offer, and his long-standing reputation in the anti-Communist cause. Gurney recommended resumption of diplomatic relations with Franco Spain.[48]

At the UN General Assembly meeting in Paris in October, Secretary Marshall noted in his talks with Schuman and Bevin that recognition of Spain was not a particular problem for the United States but recognized the difficulties such an action would make for Britain and France. Acting Secretary of State Lovett nonetheless had to clarify Marshall's remarks, saying that there was no intention to reverse the government's policy toward Spain even though the United States had doubts about the effectiveness of the UN's resolution recommending cessation of diplomatic relations with Spain.[49]

Marshall must have been well aware of congressional pressure to bring Spain into the Marshall Plan. Liberal Democratic Senator Dennis Chavez of New Mexico did not approve of the Fascist state, and claimed that he might have been jailed had he been a Spaniard. But "we are fighting communism. . . . Why should we tell the Spanish people or any other people what kind of government they should have? If Greece or Portugal are acceptable as beneficiaries in the fight against communism, why not Spain?" Although conservative Democrat Walter George of Georgia agreed with Chavez's sentiments, he pointed out that the Western European countries did not invite Spain to the conference on the Marshall Plan, which prevented Spain from becoming a beneficiary of this form of U.S. aid.[50] Congressman L. Mendel Rivers of South Carolina was outraged that the United States was held hostage to the judgments of Europeans. After a visit to Spain, he wanted to help that country economically and militarily: "We must help people we know we can trust." His implication was that Franco with his anti-Communist history was a more reliable partner than the Western Union allies, a stance that perplexed the *New York Times* military correspondent Hanson Baldwin, given Spain's role in World War II.[51]

In light of the differences between Europe and the United States over the role of Spain, Franco had hopes of using the Soviet threat to establish a special tie with the United States, if not with the Western Union. He managed to do just that with the United States but not with the Western Europeans.[52] As the year ended, Spain would not be either a beneficiary of the Marshall Plan or a member with Portugal in the Atlantic alliance. Spain remained one more grievance in transatlantic relations as the alliance was being framed.

THE CASE OF ITALY

"The case of Italy presents a particular problem." These were the words of
the Washington Paper of 9 September.[53] Italy had been perplexing Europeans and the United States from the beginning of negotiations for the
Brussels Pact. That its fate was important was demonstrated in the winter
and early spring of 1948 when a Communist victory was possible. Once
that crisis had passed, there was the question of where Italy fitted into the
larger scheme of European security.

That country's future had been a frequent subject of discussion in the exploratory talks of the summer, one without resolution. The United States
was its primary champion, but its position was not at all clear to the Western Union allies. Hickerson was a stalwart backer of Italian membership in
the alliance as a means of preventing the resurgence of Communism and of
ensuring the security of France's flank, while Kennan wanted to restrict
membership to Atlantic rim countries.[54] West Europeans in general were as
cool as Kennan to Italian membership either in the Western Union or in the
Atlantic alliance. As the Washington Paper emphasized, Italy was not a
North Atlantic country, and besides, it was subject to military limitations in
the peace treaty with this former Axis nation. How much help could it give
the alliance?[55] The summer ended with no resolution to the question beyond Hickerson's statement that the U.S. government preferred that the
Western Union partners take the initiative in resolving Italy's relationship to
the North Atlantic security pact.[56]

The Italian question did not end here. Europeans had little incentive to move
on the issue in the fall. Italian leaders had the impression, and accurately, one
could say, that the Western Union did not want them. They preferred then a bilateral arrangement for U.S. aid and a security guarantee. Moreover, Ambassador James Dunn sensed a reluctance on the Italian side to become too involved with the Brussels Pact for fear that Italy might have to give up hopes for
regaining its former African colonies as the price of admission.[57]

Irrespective of Italian or Western Union preferences, Hickerson had no
intention of giving up his plans to bring Italy into the alliance, and in November he emphasized to the embassy in Belgium that the United States
was anxious to see Italy included as an original member. As for membership in the Brussels Pact, that would be up to the partners to decide, but
stalling over revision of the World War II treaties was unacceptable. To make
the inclusion of Italy more palatable to the allies, he agreed that participation "must be on the basis of existing military clauses of [the] peace
treaty."[58] France's seemingly abrupt reversal of its opposition to Italy at the
same time bolstered Hickerson's advocacy, although France had its own reason for the change: Italy's membership would strengthen its own case for
the inclusion of Algeria.

Hickerson's seeming triumph over Kennan was short-lived as Canada's Reid noted.[59] The policy planning committee's chairman was persuasive enough to force the working group's report at the end of the year to admit that there was no agreement to bring Italy into the pact as an original member. Only the French representatives were left as Italy's supporters, although the Benelux countries were not opposed in principle. The United States settled for reinforcing "Italy's natural ties with the West . . . preferably by simultaneous association in some mutually acceptable form with the Brussels and Atlantic Pacts." This Delphic judgment was made easier by a recogniton that Italy's membership would arouse undue expectations in Greece and Turkey.[60]

The Turkish government based its case in part on Italian adherence to the alliance, asserting that any mutual defense undertaking by Western Europe must take into account the Mediterranean area and include Turkey. Under ordinary circumstances, an Atlantic alliance with Turkey "would have seemed abnormal. . . . Today such an alliance can seriously be contemplated."[61] Turkey's appeal only assured postponement of Italy's participation. So as 1948 ended, Italy, like Portugal, remained in limbo.

EUROPEAN FEDERATION REDUX

The pause in the negotiating process for an Atlantic alliance allowed other issues left from the summer to be mulled over once more, sometimes—but not always—to good effect. A major problem centered on the differences between the British and French approaches to European unity, although as noted previously, it intruded into the presidential campaign as well. Bevin had told the cabinet on 10 September that he wanted to display a positive British face toward European unification, and five days later talked to the House of Commons about building a European Union free from control of both the United States and Russia. This was language that the Western Union allies could appreciate, but it was qualified by requiring a British connection to the Commonwealth. Still, it could appeal particularly to the French at a time when *Le Monde* had identified both the United States and the Soviet Union as menaces to Western Europe, even if the U.S. menace was less dangerous than the Russian. Both threatened "the European spirit."[62] But Bevin's language also meant no immediate action on a European constitution, which would be "putting a roof on before we have built the building." This position, in the opinion of R. W. G. Mackay, a dedicated Europeanist and dissident Labour MP, placed Bevin and the Labour Party as the chief stumbling blocks to European federation.[63]

Throughout September and October, Bevin continued to talk with the French and to a lesser extent with the United States about European cooperation. When the UN met in Paris in October, Bevin tried to press upon the unreceptive French a proposal for regular high level Western Union meetings on the subject to show the public his continuing interest. The French wanted more and continued to assert that an assembly should be a specific objective that would impress the U.S. as well as the European public; an assembly would also bind the Germans more closely to a united Western Europe.[64]

Both sides backed off a little. Schuman agreed to abandon the Franco-Belgian idea of a European assembly if no satisfactory arrangement could be made, while Bevin proposed creating a new body, a council of Europe.[65] Bevin's language and sentiment were typically British. The new council would grow over the years, without a written constitution. It would achieve a distinct European identity by evolutionary rather than legal formulas. The council would resemble a miniature assembly of the UN but without vetoes and without limitations on the sovereignty of the member nations.

The result once more was a special Western Union committee to consider a greater measure of unity among the European counries with a subsequent report to the governments of the five Brussels Pact countries. Headed by Edouard Herriot, president of the French assembly, it ran into the familiar roadblocks, namely, the differing views of Britain and France.[66]

Had Churchill been appointed a member of the British delegation, chances of resolving the differences might have been brighter. Churchill certainly wanted to participate. Writing to Prime Minister Clement Attlee, he assumed that political parties would be represented and that he would "be glad to be consulted about the choice of suitable members of the Conservative Party." Attlee not only rejected Churchill's advice but made it clear that the British delegation would not be bipartisan; the committee would be represented by governments and be responsible to governments. Churchill responded that it would be "a misfortune if His Majesty's Government persists in trying to treat this great cause as a monopoly of the British Socialist Party." Churchill's reference to "Socialist" was intended as an insult, and Attlee responded in kind; he chose Hugh Dalton to be head of the British delegation with his well-known opposition to the French version of European unity.[67]

Even though *Le Monde* saw some hope for the prospects of the new Herriot committee, it was obvious by the end of the year that Anglo-French differences over steps toward European federation had not been bridged.[68] Jean Chauvel, secretary-general of the French Ministry of Foreign Affairs, made a point of contrasting Britain's lukewarm support of a European assembly with Belgium's enthusiastic endorsement.[69] Ultimately, Bevin accepted Schuman's consultative assembly, and Schuman accepted Bevin's council of Europe, but the French grand vision that had been floated at the Hague Congress in July was never realized. Arguably, the most that France gained from its position was moving Belgium from its position as the suspicious junior partner that it had been during the framing of the Brussels Pact in the winter of 1948. Massigli gave credit to Spaak for brokering a compromise on the authority to be granted a European assembly, allowing *"les details viendraient plus tard."*[70]

THE PERENNIAL GERMAN QUESTION

In this atmosphere of mutual suspicion, Anglo-French rivalry simmered during the doldrums of September and October. Conflict over the future of Germany was a volatile issue between the two nations and between France and the United States as well. While Britain was a source of annoyance to the French, their major adversary was the United States. On the surface the settlement of control of the Ruhr with its traditional industrial might was the most contentious problem. Certainly, it was the most visible one in the autumn months of the hiatus. The nub of French protest was over the Anglo-U.S. initiative to have the trusteeship of the Ruhr's coal, iron, and steel industries ultimately dissolved. Its eventual ownership would be left to the determination of a freely elected German government. The issue of the trusteeship itself with its international controls was seemingly settled in June, but in fact was unsettling enough to French public opinion to contribute to Bidault's removal from office in July. But to have a solution that explicitly returned sovereignty to a future German state was more than any French official could accept in the fall of 1948.[71]

When General Lucius Clay preempted the work of the London conference on the Ruhr, scheduled for November and December, he infuriated the French and united all their fractious parties against the United States. On Armistice Day, a particularly poor choice of timing, he issued Law No. 75 that handed over interim management of Ruhr industries to German trustees along with a reassurance of Germany's final ownership. His action ignited a firestorm in France. Reston perceived the State Department that usually deplored Clay's "parade-ground diplomacy" quietly applauding his initiative.[72] Schuman, Bidault's successor as foreign minister, berated his allies for imposing a fait accompli just two days before the conference was to meet. While admitting that much of French policy toward Germany was not realistic, he was aware that the French people did not realize that France would have to abandon some of its positions with respect to Germany. His opposition to the action of the military commander was primarily over the timing of the affair.[73]

The U.S. response to France's reaction was to underscore its conviction that the international ownership that France wanted would not increase the nation's security; it would just add another financial burden for the U.S.

taxpayer. Beyond this reality, the United States professed that continued internationalization of the Ruhr would hurt both the French and German economies as well as stoke the fires of German nationalism. France's security should be embedded in a stronger economic and political organization in Western Europe.[74]

France was not placated. In Washington, Bonnet repeated the familiar French line, namely, that adequate security in the Ruhr could only be achieved through international ownership.[75] When the London conference opened, Hervé Alphand, director of economic services at the Quai d'Orsay, began with a strong condemnation of the U.S.-UK bizonal Law no. 75 for its decision to allow a German government to determine the final settlement of the ownership of the coal and steel industries. Foreign Minister Schuman was less strident in his criticism. While he conceded that it was necessary to revive and promote German production for the general benefit of European recovery, it was dangerous to follow the path the military governors took upon themselves in giving excessive powers to a future German government.[76]

Clay, fearing that the diplomats would try to water down the law in the face of French protests, emphasized that it would be a serious error to undermine the authority of a "single U.S. head" in Germany. He pointed out that the U.S. representative of the Ruhr Authority must be responsible to the military governor as long as he was responsible for U.S. expenditures in Germany.[77] Clay received some backhanded endorsement for his undiplomatic posture when Marshall made it clear that the general was speaking for the U.S. government, even if his actions "might have been somewhat clumsy."[78] But the United States did soften its position on control of the Ruhr when the British agreed with Marshall to include a French representative in the control group for the Ruhr without prejudging a final determination about the future.

Whatever the composition of the provisional government in West Germany, the Anglo-U.S. allies assured France that it could make no final decision about the ownership of the Ruhr's basic industries before a final peace settlement had been made. This was the response to Schuman's conciliatory remarks on 19 November, recognizing the identity of purposes among the the Western powers in preventing Germany from starting an aggressive war in the future.[79] At the same time he reminded his colleagues of the solidity of French opinion, clearly expressed by President Vincent Auriol who warned against repeating the errors of 1918: "It would be unpardonable to return the arsenal of the Ruhr to the accomplices of Hitler or to a German regime that might use it against the peace of the world."[80]

The communiqué of the London conference on the Ruhr, issued on 28 December, offered another level of assurance to France in the form of a military security board. It would monitor not only progress of disarmament and demilitarization but also "the necessary prohibitions and limitations on German industry." German participation in a new international Ruhr Authority would be cautiously advanced. The authority itself would have a council composed of representatives of the member governments. Only when a German government was established would Germans have a vote. In this way, the Anglo-U.S. insistence of ultimate German ownership would be respected while France would have the protections it demanded.[81]

Whether French fears would be permanently set at rest was doubtful. The Ruhr, after all, was not the only problem separating the allies. More critical was the direction the West German parliamentary council, consisting of the eleven *Laender* [federal states] and divided by party affiliation, would be taking when it began its sessions on 1 September.[82] As the body that would draft a constitution for the federal republic, its policies were obviously of considerable concern to the French.

The French centered their opposition not on the existence of the council itself but on the representation from Berlin. They objected to the presence of Berlin delegates even on an informal basis without the right to vote. The ostensible obstacle was the potential aggravation of relations with Moscow this would present.[83] There was some justification for concern that the parliamentary conference was extending its activities beyond its mandate. Clay, in fact, had lost his temper over the council's dealing with reparations and presuming that it had the power to condemn Communist repression in East Germany. Robert Murphy, the U.S. political adviser in Germany, dissuaded Clay from issuing a public rebuke but urged him to advise the German leaders that "they were doing their own cause damage" by distorting the use of the parliamentary council to purposes for which it was not intended.[84]

If the Germans annoyed the United States with their ambitions, one can understand the distress of the French and the reasons for their use of Berlin as an excuse for hobbling the political reconstruction of Germany. Murphy worried about continuing French obstructionism. It should not have been a surprise to him that they "really did not want a united Germany with Berlin as its capital."[85] Indeed, it should have been clear to him long before 22 November that the French really did not want a united Germany at all and certainly not a Germany with a strong central government. But this was a position that the United States could not adopt without losing influence in Germany. The U.S. answer was to move ahead with plans for a federal republic in the West while accommodating as best it could France's seemingly paranoid demand for security.

At the end of 1948, France had accepted U.S. assurances, at least to the point of going along with movement toward a North Atlantic Treaty. Consensus among the Western powers on dealing with the Soviets over Berlin helped to soften the conflicts between France and its Anglo-U.S. allies. The three nations agreed to a "neutral powers" resolution presented by

Argentina, Belgium, Canada, China, Colombia, and Syria on 2 October—vetoed by the Soviets—that would end the Berlin blockade and begin new talks. They rejected the Soviet effort to make the currency of the Soviet zone the sole currency for Berlin, and acting through their military commanders they planned to introduce the West German mark by the end of the year that would make a trizonal currency to serve as the only legal currency for West Berlin.[86] The Berlin blockade remained in place, but France, Britain, and the United States were functioning as a team as 1948 came to a close.

THE IMPACT OF THE TRUMAN ELECTION

Given the expectations of Republicans and Democrats alike, the election results on 2 November were a shock. It is difficult to fault the *Chicago Tribune* for its headline proclaiming Dewey's victory over Truman. If the political class was surprised by Truman's victory, the president himself was not. He had run an energetic campaign against the Washington establishment, and he came out on top. His "whistle-stop" train tour covered some thirty-one thousand miles and an audience of six million people. He was a feisty campaigner, energized by his attack on "that no-account, do-nothing, Republican 80th Congress."

Hyperbole was not in short supply. Truman blamed his opponents for their record on inflation, housing, farm, and labor issues. Foreign affairs were not high on that list, appropriately, considering the role played by the Vandenberg Republicans in that Eightieth Congress. Only in the last days of the campaign did Truman add foreign policy to his assault on the Republican Party as a force of isolationism and reaction. He suggested that the Communists wanted a Republican in the White House.[87] It was unlikely that either party's stance on foreign affairs affected the results. The *New York Times* congratulated the president in a gracious editorial but at the same time praised the bipartisan foreign policy as evidence of the voters' wisdom.[88]

Almost as important as the Democratic presidential victory was the party's emphatic victory in both houses of Congress. By winning nine Republican seats, the Democrats in the Eighty-first Congress had a majority in the Senate of fifty-four to forty-eight. Its effect on the administration's and the Congress's positions on the future alliance was palpable, but whether it would accelerate the negotiations for the Atlantic alliance was not at all clear in November. A new team of leaders in both the executive and legislative branches took office, but in some ways the transition would be more difficult than it might have been if the Republicans had won the election. A Dewey administration accompanying a Republican congressional victory would have put in place administration figures such as Dulles and keep in place Senator Vandenberg as chairman of the Foreign Relations Committee, leaders familiar with the gradual movement of the nation from nonentanglement to an entangling alliance.

Truman's retention of his office signified a more drastic change of personalities. Marshall had signaled his intention to retire, whichever party had won; he was scheduled for a long delayed kidney operation at Walter Reed Hospital when he returned from Paris in late November and a long period of recuperation after that. Lovett, his surrogate in the State Department, would follow him out of office. The new secretary of state, Dean Acheson, was hardly a novice in foreign relations and certainly not an opponent of the direction the administration was going. But he had been out of office since his important service to the Truman Doctrine and Marshall Plan, and his acerbic personality could make relations with the Senate more difficult than they had been under Marshall and Lovett. On Capitol Hill, Tom Connally, long a jealous rival of Vandenberg, would be the new chairman of the Senate Foreign Relations Committee. He had limited familiarity with the evolution of the Atlantic alliance. Given the personality factors, Connally would be inclined to play down Vandenberg's approach, while Acheson's hauteur would raise hackles of Senate collaborators.

Although Connally would back the Truman agenda as a loyal Democrat, he lacked Vandenberg's stature and interest in the concepts behind a North Atlantic treaty.[89] He would have to be wooed as Lovett had done so effectively with his predecessor. Acheson, by contrast, was constitutionally unfit to perform this function smoothly. One of Lovett's last acts of service as acting secretary of state, one week after the election, was to flatter Connally by asking his advice in language and spirit reminiscent of his treatment of Vandenberg: "I am sorry to bother you while you are away from your office but I need some fatherly advice as to the most effective procedures to follow in connection with further talks on North Atlantic regional pact." Referring to the recent statements of the Brussels Pact countries and Canada in support of an Atlantic alliance, he asked Connally about how far he should presume to go in informal talks with the future allies. Lovett in his artful way stated that he "would like very much to have an opportunity to brief you, bring you fully up to date, and get your guidelines on tactics."[90] Even if he would not be around to complete arrangements, he could foster an atmosphere of cooperation with the Senate to facilitate the State Department's pretense of relying on the Senator's superior wisdom.

If there were questions about how the election would affect U.S. internal management of alliance negotiations, there were fewer questions about transatlantic negotiations. A new dynamic was at work. The U.S. public had become attuned to a new direction in U.S. foreign policy, despite the official secrecy that prevailed in the Washington talks. Achilles quietly assisted the public's educaton by leaking information to the State Department's correspondents at the Associated Press and the United Press. He would call them to his office every few days to say that while he could not give out specific information, he could say that the Rio pact, a model of a collective defense pact, had particular articles of interest. They could then draw their own conclusions from these elliptical conversations.[91] The campaign for public support, despite a few discordant notes, was further assisted by the bipartisan concern for a united Europe that with U.S. involvement could cope with such Soviet challenges as the Berlin blockade.[92]

The election freed Lovett from the caution he usually displayed with Europeans. Nicholas Henderson noted his changed attitude after the Western Union's permanent commission produced its draft of the treaty on 26 November. The Brussels Pact members were ready to resume what they hoped to be the final act in the negotiations for a treaty. Lovett was energized by the need to have a text ready early in the new year to present to the Senate at a time when the new Congress would be most susceptible to the administration's proposals. He feared a loss of momentum, if the allies continued the leisurely pace of September and October, and so was ready to circulate the Western Union's text as quickly as possible.[93]

Lovett's new enthusiasm took the Europeans by surprise, as did his initiative in asking them for their text. According to Henderson, "They at first flayed the ground wildly like characters in a Mickey Mouse film who have been chasing something and are suddenly called upon to change direction." Actually, the Brussels powers' spokesmen in Washington backed off from their plans to circulate the draft treaty after Hickerson and Achilles warned them not to give the impression that they were forcing the treaty on the United States.[94] The Western Union's draft had excluded issues such as membership of other countries that the United States wished to include.

There were other constraints that inhibited a rapid advance in November. Achilles had told Frederick Hoyer Millar of the British Embassy the day after the Western Union had presented its draft that the United States did not want to have too close a connection with the Brussels Pact document before talking with other governments that might join the alliance. They could be offended by their exclusion from the inner circle. Moreover, the Europeans' rush to the conclusion they wanted would be slowed by the time-consuming process of talks with the Congress. Three months at least would be required to come up with a treaty acceptable to the United States.[95] Lovett, reverting to his customary caution, made this point when Spaak, normally the most sensitive of European statesmen, in late November assumed that the treaty would be completed in January 1949. If this were possible it could only be done by brushing aside potential peripheral members and making the treaty essentially with the Brussels Pact nations alone.[96]

Kennan not surprisingly added his own reservations when the JCS gave their reluctant approval to Western Union's inadequate defense plans.[97] His policy planning staff warned against excessive attention to military considerations at the expense of economic recovery. If there must be military preparations to stiffen European morale, Kennan asserted, they should clearly be tools to gain economic and political security. Preoccupation with a military solution could result in greater insecurity if it tempted the treaty's planners to extend the commitment indiscriminately: "Either all these alliances become meaningless declarations, after the pattern of the Kellogg Pact and join the long array of dead-letter pronouncements through which governments have professed their devotion to peace in the past; or this country becomes still further over-extended, politically and militarily." The policy planning staff did endorse the Atlantic pact for "its specific short-term value" in assuring the security of Europeans but then undercut the endorsement with a caveat noting that "the Pact is not the main answer to the Russian effort to achieve domination over Western Europe."[98]

A genuine shift of atmosphere only became evident after the Ambassadors' Committee reconvened on 10 December. This committee became as enmeshed in generalities in December as they had been in July and quickly turned to the working group just as they had in the summer. The ambassadors agreed that speed was essential, but only the United States and Canada could decide how to manage it. Lovett's impatience with the group was obvious; exploratory discussions had gone on long enough. Rather than proceed as in the past solely item by item, he wanted a summary of the work of the permanent commissions to be presented.[99] Lovett was annoyed over the Western Union's permanent commission publicizing as fact that the treaty was already drawn up. This preemption invited questions from the press and the Congress about just what was in the treaty before the United States was officially involved. Such questions would be embarrassing to the administration, and so Lovett claimed that "It had not occurred to the U.S. and Canada that the suggestions received from the Permanent Commission would be something in the nature of a blueprint."[100] His show of surprise must have been for the benefit of the European partners or to cover himself in the event of newpapers leaks.

Because the Ambassador's Committtee was essentially spinning its wheels, it was not until its second meeting on 13 December that the committee recognized that no decisions would be made on such questions as the duration of the treaty, the security area, the participation of other countries, and how to negotiate with them. These questions remained unanswered at the end of the year. What could be produced was a draft of those articles agreed on and a list of alternatives on those where there was agreement. At the suggestion of British Ambassador Oliver Franks, the drafting was turned over to the working group.[101]

It was at this point that the long pause was succeeded, as Henderson put it, by a sprint to a conclusion of sorts. In terms of time, the pace of the working group could not have been more rapid. Within ten days from 13 to 24 December the work was finished. In fact, the working group delivered its report to the ambassadors on 21 December.[102] The group took care of some of the issues left hanging in the Washington Paper of 9 September and left others for resolution early in 1949.

Certainly the most sensitive problem was the wording of Article 5. In September the Washington Paper had proposed alternate versions reflecting the U.S. and European divisions. The United States wanted the pledge to state explicitly the right of each ally to decide for iself whether an attack occurred and to make no specific reference to military aid to an ally under attack. The European partners wanted an explicit mention of military aid to the victim, as written into the Brussels Pact, a position understood by Kennan, the chairman of the U.S. delegation to the working group.[103] The United States conceded both points but with a caveat that the allies could take "military or other action . . . as may be necessary to restore and assure the security of the North Atlantic area." This language, pressed by the JCS, would permit the allies, especially the United States, to respond according to strategic concepts rather than by sending armed forces to the area under attack. Major General Alfred M. Gruenther, director of the Joint Staff of the JCS, had made this point in the Pentagon conversations of March.[104]

Other issues were not necessarily solved but were less contentious. The Western Union partners had already agreed to approach the Scandinavian countries, a decision that had to be made if they did not want to risk U.S. defection from the alliance. The admission of Italy was left open as the negotiators continued the old debate marshaling familiar reasons for and against Italy's participation. Greece and Turkey presented no such problem; they would be excluded but with the promise of steps to assure their security.[105]

A lesser question, but a French one, was the duration of the alliance. Bonnet invoked American history, presumably with reference to the lend-lease arrangements of World War II, to recommend a ninety-nine-year time span. Decision on duration was deferred. Hickerson was amused as he dismissed Bonnet's suggestion, but the matter of France's North African departments was no laughing matter. These remained unresolved.[106]

Although no decision was made on the wording of the preamble, the Europeans came around to the U.S. and Canadian's belief that the Brussels Treaty's "High Contracting Party" was too pretentious. Simple language, as Hickerson and Achilles preached, was necessary to reach the average man, that "Omaha Milkman."[107] Still, gaps were not filled. The U.S. Senate had to be heard, and this required the convening of the Eighty-first Congress in January 1949.

Nevertheless, the year 1948 had witnessed the patient application of statecraft on both sides of the Atlantic that led to the brink of a transatlantic relationship that Hickerson and Achilles only hoped for but had not anticipated, a year before. They would have been justified in repeating the toasts they had made at the Metropolitan Club on New Year's Eve the year before.

NOTES

1. Donald B. Johnson and Kirk H. Porter, *National Party Platforms, 1840–1972* (Urbana: University of Illinois Press, 1973), 453.

2. Johnson and Porter, *National Party Platforms*, 432.

3. Clark Clifford, with Richard Holbrooke, *Counsel to the President: A Memoir* (New York: Random House, 1991), 234.

4. Clifford, *Counsel to the President*, 234–35.

5. *New York Times*, October 18, 1948, 1.

6. Robert H. Ferrell, *Harry S. Truman: A Life* (Columbia: University of Missouri Press, 1994), 272; Robert J. Donovan, *Conflct and Crisis: The Presidency of Harry S Truman* (New York: W. W. Norton & Co., 1977), 422.

7. Clifford, *Counsel to the President*, 225.

8. *U.S. News and World Report* 25, no. 12, September 17, 1948, 13ff.

9. Ferrell, *Truman*, 268; Donovan, *Conflict and Crisis*, 388.

10. Editorial, *New York Times*, October 13, 1948, 24.

11. James T. Patterson, *Mr. Republican: A Biography of Robert A. Taft* (Boston: Houghton Mifflin Co., 1972), 424.

12. *New York Times*, September 23, 1948, 1.

13. Memorandum of conversation, October 4, 1948: George Marshall, Jefferson Caffery, Charles Bohlen, Ernest Bevin, Frank Roberts, sub: Western Union, 840.00/1/10–448, RG 59, NARA.

14. Memorandum of conversation, October 4, 1948, Marshall, Caffery, Bohlen, Bevin, Roberts, sub: Western Union, 840.00/1/10–448, RG 59, NARA.

15. "Comments on Train to New York City," *New York Times*, October 30, 1948, 16.

16. "Text of Dewey Speech in Louisville on 12 October, 1948," *New York Times*, October 13, 1948, 17.

17. Cordell Hull, *Memoirs of Cordell Hull*, 2 vols. (New York: Macmillan, 1948), II: 1697.

18. "Dewey Speech in Louisville," *New York Times*, October 13, 1948, 1.

19. *Facts on File* 8, no. 14 (October 3–9, 1948 8), 321.

20. Arthur H. Vandenberg, Jr., ed., *The Private Papers of Arthur H. Vandenberg* (Boston: Houghton Mifflin, 1952), 457–58.

21. "Taft Speech in Nashville, October 11, 1948," *New York Times*, October 12, 1948, 22.

22. "Text of Dewey Speech in Cleveland, October 27, 1948," *New York Times*, October 28, 1948, 24.

23. Quoted in Donovan, *Conflict and Crisis*, 425.

24. Minutes of the Seventh Meeting of the Washington Exploratory Talks on Security, September 10, 1948, *FRUS*, 1948, III: 250.

25. Memorandum of conversation, Achilles and Henderson, September 30, 1948, *FRUS*, 1948, III: 257–58.

26. Memorandum by ambassadors of the WU members to Department of State, October 29, 1948, with Hickerson memorandum of conversation with Jean Daridan, Counselor of French Embassy, October 29, 1948, *FRUS*, 1948, III:, 270; memorandum, Executive Secretary, National Security Council to Lovett, November 1948, JCS 1868/28, 159, RG 218, NARA.

27. Sir Nicholas Henderson, *Birth of NATO* (Boulder, CO: Westview Press, 1983), 65.

28. *New York Times*, October 31, 1948.

29. René Massigli, *Une comedie des erreurs, 1943–1946* (Paris: Plon, 1978), 137.

30. See chapter 5.

31. Washington Paper, September 9, 1948, *FRUS*, 1948, III: 240–41.

32. Tel Ambassador to Denmark (Josiah Marvel) to Secretary of State, September 14, 1948, *FRUS*, 1948, no. 861, III: 251–52.

33. Tel Ambassador to Sweden (H. Freeman Matthews) to Secretary of State, September 17, 1948, *FRUS*, 1948, no. 1065, III: 252.

34. Theodore C. Achilles, *Fingerprints on History: The NATO Memoirs of Theodore C. Achilles*, edited by Lawrence S. Kaplan and Sidney B. Snyder (Kent, OH: Lyman L. Lemnitzer Center for NATO and European Community Affairs, Kent State University, 1992), 28.

35. Tel Acting Secretary of State to Embassy in Sweden, November 17, 1948, *FRUS*, 1948, no. 799, III: 272.

36. Memorandum of conversation, October 6, 1948: Marshall, Halvond Lange, *FRUS*, 1948, III: 260; Henderson, *Birth of NATO*, 84.

37. Memorandum of conversation, September 29, 1948, subject: Norweigan Query Re North Atlantic Pact, 840.00/9–2948, RG 59, NARA; Achilles, *Fingerprints on History*, 28.

38. Minister to Iceland (Richard Butrick) to Secretary of State, December 11, 1948, *FRUS*, 1948, no. 304, III: 315.

39. Metro Document 162, Record of the Third Meeting of the Consultative Council of Paris, October 25–26, 1948, WEU Archives, PRO, London, PRO.

40. Escott Reid, *Time of Fear and Hope: The Making of the North Atlantic Treaty, 1947–1949* (Toronto: McClelland and Stewart, 1977), 198; memorandum by the participants in the Washington Security Talks, July 6 to September 9 (Washington Paper), September 9, 1948, *FRUS*, 1948, III: 241.

41. Reid, *Time of Fear and Hope*, 200.

42. Tel Ambassador in Portugal (Lincoln MacVeagh) to Secretary of State, September 8, 1948, *FRUS*, 1948, no. 352, III: 1002–5.

43. Tel Ambassador in Portugal to Secretary of State, November 8, 1948, *FRUS*, 1948, no. 402, III, quote on 1015; tel Ambassdor in Belgium (Alan G. Kirk) to Secretary of State, November 29, 1948, *FRUS*, 1948, no. 2087, III: 298–99.

44. Achilles, *Fingerprints on History*, 28.

45. Tel Frances E. Willis, First Secretary American Embassy in London, to Secretary of State, October 25, 1948, no. 2117, sub: Spain and Western Europe, 840.00/10–2548, RG 59, NARA.

46. Tel American Embassy in Norway (Henry Villard) to Secretary of State, October 25, 1948, no. A-630, 840.00/10–2548, RG 59, NARA.

47. Tel American Embassy to London (Holmes) to Secretary of State, 18 October, 18, no. A-1895, sub: France Spain and Western Union, 840.00/10–1248, RG 59, NARA.

48. Donald MacLachlan, "Western Europe and the Spanish Question, broadcast on October 15, 1948 from London, enclosed in Willis cable, see footnote 45.

49. Memorandum of conversation, October 4, 1948, George Marshall, Robert Schuman, Ernest Bevin, *FRUS*, 1948, III: 1053; Ltr., Robert Lovett to Rep. Jacob K. Javits, *FRUS*, 1948, III: 1055–56.

50. *Congressional Record*, 94, pt. 2 80th Cong., 2nd sess., 4044–55.

51. *New York Times*, December 4, 1948, 4.

52. *New York Times*, November 28, 1948.

53. Washington Paper, September 9, 1948, *FRUS*, 1948, III: 241.

54. See chapter 5.

55. Washington Paper, III: 241.

56. Memorandum of the Thirteenth Meeting of the Working Group Participating in the Washington Exploratory Talks on Security, September 2, 1948, *FRUS*, 1948, III: 227.

57. Tel Ambassador to Italy (James Dunn) to Secretary of State, October 22, 1948, *FRUS*, 1948, no. 4081, III: 810.

58. Tel Lovett to the Embassy in Belgium, November 22, 1948, *FRUS*, 1948, no. 1546, III: 282, quote on 283.

59. Reid, *Time of Fear and Hope*, 203.

60. Henderson, *Birth of NATO*, 73; Report of the International Working Group to the Ambassadors' Committee, December 24, 1948, Annex C, *FRUS*, III: 342.

61. Tel Ambassador to Turkey (George Wadsworth) to Secretary of State, November 26, 1948, *FRUS*, 1948, no. 839, III: 294; Randolph Harrison, First Secretary of Embassy in Turkey to Secretary of State, November 26, 1948, no. 451, sub: Transmission of Text from Acting Foreign Minister Regarding Turkey's Desire to Be Associated with Atlantic Pact, 840.00/11–2648, RG 59, NARA.

62. Harold Callender, "Europe Remains a Divided House, *New York Times*, September 5, 1948.

63. Quoted in John W. Young, *Britain, France, and the Unity of Europe* (Leicester: Leicester University Press, 1984), 112; tel Douglas to Secretary of State, September 9, 1948, no. 4045, 840.00/9–948, RG 59, NARA; tel Don C. Bliss, interim Charge d'Affaires, American embassy, London to Secretary of State, September 28, 1948, no. 1097, sub: European Federal Union, 840.00/9–2848, RG 59, NARA.

64. Young, *Britain, France, and the Unity of Europe*, 112.

65. Massigli, *Comédie*, 160–61; tel Douglas to Secetary of State, 1 December 1948, no. A-2212, sub: British Proposal of the Establishment of a Council of Europe, 840.00/12–148, RG 59, NARA.

66. Tel Jefferson Caffery to Secretary of State, November 29, 1948, no. 6084, 840.00/11–2948, RG 59, NARA.

67. Tel Willis, London, to Secetary of State, November 14, 1948, no.2289, sub: Correspondence between Mr. Attlee and Mr. Churchill concerning British Delegation to Study Proposals for European Unity, 840.00/11–1448, RG 59, NARA.

68. Tel Caffery to Secretary of State, November 30, 1948, A1365, 840.000/1-3048, RG 59, NARA.

69. Jean Chauvel, *Commentaire: d'Alger a Berne, 1944-1952* (Paris: Fayard, 1972), 210-11.

70. Young, *Britain, France, and the Unity of Europe,* 116-17; Massigli, *Comedie,* 116-17.

71. See chapter 5.

72. Editorial note, *FRUS,* 1948, II: 465; James Reston, "Comment," *New York Times,* December 29, 1948.

73. Tel Caffery to Acting Secetary of State, November 12, 1948, *FRUS,* 1948, no. 5847, II: 479.

74. Tel Acting Secretary of State to Secretary of State, at Paris, November 13, 1948, *FRUS,* 1948, no. 4400, II: 493; Ltr, Caffery to Schuman, November 16, 1948, *FRUS,* 1948, II: 501.

75. Memorandum of conversation by Lovett, November 16, 1948: Lovett, Bonnet, Jacob Beam, Chief, Division of Central European Affairs, *FRUS,* 1948, III: 502-3.

76. Murphy for Embassy in UK, November 18, 1948, *FRUS,* 1948, no. 862, II: 512; Minutes of Meeting of Foreign Ministers at Quai d'Orsay: Marshall, Schuman, Wilfred McNeil (representing Bevin) and members of respective foreign ministries, November 19, 1948, *FRUS,* 1948, II: 518-19.

77. Tel Clay to Department of Army, November 15, 1948, FMPC-1008, *FRUS,* 1948, III: 498; tel Murphy to Embassy in UK, November 18, 1948, no. 862, enclosing Clays' reactions, *FRUS,* 1948, II: 508-9.

78. Tel Deputy Administrator of ECA (David Bruce) to ECA Mission in UK, November 19, 1948, ECA TO 14, *FRUS,* 1948, II: 519.

79. Tel Marshall to Embassy in France, November 29, 1948, *FRUS,* 1948, no. 4565, III: 634-35; Minutes of Meetings of Foreign Ministers November 19, 1948, *FRUS,* 1948, III: 517.

80. *New York Times,* November 12, 1948, 9.

81. Communiqué of London Conference on the Ruhr, December 28, 1948, *FRUS,* 1948, II: 577-81.

82. Tel Murphy to Secretary of State, September 1, 1948, *FRUS,* 1948, no. 2213, II: 420-21.

83. Tel Secretary of State to Murphy, 27 August 1948, no. 1543, *FRUS,* 1948, II: 416.

84. Quoted in ltr Murphy to Beam, personal and secret, September 16, 1948, *FRUS,* 1948, II: 422.

85. Quoted in tel Clay to Department of the army, November 22, 1948, *FRUS,* 1948, II: 526.

86. Editorial note, *FRUS,* 1948, III: 1233-34; tel Douglas to Secretary of State, October 26, 1948, *FRUS,* 1948, no. 4622, III: 1234-35; tel Secretary of State to Douglas, December 29, 1948, *FRUS,* 1948, no. 4814, III: 1282-84.

87. "Truman Speeches in Brooklyn and Harlem," *New York Times,* October 30, 1948.

88. Charles C. Euchner and John A. Maltese, *Electing the President: From Washington to Bush* (Washington, D.C.: Congressional Quarterly, 1992), 269-70; Editorial, *New York Times,* November 4, 1948.

89. Don Cook, *Forging the Alliance: NATO, 1945–1949* (New York: Arbor House/William Morris, 1989), 200.

90. Ltr, Lovett to Tom Connally, November 12, 1948, 840.00/11–1248, RG 59, NARA.

91. Achilles, *Fingerprints on History*, 29.

92. Cook, *Forging the Alliance*, 201.

93. Henderson, *Birth of NATO*, 67.

94. Henderson, *Birth of NATO*, 68.

95. Memo of conversation by Achilles, November 27, 1948: Achilles, Frederick Hoyer Millar, *FRUS*, 1948, III: 197.

96. Tel Lovett to embassy in Belgium, November 22, 1948, *FRUS*, 1948, no. 1566, III: 282.

97. See chapter 6.

98. Quoted in Memorandum by Director of Policy Planning Staff (Kennan), November 24, 1948, with enclosure, "Considerations affecting the Conclusion of a North Atlantic Security Pact," *FRUS*, 1948, III: 286, 288. Identified as Policy Planning Paper 43, it was accepted orally by the secretary of state, *FRUS*, 1948, III: 286, footnote 284.

99. Minutes of the Eighth Meeting of the Washington Exploratory Talks, December 10, 1948, *FRUS*, 1948, III: 312.

100. Quoted in *FRUS*, 1948, III: 313.

101. Minutes of the Ninth Meeting of the Washington Exploratory Talks, December 13, 1948, *FRUS*, 1948: 318–19.

102. Henderson, *Birth of NATO*, 65; Minutes Tenth Meeting of the Washington Exploratory Talks, December 22, 1948, *FRUS*, 1948, III: 324.

103. Henderson, *Birth of NATO*, 70.

104. Alfred Gruenther's emphasis in Minutes of the Fourth Meeting of the United States—United Kingdom—Canada Security Conversations, March 29, 1948, *FRUS*, 1948, III: 69–70; Report of the International Working Group to the Ambassadors' Committee, December 24, 1948, *FRUS*, 1948, III: 335; Reid, *Time of Fear and Hope*, 147–48.

105. Report of the International Working Group, December 24, 1948, *FRUS*, 1948, III: 339–42.

106. Oral history interview, John D. Hickerson, Harry S. Truman Library, Independence, MO, in Sidney R. Snyder, "The Role of the International Working Group in the Creation of the North Atlantic Treaty" (Ph.D. dissertation, Kent State University, 1992), 150; Henderson, *Birth of NATO*, 70.

107. Minutes of the Tenth Meeting of the Washington Exploratory Talks, December 22, 1948, *FRUS*, 1948, III: 325; Achilles, *Fingerprints on History*, 21–22.

8

Toward the Treaty of Washington, January–April 1949

THE LONGEST LAP

Sir Nicholas Henderson, recalling his insider's knowledge of the pace of negotiations, identified the first three months of 1949 as "the last lap."[1] It was an accurate assessment. The treaty, signed on 4 April, was a variation of the 9 September and 24 December drafts produced by the Ambassadors' Committee in 1948. But the devil resided in the differences between the final text of the treaty and the new questions raised in the Senate in the winter of 1949. These constituted a much longer lap than the transatlantic framers had anticipated.

Before the end of January, less than a week after a new team of policymakers had taken office, the expectation was that the pact would become a reality within thirty days. Almost all the details of the treaty had been agreed on, even if they could not yet be announced. But as one anonymous U.S. official reported, "The details of the Atlantic Pact are of far less importance than the fact that the United States has agreed to join it."[2]

This judgment was true enough, but it was not enough to make the final lap as easy to complete as U.S. and European negotiators had assumed.

Reasons for optimism about a quick conclusion were abundant. The Western Union partners seemed to be reconciled for a duration of less than the fifty-year period of the Brussels Pact. The Soviets appeared to be retreating from their adamancy over Berlin, perhaps even looking for a way out of the conflict. Even Secretary of Defense James V. Forrestal was convinced that the Soviet threat had lessened to the point where he could ask the Congress for a smaller military budget than the year before.[3] France was more receptive to a future German government than it had been earlier, albeit with appropriate safeguards. At least Foreign Minister Robert Schuman recognized the obstacles France faced in hindering West Germany's movement toward sovereignty.[4]

Other questions left over from the fall of 1948 revolved around whether Italy would join the pact as a charter member and when Norway and Denmark would be ready to abandon a Swedish-led defense alliance to join the West. Both appeared solvable. The most important issue at stake was the U.S. position on Article 5. The U.S. agreement, written into the working group's report to the Ambassadors' Committee on 24 December, to include military action in considering an attack on any member of the alliance as an attack on the United States itself, seemingly set at rest European concerns.[5] Despite these positive signs, the North Atlantic Treaty evoked reactions in the Senate, in the administration, and among the allies that pushed back the final signing of the treaty.

DEAN ACHESON VERSUS THE U.S. SENATE

That Acheson would encounter difficulties in replacing the team of George Marshall and Robert Lovett was hardly surprising. His imperious manner was made all the more intimidating by a guardsman's mustache, which suggested he did not suffer fools gladly. And he made it clear that the senators he had to deal with merited the low opinion he assigned to most of them. Unlike the soothing manner of Lovett, Acheson could not pander easily to the egos of such prima donnas as Arthur H. Vandenberg and his successor, Tom Connally of Texas. And he could not tolerate senators such as Forrest Donnell of Missouri, whom he wrote off as a crackpot. Yet he had no choice but to deal with them. He considered Vandenberg the most rational of the congressional leaders. In a declaration on 10 February 1949, the former chairman of the Senate Foreign Relations Committee recommended that the Republicans serve as the "loyal opposition," stressing the party's own major role in making an Atlantic alliance possible while ensuring that the administration did not make promises it could not keep. Deviation from such a course, he warned, would "serve neither their country nor their party nor themselves."[6]

Acheson's appreciation of Vandenberg's moderation had its limits. He had formed his opinion of Vandenberg during the debate over the Truman Doctrine in 1947 and could never develop the kind of relationship with him that Lovett had made. The secretary of state considered the Michigan senator to be something of a windbag—and a vain one at that—"who was born to lead a reluctant opposition into support of governmental proposals that he came to believe were in the national interest," but only after he played legislative games that would end with his name on a document, such as the Vandenberg Resolution.[7] Lovett had been willing to play those games to win over skeptical or ignorant senators and had even come to appreciate their friendship as well as their support. George Kennan, who differed on many issues with Acheson, was equally annoyed with the "elaborate deference" that Lovett paid to Vandenberg.[8] The senator certainly missed the courtship after Lovett left office in January. He admitted that Acheson made some effort to keep up appearances and recalled that after the treaty had been passed, "Dean called up . . . and asked if he could drop in at the flat for a drink on his way home—and drop in he did. It was *slightly* reminiscent of the old Lovett days."[9]

Although no longer chairman of the Senate Foreign Relations Committee, Vandenberg retained some of the authority he had enjoyed in the Eightieth Congress, particularly after he coupled his appeal for national unity with his intention to retire in 1952. At the hearings on Acheson's confirmation as secretary of state, he could not restrain colleagues from attacking the candidate. Hard-core Republican isolationist Kenneth Wherry of Nebraska claimed that as assistant secretary of state, "he has carried out an appeasement policy toward Russia." And Indiana's Republican Senator Homer Capehart added the charge that Acheson was the kind of "Wall Streeter" that Truman had attacked in the election campaign of 1948.[10] Countering these objections, Vandenberg came to the secretary designate's defense, noting that he had responded to all questions asked of him "with complete and commendable candor."[11] Acheson was confirmed by a vote of eighty-three to three.

As senators began an intensive examination of the contents of the treaty, it was only a matter of time before their behavior would test Acheson's temper and uncork his deadly wit. When Donnell appeared ready to undermine negotiations by citing a story in the *Kansas City Times* in which Acheson made a moral commitment to any European nation attacked without congressional authorization, the secretary saw this as the work of "an irresponsible senator reading the gossip of an irresponsible reporter." His irritation triggered a description of Donnell, whom he found combining "the courtliness of Mr. Pickwick and the suavity of an experienced waiter with the manner of a prosecuting attorney in the movies—the gimlet eye, the piercing question. In administering the *coup de grace*, he would do it with a napkin over his arms and his ears sticking out like an alert elephant's."[12] So much for the senior senator from Missouri.

Connally never suffered this kind of treatment, but Acheson was as contemptuous of his pretensions as he had been of Vandenberg's. The Texas Democrat was not easy to handle. He took over the chairmanship of the Foreign Relations Committee, making sure that no one would doubt who was in charge. Vandenberg was amused by a comment of pundit Joseph Alsop who asserted that Connally "openly resented" his predecessor's preeminence: "This will make old Tawm fairly burn in his boots."[13] British Ambassador Sir Oliver Franks saw little humor in their relationship. He reported to the foreign office that "Connally is of course a man of lesser caliber and may not fully understand the issues involved. But I suspect that he is jealous of Vandenberg and disposed to be difficult about the North Atlantic Pact on the grounds that it derives largely from the Vandenberg Resolution."[14] Franks and his Western Union colleagues feared that the personality conflict between Connally and Vandenberg could unravel the careful understandings about the prospective treaty that all parties had reached in 1948.

ACHESON AND THE WESTERN EUROPEANS

More than personality issues disturbed Europeans. The position of the U.S. military establishment provided other grounds for concern. On the one hand, the JCS informed Lovett, still acting secretary of state, on 6 January that they were "in complete agreement with the wording of Article 5, including the first paragraph that agreed 'to such military and other action . . . as may be necessary to restore and assure the security of the North Atlantic Area.' Wording less general in nature might tend dangerously to affect our freedom of planning and action with respect to global strategy that direct assistance alone might well be neither so practicable nor so effective as steps taken in consonance with the over-all strategic concepts. It is hoped that article 5 in its final form will retain the excellent terminology quoted above."[15]

On the other hand, the JCS had planned a defense of Europe under the name of Offtackle, which would not extend beyond the Rhine, and even this area was in doubt. In the short run, the JCS assumed that evacuation to French and Italian seaports would be necessary, a modest improvement over the emergency war plan Halfmoon of 1948. That plan envisioned the loss of almost all of Europe and so concentrated on such vital bases as Britain and the Suez as staging grounds for future action against the Soviets.[16] There was some, but not enough, consolation in the emergency recommendations of General Dwight D. Eisenhower, who had been brought back to the Pentagon temporarily from the presidency of Columbia University. Given the presumed indefensibility of the Rhine, on 15 February he called for a "substantial bridgehead" to be held in Western Europe. If this would not be possible, at least the United States should plan for "a return, at the earliest possible moment, to Western Europe in order to prevent the communization of that area with long term disastrous effects on U.S. national interests."[17]

Despite the solicitous tone, this kind of thinking gave little comfort to Europeans who would have to be liberated after Soviet occupation. Although the Western Union partners were not privy to the details of JCS plans, they were aware of their general drift. In a major statement to the United Press at the time of Eisenhower's policy memorandum, French Premier Henri Queille made a gloomy reference to the consequences of a Soviet occupation of Europe: "The next time the U.S. would probably be liberating a corpse and civilization would be dead."[18] Their demand for a credible deterrent made a specific U.S. commitment all the more essential.

While the secretary of state was indifferent to the clash of senatorial egos over the management of an Atlantic security pact, he could not be indifferent to the new doubts about the U.S. commitment that were disturbing the European allies in the winter of 1949. Acheson himself was responsible, in part at least, for the confusion in Europe. He was unfamiliar with the terms of the 24 December draft of the treaty that James Reston had mentioned in the *New York Times* in early January.[19] The Senate was no better informed. Lovett had failed to communicate the contents of the draft to the Foreign Relations Committee. As a consequence, Acheson quickly heard rumblings of discontent from those who suspected that an automatic commitment to war would follow from an attack on one of the allies, an action that would violate Congress's constitutional authority to declare war. The treaty's prospects appeared to suffer further damage when Walter Lippmann, the nation's most influential political analyst, returned from Europe in January to open his own campaign against the North Atlantic Treaty. He claimed to be appalled at the prospect of "zealous cold warriors" determined to "draft into a western coalition any country not occupied by the Red Army." Lippmann was convinced that Soviet aggression could be held in check by the threat of U.S. atomic retaliation and not by a collection of "weak and dubious allies."[20]

It was not until February that the new administration shocked the future allies by revealing the Senate's complaints. Inauguration of the president and confirmation of Acheson as secretary of state occupied the last two weeks of January. When Acheson began consultations with Connally and Vandenberg in early February, he recognized that the Senate knew little about the long and difficult discussion over the language of Article 5 that had consumed so much time at the meetings of the Ambassadors' Committee and the working group. Without knowing of the compromises on the subject, Connally wanted to remove such key words as "forthwith" and "military and other action," and even get rid of "as may be necessary." He appeared to join the former isolationists in seeing evidence of an automatic military action in the event of an attack on any member.[21]

Connally's initiatives disturbed the Ambassadors' Committee when Acheson explained the senators' objections. He did point out that their complaints were not directed against the objectives of Article 5 but simply against language that would impinge on their constitutional obligations. The European ambassadors responded negatively to this news. Franks spoke for his colleagues in addressing the depressing effects his weakening of Article 5 would have on their publics. If a toothless text were produced, the Soviets might see this as a symbol of the West's inability to unite.[22]

Instead of empathizing with the Europeans on this matter, the secretary seemed to side with senatorial critics. Acheson did stand fast against the efforts of the House of Representatives to have a say in the formulation of the treaty; he made it clear that the Atlantic pact would be a treaty, and treaties were, under the U.S. Constitution, exclusively the business of the Senate.[23] He was much less firm in dealing with the senators' objections to the treaty's terms. In fact, he shared their suspicions that Article 5 would commit the United States automatically to military action.[24] He asserted in his meeting on 8 February with the Ambassadors' Committee, that "military or other action" was "an unnecessary embellishment; the words merely meant 'action', i.e., military, diplomatic, economic, and any other kind of action in concert with any other Parties as may be necessary to restore security."[25] It was hardly surprising that the European diplomats would regard Acheson's words as watering down the message of Article 5.

Not privy to the protracted debates over the article, the secretary of state was less attuned to European sensibilities and more open to senators' criticisms than Lovett would have been. But he was not part of any senatorial cabal to torpedo the negotiations. As Escott Reid pointed out, it was his "arrogance of expression" that needlessly offended his European counterparts.[26] Even if he had been personally more sympathetic, the problem of reconciling an entangling alliance with the war powers of Congress would have remained. French Ambassador Henri Bonnet maintained that the draft as it stood had been arrived at after much thought and debate. He felt that the text was not in any way radical; other treaties had been more binding. But in view of the strong feelings in the Senate, tweaking the text with a word or two would be acceptable, but nothing beyond that. The European partners were afraid that the senators' proposed changes in the language of the article would reduce and possibly nullify the value of the treaty. Popular expectations in Europe had been raised to such a high level that dashing them could have a catastrophic effect. The timing itself of the Senate debate was deplorable in the eyes of the allies. The Foreign Relations Committee appeared to be backing away from its commitments just when the Soviets were putting pressure on Norway to reject participation in the Atlantic pact.[27]

The storm over Article 5, whipped up by Senator Donnell's provocative remarks on the Senate floor, gathered strength in mid-February. He touched off an isolationist reaction reminiscent of the debate over the League of Nations in 1919. Connally rushed to join the irreconcilables in disclaiming either legal or moral obligation to go to war on behalf of Europe. Connally was carried away by his own overblown rhetoric to imply that the Euro-

peans had trapped the naïve members of the State Department: "We cannot
. . . be Sir Galahads, and every time we hear a gun fired plunge into war and
take sides without knowing what we are doing and without knowing the issues involved."[28] Ambassador Franks felt that Connally's intervention
"served only to make matters infinitely worse. Senator Borah [in 1919] himself could hardly have done better with his remarks cautioning the United
States against playing the role of Sir Galahad . . . and [uttering] similar inani-
ties such as letting the Europeans declare war and letting us fight."[29]

By his relative silence, Vandenberg appeared to acquiesce in his colleague's views, both on the Senate floor and in conversations with Acheson.
He wanted action to be a matter of individual interpretation and the word
military to be omitted. Still, he could not go along with Connally's wish to
replace the key statement in Article 5 making "an armed attack against one
or more of them . . . be considered an attack against them all" with "an attack against one would be regarded as a threat to peace of all." The Rio
Treaty had included this phrase with the Senate's blessing.[30] Franks was
more tolerant of Vandenberg's language than he was of Connally's: "He un-
doubtedly wants a strong pact and I am not too worried about what he said
yesterday in the Senate. It is part of his technique, if he wants something
badly, to avoid showing his feelings too obviously in the early stages. He
may have felt yesterday that he would only have stultified his position had
he disclosed his full support of the pact."[31]

The British foreign secretary was not as complacent about the Senate's behavior or as appreciative of Vandenberg's tactics as his ambassador was. By inserting the clause "as it deems necessary" and omitting the emotive word *military*, Ernest Bevin found Connally altering a crucial sentence in Article 5. He
was ready to tell the United States that the Brussels Pact parliaments might
not accept a treaty that included the language imposed by the Senate.[32]

After some reflection, however, Bevin changed his mind. He would prefer a watered-down treaty to no treaty at all, if only because "even with a fee-
ble version of Article 5 we should presumably secure consultative machinery and above all the establishment of a military committee which would
be capable of drawing up plans and dividing up the available arms among
the signatory powers." The language of Article 5 would not matter in the
event of war, he felt, because "the United States would not be able to avoid
being involved in the conflict whatever the view the senate took as to its
technical right to the declaration of war."[33]

As a result of the Senate pressures, John Hickerson and Theodore Achilles
panicked briefly, succumbing to the Senate's position. Arguably, they may
have been motivated by a guilty conscience. It was Achilles, after a year of
protecting the secrecy of negotiations, who now recognized the need to prepare U.S. public opinion for a drastic change in foreign policy. He arranged
to do this by releasing selective information about the prospective pact to

influential journalists, particularly to James Reston of the *New York Times* who had been so discreet in his columns in 1948.[34]

The tactic succeeded in moving U.S. public opinion in the administration's direction, but it angered allies whose publics had not been exposed to details Reston was now regularly publishing in his paper.[35] Acheson confessed that he was caught in "the bureaucrat's dilemma," balancing conflicting pressures for publicity and secrecy in formulating the North Atlantic Treaty. The State Department tried to paper over the issue by saying that there were "no differences" between the administration and the Senate on the objectives of the pact; "It is simply a matter of finding the best possible way to meet those objectives."[36] For the moment these soothing words failed to appease the Europeans.

ACHESON AND THE U.S. EUROPEANISTS

The secretary of state had another bloc to cope with, namely, those in the Congress and in the country who felt that the prospective treaty did not go far enough in support of the unification of Europe. Senator J. William Fulbright, spokesman for Richard Coudenhove-Kalergi's European parliamentary union, was the leader of this faction. He returned to the subject of European unification when the ECA came up for renewal in February 1949. Although Fulbright had failed to insert a statement on European unity into the original act in 1948, he had not lost his fervor for the cause. He was particularly annoyed at Acheson's casual remark before the Senate Foreign Relations Committee that the projected council of Europe would be a useful forum for developing economic unity. Like many European federationists, the senator had hoped the council would concentrate on promoting the elusive political unity of Europe. In response to Fulbright's query about the nation delegating genuine political powers to the new council, Acheson blandly asserted that no serious reduction of national sovereignty would be involved. But to Fulbright the erosion of national sovereignty should be the primary function of the council. He was convinced that economic integration could not be separated from political integration. As he had said in the past, the ECA, for all its good intentions, tended to encourage nationalism rather than integration through its plans for economic reconstruction of Europe.[37]

Acheson's conception of the Council of Europe, which had been formally launched on 28 January, was close to the British position. The council itself was the product of a British counterproposal in December 1948 to a much more integrated Franco-Belgian plan. In fact, they put forth a compromise that would create the shell of a united Europe without any substance.[38] The French were justified in believing that British behavior undermined the movement toward the unification of the continent. Bevin wanted the delegates for a council, not an assembly, as the French and Belgians wanted. They would vote as representatives of their country, not as individuals. The British ambassador to France, Sir Oliver Harvey, observed that the French were convinced that "we shall in fact prevent anything being established at all and make the idea of European unity still-born."[39]

The French did get their assembly; A Consultative Assembly of the Council of Europe after the Western Union's Consultative Council met at the end of January. But it was an empty victory, because the assembly would lack legislative powers and could not deal with matters of national defense. Only the council of ministers would make decisions about defense and then only if these were unanimous.[40]

In the ongoing Anglo-French contest over the unification of Europe, Acheson reflected the British approach when he responded to Fulbright's recommendations. Connally agreed with the secretary's views and accused Fulbright of being "quite unfair and quite wrong" in considering the State Department to be indifferent to the political unification of Europe. The Council of Europe would be only one of many steps, he suggested, "that will bring about conditions which will enable these countries to go beyond the present steps which have been taken towards economic integration. They will enable them to go further, perhaps in the direction of political unity."[41] This was hardly the spirit that Fulbright and Coudenhove-Kalergi felt was appropriate. It seemed half-hearted, and it was.

That the secretary was aware of the segment of public opinion represented by Fulbright was apparent in the reports of Ambassador Franks to the foreign office. He recognized that Acheson needed ammunition to answer critics.[42] In Paris, Ambassador Harvey worried that the French would blame Britain for the failure of Europeans to move more quickly toward unity. The French touched a sensitive nerve when Foreign Minister Schuman went to London to point out the importance of European unification to U.S. public opinion.[43] Although the exchange between Acheson and Fulbright never focused specifically on Britain, the British were correct in assuming that the Arkansas senator identified their behavior as a primary obstacle to European unity. His principal European informant, Coudenhove-Kalergi, reinforced his perceptions. The aging visionary of a new Europe was convinced that a British plot accounted for an attempt to remove his name from the letterhead of the American Committee for a Free and United Europe. He associated this insult with the activities of a new British-led group calling itself "the European movement" that favored a vague European commonwealth as opposed to a more genuine federation.[44]

Coudenhove-Kalergi's suspicions of British subversion impressed the former Rhodes Scholar. In letters to friends, Fulbright observed that "from recent developments here and from the discussions I have had, it seems the British are pretty definitely opposed to a political federation of Europe. In view of the great influence of the British in our Department of state, I am afraid the prospects for constructive action are remoter."[45]

Franks's concern about Fulbright's ability to mobilize the Senate against the British conception of European unity was excessive. Acheson was far closer to the mood of the Congress than was the Arkansas senator. He argued that the United States should not appear to be dictating to the Europeans. "The Europeans must devise these measures themselves," he believed, "and that our attitude is one of helping them and not trying to direct them and tell them what to do." As chairman of the Foreign Relations Committee, Connally made this point more bluntly in speaking about the ECA bill, "which deals only with economics. I would be disposed to take disciplinary action against anybody in the ECA who exceeded his authority and began to meddle with the politics of Europe, either for a union or against a union or half-way between them."[46]

It is obvious that Acheson and Connally operated on a different wavelength from Fulbright's. They missed his point entirely, namely, that without a political framework, economic aid becomes a species of charity. And should such aid revive European economies, the beneficiaries would lose the incentive to change the current destructive structure of international relations. The Foreign Relations Committee, he felt, "rejected the cement . . . indispensable for the salvation of the West and the prevention of another world war."[47] Although there were few in Congress or elsewhere in the United States who would oppose the idea of a European federation, there were even fewer who considered it a vital issue for either Europeans or the United States. Even such warm friends as Fulbright rested their case for a federal Europe on the grounds that its absence would waste Marshall Plan aid.[48] Fulbright ultimately voted both for the ECA bill and the North Atlantic Treaty.

ACHESON BRIDGES GAPS

The uproar on both sides of the Atlantic subsided by the end of February. Acheson quickly took charge of dampening the senators' criticisms and allaying the fears of Europeans. He was able to explain to the Foreign Relations Committee on 19 February that while there could be no obligation for automatic use of U.S. armed forces in the event of aggression against any member, the language of the pact need not exclude reference to military assistance. This feature was embedded in Article 3 and was appreciated by all the allies, even if the "pledge" of Article 5 remained the most critical element in the alliance.[49]

The secretary won support from two major sources, one predictable, the other a happy surprise. That the president would bring to bear the weight of his office was not a surprise. While the outspoken Truman was no "hidden hand" leader in the Eisenhower mold of the 1950s, he was on this issue a modest, often silent, champion of an Atlantic alliance, preferring to work through Lovett and later Acheson. His willingness to grant credit to Vandenberg in the Eightieth Congress reflected his understanding of the importance of bipartisanship to win over the Senate.

Although his inaugural address in January 1949 highlighted Point 4—technical aid to underdeveloped nations—the Atlantic pact was not neglected. He told the nation on 10 January that "to further this objective [the security of the North Atlantic area] I expect later to request funds for providing military supplies to those countries."[50] His notice might have been even more central had he not blamed Hickerson and Achilles for premature release early in January of outlines of the projected treaty's provisions. Needing something new to replace the Atlantic alliance, the president emphasized Point 4.

Yet Europe was not neglected. Inviting Connally and his wife to dinner at the Blair House, Truman fed his ego, pointing out that he was the ideal man to lead the nation into a new age. The campaign worked. Connally was converted, and Acheson secured an agreement from the Foreign Relations Committee over the wording of Article 5. There was one change in the text of 24 December 1948: ". . . such action as it deems necessary, including the use of armed force" would be substituted for "such military or other action . . . as may be necessary."[51] The curse of "deems necessary," as the Europeans saw it, was mitigated by the insertion of "forthwith" into the clause. This version, as Sidney Snyder noted, represented "the minimal commitment that Europe would accept and the maximum that Vandenberg and Connally would endorse."[52]

The surprise was Senator Robert Taft's apparent endorsement of the pact. He told a reporter that he would favor a treaty similar to the Rio de Janeiro Treaty of 1947 that was based on the principle that an attack on any U.S. nation would be an attack on all. Extending the mutual defense principle to the democracies of Western Europe "has been my idea all along." Whether the Rio pact itself was an acceptable model for Europeans may have been open to question, as was Taft's enduring commitment to Western Europe's defense. Taft's new tone reflected a *Washington Post* poll of the Senate, when fifty members said they would vote to respond to any attack on Western Europe. Although thirty-seven senators declined to answer at the time, only one indicated that he probably would not vote for war. Homer Capehart of Indiana saw the North Atlantic Treaty as an opportunity to switch funds from the ECA program to military assistance: "If the threat of communism still exists at this time, I think we could well use some of this ECA money to pay for arms for our friends."[53]

There was uneasiness over the new text on both sides of the Atlantic. Vandenberg, who thought of himself as father of the alliance, never overcame his discomfort over the possibility of the Senate losing war powers. As late as the third week of March, he retracted his endorsement of a speech John Foster Dulles was scheduled to present in Philadelphia, because it seemed to make "instant war action by the president automatic and inevitable if there is an armed attack on someone else." The senator insisted that there would be a considerable difference in the U.S. reaction to an attack on Pearl Harbor and an attack on Norway. The former would require instant response, while the latter would require no more than "instant consideration." Dulles responded in a way that would have soothed Europeans; by observing that even if the U.S. response was not automatic, the results must be the same as if they were.[54] In effect, Dulles underscored Bevin's point that any treaty, no matter how flawed, would set up the machinery of entanglement. This tacit understanding would be the key to the success of the negotiations.[55]

That the Western Union members would have preferred the wording of Article 5 to replicate the unequivocal language of the Brussels Treaty's Article IV was obvious. But they were willing to settle for what they could get. The permanent commission of the Western Union quickly approved, in principle, the changes proposed in the Senate.

Senator Donnell, joined by Senator Arthur Watkins of Utah, continued efforts to slow down the process. As late as 25 March they were demanding more information about the treaty from the Foreign Relations Committee and the State Department. They insisted also that the committee permit every senator "to participate as fully as if every member of the Senate were a member of the Foreign Relations Committee."[56] Although they got their wish, their last ditch efforts to stop the signing were too late. Still, their sentiments suggested that the administration would have trouble ahead with ratification of the treaty.

BRINGING IN THE STEPPING-STONE COUNTRIES

In February, the agitation in the Senate tended to obscure other issues involved in the framing of the treaty, none more pressing than the admittance of the Scandinavian countries and Portugal into the alliance as founding members. These were finally resolved in the Senate and Ambassadors' Committee without the passions attending the debate over Article 5. Ironically, unlike the wrangling between the United States on the one side and Europeans on the other, many of the problems over the scope of the alliance that peaked in the winter of 1949 devolved on internal objections within the stepping-stone countries.

The United States had fewer hesitations about the importance of admitting countries whose territories or possessions were vital as conduits for military aid to Europe than did the potential new allies themselves. And whatever reservations the Western Union had about enlarging the alliance—and they were numerous—they deferred to U.S. pressure.

Of the four Nordic countries considered for membership—Norway, Denmark, Sweden, and Iceland (newly separated from Denmark)—Norway was the most eager to participate in an Atlantic alliance. Its historic ties with Britain and its painful experience in World War II accentuated Norway's sense of vulnerability. But two major obstacles stood in the way of Norway's allegiance to an Atlantic alliance. One was the ongoing efforts of Sweden to create a Nordic bloc that would be a neutral entity between East and West. Sweden's successful neutrality in World War II was an attractive model, and if neutrality could be combined with U.S. military aid, Norway might have made this choice. A further inducement would be the recognition that the Soviets would be less hostile to a Nordic bloc than to an Atlantic bloc.[57]

The United States rejected the Swedish request for military aid on the grounds that it would violate the spirit of the Vandenberg Resolution as well as have a negative impact on members of the Atlantic alliance. Only in the unlikely circumstance that there would be funds left over after the signatories of the pact had been helped would Nordic nations be aided.[58] But the State Department in no uncertain terms judged that the Nordic proposal, devised at Karlstad, Sweden, in early January, was not an option the United States would accept.[59]

The Norwegians confronted the problem of its geographic location. The Soviet Union was their neighbor, and they needed an assurance that no military bases would be placed on Norwegian territory if they should join the alliance. They had received this promise in December, but it was not enough to satisfy the Soviets. They asked, specifically, if Norway intended to sign the North Atlantic Treaty and if so, would they allow bases for foreign air and naval forces. Norway replied that it "will not open bases for the armed forces of foreign countries unless attacked or threatened with aggression." Alarmed by the Soviet tone, Foreign Minister Halvard Lange, a strong supporter of an Atlantic alliance, asked the State Department if such bases would be required under the North Atlantic Treaty. He was told that while there was no requirement, it would be left open for Norway to decide how to respond if the future North Atlantic Council requested facilities.[60]

At least one prominent U.S. diplomatist was uncomfortable with this situation. Dulles, as a delegate to the UN General Assembly, addressed on 8 March a study conference on world order sponsored by the Federal Council of Churches, where he warned the Atlantic Pact negotiators to avoid any commitment that the Soviets might construe as "bringing the United States military might directly to Russia's Scandinavian border."[61] While turning down once again a Soviet offer of a nonaggression pact, Norway declared that membership in the Atlantic alliance would carry an understanding that no foreign military bases would be installed in peace time. Despite this caveat, the Norwegian ambassador to the United States, Wilhelm Munthe Morgenstierne, explained on 4 March just why his country was allying itself with the West. "Norway learned her lesson in 1940" when German invaded, and "today does not believe that 'neutrality' has any relation to the facts of life."[62]

Denmark was more hesitant than Norway to embrace the West. It would have preferred the Swedish arrangement if a Nordic pact could have maintained neutrality and at the same time extracted a pledge of U.S. military aid. At the Karlstad conference, the Danish delegation was split between the Conservatives and the Social Democrats, with the former arguing for the Norwegian stance and the latter veering toward the Swedish proposal to defend Danish territory without a concomitant Western military commitment.[63]

Foreign Minister Gustav Rasmussen was caught in the middle. Lashing out at U.S. insensitivity to Denmark's internal political situation, he asserted that the United States was not serving the cause of world peace. Plaintively, he asked U.S. correspondents visiting Denmark in February under ECA's auspices, "Does it further the cause of peace better if the countries of Scandinavia stand divided?"[64] But recognizing that a united Scandinavia following Sweden's lead would not have sufficient means to defend itself, Denmark joined Norway in accepting the North Atlantic Treaty. As political scientist Nikolaj Petersen pointed out, the decision was made "somewhat half-heartedly," largely because the alternative was unacceptable isolation.[65] And it was made less than two weeks before the treaty was signed.

For the United States, the role of Greenland trumped Danish hesitations and the Western Union's reservations, although that Danish territory would have been covered under the Rio umbrella even if Denmark chose not to participate in the alliance. It served Denmark's political interests, however, for Rasmussen to inform the Danish Parliament that Greenland's facilities would be used purely for defense and not for aggressive purposes.[66]

It was ironic, as historian Valur Ingimundarson observed, that "Iceland, the only unarmed member of the Atlantic Alliance, witnessed the most serious disturbances when it joined NATO as a founding member." Iceland, without an army and with a history of U.S. preventive occupation in World War II, had special objections to membership. Icelanders were well aware of the strategic importance of their country. It was with their consent that it had been occupied by U.S. troops, replacing a British contingent, as a preemptive move against Germany. They did not leave until 1946. Newly aroused nationalism, accompanying independence from Denmark in 1944, inspired a rejection of the U.S. bid to prolong its wartime presence by means of a long-term base lease. The most that the government would tolerate was the Keflavik Agreement of 1946 that allowed transit landing rights for U.S. military aircraft. A pro-Moscow Socialist party with neutralist sentiments replaced a conservative government and proclaimed its wish to avoid Iceland's integration into the North Atlantic alliance.[67]

But Iceland's strategic importance would not permit the United States to allow either friends of the Soviet Union or adherents of a Swedish-style neutralism to prevail. Acheson assured the government that "we were well aware of the special situation in Iceland which has no defense forces and does not desire foreign defense forces on its territory in peacetime," and that there would be "no impairment of the sovereignty of any member."[68] It was not simply bases for defense or for support of future aid to Europe that animated U.S. diplomatists. Iceland's membership would assure the United States that NATO would be an Atlantic, not a European institution. Iceland finally joined Norway and Denmark, when its Parliament voted thirty-seven to eighteen to participate only five days before the treaty was signed and did so amid Communist rioters challenging club-wielding policy.[69]

Norway and Denmark's precondition for joining the alliance was an understanding that there would be no military presence in peacetime. Iceland would have preferred something more binding, such as an explicit statement that "it was unable to declare war." Acheson recommended that if a phrase had to be included, it might note that the country's "special position" as an unarmed nation would affect the action it might take under Article 5.[70]

Ireland, like Sweden, was not a stepping-stone country and, like Sweden, might have been a desirable member of the alliance. But Ireland, too, ruled itself out of the alignment. It precluded any association with NATO as long as Northern Ireland remained part of the United Kingdom.[71] Initially, the British were worried about the prospect of U.S. anglophobia being aroused once again by the intrusion of the Irish question into Anglo-U.S. relations. They need not have been alarmed. There was no uproar in the Senate over the British presence in Northern Ireland.

Nor did U.S. diplomas take up the Irish cause. In an informal conversation with his British counterpart, Spencer Chapin, the counselor at the U.S. Embassy in Dublin, claimed that the Eire government was indulging in "wishful thinking that the Atlantic Pact powers would be prepared to pull the Partition plums out for them."[72] The Irish foreign minister, Sean MacBride, later reproached Acheson for "losing an opportunity for the United States in some tactful way of assisting in the solution of the problem." The secretary of state replied that involvement in "the Irish partition question would be to bring us into a matter which was not an American concern, which would be resented in England and which in my judgment would cause far more harm than it could possibly do good."[73] In the nineteenth century, the Irish-U.S. lobby would not have permitted Anglophile U.S. diplomats to dismiss their cause so cavalierly.

To the United States, Portugal was as important as Norway and Denmark for the bases it could provide in the Atlantic. Acheson took pains to assure the Portuguese that their membership in NATO would not be inconsistent with existing of future Spanish-Portuguese agreements. The traditional Anglo-Portuguese connections helped soften European discomfort with the idea of Portugal as an ally in NATO. Western Union opposition, though, was inevitable considering the undemocratic character of dictator Antonio Salazar's regime and his close ties to Fascist Spain. Salazar's wish to bring Spain into the alliance intensified the misgivings of the Brussels Pact powers.[74] But as with the Scandinavian countries, the United States was prepared to risk antagonizing its future allies to get its way.

Portugal had its grievances against the allies. Despite Britain's historic role as Portugal's oldest ally, the Portuguese harbored suspicions that France and Britain had designs on their territories and professed to believe that their security was tied to Spain's, not to the continent's. Achilles helped to soften this hostility by drafting a letter from Truman to Salazar stating that the United States shared his reluctance to involve itself in continental affairs, "as our history showed. Like Portugal, we were an oceanic, seafaring, Atlantic power with a great interest in maintaining the security of the Atlantic area and not just the continent."[75]

Unlike the case of Ireland, U.S. pressure reflected the need for base facilities in the Azores. The absence of democracy in an alliance "founded on the principles of democracy," as proclaimed in the North Atlantic Treaty's preamble, was naturally a matter of concern to senators and framers of the treaty alike. They were able to indulge in semantics as they finessed the problem of dictatorship. When Senator Henry Cabot Lodge of Massachusetts asked in executive session how we could square "the common heritage of freedom" with Portugal's Fascist regime, Achilles responded that "although its government is not the same form of democracy as we have, it is authoritarian, but it is not totalitarian. . . . If it is a dictatorship, it is because the people freely voted for it." This language was later employed in the Ronald Reagan administration to distinguish friendly authoritarian dictatorships from unfriendly totalitarian dictatorships. Senators Connally and Theodore Green of Rhode Island then chimed in with helpful rhetorical questions, such as Connally's "Don't we owe her a little for Vasco da Gama," and Green's "Didn't she found Massachusetts?" The Texan Connally may be excused for his limited knowledge of fifteenth-century history, but it is more difficult to explain the New Englander's interpretation of the origins of neighboring Massachusetts.[76]

Despite these effusive expressions of solidarity with Portugal, Salazar, as late as two weeks before the scheduled signing of the treaty, still felt that Portuguese national interests were insufficiently protected. When dictator Francisco Franco recognized that Portugal's admission to NATO might pave the way for Spain's entry in the future, the last barrier was removed.[77] Portugal signed the treaty on 4 April as a charter member.

THE MEDITERRANEAN ISSUE

Italy was the political as well as the geographical center of the Mediterranean. If it were not for the unlikely alliance between Hickerson and the French government, Italy, at best, would have been part of a Mediterranean bloc related to, but not part of, NATO. This was Britain's preference. The other European allies wished that the Italian question would just go away. The subject was as wearying as it was contentious. In March, Connally and Vandenberg as well as the president were ready to exclude Italy from the pact as an original signatory. President Harry S. Truman and Acheson might have accepted Italian membership in a related Mediterranean treaty as an alternative, while the Senate was of a mixed mind. The reflex response of the two leaders of the Foreign Relations Committee was negative; they feared both overextending the alliance's geographic commitments and setting a dangerous precedent with respect to Greek and Turkish requests for admission.[78]

Italy had consumed considerable time in the Ambassadors' Committee and the working group's deliberations in the fall of 1948, and it continued to be a major headache for the Brussels Pact allies in the winter of 1949. Most of the negotiators agreed that Italy should have been an unlikely candidate for membership in the Atlantic alliance. Its geographic location was far from the Atlantic; the terms of the Italian peace treaty of 1947 would restrict its military involvement; and the strong Communist presence raised questions about its reliability as a partner. The Ambassadors' draft of 24 December did not set the issue at rest. The ambassadors left it to be settled in the new year.

France had already determined to support Italy's membership as part of its campaign to include the Algerian departments in NATO. The movement of the Scandinavian countries toward the alliance in February and March raised the volume of France's advocacy of Italy. It would vote for Norway only in company with Italy; Bonnet stated bluntly at the 1 March meeting of the Ambassadors' Committee that if Italy was not linked to Norway, "then the French Government would have to reconsider its position as far as its own participation was concerned." The next day the British ambassador to France informed Bevin that there was little chance of French approval of the North Atlantic Treaty "if Norway was a member and Italy was not." The British then took the position that "we ourselves are not, repeat, not keen on Italy acceding, but if both the Americans and French wish her to accede, we should have no objection."[79]

This was hardly an enthusiastic endorsement of Italy's membership. The British were well aware of France's twofold intention of using Italy to advance its Algerian agenda and to serve as a counterweight to Scandinavia in northern Europe. The British had been informed of France's inflexible stance on Algeria at the meeting of the Western Union's Consultative Council on 28 January when Schuman told his colleagues that it would be impossible to get the French parliament's approval "if the pact included such places as Alaska and excluded Algeria."[80]

It was not France's insistence alone that gained Italy charter membership in NATO. The U.S. role was preeminent. In the State Department, Hickerson's influence was a critical factor in overcoming the objections Kennan had made in 1948. He now had the implicit backing of the JCS. While they felt that the Brussels Pact rather than NATO was the appropriate vehicle for Italian membership, so that "the whole pattern of defense of Western Europe be more properly integrated," they recognized that "it will be harmful from the military point of views for her to be a member of neither." They shared Hickerson's concern that if Italy were excluded, Italians might lose heart and succumb to a Communist regime in the event of war with the Soviet Union.[81]

One of the obstacles Hickerson had to surmount stemmed from Italy's own ambivalence about membership. While Acheson was able to marshal sufficient argument in favor of admission, including the damage France might inflict on the alliance if Italy was snubbed, he had to contend with Italy's internal debates over the treaty. Elements of the Socialist Party, which was part of the governing coalition, publicly repudiated the party's advocacy of the alliance. Combined with the Communists who followed the familiar paths of violence in the streets and fist fights on the floor of the Chamber of Deputies, they constituted an often daunting challenge to the Alcide de Gasperi government's entry into NATO.[82]

Subsumed under the political struggles in Rome was a more positive reason for participation: it would accelerate the pace of Italy's return to respectability if not to power after the debacle in World War II. But it also tempted Italy to link membership in the Atlantic alliance to retention of Trieste and the return of its former African colonies. This tactic was abandoned when Foreign Minister Carlo Sforza agreed not to complicate Italy's application by raising contentious and extraneous issues that might have alienated their champions in the United States and France.[83] There was a cognate matter that served Italy's cause: participating in the council of Europe, as historian E. Timothy Smith noted, "was a way by which a Mediterranean nation could justify joining a North Atlantic regional security system."[84]

This opportunity was not open to Greece and Turkey. Despite Turkish protests that the acceptance of Italy, a non-Atlantic power, would increase their vulnerability to Soviet pressure, none of the Atlantic powers would consider them as suitable applicants at this time. They had to settle for a declaration by the signers of the North Atlantic Treaty in defense of Greece and Turkey—and Iran as well—that would be issued simultaneously with the completion of the treaty.[85]

WESTERN UNION AND THE MILITARY ASSISTANCE PROGRAM

The long journey to the completion of treaty negotiations was approaching in March 1949. But there were a few major issues unresolved as well as repercussions to be anticipated. How the treaty would fit the terms of the UN charter and how the Soviet Union would react to the alliance were still in doubt. But before these problems were faced, the United States had to deal with the ongoing aspirations of the European allies for military aid—massive and immediate. While not expressed as openly, it seemed that Article 3, calling for "mutual and effective self-help and mutual aid," was as important as Article 5 to the five members of the Western Union. They equated mutual aid exclusively with U.S. aid, and to secure this was the impetus behind most of the activities of the Western Union's defense organization (WUDO).

By the end of 1948, it was obvious that WUDO had accomplished as much as it could to demonstrate to the United States that the Brussels Pact members were worthy beneficiaries of U.S. military assistance. On 29 December 1948, WUDO's chiefs of staff committee produced a report that celebrated the progress Europeans had made through their own efforts. At the same time, it presented a case for external assistance that only the United States could supply. And in its presentation, they benefited from collaboration with U.S. advisers whose voices were expected to be heard in the Pentagon and in the Congress.[86]

The joint effort showed signs of success. The president's third point in his inaugural address spoke to the provision of "military advice and equipment to free nations which will cooperate in maintenance of peace and security."[87] This was a clear link between the North Atlantic Treaty and military assistance program (MAP). A Foreign Assistance Correlation Committee (FACC), under State Department leadership, had been established on 3 January to work out policies for considerations of the steering committee, composed of the Secretaries of State and Defense and the ECA administrator. Major General Lyman Lemnitzer was the Defense Department's representative on the FACC. Its object was to consider aid to countries worldwide, but its focus was on Western Europe and the contributions each country could make to the security of the United States in the event of war.[88]

Although the FACC accepted the JCS interim program for fiscal year 1950, the inadequate information provided by WUDO was no help in developing an efficient supply system. But because the Western Union's defense policy, such as it was, fitted the strategic thinking of the JCS, its lists would serve as the basis for budgeting, until a more careful and more complete evaluation could be made. The interim supply program had to satisfy two criteria: a) It must not affect the economic recovery of individual countries, and b) The MAP must not breach the minimum requirements of each armed service. Both the U.S. and European military agreed that they could live with these caveats, at least until the programs were implemented.[89]

On another level, the MAP ran into trouble with European expectations. To aid coordination of European efforts, the U.S. ambassador to Britain, Lewis W. Douglas, was appointed chief of a European Coordinating Committee in February. As such, he was the point man and uncomfortable mediator between the United States and Europeans on all matters of U.S. military aid. He first had to contend with the hesitant response of the Brussels Pact powers to the U.S. requirement of coordination requests. And while he used Bevin as a conduit to other members of the Western Union, Bevin was a wary partner.[90]

When Douglas and W. Averell Harriman, U.S. Special Representative in Europe for the ECA, presented plans for military assistance on 1 March, these contained principles that should not have been a surprise to Europeans. They comprised such familiar concerns as a need for "a steady, if moderate expansion of their arms and equipment" and an understanding that "over a long period, they should be increasingly produced and financed by European economies." Nor should they have been surprised at the U.S. insistence on reciprocal aid, given the terms of the ECA. Yet this statement of principles implied pressure that Bevin resented. As Douglas noted, he resisted the general principle of reciprocity and was "adamant against the [U.S.] even informally viewing and commenting on the WU Consultative Council's draft paper before it was approved in London."[91] It was obvious that the State Department was not going to engage in the mutually satisfying games that the European and U.S. military were playing.

At its plenary session on 14 March 1949, the Western Union's consultative council complained that it was impossible even to agree in principle "until we had some idea of how we could apply this principle."[92] The council, in fact, did agree, in general, to reciprocation but balked at U.S. demand for examination and approval of Western Union's requirements. Although Douglas, after conferring with other Brussels Pact foreign ministers, doubted that Bevin was speaking for them, they insisted that he had stated a common position accurately.[93]

There were two especially contentious issues that the Western Union partners raised. One was the charge of discrimination inherent in the U.S. refusal to provide aid to the Netherlands because of Dutch opposition to Indonesian independence. Disclaiming any intention to coerce the Dutch government, the U.S. ambassador to the Netherlands had pointed out that "certain obligations resting on our government because of its UN membership might make it impossible to furnish military equipment assistance under MAP."[94] The European allies bristled at this judgment, which they felt masked U.S. suspicion that U.S. arms in Dutch hands would be used to suppress Indonesian forces.

That U.S. public opinion saw the Dutch repression of the Indonesian struggle for independence as a violation of the UN charter was reflected in an appeal by Senator Margaret Chase Smith of Maine to Queen Juliana, "woman-to-woman," to stop the war. To the Dutch government and their allies in the Western Union, however, the U.S. position appeared as an unwarranted interference in the internal affairs of an ally and an inappropriate interpretation of UN obligations.[95]

Proclaiming that the Western Union should "deal with [the] US on a basis of oneness," other members of the Brussels Pact rallied behind the Netherlands, partly out of concern that similar punishment might be meted out to them in the future and partly out of umbrage at the tone of moral superiority displayed in the anticolonial sentiments of the United States. Bevin spoke for all his allies in observing that "Whatever the merits or demerits we may feel about the present situation in Indonesia, we felt we couldn't isolate it from the general reaction that might happen upon any one of us in similar circumstances."[96] This complaint was made just two days before the signing of the treaty.

Both sides then backed off. The United States appreciated the threat to the North Atlantic Treaty if the allies lost confidence in the senior partner's commitment to their security. And while the Dutch were grateful for the extent to which their European colleagues rallied to their defense, no member of the new alliance wanted to risk blame for sabotaging the treaty in its final stages. Eleven days before this protest was made, Ambassador Douglas as European Correlation Coordinator, had already made a convincing case to the Truman administration for accepting Dutch professions of good faith.[97]

The second complication in the planning for the MAP was over U.S. policy on reciprocity. Base facilities were to be the quid pro quo of military assistance. This equation raised the image of nineteenth-century territorial concessions, as if Europe were some sort of inferior outpost. It also focused on bilateral rather than multilateral negotiations, deviating from Western Union's wish to be considered an equal and as exclusive bargaining partner of the United States. There was more than an implied threat in the words of the FACC document of 7 February: The United States "should require as a matter of principle, that reciprocal assistance, such as base rights . . . be granted, where necessary." Should the allies fail to cooperate, "this would mean no military aid at all."[98] Some modification was made later in the month when the United States agreed that after ratification of the treaty, the member nations would decide whether negotiations should be continued on a bilateral basis.[99]

Ambassador Douglas did his best to minimize transatlantic quarrels and offered balm to wounded sensibilities, even when he failed to soften U.S. positions. As he warned Acheson, "Although all recognize that we will and should have bilateral arrangements on certain matters with individual countries, if U.S. over-emphasizes attitude . . . we can and will be accused of pursuing same tactics as Kremlin vis-à-vis satellites, i.e., those of the great power dictating to smaller powers." The United States could weaken the Western Union just as it was in the process of being absorbed into "a more diffused North Atlantic Pact organization."[100] At the same time, he recognized the political and military realities behind the congressional demand for reciprocation and the military's insistence on bases as prerequisites for defense of the West.

Bevin made the best case he could in explaining why a revision of the Consultative Council's request for U.S. aid was inadvisable. Full compliance with U.S. requirements would embarrass Western Union members and create delays that could upset the MAP timetable. But Bevin also admitted that the terms of the Western Union request did not rule out bilateral agreements of the kind the United States wanted. From his perch in London, Douglas was more sympathetic to the political problems of the allies than his colleagues in Washington. He was convinced that pervasive fear of Soviet power, more than nationalist passions, explained their reluctance to identify possible U.S. bases in their countries.[101]

The interplay of the United States and Europeans over negotiations for the MAP at this point resembled an orchestrated minuet. The Western Union would take a short step indicating its general needs and insufficient resources; the United States would counter the step with strict conditions that had to be met; and both sides would follow with a slow, ceremonious, and mutually satisfying conclusion. In mid-March, the Europeans knew that the Truman administration wanted a document to be ready for public release immediately after the signing of the North Atlantic Treaty. Neither side was under any illusion about Europe's readiness to do its share. The JCS might bluster about their particular needs, but before the end of 1948 they had accepted WUDO's pretense of compliance. The unity and cooperation of Western Europe were more important than public concessions to U.S. interests.

What the State Department wanted was enough credibility for Western Union requests to pass muster in the Senate. It did not succeed. When the European package of military needs was submitted on 5 April, one day after the signing ceremonies, it became clear that the transatlantic allies had overestimated their chances for success with the Senate.[102] Too many lacunae had not been filled in during the campaign for a quick resolution of the MAP, ranging from Senate displeasure over the omission of non-Western Union members of the alliance to unhappiness with excessive militarization of the new organization. Senator Taft forewarned the policymakers when he told reporters on 18 March about his concern that the treaty seemed to be "inseparable" from the issue of arms aid. And Senator Wherry signaled that his vote on the ratification of the treaty would depend on the State Department laying down "for inspection any separate legislation that goes along with it."[103] It took six months of difficult bargaining before Congress was willing to approve MAP for the NATO allies.

MEETING THE TERMS OF THE UN CHARTER

There was still one more obstacle to the completion of the treaty, namely, its compatibility with the UN charter. This was not a new problem. Vandenberg had confronted it in his resolution in the spring of 1948. No one reading the text of the Senate Resolution 239 could have had any doubt of his dedication to the vital role he assigned to the UN in securing a peaceful postwar future. Its preamble resolved that the Senate reaffirm the policy of the United States "to achieve international peace and security through the United Nations." No matter how badly the Soviets might abuse their position on the Security Council, Vandenberg believed that the proposed association of the United States with Western Europe must conform to the terms of the charter. It was no coincidence that all but one of the six paragraphs of the resolution mentioned the charter.

In this context "progressive development of regional and other collective arrangements for individual and collective self-defense" rested on its compatibility with Article 51 of the charter. It is worth noting that this article, dealing with collective defense, was a fundamental right under international law, irrespective of its inclusion in the UN's charter.

The UN's obvious failure to function in the way the charter had intended was proclaimed as the primary reason for an Atlantic security pact. Soviet abuse of its veto power in the Security Council in the eyes of the other victors in World War II was an unintended byproduct of the UN in action. The framers of the North Atlantic Treaty regularly insisted that the treaty would support and not undermine the charter by strengthening the defense capabilities of its members. An assumption of compatibility between the treaty and the charter ran as an undercurrent throughout the long deliberations over the treaty. The first major draft, the White Paper in September 1948, finessed the issue by noting that its articles would place the treaty "within the framework of the United Nations Charter" as well as "demonstrate the determination of the parties fully to meet their obligations under the Charter.[104] The working group professed to find no problem in linking the treaty to the charter in its report on 14 December 1948. The treaty presumably would be placed under the rubric of Chapter VIII, embracing Articles 51 to 54 of the charter, identifying the alliance as a regional organization. However, Articles 53 and 54, the pertinent models in Chapter VIII, required that regional organizations report to the Security Council where their activities would be scrutinized. This would also mean that their operations would be subject to a Soviet veto, which was an intolerable prospect. The allies did not deal with this problem in 1948.[105]

The question of compatibility could not be evaded in 1949 as negotiations were coming to a close. If the treaty created a genuinely regional organization, then Articles 53 and 54 would impose serious problems for the allies. The allies did not meet the conflict head on until the sixteenth meeting of the Ambassadors' Committee on 7 March. Obviously, the projected treaty could not fit into the charter's Article 53. But to admit that the North Atlantic Treaty was not a regional organization would guarantee "endless confusion," according to Secretary Acheson. Although he was impatient with the ambassadors' agonizing over the language of Article 53, he devised a legal distinction between "enforcement action" under Article 53 of the charter, which would be the responsibility of the Security Council and collective defense under Article 51, which permitted individual states to work together to deter aggression without necessarily reporting to the UN council.[106]

The approach here was to avoid controversy by refraining from asking if the North Atlantic Treaty was or was not a regional organization. The text would simply assert conformity with the charter without subjecting it to the judgments of the Soviet Union.[107] The final version of the treaty then reprised the language of the Vandenberg Resolution if not its spirit. Four of the fourteen articles, in addition to the preamble, referred to the charter by name, and Article 7 piously respected the primary responsibility of the Security Council for the maintenance of international peace and security.

While the treaty partners had hoped to dismiss the problem of its compatibility with the UN charter, their assertions provided an opening for their adversaries, notably the Soviet bloc, to charge them with violating the charter. Soviet reactions initially were low-key. Joseph Stalin was engaged in a peace offensive in January and February that was marked by hints of a settlement of the Berlin blockade. In January, he raised this possibility in an interview he gave to International News Service correspondent Kingsbury Smith.[108]

The Soviets were coming around to recognize that the Berlin airlift was a success and was more than a prop to German morale. The unification of West Germany under trizonal auspices was a reality. When Acheson noted that Stalin had answered Smith's question about the blockade without mentioning the currency reforms that presumably precipitated it, he perceived a new mood. Stalin spoke favorably about a mutual declaration against going to war with each other and responded to Smith's question about gradual disarmament with the comment, "naturally." Acheson recorded in his memoirs that "we judged the episode to be a cautious signal from Moscow."[109] In the absence of documentary evidence, one may speculate that the Donald Maclean reports to Moscow from inside the British Embassy in Washington were seriously considered and served to quiet Soviet fears about Western intentions.

Still, caution was the appropriate word to apply to Soviet treatment of the Berlin blockade, a West German state, and the establishment of NATO. Certainly, the harsh dismissal of Norway's promise not to permit regional bases on their territory indicated a hard line toward the Atlantic alliance, even if in this instance its ire was not directed against the United States. At the same time, the Soviets threatened to suspend the Anglo-Russian and Franco-Russian accords of World War II in which the signatories agreed "not to conclude any alliance and not to take part in any coalition directed against one of the High Contracting Parties." They intended to equate the North Atlantic Treaty with an aggressive coalition that would undermine the UN.[110]

The Communist charges of violations of the UN charter picked up steam as the allies concluded their negotiations. The Soviet press made a point of printing the full text of the treaty on 29 March to expose the hollowness of its claim of its harmony with the charter. And on 31 March, just five days before the official signing, the Soviets issued a formal protest, asserting that Article 5 would unleash aggressive armies "without any authority whatsoever of the Security Council." Nor could the treaty be justified under Article 51, which was designed to be used only in the case of an armed attack upon a UN member, not as a cover for aggressive aims.[111]

The Soviet argument won some backing from uneasy UN officials, including the Secretary General himself. In examining NATO as part of the UN's collective security system, Trygve Lie warned that "no regional arrangement can ever be a satisfactory substitute for the United Nations." If the world comes to regard alliances as a substitute for the genuine worldwide collective security, "it would undo the hope of a lasting peace."[112]

All twelve NATO partners present in Washington for formal signing of the pact rejected the Soviet protest. Their joint statement on 2 April stood firm in the conviction that the defensive nature of the treaty accommodated both the spirit and the letter of the UN charter.[113] But anticipating that the Soviets would arraign the United States as an aggressor at the forthcoming session of the UN General Assembly, the staff of the U.S. delegation prepared a paper recommending that the European allies take the lead in refuting the charges.[114]

Their worries about a violent Soviet outburst were excessive at this time. With all their bombast against the transatlantic alliance, Soviet violence was verbal. The Communists had a stake in a peaceful front. A Soviet-inspired Cultural and Scientific Confederation for World Peace convened at the Waldorf Astoria in New York from 25 to 17 March to alert the dangers of a new war that the United States was causing. Elsewhere, peace conferences were held in Bucharest, Tokyo, Mexico City, Paris, and Moscow. The Soviet press also made a point of reproducing comments from U.S. sources—editorials in the *Chicago Tribune*, a resolution from the Society of Friends, and pronouncements from Henry Wallace's Progressive Party—depicting the alliance as provocative and the United States as an enemy of the UN. In this environment, Communist incitements to civil strife were sacrificed to the image of the Soviet Union as the defender of the UN Charter. The Joint Intelligence Committee of the U.S. Embassy in Moscow concluded on 1 April that the Soviets "will not resort to direct military action against the West in the near future and counts on a period of several years of peace."[115]

RACING TO THE FINISH LINE

Senator Vandenberg's blessing to the publication of the State Department's White Paper on the North Atlantic Treaty seemed to solidify U.S. public opinion on the subject. Addressing the U.S. Conference of Mayors on 23 March, he hailed the treaty as "the most important step in American foreign policy since the promulgation of the Monroe Doctrine."[116] By the end of March, almost all the problems carried over from 1948, as well as a few new questions asked in 1949, had been addressed. The stepping-stone countries came in just under the wire. Only a few stray strands remained to be tied into the text.

Not all the signatories achieved full satisfaction of their aspirations and grievances, but the compromises were acceptable. Canada had never given up its wish for an Article 2 that would emphasize the social and economic dimension of NATO. As Ambassador Hume Wrong asserted in the Ambassadors' Committee in February, "It would cause great political difficulty in Canada, if there were no article in the treaty of a non-military nature. There was need for something which reflected the ideological unity of the Atlantic powers."[117]

But just as the Canadians were urging the strengthening of the article, Acheson was intensifying his distaste for what he considered its vague generalities without practical application. He was also sensitive to the Senate's hostility to the phrase "to promote the general welfare." It aroused visions of endless handouts to beneficiaries. Achilles recalled Connally saying that "the reference to the general welfare in the United States Constitution had caused more litigation than any other provision in it. Get it the hell out of this treaty."[118] That clause was removed, but reference to "economic collaboration" remained in Article 2.

The duration of the alliance was another remnant left over from the debates in 1948. The fifty-year model of the Brussels Pact, championed by France, was unacceptable to the United States and Canadians. Lester Pearson, Canada's deputy undersecretary of state for external relations, recommended a five-year period on the assumption that a new schedule would be set following the temporary emphasis on the organization's military functions. He envisioned the withering away of the security aspects of the alliance, while economic and cultural aspects of the alliance would have been developing within the organization.[119] Although Dutch Ambassador Eelco van Kleffens would have preferred the French proposal of a fifty-year period to lock the United States firmly into the alliance, the signatories accepted in Articles 12 and 13 a twenty-year period as sufficient to effect this result. As for U.S. senators, the curse of a permanent entanglement was alleviated by incorporating a review of the treaty after ten years, and after twenty years any member could leave the alliance on giving one year's notice. The wording of the preamble, also disputed in 1948, was easily resolved with the expected deference to the UN but without rhetorical flourishes.[120]

Not surprisingly, French reservations loomed larger than those of the other allies. Although their sponsorship of Italy as a charter member was successful, they had no chance of willing coverage of all their colonial possessions. The stigma of colonialism had to be erased before the U.S. Senate would ratify the treaty. But their demand to place Algeria under Article 6 required a compromise that Achilles claimed to have supplied: "I picked the Tropic of Cancer, running between Florida and Cuba, as a convenient southern boundary to avoid complications with the Good Neighborhood."[121] This permitted the French to include the three northern departments of Algeria that were constitutionally part of metropolitan France.

There was still one more problem that was always on France's mind. It entered the alliance with a wary eye on Germany. Under Schuman's leadership, the French agreed to German control of the Ruhr with appropriate safeguards, but they still harbored suspicions that the Anglo-U.S. allies would grant more authority to the prospective West German government than they could tolerate. To resolve their doubts, the French wanted a

high-level conference with the British and the United States that would better coordinate a German policy. This request alarmed the allies who feared
that the real French aim was to undo plans for a West German constitution.
It seemed obvious that the North Atlantic Treaty had not exorcised the old
fears of a powerful Germany. When Schuman met with Acheson on 1 April
in Washington, they left open the matter of further tripartite talks over Germany.[122]

The French also challenged their Anglo-U.S. allies to share military authority within NATO. They persisted in believing that the combined chiefs
of staff of World War II, which had excluded French participation, did not
dissolve with the end of the war. They wanted to ensure that any military
committee established under the aegis of a North Atlantic Council authorized in Article 9 would be headed by a tripartite standing group, with France
as the third partner.[123] France won this particular contest. Suspicious
though the French still were about an Anglo-U.S. conspiracy to dominate
the alliance, Schuman did not refrain from joining the foreign ministers of
the other eleven member nations in the signing ceremony conducted at the
imposing Inter-Departmental Auditorium on Constitution Avenue.

The location inevitably was Washington. Acheson was more attuned to
the beneficial impact the site would have on U.S. public opinion than he
was to European preferences. The British and Canadians would have preferred Bermuda or the Azores as suitable Atlantic symbols but had to defer
to U.S. priorities. While acknowledging that it would be difficult to justify
a visit to Bermuda simply to sign the document, the "scant courtesy" with
which the United States greeted their proposal annoyed the British. But because there was no chance of getting their way, "we had better swallow the
pill smilingly."[124]

The Europeans had little choice about accepting the U.S. decision. But given
the United States responsibility for prolonging negotiations in the six months
preceding the ceremony, it seemed inappropriate for the United States to demand immediate actions on the time and place for the signing of the treaty in
mid-March. Even more irritating to the Brussels Pact allies was the invitation
to the formerly peripheral nations to participate as equals without proper consultation. The United States "jumped the gun," according to the disgruntled
British Foreign Office. As for the Western Union permanent commission, it
had envisioned their accession only after the treaty was signed, thereby assuring a superior position in the alliance for the core powers.[125]

There was discontent in the Congress as well when the State Department's invitation to attend the ceremony excluded most of that body's
membership. The original plan was to invite only the leaders of both parties and members of the Senate Foreign Relations and House Foreign Affairs
Committees. Connally accused the State Department of "poor taste and bad
finesse." Acheson sardonically wondered if the Marine Corps band had

caught the spirit of the occasion when it accompanied the solemn and dignified proceedings with George Gershwin's "I've Got Plenty of Nothin'" and "It Ain't Necessarily So." But given the euphoria of that moment, Canadian Foreign minister Pearson recalled that "we were not even disturbed by the regrettable musical selections of the band."[126]

Despite all the hurdles that had to be vaulted en route to the final entanglement, Hickerson and Achilles had every right to celebrate the end of their fifteen-month journey as they headed for the nearest bar in the basement of the Willard Hotel. Now "they could relax, grin at each other, and really enjoy a couple of bourbons."[127]

Appropriately, their creation was the "Treaty of Washington" rather than an extension of the Western Union. The Europeans may have initiated the process, but bipartisan U.S. advocates brought it to a conclusion and terminated America's 149-year tradition of political and military non-entanglement with Europe.

NOTES

1. Sir Nicholas Henderson, *Birth of NATO* (Boulder, CO: Westview Press, 1983), 77.

2. *New York Times*, January 26, 1949, 20.

3. James V. Forrestal, "Talk to National Press Club," *New York Times*, February 2, 1949.

4. John W. Young, *Britain, France, and the Unity of Europe* (Leicester: Leicester University Press, 1984), 209.

5. See chapter 7.

6. *New York Times*, February 11, 1949, 15.

7. Dean Acheson, *Present at the Creation: My Years in the State Department* (New York: W. W. Norton & Co., 1969), 233.

8. George F. Kennan, *Memoirs, 1925–1950* (Boston: Little, Brown and Co., 1967), 427–28.

9. Arthur H. Vandenberg, Jr., ed., *The Private Papers of Arthur H. Vandenberg* (Boston: Houghton Mifflin, 1952), 500.

10. *Congressional Record*, 81st Cong., 1st sess., January 18, 1949, 95: 465; *New York Times*, January 19, 1949, 1, 14.

11. *Congressional Record*, 81st Cong., 1st sess., January 18, 1949, 95: 460.

12. Acheson, *Present at the Creation*, 281.

13. Vandenberg, *Private Papers of Senator Vandenberg*, 506.

14. Franks to FO, February 15, 1949, no. 939, FO 371/79225 8630, PRO.

15. JCS memorandum for Secretary of Defense (James Forrestal), January 5, 1949, Sub: North Atlantic Pact, *FRUS*, 1949, IV: 12.

16. Steven L. Rearden, *History of the Office of the Secretary of Defense: The Formative Years, 1947–1950* (Washington, D.C.: Historical Office, Office of the Secretary of Defense, 1984), I: 365.

17. Kenneth W. Condit, *The History of the Joint Chiefs of Staff: The Joint Chiefs of Staff and National Policy* (Washington, D.C.: Historical Division, JCS, 1992), II: 365.

18. Quoted in cable from British ambassador to France to FO, February 26, 1949, no.49, FO 371/79250, PRO.

19. James Reston, *New York Times,* January 11, 1949.

20. Quoted in Ronald Steel, *Walter Lippmann and the American Century* (Boston: Little, Brown, 1980), 458–59.

21. Escott Reid, *Time of Fear and Hope: The Making of the North Atlantic Treaty, 1947–1949* (Toronto: McClelland and Stewart, 1977), 148.

22. Minutes of the Twelfth Meeting of the Washington Exploratory Talks, February 8, 1949, *FRUS,* 1949, IV: 73–74; Henderson, *Birth of NATO,* 89–90.

23. Sidney R. Snyder, "The Role of the International Working Group in the Creation of the North Atlantic Treaty" (Ph.D. dissertation, Kent State University, 1992), 169.

24. Memorandum of Conversation by Secretary of State, February 14, 1949, Charles Bohlen, Tom Connally, Vandenberg, *FRUS,* 1949, IV: 109–110.

25. Minutes of the Twelfth Meeting of the Washington Exploratory Talks, February 8, 1949, *FRUS,* 1949, IV: 85.

26. Reid, *Time of Fear and Hope,* 150.

27. Minutes of the Twelfth Meeting of the Washington Exploratory Talks, February 8, 1949, *FRUS,* IV: 76; *New York Times,* February 17, 1949.

28. *Congressional Record,* 81st Cong., 1st sess., February 14, 1949, 95: 1163.

29. Oliver Franks to FO, February 15, 1949, no. 938, FO 371/ 79225, PRO.

30. Memorandum of Conversation by Secretary of State, February 14, 1949, Bohlen, Connally, Vandenberg, *FRUS* 1949, IV: 109.

31. Franks to FO, February 15, 1949, no. 939, FO371/79925, PRO.

32. Snyder, "The Role of the International Working Group," 172.

33. Memorandum by Secretary of State for Foreign Affairs, February 19, 1949, C. P. (49) 34, 1–2, CAB 129/32 8605, PRO.

34. Reid, *Time of Fear and Hope,* 153; Theodore C. Achilles, *Fingerprints on History: The NATO Memoirs of Theodore C. Achilles,* edited by Lawrence S. Kaplan and Sidney B. Snyder (Kent, OH: Lyman L. Lemnitzer Center for NATO and European Community Affairs, Kent State University, 1992), 29.

35. Memorandum of Conversation by the Secretary of State, February 14, 1949, Henri Bonnet, Achilles, *FRUS* 1949, IV: 107.

36. *New York Times,* February 17, 1949, 1, 4.

37. Extension of European Recovery Program, *Hearings,* February 11, 1949, Senate Committee on Foreign Relations, 81st Cong., 1st sess., 198–99.

38. See chapter 7.

39. Oliver Harvey to FO, January 22, 1948, no. 96, FO 371/7214, PRO.

40. Metric Document No. 217, Record of the Fourth Meeting of the Consultative Council, London, 2 January 28, 1949 Annex II, Document No. A/143, PRO; Frances E. Willis, U.S. Embassy in London, to Secretary of State, March 7, 1949, No. 377, "Draft Proposal for a Council of Europe," 800.00/3, RG 59, NARA.

41. Extension of European Recovery Program, *Hearings,* February 11, 1949, 200–1.

42. Franks to FO, January 31, 1949, no. 611, FO371/79243, PRO.

43. France's President Vincent Auriol noted that Robert Schuman was going to London to point out to the British how important European unity was to American public opinion. Auriol, *Journal du Septennat*, II: January 12, 1949, III: 9.

44. Richard Coudenhove-Kalergi to J. William Fulbright, February 2, 1949, Fulbright Papers, University of Arkansas Library, Fayetteville.

45. Fulbright to Coudenhove-Kalergi, February 12, 1949, Fulbright Papers.

46. Extension of European Recovery Program, *Hearings*, February 11, 1949, 198–99.

47. *Congressional Record*, March 30, 1948, 81st Cong., 1st sess., 95: 3457.

48. Extension of European Recovery Program, *Hearings*, February 11, 1949, 199.

49. Dean Acheson, *New York Times*, February 19, 1949.

50. Annual Budget Message to the Congress, Fiscal Year 1950, January 10, 1949, *Public Papers of the Presidents: Harry S. Truman* (Washington, D.C.: Government Printing Office, 1964), 46; Snyder, "The Role of the International Working Group," 167–68.

51. Oral history interview, John D. Hickerson, Harry S. Truman Library, Independence, Miss., in Sidney R. Snyder, "The Role of the International Working Group in the Creation of the North Atlantic Treaty" (Ph.D. dissertation, Kent State University, 1992), 74–75.

52. Snyder, "The Role of the International Working Group," 175.

53. *New York Times*, February 1, 1949; *New York Times*, February 19, 1949.

54. Arthur Vandenberg to John Foster Dulles, March 19, 1949; Dulles to Vandenberg, March 21, 1949, John Foster Dulles Collection, Seeley G. Mudd Library, Princeton University.

55. Memorandum by Secretary of State for Foreign Affairs, February 19, 1949, C. P. (49) 34, 1–2, CAB 129/32 8605, PRO.

56. *Congressional Record*, 81st Cong., 1st sess., March 25, 1949, 3154.

57. Tel Acting Secretary of State to Embassy in Norway, January 14, 1949, *FRUS*, 1949, no. 17, IV: 27.

58. Tel Ambassador to Denmark (Josiah Marvel) to Acting Secretary of State, January 10, 1949, *FRUS*, 1949, no. 20, IV: 17.

59. Tel Ambassador to Sweden (Matthews) to Acting Secretary of State, January 14, 1949, *FRUS*, 1949, no. 53, IV: 25.

60. Russian Declaration Delivered to Foreign Minister (Norway), February 5, 1949, Proposing a Non-Aggression Pact, *FRUS*, 1949, IV: 91–93; quoted in Olav Riste, "NATO, the Northern Flank, and the Neutrals," *A History of NATO: the First Fifty Years*, ed. Gustav Schmidt, 3 vols. (London: Palgrave Publishers, Ltd., 2001), III: 250.

61. *New York Times*, March 9, 1949, 5.

62. *Facts on File Yearbook, 1949*, vol. IX, no. 435, February 27–March 5, 1949, 71; *New York Times*, March 5, 1949, 3.

63. *New York Times*, January 24, 1949.

64. *New York Times*, February 26, 1949, 1.

65. *New York Times*, March 26, 1949; Nikolaj Petersen, "The Dilemmas of Alliance: Denmark's Years with NATO," in Schmidt, *History of NATO*, III: 277.

66. Memorandum of Conversation, by the Counselor of the State Department (Charles Bohlen) Gustav Rasmussen, Henrik de Kauffmann et al., *FRUS*, 1949, IV: 200.

67. Valur Ingimundarson, "The Role of NATO and US Military Bases in Ice-landic Domestic Politics," in Schmidt, *History of NATO*, II: 285–86; Gunnar Karls-son, *The History of Iceland* (Minneapolis: University of Minnesota Press, 2000), 317–18.

68. Memorandum of conversation by Secretary of State, March 14, 1949: Bjarni Benediktsson et al., *FRUS*, 1949, IV: 203.

69. Lawrence S. Kaplan, "The Atlantic Component of NATO," *The Long Entangle-ment: NATO's First Fifty Years* (Westport, CT: Praeger, 1999), 29–35; *New York Times*, March 31, 1949, 2.

70. Acheson to legation in Iceland, March 26, 1949, *FRUS*, 1949, IV: 248. Mem-orandum of conversation by Director of Office of European Affairs (John Hicker-son): Irish Minister Sean Nunan, *FRUS*, 1949, IV: 890.

71. Extract of letter from N. Pritchard, Office of UK Representative, to Eire, to N. E. Archer, Commonwealth Relations Office, March 7, 1949, FO 371/79235, PRO.

72. Extract of letter from N. Pritchard, Office of UK Representative, to Eire, to N. E. Archer, Commonwealth Relations Office, March 7, 1949, FO 371/79235, PRO.

73. Memorandum of conversation by the Secretary of State, April 11, 1949: Sean MacBride, *FRUS*, 1949, IV: 293; Achilles, *Fingerprints on History*, 28.

74. Tel Secretary of State to the Embassy in Portugal, March 11, 1949, *FRUS*, 1949, no. 68, IV: 201–2.

75. Tel Ambassador to Portugal (Lincoln MacVeagh) to Secretary of State, March 9, 1949, *FRUS*, 1949, no. 85, IV 180–82. Achilles, *Fingerprints on History*, 28.

76. Vandenberg and North Atlantic Treaty, *Hearings*, in Executive Session before Senate Committee on Foreign Relations, February 18, 1949, 81st Cong., 1st sess., 89.

77. Tel Ambassador to Portugal to Secretary of State, March 19, 1949, *FRUS*, 1949, no. 99, IV: 239; Memorandum of conversation by Ambassador in Portugal, March 30, 1948: Spanish Ambassador Nicolas Franco, *FRUS*, 1949, IV: 255.

78. Memorandum of conversation by Secretary of State, February 28, 1949: Pres-ident, Connally, George, Vandenberg, 840.20/11–2448, RG 59, NARA.

79. Minutes of the Fourteenth Meeting of the Washington Exploratory Talks, March 1, 1949, *FRUS*, 1949, IV: 128–29; Harvey to Bevin, March 2,1949, FO 371/7929, PRO; Crosthwaite to Mallet and Shuckburgh, March 1, 1949, FO 371/7929, PRO.

80. Metric Document No. 214, Negotiations Relating to the Conclusion of a North Atlantic Pact, in Metric Document No. 217, Record of the Fourth Meeting of the WU Consultative Council, London, January 27–28, 1949, PRO.

81. JCS memorandum for Secretary of Defense, January 5, 1949, *FRUS*, 1949, IV:13; E. Timothy Smith, *The United States, Italy, and NATO, 1947–1952* (New York: St. Martin's Press, 1991), 76–77.

82. *New York Times*, March 4, 1949.

83. Smith, *The United States, Italy, and NATO*, 89.

84. Smith, *The United States, Italy, and NATO*, 89.

85. Tel Secretary of State to Embassy in Turkey, March 16, 1949, *FRUS*, 1949, no. 102, IV: 234; tel Secretary of State to Certain Diplomatic Offices, April 2, 1948, *FRUS*, 1949, IV: 270–71.

86. F.C. (48)33, December 29, 1948, Western Union Chiefs of Staff Committee, memorandum by French Minister of Defence, sub: Defence Efforts of the Five Powers, WEU Archives, PRO.

87. Inaugural Address, January 20, 1948, Public Papers of the Presidents, Harry S. Truman, 1949, 114.

88. *FRUS*, 1949, IV: 1: 250 n.

89. Report, JCS 1868/58/11 February 1949, enc. B, 387, CD 6-2-46, RG 330, NARA.

90. Record of Meeting with Bevin, March 1, 1949, Assistant to Secretary of State for Foreign Military Affairs files, 1949, N7-1, N7-1(61)-A-1, Box 2, RG 330, NARA.

91. Memorandum presented by Avenell Harriman and Lewis Douglas to Bevin, March 3, 1949, Assistant to Secretary of State for Foreign Military Affairs files, 1949, N7-1 N7-1(61)-A-1, RG 330, NARA.

92. Metro Document No. 257, Item 2—Action to be taken with regard to Mr. Harriman's Memorandum (Metro document No. 243), 173, Minutes of the Fifth Session of WU's Consultative Council, London, March 14–15, 1949, PRO.

93. Tel Douglas to Secretary of State, March 16, 1949, *FRUS*, 1949, no. 983, IV: 229–33.

94. Tel Ambassador to the Netherlands (Herman Baruch) to Secretary of State, March 8, 1949, no. 225; Baruch to Assistant to Secretary for Foreign Military Assistance, March 8, 1949, N7-1, N7-1 (1)-A-1, RG 330, NARA.

95. *New York Times*, January 4, 1949, 3; tel Douglas to Secretary of State, March 7, 1949, *FRUS*, 1949, no. 821, IV: 165–66.

96. Tel Douglas to Secretary of State, March 16, 1949, *FRUS*, 1949, no. 983, IV: 230; quoted in Lawrence S. Kaplan, *A Community of Interest: NATO and the Military Assistance Program, 1948–1951* (Washington, D.C.: Office of the Secretary of Defense Historical Office, 1980), 30.

97. Tel Douglas to Secretary of State, March 27, 1949, *FRUS*, 1949, no. 1220, IV: 251–53.

98. FACC D-3, February 7, 1949, sub: Basic Policies of the Military Assistance Program, *FRUS*, 1948, I: 256.

99. John Sherman, Secretary of the War Council, to Service Secretaries and Chiefs of Staff, February 24, 1949, sub: Significant Actions of the Meeting of the War Council on February 18, 1949, N7-1, N-71(1)-A-1, Box 2, RG 330, NARA.

100. Tel Douglas to Secretary of State, March 26, 1949, *FRUS*, 1949, no. 213, IV: 251.

101. Minutes of the First Meeting of the European Correlation Committee London, March 25, 1949: Douglas, Harriman, et al., *FRUS*, 1948, IV: 244–46; Douglas to Secretary of State, March 27, 1949, *FRUS*, 1949, no. 1220, IV: 251–53.

102. Requests from the Brussels Treaty Powers . . . for Military Assistance, April 5, 1949, *FRUS*, 1949, IV: 285–87; Reply . . . to the request, April 6, 1949, *FRUS*, 1949, IV: 287–88.

103. *New York Times*, March 20, 1949.

104. Memorandum of Participants in the Washington Security Talks, July 6 to September 9, 1948, *FRUS*, 1948, III: 243.

105. Report of the International Working Group to the Ambassadors' Committee, December 24, 1948, *FRUS*, 1948, III: 336.

106. Minutes of the Sixteenth Meeting of the Washington Exploratory Talks, March 7, 1949, *FRUS*, 1949, IV: 169.

107. Minutes of the Sixteenth Meeting, 171; Minutes of the Eighteenth Meeting, March 15, 1949, 218–19.

108. Tel Chargé in the Soviet Union (Fay D. Kohler) to Secretary of State, January 31, 1949, *FRUS*, 1949, no. 242, III: 563–64.

109. Acheson, *Present at the Creation*, 267–68.

110. Tel Chargé in the Soviet Union (Kohler) to Secretary of State, January 29, 1949, *FRUS*, 1949, IV: 51–52, citing statement of Soviet Minister of Foreign Affairs on the North Atlantic Pact; memorandum of Soviet government on the North Atlantic Treaty, March 31, in Alvin Z. Rubinstein, ed., *The Foreign Policy of Soviet Union* (New York: Random House, 1969), 268–69.

111. Tel Ambassador of the Soviet Union to Secretary of State, March 31, 1949, no. 32, encl. Memorandum of the Government of the USSR Concerning the North Atlantic Treaty, *FRUS*, 1949, IV: 264.

112. *New York Times*, April 2, 1949, 4; Trygve Lie, *Seven Years with the United Nations* (New York: Macmillan, 1954), 439–40.

113. *Facts on File Yearbook*, March 27–April 2, 1949, 105.

114. Preliminary Position Paper Proposed by Staff of U.S. Delegation to the General Assembly, March 30, 1949, *FRUS*, 1949, II: 72–73.

115. *Current Digest of the Soviet Press* (May 13, 949), I, 14: 35–39; Chargé in the Soviet Union (Kohler) to Secretary of State, April 6, 1949, *FRUS*, 1949, no. 202, V: 603.

116. *New York Times*, March 23, 1949, 1.

117. Minutes of the Twelfth Meeting of the Washington Exploratory Talks, February 8, 1949, *FRUS*, 1949, IV: 86.

118. Quoted in Reid, *Time of Fear and Hope*, 173.

119. Reid, *Time of Fear and Hope*, 187–89.

120. Minutes of the Eleventh Meeting of the Washington Exploratory Talks, January 14, 1949, *FRUS*, 1949 IV: 33.

121. Achilles, *Fingerprints on History*, 23.

122. Memorandum of conversation by Secretary of State, April 1, 1949—, Schuman, Bonnet, et al., *FRUS*, 1949, III: 265–66.

123. Achilles, *Fingerprints on History*, 29.

124. Memorandum, Schuckburgh to Gladwyn Jebb, March 14, 1949, FO 371/79231, PRO.

125. FO to Embassy in Washington, March 7, 1949, no. 2589; Franks to FO, March 8, 1949, no. 2589.

126. *New York Times*, April 5, 1949, 2; Acheson, *Present at the Creation*, 274; Henderson, *Birth of NATO*, 112; John A. Monroe and Alex I. Inglis, eds., *Mike: Memoirs of Right Honourable Lester B. Pearson*, 3 vols. (Toronto: University of Toronto Press, 1972), III: 60.

127. Achilles, *Fingerprints on History*, 31.

9

The Relevance of NATO in the Post-Cold War Era

Looking back on the impact that the events of 1948 have had on Europe and the United States in the past sixty years, observers will come up with a mixed verdict about the achievements of NATO's founding fathers. The allies met their initial goal of containing and ultimately outlasting the Soviet empire and the Communist system it sheltered. NATO survived; the Warsaw Pact did not. Communist regimes persist in Cuba and China, but in the former, it is not a threat to the West, and in the latter, its future challenge to the United States and Europe derives from its capitalist energies rather than from ideological ardor. The longer goal of a harmonious Western community under U.S. leadership has been more elusive.

A PATH NOT TAKEN

There are critics today as well as from two generations ago who believe that accommodation rather than confrontation with the Soviet Union might have yielded peace without the costs that the militarization of NATO incurred. One of the prices for the path the United States chose to take in 1949 was the creation of a massive national security apparatus with concurrent infringement on individual liberties. The concomitant increase in executive power deriving from the president's position as commander-in-chief was a legacy of NATO as was the vast permanent growth of the U.S. military establishment.

How an accommodation might have been reached was easily answered by the Progressive Party of Henry A. Wallace as the North Atlantic Treaty was being framed. It involved first an appreciation of the enormous losses

suffered by the Soviet Union in World War II and the contribution that nation made to the victory over Nazi Germany. It would also recognize the defensive nature of the Soviet reaction to the Anglo-U.S. activities in Western
Europe. Given the barbarity of the Nazi wartime occupation of Russia, it
was understandable that the Soviets would share France's fear of a revived
militant Germany. From the Soviet perspective, the U.S. and British rebuilding of the West German economy was a prelude to the creation of a
state that would be a threat to the Soviet Union and its control of Eastern
Europe, including territory taken from Germany at the end of World War II.
Instead of interpreting the Berlin blockade of 1948 as the Soviet means of
severing all of Berlin from the West, critics could consider it a response to
the perceived Western intention of recreating a German threat to the Soviets. In brief, a badly wounded Soviet Union was in no position to challenge
U.S. power in Europe. Its aim in the postwar years was primarily to secure
a buffer zone in central Europe against a hostile Western alliance in the
making.

Would a more accommodating U.S. approach have cut short a Cold
War? This seemed possible, if not in 1949 then in the early 1950s after
Joseph Stalin's death, when his successors offered to reach a détente on
the basis of an unarmed Germany. The example of Austria removed from
the Cold War by mutual consent in 1955 may have been the solution
Nikita Khrushchev, General Secretary of the Soviet Communist Party,
would have found acceptable. These were the years of the Soviet actively
pressing for denuclearization of Germany—East and West—and the removal of U.S. troops from Western Europe. The Soviet objective was to undermine the rationale for NATO by appealing to Western Europeans on
behalf of a denuclearized Europe and a neutralized Germany. When the
Soviets created the Warsaw Pact in 1955, a military alliance linking the nations of central and Eastern Europe under their leadership, they clearly intended it to be a temporary arrangement. The last article of the pact noted
that it would "cease to be operative from the day a General European
Treaty enters into force."

Lacking Wallace's faith in the essential good intentions of the Soviet adversary, George Kennan shared his concern about the militarization of the
alliance. His was a reluctant endorsement of NATO in 1949. Kennan was
under no illusion about the ultimate objectives of Soviet Communism; he
agreed that the ideological fervor spread throughout Europe under
Moscow's patronage was a genuine threat to Western democratic governments. His response was to contain Communist expansion, as he had ex-
pounded in his long telegram in 1946, through economic and political
means until the internal contradictions within the system would destroy the
Communist system.

Although Kennan lived long enough to witness the dissolution of the Warsaw Pact and the implosion of the Soviet empire, his views failed to convince Secretary of State Dean Acheson in the Harry S. Truman administration or Secretary of State John Foster Dulles in the Dwight D. Eisenhower administration. With the exception of a brief period in the John F. Kennedy administration, when he was ambassador to Yugoslavia, he had to witness U.S. foreign relations from Princeton, where he studied European history and issued philippics from his office at the Institute for Advanced Studies. The militarization of containment, he wrote in 1958, had become too rigid to respond to new trends in the Soviet Union as well as to changes in Western Europe.[1] The transatlantic allies ignored the advice from the father of the containment doctrine.

The consequences of a militarized NATO under firm U.S. leadership, according to critics of the alliance, were first an uncomfortable embrace of Fascist Portugal in 1949, informal accommodation with Franco Spain in the 1950s, and acceptance of a Greek military junta in the 1970s. These Faustian arrangements were based on the necessity of using every means of coping with the Soviet adversary, even if they subverted the principles on which alliance had been made. As the Senate debate in 1949 reflected, a distinction was made between "authoritarian" friends and "totalitarian" enemies. They rationalized their double standards as a necessity in the face of an aggressive Soviet Union.

Given the challenges of the Cold War, it was not surprising that critical commentators such as Johns Hopkins political scientist David Calleo would characterize the Supreme Allied Commander in Europe as a U.S. proconsul controlling the governments of the Western European allies in 1970.[2] An even darker picture of NATO's behavior in the Cold War—and after—appeared in the 2005 charge of Swiss scholar Daniele Gensler that NATO collaborated repeatedly with right-wing elements to subvert democratic governments of every member nation.[3]

THE PREFERRED PATH

This view of negative consequences of the decision to build Western defenses against potential Soviet aggression may have some merit, but it does not cover the totality of the circumstances that led to the creation of the alliance. It does not do justice to the sense of despair that pervaded the West in the wake of World War II. The *cri de coeur* of the Brussels Pact powers required a military, not just an economic, response from the United States in 1948. The U.S. reaction was hesitant initially and at no time signified an opportunity to assert an imperial presence in Europe. It was, as Norwegian historian Geir Lundestad described it, an empire by invitation. Without the "pledge" of Article 5, the revival of Western Europe would not have taken place.[4] The Marshall Plan would have failed because of political insecurity of its beneficiaries. Soviet acquisition of an atomic bomb and the loss of China to Communism in 1949 combined with the Korean War in 1950 to increase the role of the military—and this meant the U.S. military—to contain Soviet expansion.

The European allies accepted a junior status in the first dozen years of NATO's history, partly because of their dependence on U.S. deterrent power and partly because of the governance of the new organization. Decisions were to be made by consensus, "the NATO method." But if unanimity was required, it frequently was achieved by a willingness on the part of the allies to accept the judgments of the senior partner. Still, the United States made an effort to avoid the taint of an occupying power in Europe by its status of forces agreements in the 1950s. These bilateral agreements allowed U.S. troops charged with crimes off duty to be tried in the courts of the host nation. Such actions demonstrated U.S. reluctance to become a permanent military presence in Europe, a position that would have been heartily endorsed by NATO's founding fathers. The extensive debates in the United States over the nature of its commitment to Europe before the signing of the treaty, particularly over the wording of Article 5, reflected an ongoing worry about being forced into wars that neither the Truman administration nor the senators wanted. Their hopes rested not on U.S. ground forces but on the deterrent power: what a U.S. commitment in the region was expected to have on Soviet behavior.

THE UNILATERAL TEMPTATIONS IN THE COLD WAR

The U.S. objective in 1949 was to help Western Europe recover from the devastation of World War II and then reform its institutions, so that ultimately it could defend itself independent of U.S. support. Until that time, the principles of self-help and mutual aid, as explicit in the treaty's Article 3 as it was in the Marshall Plan, would apply. While the Brussels Pact members had made military aid seem almost as important as Article 5, it was of lesser significance to the United States and ultimately to the Europeans themselves. What counted was the U.S. commitment, which the Korean War transformed from psychological support into a troop deployment in 1951: four new divisions that were intended to be temporary. The divided Germany in Europe appeared to be a constant temptation for Communist intervention, just as a divided Korea had invited Communist aggression in Asia. The presence of some sixty thousand U.S. armed forces in Europe currently, long after the end of the Cold War, is an unintended consequence of the treaty.

That there would be friction between the senior partner and its allies, even at the height of the perceived Communist threat—in the 1950s and 1960s—was hardly a surprise, despite U.S. efforts to respond to European sensibilities. As early as 1948, Europeans expressed their resentment over the contradiction between U.S. demands for integrated European military use of U.S. assistance and the U.S. insistence on bilateral negotiations for base rights on the territory of member nations. These negotiations included the stationing of U.S. inspectors to ensure proper management of the military aid being supplied. The allies regarded the former demand as establishing a double standard; the United States operated on a binational plane, while requiring Europeans to function multilaterally. The latter was an insult to their pride. The U.S. inspectors were abusing the sovereignty of presumably equal partners in the alliance.

The larger powers felt the slights more keenly when France blamed the senior ally for the loss of Indochina in 1954, and both France and Britain lost face in the Suez crisis of 1956. The smaller members in turn felt excluded from consultation about major decisions despite the NATO method of consensus. Only the United States, Britain, and France had representation on the standing group of the military committee. The report of the Three Wise Men in 1956—from Canada, Italy, and Norway—that asked for greater involvement of the smaller powers was ignored as the crisis over the botched Anglo-French intervention in the Suez Canal diverted NATO's attention from their concerns.

While these grievances were genuine, they did not disrupt the alliance. Not one of the allies—large or small—sought to activate Article 12 of the treaty that permitted any member to request a review of its terms after it had been in force for ten years. The menace of Soviet Communism under the erratic leadership of Khrushchev served as a centripetal force. The Soviet threat to incorporate West Berlin into East Germany in 1958 and 1961 and the placement of Soviet missiles in Castro's Cuba reminded the allies of the importance of U.S. nuclear power in the defense of Europe.

The successful conclusion of both crises did not make the alliance irrelevant, but by the mid-1960s, there were differences within NATO that altered the nature of the transatlantic relationship. One of them was an increasing U.S. discontent with Europe's role in the alliance, a sense that it was not sharing the costs of defending Western Europe—to the extent that its economic revival—the *Wirtschaftswunder*—should have afforded. This U.S. grievance was compounded by the unwillingness of the allies to support the U.S. war in Southeast Asia. The United States claimed that its participation in South Vietnam's war against the Communist North served the common cause against Communist aggression; Europeans should have appreciated that Moscow was still the mastermind behind Communist subversion everywhere in the world. They disagreed with this judgment. The allies, by contrast, felt that the United States was diverting its resources from Europe to uphold its historic interests in Asia and so putting European security in jeopardy. But because the alliance remained vital to the West, particularly to Germany, which was more vulnerable than the others to a Soviet attack, NATO allies increased their contributions to U.S. military expenses in Europe.

The more significant change derived from a sense among the European allies that the threat of a Soviet invasion of the West had diminished to the point where the Warsaw Pact bloc was an adversary that Western Europe could live with. The concept of détente dominated the alliance from the late 1960s into the mid-1970s. The smaller nations led the way. A new report chaired by Belgium's Pierre Harmel in 1967 made détente equal to defense as a NATO goal. And the United States, whose authority was weakened by the Vietnam War, agreed to accept this direction, even though it did not share fully the optimism of the European colleagues. The departure of France from the military structure of the alliance helped to ease the way for greater sharing of nuclear information with all the allies. The United States may have resented paying as much as it did for the defense of Europe, but it was aware of the need to consult with its allies about nuclear matters, even if the decision-making process was excluded from their discussions. To keep the alliance alive, the United States made concessions to the sensitivities of Europeans as it dealt with the Soviet bloc.

The Cold War did not end with détente. Détente itself was shoved into the background by the end of the 1970s, when it was apparent that the Soviets not only had stymied negotiations over asymmetrical troop reduction but were steadily building a war machine at a time when NATO had reduced its military budgets. The Soviets were now specifically targeting new medium-range nuclear missiles on Western European cities, and so thirty years after the signing of the North Atlantic Treaty, the European allies were demanding a U.S. response once again to an unsettling military threat. A new Cold War was in progress.

Although the United States had proceeded in the Jimmy Carter administration to increase its defense budgets, which were massively expanded during the Ronald Reagan years, the allies did not respond to NATO's request to increase their budgets by at least 3 percent. Once again, Europe turned to the United States for its protection and demanded deployment of U.S. intermediate-range nuclear missiles to cope with the Soviet adversary. At the same time, the allies wanted to continue the dialogue with the Communists over mutual reduction of nuclear and conventional weaponry and were repelled by the militant tone of President Reagan's dealings with the Warsaw Pact adversary. European dependence on U.S. nuclear power did not mean acquiescence in the superpower's leadership in the manner of the 1950s. Western Europe was now in a situation of economic, if not military, strength, and after a generation's experience with the United States as the senior partner, its governments did not trust its discretion to maintain peace with the East. Once the new missiles were in place in 1983, they wanted diplomacy to resolve East-West differences, while the U.S. president continued to rail against the evil Soviet empire.

The arrival of Mikhail Gorbachev to power in 1985 transformed relations between NATO and the Warsaw Pact. Recognizing the heavy costs in competing with NATO, as well as the relative backwardness of the Soviet economy, the new leader consciously set out to reform his own society and terminate the second Cold War with the West. Surprisingly, he seemed to find a soul mate in Reagan, who responded wholeheartedly to Gorbachev's overtures; they both looked for ways to reduce, if not to remove, nuclear weaponry from their arsenals. Rather than expressing relief over the new Soviet-U.S. entente, the NATO partners were anxious about its effects on their security.

Reagan, not NATO's secretary-general, met with the Soviet general secretary, and the allies wondered if their interests were being sacrificed on the altar of Soviet-U.S. friendship. A unilateral U.S. initiative to destroy all nuclear weapons would leave Western Europe vulnerable to Soviet superiority in conventional weaponry. Suspicion of U.S. behavior, even if based on U.S. naïveté, persisted until the end of the decade, even though U.S. troops in Europe remained in place, though in reduced numbers. They would continue to guarantee U.S. engagement in the event of war. The pledge of 1949 remained valid forty years later.

The sudden implosion of the Soviet Union and the dissolution of the Warsaw Pact in 1991 was an unexpected by-product of Gorbachev's reforms. These exposed the internal contradictions within the Communist system and accentuated the disaffection of the subordinate states, much as Kennan had predicted almost a half-century before. The contrast between the successful economies of the West, made possible by the sense of security supplied by NATO and the failed Communist economies, was striking. Equally striking was the example NATO also supplied of an alliance of free nations whose continuing quarrels, most notably between Europe and the United States, obscured the common bonds that permitted its survival when the rival Warsaw bloc collapsed.

NEW MISSIONS, OLD QUARRELS

The question why NATO should continue to exist arose inevitably after the disappearance of the Soviet empire. Its *raison d'être* had rested on the fate of a devastated Europe threatened internally and externally by aggressive Communist forces. In the 1990s, Western Europe had survived and prospered and no longer faced threats to its survival. Alternative organizations were considered as possible replacement for the Atlantic alliance—the Organization for Security and Cooperation in Europe (OSCE), embracing the Warsaw Pact organization as well as NATO; the expanding European Economic Community (EEC), that included most of the members of NATO; and even the UN itself, now freed from the veto power of the Soviet Union. None was suitable. For all its internal tensions, NATO, under the leadership of the superpower, had the military capability of attending to what the allies felt would be new challenge in the years ahead, namely, crisis management in areas bordering the member countries or in situations where the security of a member was threatened. Under the rubric of Article 4, NATO would be justified in extending its reach to what was awkwardly called "out-of-area" regions. Such was the judgment of the North Atlantic Council's meeting in Rome in 1991.

This seemed to be a reasonable new mission for the alliance. It would keep the United States involved in Europe, an important consideration when the remnants of the Soviet Union still possessed nuclear weapons that could be a danger in the future. It would also safeguard its members from of outbreaks of violence outside NATO's boundaries.

Out-of-area problems did arise in the 1990s, and NATO managed Balkan crises but only after considerable delay and consequent friction within the alliance. Given the proximity of Yugoslavia to its NATO neighbors, the wars that erupted from its dissolution should have been the perfect occasion for the organization's intervention. When the UN failed to stop the Serbian president's aggression against Croatia and Bosnia, the European allies were expected to take the initiative in coping with the crisis.

They failed to act, and essentially left it to the United States to strike at Slobodan Milosevic in 1995 and again in 1999. Air strikes against Serbia in those years were the first times that NATO employed military force against an aggressor and not under the auspices of Article 5, but under Article 4, which authorized consultation if the security of any member were threatened.

NATO succeeded in restoring order in the Balkans but at a heavy cost. One part of it was the continuing need for peacekeeping troops in the area. Yet, there is room for some optimism in the relationships among the former Yugoslav republics and in the work of the various peacekeeping agencies over the past decade. There is less optimism over the frictions between the superpower and its transatlantic allies that accompanied their operations. The United States resented the inability of the European partners to meet the challenge in the Balkans. The Europeans were unable or unwilling to make the financial sacrifices to pay for communications and intelligence systems and airlifts, all prerequisites to the rapid responses needed to manage crises. They refused to raise even minimal armed forces to supplement those supplied by the United States. U.S. frustration was clearly expressed in conflict over Kosovo in 1999, when the Supreme Allied Commander felt that the North Atlantic Council in Brussels tied his hands until late in the contest by holding back the threat of ground troops and air strikes against Belgrade. Europeans, for their part, raised the familiar and understandable argument against excessive U.S. aggressiveness and an unwillingness to give more rein to diplomacy in dealing with crises.

This transatlantic gap widened into a schism in the twenty-first century after the Al Qaeda assault on New York and Washington on 9/11. This situation may have been avoidable. NATO's immediate response was solidarity under Article 5. Ironic as it was, Europeans and the United States spoke with one voice in September 2001 when the North Atlantic council invoked the article, not on behalf of a European ally as envisioned in 1948 but of the superpower itself. The United States squandered the opportunity for continued consensus by refusing to use allied help in taking on the Taliban in Afghanistan.

The U.S. military command in Tampa, Florida, remembered that allied involvement in 1999 had prolonged the war and felt no need for NATO help in 2001. This unilateral impulse reflected the general approach of the Bush administration toward the world at large and alienated its NATO allies. European resentment at being shunted aside in Afghanistan increased in 2002 as the Bush administration identified Iraq's weapons of mass destruction as an appropriate target against Al Qaeda. The United States appeared-to part ways from is allies in the UN when France and Germany conspicuously opposed U.S. intervention in Iraq. France would have opposed action even if the UN had given its blessing in 2003.

The Iraq war illuminated fault lines in NATO that had origins in the negotiations over the North Atlantic Treaty in 1948. It was no coincidence that France, with considerable support from the peoples of almost all the NATO members, led Europe in opposing the U.S. intervention in Iraq in 2003. There had always been an undercurrent of discontent with U.S. power among Europeans, centered on the inappropriateness of an upstart society asserting superiority over the great civilizations of the Old World. Britain's Alistair Buchan has rationalized this situation by comparing the United States to ancient Rome and Britain to ancient Greece, when intelligent Greek slaves guided the empire of the stronger but less civilized Romans.[5] President Jacques Chirac of France and former Chancellor Gerhard Schroeder were less diplomatic in their disdain for U.S. pretensions of leadership of the West.

Their U.S. counterparts were just as dismissive of Europeans. Pundit Robert Kagan characterized Western Europe as effete, vainly expecting the soft power of diplomacy to solve hard geopolitical problems, underscoring the notion that Europeans were from Venus while the United States was from Mars.[6] Secretary of Defense Donald Rumsfeld looked for a new breed of European allies from the former Warsaw bloc to replace Old Europe of the West as U.S. supporters.

Conceivably, NATO might have dissolved over the differences within the alliance. Charles de Gaulle's assumptions that the United States was neither a reliable partner nor a worthy leader could be validated a generation after his death. But this has not yet occurred and may not. NATO is still too important for all its members to go the way of the League of Nations. Once Iraq appeared to be in danger of replicating the U.S. debacle in Vietnam, the George W. Bush administration and Congress qualified their unilateral approach to foreign affairs and turned to NATO for help in Iraq and Afghanistan. The allied response often has been reluctant and inadequate, but at least NATO has a presence in both countries today. The United States needs the support of the allies, and they in turn need the United States to compensate for their minimal defense budgets and insufficient military forces. The circumstances today do not replicate those of 1948, but the importance of allied solidarity does.

NATO VERSUS THE EUROPEAN UNION

Defense of the West was not the only aspiration expressed in the negotiations of 1948. A federated Europe, even a United States of Europe in the U.S. model, was to be an end product of the transatlantic alliance. Although some advocates of this goal were interested solely as a means of ridding the United States of its obligations, the majority welcomed the prospect of a democratic West as a partner in maintaining peace and prosperity that the UN had failed to provide. This explains the United States' backing of the many steps toward European unity during the Cold War, ranging from the integration of West Germany into the European Coal and Steel Community and into NATO itself to the Treaty of Rome in 1957 that created the European Economic Community, and finally to the European Union (EU) in 1991 that would develop a military as well as political dimension side by side with NATO. U.S. leaders, through much of this period, continued to believe that the interests of a united Europe would always accord with those of the United States. That U.S. efforts might be helping to create a Frankenstein monster did not fully penetrate policymakers' consciousness until the Cold War had ended.

By the 1990s the fitful movements toward a United States of Europe had produced a common currency, the euro, and the European Economic Community, renamed the European Union in 1991. Apart from Ireland, Sweden, Finland, and Switzerland, the members of the EU are also members of NATO. Under Franco-German leadership, the European powers surpassed the United States in population and resources. The new NATO members from central and Eastern Europe were as anxious to join the European Union as they were the Atlantic alliance. A united Europe promised them economic benefits that conceivably could be more valuable than the political and military protection offered by the NATO umbrella.

The rise of the EU inevitably posed a conflict between the U.S.-dominated NATO and the Franco-German conception of a united Europe. While there were always economic rivalries within Europe, they paled in contrast to conflict with the United States over tariffs and subsidies that contributed to transatlantic tensions. But the major source of difficulty in the twenty-first century revolves on the military dimension that NATO has in abundance and the EU still lacks. Granted, the old Brussels Pact of 1948 had morphed first into a Western European Union in 1954 to encompass Britain, West Germany, and Italy and then was incorporated into the EU as is official military arm in 1999. Yet the disparity between the military capabilities of NATO and those of the EU has not been bridged. Its existence raises the question about the need for the two organizations to have a military component; NATO's could serve the EU, because almost all its members were inside NATO.

The competition between the two organizations reflects a long-standing European resentment of U.S. power, most vigorously expressed by France from the inception of the Atlantic alliance. The Iraq war was only the most visible occasion to demonstrate differences. The idea of a European identity separate from the U.S.-dominated NATO was an integral part of the intra-European debates in 1948, when Britain's Ernest Bevin often joined with France in wistful hopes of Western Europe becoming a "third force" between the superpowers. While most of the European allies recognized its illusory aspects, France kept it alive throughout the Cold War, most notably in de Gaulle's scenario of a Europe from the Atlantic to the Urals, free of U.S. and ultimately Soviet control.

Since 1990, the rapid evolution of a European identity had sharpened the differences between the two organizations to the extent that the future of NATO itself seemed to have been at stake. Yet there are mitigating elements in the relationship that could promote collaboration rather than discord. The most persuasive is the disparity in military power between the two. The EU could talk, as it did in 1999 when the evolved Brussels Pact (the Western European Union since 1954) was officially named the military arm of Europe, with plans for a rapid response force in place within three years. But the EU's concentration on soft power, necessitated by the costs of social benefits in their constituent states, made it impossible for it to provide the military muscle that NATO possesses. With tensions mounting in many parts of the world from the ambitions of radical Islam and with Russia and China ambivalent about relations with the West, a NATO military, smaller in size than in the Cold War but more flexible in its movements, is better equipped to manage global crises that come under the aegis of Article 4. That NATO had to deal with crises in Africa and Asia as well as the Middle East inspired former Spanish Prime Minister Jose Maria Aznar's research center in 2005 to recommend a transformation of NATO into a global organization.[7]

Another consideration that dampens conflict is the attitude of the new members of the EU toward NATO. The EU, like NATO, expanded in the last ten years, drawing from the same pool of countries in central and Eastern Europe. Enlargement was not in itself a new phenomenon. The negotiations over the scope of the alliance in 1948 devolved on U.S. demands for stepping-stone countries to participate, and the Brussels Pact members reluctantly agreed. By the end of the Cold War four countries had joined NATO, and two of them—Greece and Turkey—only for Cold War reasons. This consideration was true in part for West Germany. But the Federal Republic's membership in 1955 and Spain's in 1982 had the broader purpose of encouraging European integration and promoting the spread of democracy. Those two goals animated the drive for incorporating former Soviet satellites into NATO in 1999 and 2004, bringing the total number to twenty-six. How many more members may be absorbed by the alliance is an open question in 2007, but the linkage of new allies to the advancement of democratic values is more fixed today than it was during the Cold War.

The newcomers do not share the resentments of the older members against U.S. leadership. In fact, an incentive for membership on the part of Poland, Hungary, and the Baltic nations was the kind of security Western Europeans had sought in 1948. U.S., not European, pressure was responsible for their admission into NATO in 1999 and 2002. The United States, not the EU, is the bulwark against a revival of Russian reassertion of authority over former satellites and former republics of the Soviet Union. It was no coincidence that these newer members of NATO have been more supportive of the United States in Iraq than any of the older members of the alliance, notwithstanding reservations on the part of their publics. They are not likely to follow the path of confrontation within NATO led by France and Germany. And within the EU itself, the continuing uneasy British and Scandinavian involvement in the EU, along with its members' rejection of a European constitution, suggested in 2005 that the EU may be more open to cooperation with NATO than it was a few years before.

There is already evidence that some of the early expectations of the EU may be realized. In the 1990s, NATO leaders had hoped that the EU would serve NATO's interests by managing crises that would be of greater concern to its members than to the United States or to NATO. This concept was implicitly advanced at the Brussels meeting of the North Atlantic Council in 1994 when the Council decided to make NATO assets available to the Western European Union, provided that they report to NATO how the materiel or facilities were used. A dozen years later, the EU has taken responsibility for peacekeeping in Kosovo. Collaboration rather than conflict between the United States and a federated Europe was the assumption in transatlantic relations in 1948. This assumption remains alive in 2007.

THE NORTH ATLANTIC TREATY TODAY

From the foregoing sketch of NATO's history, it is obvious that the questions raised in the lengthy negotiations among the United States, Canada, and the Brussels Pact nations were answered in one way or another over the past sixty years. The Brussels Pact itself may have lost its initial functions, but it reappeared in 1954 to deal with the German issue and in 1999 to reinforce the EU. Article 2, the Canadian initiative that sought economic and cultural roles for NATO, never recovered from U.S. criticism in 1948, but other organizations were in place to serve those functions. The bedrock of the alliance through the Cold War, however, was Article 5 of the North Atlantic Treaty. It lost its primacy after the United States became the sole superpower in the 1990s.

It was Article 4, almost an afterthought in the negotiations of 1948, which became prominent in post–Cold War years. This article opened consultations "whenever, in the opinion of any of them, the territorial integrity, political independence or security of any one of the Parties are threatened." NATO's intervention, or more properly U.S. intervention, in the Balkan crises in 1995 and 1999 was made under the rubric of this article. These post–Cold War crises marked NATO's use of force without recourse to Article 5. Violence in the Yugoslav states bordering NATO members was sufficiently close to NATO territories to justify its invocation at this time. In 1948 Article 4 was obscured by seemingly more relevant articles.

Similarly, Article 10, inviting other European states to accede to the treaty if the charter members agreed, was not a contentious issue in 1948. But it was under aegis of this article that NATO enlargement was permitted, "by unanimous agreement" of all the signatories. In NATO's first generation, Greece and Turkey were able to join in 1951. The exigencies of the Cold War in 1951 had made a southeastern European anchor seem vital for the effectiveness of the reorganized military command of NATO. And membership of West Germany in 1955 in the face of long-standing French opposition symbolized the rapprochement of historic enemies inside the Atlantic alliance. The new Franco-German relationship had some setbacks over the course of the next generation, notably in the initial French reluctance in 1990 to accept German reunification, but its accomplishment was ultimately a tribute to the solidity of the new European order that NATO ushered into being in the generation before. NATO enlargements in 1999 and

2002 that embraced former Warsaw Pact states, and even the Baltic countries formerly inside the Soviet Union, were further testaments to the relevance of Article 10.

The North Atlantic Treaty of 1949, like the U.S. Constitution of 1787, was framed in such a way that loose construction of its articles could allow for growth in different directions. Only Article 9 specifically called for a council, on which each member would be represented, to consider implementation of the treaty. Just as Article 2 of the Constitution endowed the office of the president with inferior bodies without specifying them, so the North Atlantic Council was empowered to "set up such subsidiary bodies as may be necessary," and in particular a defense committee to carry out the missions of Articles 3 and 5. All subsequent offices, such as a secretary-general and supreme allied commanders, derived from the authority granted under Article 9.

It may be an act of faith to assert that the groundwork of NATO laid in 1948 had created an entity that could withstand any challenge in the future. Arguably, the most compelling evidence of the durability of the alliance has been the silence of its members with respect to terminating their membership in NATO. In 1966 France did withdraw from its military structure, as did Greece in 1966; but Greece resumed its role inside the military structure in 1980, and France made it clear that its attachment to the alliance remains firm. Under Article 13, any member after twenty years "could cease to be a Party one year after its notice of denunciation." No member has chosen to take advantage of this way out of the organization. The danger in the future lies less in the likelihood of dissolution through defections than in NATO's becoming as irrelevant as the League of Nations in the 1930s, should the United States and Europe fail to share the responsibilities of crisis management beyond the original boundaries of the treaty. No other organization can serve this function. The transatlantic bargain of 1949 continues to resonate in the twenty-first century. Whatever NATO's future may be, the changes it fostered over the past sixty years have made a permanent impact on the history of the twentieth century

NOTES

    1. George F. Kennan, *Russia, the Atom and the West* (New York: Harper & Row, 1958).

    2. David P. Calleo, *The Atlantic Fantasy: The U.S., NATO, and Europe* (Baltimore: Johns Hopkins University Press, 1970).

    3. Daniele Gansler, *NATO's Secret Armies: Operation Gadio and Terrorism in Western Europe* (New York: Frank Cass, 2005).

    4. Geir Lundestad, "Empire by Invitation? The United States and Western Europe, 1945–1952," *Journal of Peace Research* 23 (September 1986): 263–77.

5. Alistair Buchan, "Mothers and Daughters (or Greeks and Romans)" in *Two Hundred Years of American Foreign Policy*, ed. William P. Bundy (New York: New York University Press).

6. Donald Kagan, *Of Paradise and Power: America and Europe in the New World Order* (New York: Alfred A. Knopf, 2003).

7. Rafael L. Bardaji, *NATO: An Alliance for Freedom* (Madrid: FAES, 2005).

Appendix A

The Brussels Pact

Treaty of Economic, Social and Cultural Collaboration and Collective Self-Defense between the Governments of the United Kingdom and Northern Ireland, Belgium, France, Luxembourg, and the Netherlands, signed at Brussels, March 17, 1948.

ARTICLE I

Convinced of the close community of their interests and of the necessity of uniting in order to promote the economic recovery of Europe, the High Contracting Parties will so organize and coordinate their economic activities as to produce the best possible results, by the elimination of conflict in their economic policies, the co-ordination of production and the development of commercial exchanges.

The co-operation provided for in the preceding paragraph, which will be effected through the Consultative Council referred to in Article VII as well as through other bodies, shall not involve any duplication of, or prejudice to, the work of other economic organizations in which the High Contracting Parties are or may be represented but shall on the contrary assist the work of those organizations.

ARTICLE II

The High Contracting Parties will make every effort in common, both by direct consultation and in specialized agencies, to promote the attainment of a higher standard of living by their peoples and to develop on corresponding lines the social and other related services of their countries.

The High Contracting Parties will consult with the object of achieving the earliest possible application of recommendations of immediate practical interest, relating to social matters, adopted with their approval in the specialized agencies.

They will endeavour to conclude as soon as possible conventions with each other in the sphere of social security.

ARTICLE III

The High Contracting Parties will make every effort in common to lead their peoples towards a better understanding of the principles which form the basis of their common civilization and to promote cultural exchanges by conventions between themselves or by other means.

ARTICLE IV

If any of the High Contracting Parties should be the object of an armed attack in Europe, the other High Contracting Parties will, in accordance with the provisions of Article 51 of the Charter of the United Nations, afford the party so attacked all the military and other aid and assistance in their power.

ARTICLE V

All measures taken as a result of the preceding Article shall be immediately reported to the Security Council. They shall be terminated as soon as the Security Council has taken the measures necessary to maintain or restore international peace and security.

The present Treaty does not prejudice in any way the obligations of the High Contracting Parties under the provisions of the Charter of the United Nations. It shall not be interpreted as affecting in any way the authority and responsibility of the Security Council under the Charter to take at any time such action as it deems necessary in order to maintain or restore international peace and security.

ARTICLE VI

The High Contracting Parties declare, each so far as he is concerned, that none of the international engagements now in force between him and any other of the High Contracting Parties or any third State is in conflict with the provisions of the present Treaty.

None of the High Contracting Parties will conclude any alliance or participate in any coalition directed against any other of the High Contracting Parties.

ARTICLE VII

For the purpose of consulting together on all the questions dealt with in the present Treaty, the High Contracting Parties will create a Consultative Council, which shall be so organized as to be able to exercise its functions continuously. The Council shall meet at such times as it shall deem fit.

At the request of any of the High Contracting Parties, the Council shall be immediately convened in order to permit the High Contracting Parties to consult with regard to any situation which may constitute a threat to peace, in whatever area this threat should arise; with regard to the attitude to be adopted and the steps to be taken in case of a renewal by Germany of an aggressive policy; or with regard to any situation constituting a danger to economic stability.

ARTICLE VIII

In pursuance of their determination to settle disputes only by peaceful means, the High Contracting Parties will apply to disputes between themselves the following provisions:

The High Contracting Parties will, while the present Treaty remains in force, settle all disputes falling within the scope of Article 36, paragraph 2, of the Statute of the International Court of Justice by referring them to the Court, subject only, in the case of each of them, to any reservation already made by that Party when accepting this clause for compulsory jurisdiction to the extent that that Party may maintain the reservation.

In addition, the High Contracting Parties will submit to conciliation all disputes outside the scope of Article 36, paragraph 2, of the Statute of the International Court of Justice.

In the case of a mixed dispute involving both questions for which conciliation is appropriate and other questions for which judicial settlement is appropriate, any Party to the dispute shall have the right to insist that the judicial settlement of the legal questions shall precede conciliation.

The preceding provisions of this Article in no way affect the application of relevant provisions or agreements prescribing some other method of pacific settlement.

ARTICLE IX

The High Contracting Parties may, by agreement, invite any other State to accede to the present Treaty on conditions to be agreed between them and the State so invited.

Any State so invited may become a Party to the Treaty by depositing an instrument of accession with the Belgian Government.

The Belgian Government will inform each of the High Contracting Parties of the deposit of each instrument of accession.

ARTICLE X

The present Treaty shall be ratified and the instruments of ratification shall be deposited as soon as possible with the Belgian Government.

It shall enter into force on the date of the deposit of the last instrument of ratification and shall thereafter remain in force for fifty years.

After the expiry of the period of fifty years, each of the High Contracting Parties shall have the right to cease to be a party thereto provided that he shall have previously given one year's notice of denunciation to the Belgian Government.

The Belgian Government shall inform the Governments of the other High Contracting Parties of the deposit of each instrument of ratification and of each notice of denunciation.

In witness whereof, the above-mentioned Plenipotentiaries have signed the present Treaty and have affixed thereto their seals.

Done at Brussels, this seventeenth day of March 1948, in English and French, each text being equally authentic, in a single copy which shall remain deposited in the archives of the Belgian Government and of which certified copies shall be transmitted by that Government to each of the other signatories.

Appendix B

The Vandenberg
Resolution (S. 239)

Whereas peace with justice and the defense of human rights and fundamental freedoms require international cooperation through more effective use of the United Nations: Therefore be it *Resolved*, That the Senate reaffirm the policy of the United States to achieve international peace and security through the United Nations so that armed force shall not be used except in the common interest, and that the President be advised of the sense of the Senate that this Government, by constitutional process, should particularly pursue the following objectives within the United Nations Charter:

1. Voluntary agreement to remove the veto from all questions involving pacific settlements of international disputes and situations, and from the admission of new members.
2. Progressive development of regional and other collective arrangements for individual and collective self-defense in accordance with the purposes, principles, and provisions of the Charter.
3. Association of the United States, by constitutional process, with such regional and other collective arrangements as are based on continuous and effective self-help and mutual aid, and as affect its national security.
4. Contributing to the maintenance of peace by making clear its determination to exercise the right of individual or collective self-defense under article 51 should any armed attack occur affecting its national security.
5. Maximum efforts to obtain agreements to provide the United Nations with armed forces as provided by the Charter, and to obtain agreement among member nations upon universal regulation and reduc-

tion of armaments under adequate and dependable guaranty against violation.

6. If necessary, after adequate effort toward strengthening the United Nations, review of the Charter at an appropriate time by a General Conference called under article 109 or by the General Assembly.

Appendix C

The North Atlantic Treaty

The Parties to this Treaty reaffirm their faith in the purposes and principles of the Charter of the United Nations and their desire to live in peace with all peoples and all governments.

They are determined to safeguard the freedom, common heritage and civilisation of their peoples, founded on the principles of democracy, individual liberty and the rule of law. They seek to promote stability and well-being in the North Atlantic area.

They are resolved to unite their efforts for collective defence and for the preservation of peace and security.

They therefore agree to this North Atlantic Treaty:

ARTICLE 1

The Parties undertake, as set forth in the Charter of the United Nations, to settle any international dispute in which they may be involved by peaceful means in such a manner that international peace and security and justice are not endangered, and to refrain in their international relations from the threat or use of force in any manner inconsistent with the purposes of the United Nations.

ARTICLE 2

The Parties will contribute toward the further development of peaceful and friendly international relations by strengthening their free institutions, by bringing about a better understanding of the principles upon which these institutions are founded, and by promoting conditions of stability and well-being. They will seek to eliminate conflict in their international economic policies and will encourage economic collaboration between any or all of them.

ARTICLE 3

In order more effectively to achieve the objectives of this Treaty, the Parties, separately and jointly, by means of continuous and effective self-help and mutual aid, will maintain and develop their individual and collective capacity to resist armed attack.

ARTICLE 4

The Parties will consult together whenever, in the opinion of any of them, the territorial integrity, political independence or security of any of the Parties is threatened.

ARTICLE 5

The Parties agree that an armed attack against one or more of them in Europe or North America shall be considered an attack against them all and consequently they agree that, if such an armed attack occurs, each of them, in exercise of the right of individual or collective self-defence recognised by Article 51 of the Charter of the United Nations, will assist the Party or Parties so attacked by taking forthwith, individually and in concert with the other Parties, such action as it deems necessary, including the use of armed force, to restore and maintain the security of the North Atlantic area.

Any such armed attack and all measures taken as a result thereof shall immediately be reported to the Security Council. Such measures shall be terminated when the Security Council has taken the measures necessary to restore and maintain international peace and security.

ARTICLE 6

For the purpose of Article 5, an armed attack on one or more of the Parties is deemed to include an armed attack on the territory of any of the Parties in Europe or North America, on the Algerian Departments of France, on the territory of or on the Islands under the jurisdiction of any of the Parties in the North Atlantic area north of the Tropic of Cancer; on the forces, vessels, or aircraft of any of the Parties, when in or over these territories or any other area in Europe in which occupation forces of any of the Parties were stationed on the date when the Treaty entered into force or the Mediterranean Sea or the North Atlantic area north of the Tropic of Cancer.

ARTICLE 7

This Treaty does not affect, and shall not be interpreted as affecting in any way the rights and obligations under the Charter of the Parties which are members of the United Nations, or the primary responsibility of the Security Council for the maintenance of international peace and security.

ARTICLE 8

Each Party declares that none of the international engagements now in force between it and any other of the Parties or any third State is in conflict with the provisions of this Treaty, and undertakes not to enter into any international engagement in conflict with this Treaty.

ARTICLE 9

The Parties hereby establish a Council, on which each of them shall be represented, to consider matters concerning the implementation of this Treaty. The Council shall be so organised as to be able to meet promptly at any time. The Council shall set up such subsidiary bodies as may be necessary; in particular it shall establish immediately a defence committee which shall recommend measures for the implementation of Articles 3 and 5.

ARTICLE 10

The Parties may, by unanimous agreement, invite any other European State in a position to further the principles of this Treaty and to contribute to the security of the North Atlantic area to accede to this Treaty. Any State so invited may become a Party to the Treaty by depositing its instrument of accession with the Government of the United States of America. The Government of the United States of America will inform each of the Parties of the deposit of each such instrument of accession.

ARTICLE 11

This Treaty shall be ratified and its provisions carried out by the Parties in accordance with their respective constitutional processes. The instruments of ratification shall be deposited as soon as possible with the Government of the United States of America, which will notify all the other signatories of each deposit. The Treaty shall enter into force between the States which have ratified it as soon as the ratifications of the majority of the signatories, including the ratifications of Belgium, Canada, France, Luxembourg, the Netherlands, the United Kingdom and the United States, have been deposited and shall come into effect with respect to other States on the date of the deposit of their ratifications.

ARTICLE 12

After the Treaty has been in force for ten years, or at any time thereafter, the Parties shall, if any of them so requests, consult together for the purpose of reviewing the Treaty, having regard for the factors then affecting peace and security in the North Atlantic area, including the development of universal as well as regional arrangements under the Charter of the United Nations for the maintenance of international peace and security.

ARTICLE 13

After the Treaty has been in force for twenty years, any Party may cease to be a Party one year after its notice of denunciation has been given to the Government of the United States of America, which will inform the Governments of the other Parties of the deposit of each notice of denunciation.

ARTICLE 14

This Treaty, of which the English and French texts are equally authentic, shall be deposited in the archives of the Government of the United States of America. Duly certified copies will be transmitted by that Government to the Governments of other signatories.

In witness whereof, the undersigned plenipotentiaries have signed this Treaty.

Done at Washington, the fourth day of April, 1949.

Bibliographic Essay

There is a wealth of primary material easily available, both published and unpublished. For this project, I have utilized mostly documents from United States sources, partly for their accessibility but also because of the dominant role the nation played in NATO's formation. The National Archives in College Park, Maryland, were particularly useful, especially State Department correspondence in Record Group 59 and, to a lesser degree, the Defense Department's documents in Record Group 330. The most important published primary sources are the *Foreign Relations of the United States (FRUS)* volumes for 1948 and 1949, the Hearings of the Senate Foreign Relations Committee, and the *Congressional Record* for those years.

Papers of the principal U.S. actors are scattered among major libraries—Harry S. Truman's at the Truman Library, Independence, Missouri; Dean Acheson's and Robert Lovett's at the Truman Library and Yale University; George Marshall's at the George Marshall Foundation in Lexington, Virginia; Arthur Vandenberg's at the Bentley Library in Ann Arbor, Michigan; Tom Connally's at the Library of Congress; J. William Fulbright's at the University of Arkansas Library in Fayetteville; and John Foster Dulles's and James Forrestal's at Princeton University. Even more relevant to this book are the thoughts of the middle-echelon diplomatists, notably John Hickerson at the Truman Library and Theodore Achilles' thousand-page memoir at the Lyman L. Lemnitzer Center for NATO and European Union Studies at Kent State University. Achilles's major NATO reflections have been excerpted from this memoir and published by the Lemnitzer Center as *Fingerprints on History*, and edited by Sidney R. Snyder and myself in 1992.

Most of the figures cited have published their memoirs—Dean Acheson, *Present at the Creation: My Years in the State Department* (New York: Norton,

1969); Charles Bohlen, *Witness to History, 1929–1969* (New York: Norton, 1973); Walter Millis, ed., *The Forrestal Diaries* (New York: Viking Press, 1951); George F. Kennan, *Memoirs: 1925–1950* (Little, Brown & Co., 1967); Paul Nitze, *From Hiroshima to Glasnost at the Center of Decision* (New York: Grove Weidenfeld, 1989); Arthur Vandenberg, Jr., ed., *The Private Papers of Senator Vandenberg* (Boston: Houghton Mifflin, 1952); and Harry S. Truman, *Memoirs*, vol. 1, *The Years of Trial and Hope* (New York: Doubleday, 1956). The president's fingerprints are not as evident as those of his associates, but his presence was felt behind the scenes.

The *New York Times*, with its ongoing interest in the development of NATO, is the source of both facts and judgments worth recording, even when neither was always accurate. *Facts on File* supplements the paper as do the *Washington Post*, *Times of London*, and Paris's *Le Monde*. Additional information is occasionally drawn from Dutch and Norwegian publications, and journals of other future members of the alliance.

Books and monographs on the origins of NATO are present in every chapter. My own and those of my former students are identified in the preface. In the 1980s when archives of the late 1940s were being opened, U.S. scholars produced a number of significant articles and books on the Truman Doctrine, the Marshall Plan, and to a lesser degree, NATO. NATO did not—and still does not—occupy a major place in the writings of U.S. diplomatic historians.

Two important official histories are important for this book: Kenneth W. Condit, *The History of the Joint Chiefs of Staff*, vol. 2, *The Joint Chiefs of Staff and National Policy, 1947–1949* (Washington, DC: Office of Joint History, Office of the Chairman of the Joint Chiefs of Staff, 1996) and the more insightful Steven L. Rearden, *History of the Office of the Secretary of Defense*, vol. I, *The Forrestal Years, 1947–1950* (Washington, DC: Historical Office, Office of the Secretary of Defense, 1984).

Biographies of the major framers are present in abundance. There are a number of biographies of the president, but the most valuable for this book is Robert H. Ferrell, *Harry S. Truman: A Life* (Columbia: University of Missouri Press, 1994). Similarly, Acheson's career has inspired many biographies. A useful general introduction is James Chace, *Acheson: the Secretary of State Who Created the American World* (New York: Simon and Schuster, 1998). The most authoritative is Robert L. Beisner, *Dean Acheson: A Life in the Cold War* (New York: Oxford University Press, 2006). For Marshall as secretary of state, Mark A. Stoler provides a succinct appreciation of his role in *George C. Marshall, Soldier-Statesman of the American Century* (Boston: Twayne Publishers, 1989). For Forrestal as secretary of defense, see Townshend Hoopes and Douglas Brinkley, *Driven Patriot: The Life and Times of James Forrestal* (New York: Alfred A. Knopf, 1992). Wilson D. Miscamble's *George F. Kennan and the Making of American Foreign Policy* (Princeton, NJ: Princeton

University Press, 1992) ably explores his role. T. Michael Ruddy, *The Cautious Diplomat: Charles E. Bohlen and the Soviet Union, 1929–1969* (Kent, OH: Kent State University Press, 1986) discusses the similarities and differences with Kennan. Although published over thirty years ago, J. Samuel Walker's *Henry Wallace and American Foreign Policy* (Westport, CT: Greenwood Press, 1976) is still the most useful introduction to the Progressive Party in 1948. Clarence E. Wunderlin, Jr., *Robert A. Taft: Tradition and Party in U.S. Foreign Policy* (Lanham, MD: SR Books/Rowman and Littlefield, 2005) is the most recent addition to the Taft literature. Richard Immerman, *John Foster Dulles: Piety and Pragmatism in U.S. Foreign Policy* (Wilmington, DE: SR Books, 1999) captures the many facets of Dulles's foreign policy positions. Randall B. Woods, *Fulbright: A Biography* (New York: Cambridge University Press, 1995) is the most authoritative treatment of the senator.

An early perceptive treatment of the origins of the treaty, as archives were being opened, is in Alan K. Henrikson, "The Creation of the North Atlantic Alliance" *Naval War College Review* 32 (May–June 1980), 4–39. Timothy P. Ireland, *Creating the Entangling Alliance: The Origins of the North Atlantic Treaty Organization* (Westport, CT: Greenwood Press, 1981) emphasizes the German problem in making the treaty. Journalist Don Cook provides a readable popular history of how the United States abandoned its isolationist tradition in *Forging the Alliance: NATO, 1945–1949* (New York: Arbor House/William Morris, 1989). Chester J. Pach, *Arming the Free World: The Origins of the United States Military Assistance Program, 1945–1950* (Chapel Hill: University of North Carolina Press, 1991) links the MAP with NATO. Francis H. Heller and John Gillingham, eds., *NATO: The Founding of the Atlantic Alliance and the Integration of Europe* (New York: St. Martin's Press, 1992) were presentations made in Kansas City on the fortieth anniversary of NATO. Stanley R. Sloan, *NATO's Future: Toward A New Transatlantic Bargain* (Washington, DC: National Defense University Press, 1985) reinforces the idea that Harlan Cleveland, *NATO: The Transatlantic Bargain* (New York: Harper & Row, 1970) popularized.

Parliamentary records of the allies are of limited value with respect to how the alliance was put together. Of all the charter members of NATO, Britain was the most important. Its legislative journal, *Hansard*, contains debates over key issues in 1948, none more significant than Ernest Bevin's speech in January that instigated negotiations. I found foreign office records and cabinet discussion at the Public Record Office in Kew (incorporated into the National Archives of the UK in 2003) important to this study. British scholars outdid their European counterparts in contributions to NATO's origins. Their appreciation of Bevin as the major figure in the formation of the alliance helps to explain much of their scholarly activity. Alan Bullock, *Ernest Bevin, Foreign Secretary, 1945–1951* (Oxford: Oxford University Press, 1985) is his most important biographer.

The motives of British scholars may have been to counter the parochial U.S. view of NATO's origins in which the United States was not only the dominant partner but also the prime mover. Martin H. Folly, "Breaking the Vicious Circle: Britain, the United States, and the Genesis of the North Atlantic Treaty," *Diplomatic History* 12 (Winter 1988), 59–77, judges that there would have been no Atlantic alliance without Bevin's leadership. Less strident but equally positive is John Baylis, *The Diplomacy of Pragmatism: Britain and the Formation of NATO, 1942–1949* (Kent, OH: Kent State University Press, 1993). Alex Danchev, *Oliver Franks: Founding Father* (Oxford: Oxford University Press) gives considerable credit to the advices of the British ambassador to the United States. Nicholas Henderson confirms their conclusions from his perch as a minor player, but acute observer, in the treaty negotiations. His book—part memoir, part history—*The Birth of NATO* (Boulder, CO: Westview Press , 1983) draws from his manuscript, "The History of the North Atlantic Pact Negotiations," at the Public Record Office. A higher level diplomat but less engaged in NATO proceedings is Gladwyn Jebb, *Memoir of Lord Gladwyn* (New York: Weybridge and Talley, 1972).

Arguably, the best volume from any member nation on the origins of NATO is the Canadian diplomatist Escott Reid, *Time of Fear and Hope: The Making of the North Atlantic Treaty* (Toronto: McClelland and Stewart, 1977). It combines history with personal memoir and reflects Canadian ambivalence about the U.S. role in the process. Lester Pearson, the foreign secretary in 1949, provides his own gloss on the treaty's formation in John A. Munro and Alex Inglis, eds., *Mike: Memoirs of Lester D. Pearson*, 3 vols. (Toronto: University of Toronto Press, 1972), II: 50.

While France was a major player even in its customary opposition to its allies, its contribution, like its attention to the literature of NATO, was not equal to those of the United States and the United Kingdom. Of the leading French policymakers, I have consulted Georges Bidault, *Resistance: The Political Autobiography of Georges Bidault* (New York: F. A. Praeger, 1967) and Vincent Auriol, *Journal du Septennat, 1947–1954* (Paris: A.Colin, 1970). Jean Monnet, *Memoirs* (New York: Doubleday, 1978) was not a major figure in the framing of the treaty or an influence at this time at the Quai d'Orsay, but his voice was heard. More useful have been the memoirs of French diplomats in Washington, London, and Paris: Jean Chauvel, *Commentaire: d'Alger à Berne, 1944–1952* (Paris: Fayard, 1972); René Massigli, *Une comédie des erreurs, 1943–1956* (Paris: Plon, 1978); and Armand Bérard, *Une ambassadeur se souvient: Washington et Bonn, 1945–1955*, 5 vols. (Paris: Plon, 1976–1982).

French diplomatic historians have not been prominent contributors to NATO historiography, but the few who have studied the subject are leaders in the field. The most visible is Pierre Melandri whose doctoral dissertation, published as *Les Etats-Unis face a l'unification de l'Europe, 1945–1954* (Paris:

A. Pedone, 1980) was a pioneer in transatlantic studies. Frederic Bozo's *La France et l'Otan: de la guerre froide au nouvel ordre européen* (Paris: Masson, 1991) opens with a convincing examination of France's role in the birth of the alliance. In 1986, Maurice Vaisse joined Melandri and Bozo in editing and contributing to *La France et l'Otan, 1949–1996* (Paris: Editions Complexe, 1986), the most comprehensive French-sponsored study of NATO, with a hundred pages devoted to NATO's origins.

The other founding members of the alliance have had less to say about its origins. Memoirs from Belgian, Dutch, and Norwegian diplomats reveal many of the sentiments behind the participation of their governments in the negotiating process. The most influential figure in this group was Belgian foreign minister Paul-Henri Spaak whose *The Contining Battle: Memoirs of a European, 1936–1966* (Boston: Little, Brown & Co., 1971) illustrated the role of the smaller powers. Spaak's counterparts, The Netherlands' Dirk Stikker, *Men of Responsibility* (New York: Harper & Row, 1966), offers a national perspectives on the proceedings. It would have been useful to have a Soviet perspective on the formation of NATO. Regrettably, the relative Soviet archives, especially those of the KGB, have not yet been declassified. A knowledgeable secondary account may be found in Vojtech Mastny, "NATO in the Beholder's Eye: Soviet Perceptions and Policies," Working Paper No. 35, *Cold War International History Project* (Washington, DC: Woodrow Wilson International Center for Scholars, March 2002).

The Brussels Pact is not a subject that has attracted the attention of Anglo-U.S. scholars, but it did yield a major monograph by an Italian historian, Antonio Varsori, *Il Patto de Bruxelles (1948): tra integrazione europea e alleanza atlantica* (Roma: Bonacci, 1988). See also Wolfgang Krieger, "Foundation and History of the Treaty of Brussels, 1948–1950," in *The Western Security Community,* edited by Norbert Wiggershaus and Roland G. Foerster, 229–50. Oxford/Providence: Berg, 1993. Dutch political scientists, Cees Wiebes and Bert Zeeman, "The Pentagon Negotiations, March 1948: The Launching of the North Atlantic Treaty," *International Affairs* 59 (Summer 1983): 351–63, like Varsori, shed light on special aspects of NATO's history. Norwegian historian Geir Lundestad, *America, Scandinavia, and the Cold War* (New York: Columbia University Press, 1980) and Danish scholar Nikolaj Petersen, "Danish and Norwegian Alliance Policies, 1948–1949: A Comparative Analysis," *Cooperation and Conflict* 14 (June 1979): 193–210, provide Scandinavian perspectives on the formation of the alliance.

European scholars have sponsored major conferences on NATO's beginnings, and I mention three of the most useful proceedings for this project: Olav Riste, ed., *Western Security: The Formative Years, European and Atlantic Defence, 1947–1953* (Oslo: Norwegian University Press, 1985); Josef Becker and Franz Knipping, eds., *Power in Europe? Great Britain, France, Italy, and Germany in a Postwar World, 1945–1950* (New York: Walter de Gruyter,

1986); and Norbert Wiggershaus and Roland Foerster, eds., *The Western Security Community* (Oxford/Providence: Berg, 1993). Although NATO's origins receive only passing notice, Gustav Schmidt, ed., *A History of NATO: The First Fifty Years*, 3 vols. (London: Palgrave, 2001) merits attention for the scope, depth, and the dominance of European scholarship in NATO historiography. The *NATO Review* solicited articles on NATO's prehistory that were edited by Nicholas Sherwen and written by André de Staercke et al., under the title of *NATO's Anxious Birth: The Prophetic Vision of the 1940s* (London: C. Hurst and Co., 1985).

Index

About the Author

Lawrence S. Kaplan is University Professor Emeritus of History and Director Emeritus of the Lyman L. Lemnitzer Center for NATO and European Union Studies at Kent State University. He is currently a professorial lecturer in history at Georgetown University. He has been a Fulbright lecturer at the Universities of Bonn, Leuven, Nice, and Malta.